3

A CENTURY OF CO-OPERATIVE INSURANCE

by

R. G. GARNET

London
GEORGE ALLEN AND UNWIN LTD
RUSKIN HOUSE, MUSEUM STREET

7. 1968   9 ⟶

PRINTED IN GREAT BRITAIN
in 11 *on* 12 *pt Bembo Type*
by Co-operative Wholesale Society Limited, Reddish, Stockport
for the Co-operative Insurance Society Limited

A. E. F. Lovick
Chairman
Co-operative Insurance Society Limited

Dedicated to Robert Owen
— who, it was said,
never thought differently
of a book
for having read it.

PREFACE

Given the growth and ramifications of Co-operation it is remarkable how few works of independent scholarship have been published on the history of the British Co-operative Movement. It is now a generation since G. D. H. Cole's *Century of Co-operation;* almost half-a-century since *The Consumers' Co-operative Movement* by Sidney and Beatrice Webb (who pointed out that their work was not a history but a " descriptive analysis "); and sixty years since the first edition of C. R. Fay's survey of the world Co-operative Movement *Co-operation at Home and Abroad.* A. M. Carr-Saunders and P. Sargant Florence wrote on Co-operation during the inter-war years, but their contributions were more in the form of essays. Apart from these works, one must go back to the writings of Beatrice Webb and G. J. Holyoake during the nineteenth century. The central institutions of the British Co-operative Movement have been even more neglected by all those historians who are not directly associated with the Movement — with the slight exception of Albert Mansbridge who wrote a little-known pre-war history of the Co-operative Permanent Building Society.

Perhaps the present spate of self-questioning of purpose and direction within the Co-operative Movement will provoke more attention from a new generation of social commentators and historians. In this connection one looks forward with interest to the forthcoming centenary history of the Scottish Co-operative Wholesale Society which has been written by an objective observer.

This history of the Co-operative Insurance Society was commissioned by the CIS Board of Directors who, acting through Mr. Robert Dinnage, then General Manager and Secretary, gave the author complete freedom of access to archives. No business historian has been treated so laudably and accommodated so congenially: the years spent on writing were a virtual essay in co-operation, and it is impossible to mention all the people who have tendered advice, comment and explanation. The writer had little working-experience of insurance or of practical Co-operation, but Mr. Dinnage acted as mentor throughout and was unstinted of his scarce leisure time in reading successive typescripts and providing invaluable constructive criticism.

Mr. James McCairn, Superintendent of the CIS Publicity Department, was painstaking and dedicated in the unenviable task of acting as co-ordinator between printer, artist, author and management. Mr. Alex Bottomley was a *vade mecum* on early personalities of the CIS. Mr. H. Mathieson, retired CIS Branch Manager, provided the writer with valuable preliminary notes. Countless serving and retired CIS men and women agents, district and branch office staff responded to appeals for information and many were interviewed. The author is particularly indebted to Mr. J. L. Nuttall, Mr. H. H. Knighton, Mr. A. Duval, Mr. J. E. Dunkerley, Mr. H. Smith, Mr. F. H. Edwards, Mr. D. Stott, Mr. A. Mellor, and other CIS officials who completed opinion surveys.

Gratitude is also due to Professor H. B. Rose of the London Graduate School of Business for a most interesting discussion on the neglect of insurance by economic historians. Professor T. S. Ashton, to whom all students of Economic History are heavily indebted, kindly read parts of the book at proof stage. In America, Professor I. K. Steigerwalt, Dean of the School of Business Administration at Detroit Institute of Technology, stimulated the author with small-hours talk on the writing of business history. But most credit is due to my colleague Dr. R. S. Fitton who prodded and encouraged the work through many literary lapses.

The librarians of the Manchester Local History Library, the Insurance Institute of London and the Co-operative Union were most helpful, particularly Mr. Desmond Flanagan of the Co-operative Union. Lord Robens was kind enough to answer queries about his early trade union affiliations.

Immaculate abstracting, typewriting and secretarial assistance was always forthcoming at CIS Chief Office from Mrs. M. Holt, Mrs. D. McNulty, Miss Sylvia Watts, Miss B. Raftery, Mrs. F. Rothwell, Miss H. Needle. Thanks are also due to unknown typists — folios were oft-times thrown into the typing pool without warning, but the copies were always returned with decorum.

Not least, an accolade should be given to the staff at the CWS Printing Works at Reddish who gave sterling service in typesetting, proof-reading and correction.

The deepest acknowledgment is to the *uberrima fides* on the part of my wife — that the manuscript which went on many family excursions, including some months in the American Deep South, would one day appear in print.

This history relies heavily on the minute books of meetings of the CIS Board and its Committees since 1867: where other source-material has been used, annotations are given in the text.

Finally, a word of expiation and exculpation: the historian with his time-advantage and detachment has an *hauteur* denied to the busy man-of-affairs, and there is no intention by the author to reduce the stature of certain statesmen and politicians, many of whom are now dead, and of other investigators who are now older and perhaps more aware of the intricacies of the insurance industry.

One lesson only need be drawn — that politicians as well as historians need to do their homework properly before embarking on grand self-assignments.

RONALD G. GARNETT

April, 1968

CONTENTS

Preface   v
Introduction   1

PART ONE

INSURANCE AND CO-OPERATIVE MOVEMENT

The Economic and Social Background   6
Fidelity Insurance   8
Early Co-operative Movement and Life   13
    Assurance
Fire Insurance and the Co-operative Movement   17

PART TWO

EARLY YEARS OF CO-OPERATIVE INSURANCE
1867–1899

Foundation of CIC   20
Life Assurance Proposals and the Fire Tariff   53
Friendly Societies   70
Life Assurance   74
CIC and Ordinary Life Assurance from 1886   77
Social Conditions and Welfare   96
Fin de Siècle: A New Society   98

PART THREE

NEW PARTNERS

1900 – 1904   112
1905–1909   117
A New Building   125
Co-operative Controversy   136
The War Years   149
The Planet   152

PART FOUR

THE 1920S

Post-War Developments   162
Collective Life Assurance   167

Investments   170
Builders' Guilds   171
Valuation, New Business and Parmoor   173
Ireland   182
Cambridge Stamp Scheme   184
House Purchase   185
Motor and Advertising Business   188
Publicity and Investment   192
General Strike   194
New Prospects   196
Staff and Organisation   197
Fire Business   201
Industrial Assurance Act 1929   202
Strikes   203

PART FIVE
THE 1930S
" Something to Think About "   208
Funds and Interest Rates   209
Cohen and After   211
Out of Depression   216

PART SIX
NEW HORIZONS
War Years   222
Post-War   231
Proposed Nationalization of Industrial Assurance   232
Nationalization and the CIS   246
    (A Case Study in Communications)
The New Building   266
ICA and Reinsurance Bureau   280
Changing Patterns of Investment of Insurance   288
    Offices
The CIS and Investment within Co-operative   291
    Movement
Recent Trends   294

Envoi   296
Appendices   302
Personalities and Chairmen   313
Index   315

INTRODUCTION

Achieving a century calls for at least a brief pause for reflection; the centenarian, the cricketer and the business house have this much in common — it is an appropriate time to take stock and to make plans for the future. The CIS has survived 100 years and believes that its life-story may be of interest not only to past and present generations of CIS men and women, but also to Co-operators generally. There are many gaps in our knowledge of the vast social changes and developments in Britain over the past century — perhaps the history of the CIS can add a little to our awareness and understanding.

Few lives are unblemished, and a business history should not confine its chronicle to a catalogue of successes and self-congratulations. The story of the CIS has not been one of uninterrupted progress throughout its life. It does not claim that its rate of growth has been unprecedented; indeed there has been felt, at times, a sense of oppression rather more burdensome than the forces of normal market competition. Nevertheless, by 1967, the CIS has become the second largest industrial/ordinary life assurance office in Britain, and with a non-life premium income of £21m. it ranks quite high as a Fire and Casualty Office, but despite its size its name is less familiar to members of the public than many smaller insurance offices.[1]

Insurance has not received a good Press over the past century. Industrial assurance was attacked by a nineteenth-century prime minister; and the author of our national plan for social security, written during the second world war, was equally critical. The accusations of social injustice arising from the inequalities of industrial assurance have now faded with a more generally prosperous society, but during the years immediately after the second world war the control of industrial assurance became a national political issue which

---

[1] There is for instance no reference to the CIS in the chapter on insurance companies in Anthony Sampson's *Anatomy of Britain* (2nd edit. 1965).

1

involved the CIS at a critical stage in its growth. More recently, insurance has been vilified on other counts. Progressively since the 1930s, the insurance offices have become institutional investors, with large holdings of industrial securities, and there have been constant insinuations of secret manipulation of other people's business, tax-evasion, and inflation-profiteering through the capital-gains of specula-tion in real property. The coin, whether counterfeit or otherwise, is two-faced, for the critics also make up the large body of insurance policyholders (there are 12m. life policies currently underwritten by the CIS).

Being part of a large self-questioning Co-operative Movement, the CIS receives advice and criticism from within the ranks of Co-operators. However, the channels of redress remain open and the scrutiny brought to bear on the CIS as a social institution is a small price to pay for democracy.

Perhaps it is safe to suggest that the tremendous growth of the CIS was unexpected, at least in its first half-century. It is possible to visualise ordinary working men retailing groceries, but not becoming involved in the intricate contractual liabilities of insurance practice. The pioneers of the CIS were inexperienced, but they learned fast, and they created the wherewithal for the sheer professionalism which more than any other feature is the explanation of the expansion of the CIS to its present dimensions.

There are certainly a number of unique features in the development of the CIS — its experience, for instance, has been the reverse of several of the large composite offices which were founded during the second half of the nineteenth century and which began with industrial life assurance rather than with general insurance business.

Also, to some extent, insurance as an industry has suffered from lack of attention of economic historians. Banking and insurance are often dealt with as common items, with banking generally receiving the emphasis. This is a surprising oversight, for the monetary total of insurance cover and premiums alone would justify more investigation, certainly since the mid-nineteenth century. In addition, the army of insurance agents and the millions of households in their territories must have some social significance. Moreover, insurance is a growth-industry, rapidly incorporating more mechanised methods and with an enviable record of increments of productivity.

Twenty years ago, *The Economist* commented that "the CIS appears to have emerged as a leader in life assurance — a fact which has interesting social consequences . . ."

Writing a business history raises the problem of narrative versus analysis. This personal interpretation of the history of the CIS has attempted to avoid being merely a recital of day-to-day events, but the reader must be left to judge how far short the study has fallen in seeking out the paths of growth of the CIS; how far the right questions have been posed; how far there are explanations of the pace and direction of movement; how far business decisions have been conditioned by past experience, impulse or compliance with directives from the parent Co-operative Movement.

And yet a business history can never say very much that is apposite for business growth in general — it cannot be concerned with the growth or nature of all enterprise. Like all history, it is concerned with a microcosm; with the relation between the unique and the general—the historian can no more separate them than he can separate fact and interpretation.

In sum, there is so much to be deduced from the CIS about the wider social and economic world of the last 100 years that it would surely be a detriment to the CIS to confine this history to the CIS.

"If we take from history the discussion of why, how and wherefore each thing was done and whether the result was what we should reasonably have expected, what is left is a clever essay but not a lesson, and while pleasing for the moment of no possible benefit for the future."[1]

---

[1] Polybius, Greek historian (c.202 — 120 B.C.); see W. R. Paton, *Histories of Polybius*, (1922) Book III 31. 7. Vol. 2.

PART ONE

INSURANCE AND THE
CO-OPERATIVE MOVEMENT

(i) *The Economic and Social Background*

> " The theory of insurance . . . though based upon self-interest, yet it is the most enlightened and benevolent form which the projects of self-interest ever took. It is, in fact, in a limited sense, and a practicable method, the agreement of a community to consider the goods of its individual members as common."

Augustus De Morgan, *An Essay on Probabilities and on their Application to Life Contingencies and Insurance Offices* (1838), p.xv.

> " The only history that is of practical value is what may be termed Descriptive Sociology."

Herbert Spencer, *Education, Intellectual, Moral and Physical* (1861), p.36.

The growth of the British insurance industry, particularly life assurance, from the mid-nineteenth century is closely related to the major features of economic and social change. Insurance grew as a response to industrialisation and concomitant urbanisation. The new masses of city dwellers, detached from the security of the rural or small town community, sought new modes of mutual protection. In a world of uncertain employment, the industrial classes converted long-standing parochial trade clubs and societies into working-class institutions with national coverage. Of these institutions, Co-operation and Trade Unionism have grown to their present dimensions as self-generated movements and their social democracy has survived. Another predominantly nineteenth century working-class institution — the friendly society (in terms of members always larger than either Co-operation or Trade Unionism) — underwent a metamorphis. The friendly society offered protection from some of the hazards of the economic environment, but the industrial assurance companies and collecting societies, which grew apace during the second half of the nineteenth century, offered the wage-earner a fuller adjustment to the prevailing economic situation. Industrial assurance companies with their fixed premiums, air of stability, apparent efficiency of operation and professional collecting service, unadulterated with social embellishments, contrasted favourably with the friendly societies which were fraternal but often precarious.

Insurance offered the attainment of social and self-respect, for which the working-classes were prepared to pay dearly. During times of bereavement they opened their homes. After a " decent " burial the impression to be given to relatives and neighbours was respectability.

Given the growing demand for life assurance, why was the Co-operative Insurance Company content for so long to restrict its activities to providing insurance cover for the property and funds of the Co-operative Movement rather than offering life assurance to co-operators? To deal with this question at all adequately, it is necessary to examine the antecedents of the CIS, but before doing so, some indication of the prevailing economic condition of the working-classes is appropriate.

Fortunately, a survey was undertaken in the same year as the foundation of the Co-operative Insurance Company and gave an estimate of the total national income of the United Kingdom for 1867, as £814m., and the gross income of England and Wales alone as £661.9m.[1] The estimated total population of United Kingdom in 1867, based on the 1861 census, was 29.7m., of whom 10.9m. were manual wage-earners, and 12.1m. were dependants of manual wage-earners; 6.6m. were upper and middle class. (Between 1861 and 1867, more than half-a-million had been added to the working population.) The 10.9m. members of the manual labouring class earned less than £60 yearly *per capita*.

In 1866, the average number of paupers on relief at any one time was 916,000, but the total number relieved during the year was 3,206,000 (three and a half times 916,000, based on the formula given in the Appendix to Poor Law Returns of 1857). The resultant figure equalled 20 per cent of the manual labouring class. Baxter thought fully 20 per cent should be deducted from nominal full-time wages to compensate for loss of work through sickness and unemployment. Indeed, the actual level of relief was no indication of the extent of loss of work and wages, as many workers, then as now, were reluctant to call on relief.

The average income per head of the occupied population in England and Wales in 1867 was £68 per year, but with tax deductions and income per head distributed over the total population including dependants, the average was £32 per head for 21m. of the population; 4.5m. manual workers earned between £10 10s. and £36 yearly, and

[1] R. Dudley Baxter, *National Income of United Kingdom* (1868).

another 5m. earned less than £1 per week.[1] In one respect only was the national economy in a sounder position in 1867 than 1967 — "It is a wonderful thing that the gross annual income of the United Kingdom should exceed by £36,000,000 the whole £778,000,000 of the national debt."[2]

These nominal and average income-levels must be related to costs-of-living to arrive at any approximate assessment of the conditions of livelihood of the working-classes. A quarter of a century later, Charles Booth drew his (subjective) poverty line at something approaching 23s. for the weekly maintenance of a family in London. But during the intervening period, the general level of prices had been falling.[3] In the complex of movements in retail prices, wage-levels, urban rents and employment, the lot of the working-classes slowly improved in the second half of the nineteenth century and most noticeably so in the period of falling prices from 1873 to 1896.

(ii) *Fidelity Insurance*

Fidelity insurance has a lineage stretching back to antiquity. A party to a bargain or a promise was often called upon to provide a person of substance to act as surety or bond for the obligee. But it was not until recent times that the onus of responsibility for reimbursement of the injured party to a contract could be transferred to an insurance underwriter. As late as the nineteenth century, it was still usual to demand large sureties compared with the level of salaries paid to clerks and others having access to funds.

Peculation was also a grave risk to the pioneer co-operative ventures which suffered from insufficient surveillance or audit of storekeepers and cashiers. Generally, the system of book-keeping was so perfunctory that it invited dishonesty, and from the earliest days co-operative societies sought protection of their funds and stock from erring officials.

Co-operative societies were treated as partnerships, but legal protection in the early decades of the nineteenth century was largely

[1] There is, however, evidence that the propensity to save did not always vary proportionately with income levels . . .
"Again, if we analyse the accounts of the principal savings-banks in the manufacturing districts, we find that it is not so much the highly paid classes of working people who deposit money in them as those who earn comparatively moderate incomes. Thus the most numerous class of depositors in the Manchester and Salford savings-bank is the class of female domestic servants, whose money wages range from £12 to £20 a year."
"Workmen's Earnings and Savings," *Quarterly Review*, July, 1860.

[2] Dudley Baxter, op.cit., p.63.

[3] Charles Booth, *Life and Labour of the People in London* (1902 edit.).

illusory, for it was conceded that the only procedure open to a partner who wished to sue a co-partner was to file a bill in equity in the Court of Chancery, for which the legal cost was at least £60. Hence, care had to be taken in the choice of shopmen. Once appointed, it was necessary that the storekeeper should cease to remain a member of the co-operative society: to prevent him from screening himself, he had to be placed in the position of a punishable servant of the society, or of the trustees, who could then accept a bond or security from him. But the same law held good — the guarantor was not to be a joint guarantor, for the individual guarantor could then have pleaded exemption by being a joint partner. Hence a guarantor had to be an outsider, neither a member nor a trustee. A member of Glasgow Co-operative Society wrote in 1830 that notwithstanding the above legal remedies:

> "All the societies that I have known and am presently acquainted with, are generally deficient in the knowledge of ordinary business and shopkeeping. Without which knowledge societies are exposed to the frauds and embezzlements of friends and foes. The risks are great and individuals and collectively the members are apt to imbibe feelings of distrust. This state of things exposes the whole concern to sadden (sic) disillusion."[1]

Various remedies were suggested, such as members keeping the books of the local society in rotation, and more frequent stock-taking, but with limited success.

The Ripponden Co-operative Society, founded in 1832, registered its first book of rules in 1839, which stated:

> "That this Society shall have two servants at least, under the denomination of Agent and Salesman, they shall be interested with all the property of this Society in the Storerooms and for its management, and shall give joint and satisfactory security, pursuant to 10 Geo. IV for the same, and shall deliver up all money, goods, etc., belonging to the Society, at any time when requested by the General Committee or to the persons appointed to receive or examine the same."

An article in the *British Co-operator* of May, 1830, gave legal advice to the struggling societies. Licences for dealing in groceries could only be obtained for six persons in partnership; hence licences could not be taken out in the corporate capacity of all the members, and licence holders were, by law, entitled to control the purchase and

[1] *British Co-operator*, October, 1830.

disposal of the property owned by the Society. Moreover, if there were no Articles of Association for a definite period, any one of the partners could declare the partnership at an end and insist on winding-up. This could, however, be used as a device for getting rid of an obnoxious partner and then reforming the society. Trustees could be nominated from another society to enable prosecution if the local ones failed in their legal obligations. The trustees, in turn, could delegate their powers to officers — the manager or committee members — and they too could be held liable at law if they did not keep to their powers as servants of the trustees. The *British Co-operator* went on to warn societies to " observe *the management* must not be assigned to a few as in your Sick and Burial Societies. *All must* take some part, or be prepared to take some part."

Although several hundreds of co-operative societies were founded during the early 1830s, the vast majority had an extremely short life. They suffered from weaknesses of excessive competition, inadequate capital, overtrading and bad debts; but there is no evidence that they entered into contracts of fidelity insurance to protect themselves against peculation. Indeed, it should be noted that at the time there was no reputable insurance company that could undertake such class of business. In the next thirty or more years, the Co-operative Movement slowly acquired legal protection for its funds, but it had to await the founding of the Co-operative Insurance Company to provide the simple remedy of fidelity insurance as a safeguard against embezzlement. For instance, Plymouth Co-operative Society, founded in 1860, appointed their first buyer in 1862, with the task of checking the stock book which was kept by a committee of members. The buyer was fined 3d. for each item of default on his part (committee members were also liable for the same amount). He was paid 20s. for each quarter's service, having first to find a surety of £2 5s. as a guarantee of honest dealing. Other societies devised their own schemes of protection. The Rochdale Pioneers had a system whereby the salesman kept vouchers as a check on the cashier. At Halifax:

"storekeepers are put in possession of goods of a certain value; all other goods sent in from the central depot must be paid for at the retail value by the storekeeper, less 3d. in the pound, which is allowed for waste; when stock is again taken, the value of goods must be the same as when commenced, or there must be an equivalent in cash to make good the deficiency."

None of these precedents resolved the issues facing working-class institutions with funds at their disposal. In many cases, the surety required, being far in excess of the accompanying wage, was thereby difficult to meet. The guarantor was often in as vulnerable a position as the society seeking protection for its funds; the absconding of servants could bring about the dissolution of the society, and penury to the guarantor. The need for an institutional guarantor, untrammelled by personal ties with the party concerned, and having adequate financial resources to meet any contingency, was hardly contemplated during the first three decades of the nineteenth century, despite the growing division between ownership of assets and direct participation in company transactions. The Guarantee Society of London,[1] founded in 1840, sought to remedy the defects of private suretyship:

"Instances have constantly occurred in which persons of the highest respectability have been obliged to forgo valuable appointments; from either the great difficulty of obtaining security, or a repugnance to place their relatives or friends and themselves under the obligations involved therein."

[1] Now a subsidiary of the Yorkshire Insurance Company.

It was held at the time that a master would hesitate to engage an assistant who could only give the security of an insurance contract — a variation of one of the arguments then being used against the extension of limited liability. As fidelity insurance became more general, it was noticed that the confidential clerk was no more likely to turn into a rogue because an insurance company provided fidelity guarantee for him, but the clerk himself certainly became more independent. It was also found that the master could make good his claim on an insurance company more promptly than he could on a disillusioned relative or private guarantor. The Lords of the Treasury agreed in 1842 to accept fidelity guarantee policies in lieu of personal bonds or sureties, and in the same year fidelity cover was offered on advantageous terms to those persons who had taken out life assurance policies, but the scheme did not mature. Fidelity insurance premiums took into account the personal character of the individual, the nature of his duties, and the overall supervision. A proposal would be declined if the employer was careless or negligent in the protection of his own interests, so that the character of the applicant for suretyship was but one of the circumstances taken into consideration. Indeed, many employers acknowledged the direct benefits of fidelity insurance by paying the premiums for their office holders. A further development was the institution of floating policies for a group of clerks which covered any number of defaults during the currency of the policy, or assigned the limits of loss of each particular member.

A pamphleteer was percipient enough to note in 1847,

> " there is reason to believe that the system of private surety will in course of time cease to be one of the duties of life . . . and the adoption of public guarantee will be viewed as one of the great eras of civilisation from the numerous beneficial auxiliaries which institutions will afford to the community."[1]

Employers increasingly favoured public fidelity guarantee cover because the security provided was certain, and often private surety was difficult to trace. Moreover, public surety allowed the individual to avoid the onus of applying to friends to act as guarantors.

At the time of the formation of the Co-operative Insurance Company in 1867, there were only two companies undertaking fidelity insurance business to any appreciable extent. This class of insurance was still beset with difficulties, for however simple the mere guarantee of

---

[1] James Knight, *Private and Public Guarantee for Persons appointed to Offices of Trust Considered* (1847).

honesty appeared to be, it was continually resolving itself into the far more difficult question of the guarantee of commercial risk, or at least of solvency. This was obviously the case when the relations between the employer and the employed were such that the account between them assumed the form of debtor and creditor and a deficiency ceased to be felonious.

The fidelity companies were liable to be made victims of the collusive fraud, hence they had to make criminal prosecution a *sine qua non*. Fidelity differs from other forms of insurance — while other branches have an element of moral hazard, fidelity is all moral hazard. There are few branches of insurance more dependent upon accurate practice. The losses the insurance company is called upon to meet are not infrequently surrounded by circumstances involving more than a simple pecuniary relationship; the investigation into a loss incurred may disclose facts which ought to have been known to the employer and the insurer from the beginning.

By 1875, the aggregate premium income for fidelity business in the country as a whole exceeded £100,000 a year and one of the companies could show an average annual profit of over £19,000 for the years 1866 to 1871.

(iii) *Early Co-operative Movement and Life Assurance*

The first issue of the *The Economist* in January, 1821,[1] outlined a scheme for a Co-operative and Economical Society to include 250 families living in community, but continuing their individual outside employment.[2] From the wage-earner's weekly contribution of one guinea, he would receive lodging and food for family, education for children, sickness benefit and provision for old age. By the end of the year, the plans for associated living included the fitting up of a laboratory for dispensing medicine to the communal families. A medical practitioner who visited the establishment agreed to direct the dispensary. In addition, the members aimed to provide tables

> " accurately representing the condition and progress of a community as respects the births, marriages, and deaths; the ascertained or probable causes of disease and death in the

---

[1] *The Economist* (1821–22) was a weekly journal devoted to Owenism and Co-operation.

[2] For early Co-operative Movement see R. G. Garnett, *The Ideology of Early Co-operative Movement*, Endowment Lecture, University of Kent, May, 1966 and " E. T. Craig: Communitarian, Educator, Phrenologist." *The Vocational Aspect*, Vol. XV, Summer 1963.

individuals of both sexes, and the age at which dissolution takes place; the sexes of the children and their physical condition at the birth; the mode of treatment pursued as to their food, clothing, exercise, rest, etc., in health and sickness; the development of their mental and bodily powers ... this comprehensive view of a human society in all its circumstances is a desideratum ... "

This valiant exercise was never undertaken — the clinical, actuarial, and financial resources were not available, nor indeed in existence — but the lack of wherewithal does not detract from this interesting pioneer scheme which linked social welfare with statistical investigation, later to be found in the independent social surveys of Booth, Rowntree and others. The Co-operative Movement in the 1820s and 1830s was diffused and disjointed, and in neither of its main activities — community-building and small shopkeeping — did it approach a solution of the administrative problems of social security. In the Owenite New Moral World, health, wealth and plenty were concomitants of the *new* Society. With these visions, insurance arrangements were to Robert Owen as irrelevant as petty shopkeeping; although Owen took good care to insure his own life with a reputable underwriter.[1] Both could be dealt with as administrative details once the Co-operative Commonwealth was born. Later on, when co-operation turned away and adopted the new model of Rochdale,[2] it became increasingly apparent that insurance was as necessary in co-operation as it was in outside capitalist enterprise.

Although the Owenite co-operative communities collapsed in disorder, the original body founded by Robert Owen for setting up communities survived. The Association of All Classes of All Nations, founded in 1835, was metamorphosed into the Community Friendly Society in the following year — established for " the mutual relief

[1] The journal *New Moral World*, a vehicle for Owenite ideas, was published from 1834 to 1845. Robert Owen was involved in a number of community experiments in Britain and America and he is generally regarded as the inspiring force behind the Early Co-operative Movement.
Robert Owen took out a life policy for £2,500 with the Royal Exchange Assurance, London. A receipt for the 21st annual premium of £71 5s. issued 11 April, 1824, is extant. Original at Gourock Ropeworks, Port Glasgow.

[2] Cf. *Co-operator*, 1 November, 1865.
Rochdale had an Equitable Sick and Burial Society which grew out of and held its meetings and collections at the premises of the Pioneers. " The Sick Society was commenced by, and confined to, the shopmen and workmen of the Pioneers Society. In 1861, it was thrown open to the members and families of the store. At the end of the year 1864, the Sick Society had 450 members and funds amounting to £400; in December, 1865, the members roll was 550 and the funds £500; at present the number of members is 640 and the funds £620."

and maintenance of the members and for the purpose of promoting the well-being of themselves and families upon the principles of co-operation." The relief funds were to be accumulated through subscriptions and donations for maintenance in sickness, unemployment, old age and death. For instance, at an average wage of 16s. weekly, contributions to the relief fund would be 4d. with an allowance of 8s. when sick. Unemployment benefit was to be much less at 5s. 4d. weekly. The qualifying period was to be six months, and sickness or incapacity allowances of 24 times the weekly subscription would be paid "until death or until elected into any establishment of the Society." The unemployment benefit was to be fixed at 16 times, but with a maximum of six weeks' allowance in any one year and the unemployment must "not be caused by any strike or combination or any misconduct." Robert Owen was strong on industrial discipline; he had little countenance for the irresponsible activities of trade clubs.

There is no evidence that any contributions or allowances were actually made, and the Society rules merely added folios to the paper Owenite commonwealth.[1] The Community Friendly Society underwent several further transformations to its title, and after the final breaking-up of the last of the Owenite communities at Harmony Hall in Hampshire in 1845, the parent Owenite Society, now termed the Rational Society, determined that members who had sought to enter the New Moral World could remain on the books of the Rational Society on payment of an annual subscription of one shilling, which it was noted would also cover arrears. The Owenite movement was flickering out at the same time as Rochdale was demonstrating sound principles for co-operative shopkeeping. Robert Owen had little sympathy with shopkeeping, co-operative or otherwise, and the retail Co-operative Movement can hardly be traced to his paternity. The sole continuous present-day link with Robert Owen is indeed to the social insurance provision laid down in the Community Friendly Society of 1836. The Rational Society had been formed in 1843, and it too had set up a Rational Sick and Burial Association, which by 1845 included at least seven branches. In the following year there were 20 branches; by 1856, 63 branches with over 2,000 members; by 1883, over 500 branches had been formed; and by 1904, the Rational Sick and Burial Association had become the seventh largest friendly

---

[1] There was for instance a draft scheme in 1841 of "Proposals for the Adoption of the Principles of Equitable Assurance As A Means of Raising Capital to be Applied to the Formation of Communities."

society in the country in terms of members and finance. The present-day Rational Association Friendly Collecting Society still has its headquarters in Manchester.[1]

On the passing of the Industrial and Provident Societies Act, 1852, a co-operative conference was held in London at the premises of the Society for Promoting Working Men's Associations. It was called to discuss the best mode of turning co-operative labour and trade to profitable account. Twenty-five delegates attended, mainly from Working Men's Associations, but they also included Lloyd Jones, Thomas Hughes and F. J. Furnivall as delegates from co-operative societies. Thomas Hughes moved that there should be established a Co-operative Friendly Union which would act as a Benefit Society. He proposed two levels of subscription — a lower rate for admittance to such facilities as library, lectures, concerts, and a higher rate, which would insure benefits in case of sickness and death. The resolution was unanimously adopted and a committee of seven set up including Lord Goderich, J. M. Ludlow, Thomas Hughes, Lloyd Jones, William Newton, John Douthwaite and E. Vansittart Neale,[2] (who was to play such an important role in the early growth of the Co-operative Insurance Company), but as with so many of the plans for co-operative betterment, there is no evidence of any practical achievement. Presumably, the conference was either unaware of the Rational Sick and Burial Association, or they thought it far removed from its co-operative origins. Nevertheless, the proposals for sick and funeral benefit were at least an indication that insurance cover was never far from the minds of co-operators and co-operative organisations. At a further conference held in Manchester during August, 1853, at Cooper Street Mechanics' Institute, 26 delegates attended and recommended the drawing up of plans for a Co-operative Land, Building and

---

[1] The rules of the Community Friendly Society were agreed at a meeting at 94 Tottenham Court Road, on 3 February, 1836. The sick fund society was instituted on 1 January, 1837. Forty years later, the Rational Sick and Burial Association was praised by a member of the Royal Commission on Friendly Societies (1874): " Mr. Stanley speaks of it as one of the best managed societies of the smaller orders." As a rule, the business of the Society was transacted away from public houses. By the end of 1870 the Rational Society had 247 branches, with 1,437 members in Lancashire but 5,754 in Devon and over 4,300 in East Anglia. From 1861 it had worked on graduated scale of contributions, and had 14,134 members in 1871.

[2] *Vansittart Neale, Edward*, 1810–1892. Son of Reverend E. Neale. Educated Oriel College, Oxford. Called to the Bar 1837. Drafted the rules for registration of CWS and compiled model rules for Co-operative Societies published by the Co-operative Union. He was one of the principal founders of the International Co-operative Alliance.

16

Investment Society, and an Industrial and Provident Societies Union. The proposed land society would purchase building sites, erect dwellings and workshops, and the latter would be sold at cost to members with legal title to the buildings with the land remaining as security until purchase price and interest was paid. Insurance was contemplated, but it was corporate insurance — " An annual payment will be charged upon each of these establishments by way of an assurance against risk of failure." This apparently is the first evidence of thoughts which twenty years later received embodiment in the CWS Trade Insurance Fund.

Of the risks facing a co-operative society, fidelity and fire hazards were outstanding in that they could destroy the whole financial basis of the retail society. Looking severely at co-operation as a form of business organisation, the social security of its members could wait, hence in these terms, the Co-operative Insurance Company, in commencing with fire and fidelity cover, was being quite consistent.

(iv) *Fire Insurance and the Co-operative Movement*

Fire Insurance has a much longer history than fidelity insurance. Although the early co-operative societies had the choice of a large number of fire offices at their disposal, fire insurance was hardly contemplated. This was understandable, given the slender resources of many of the early co-operative stores, but with the growth of the Movement and the larger reserves of stock, housed in more adequate and costly premises, it is all the more surprising that fire insurance cover was generally lacking or grossly inadequate. A stock list of a

17

village co-operative store in 1842 is of interest not only as an indication of household items and living standards, but also for the inflammable nature of many of the commodities.[1] There is no evidence that the store was insured against fire. There were, however, some early co-operative societies who took out fire insurance and safeguarded themselves as much as possible against fire hazards. The Oldham Society minuted: " 17 September, 1855 — the Committee gave orders for a fireproof safe to be purchased." The Ripponden Society balance sheet of 1864, shows insurance of £7 7s. 6d. out of a total expenditure of £3,465, but there are no details how this premium was allocated between the various insurable risks. The Plymouth Society increased its fire insurance on stock to cover £300 in June, 1862. Nottingham thought fit to insure its whole stock-in-trade in May, 1867, with the General Life and Fire Assurance Company, at a valuation of £1,600.

[1] J. H. Priestley, *History of Ripponden Co-operative Society, 1832-1932*. List of stock of Ripponden Society on 3 October, 1842, included the following items:

	£	s.	d.		£	s.	d.
Dust and Sweepings..	1	8	0	Lute string	8	13	3
Jones parcel	3	7	0	Silk Ribbings.. ..	4	4	11
2 pieces flannel ..	3	10	0	Velvets, &c.	7	2	8
Niter or saltpeter ..	0	3	6	Silk Shawls, &c. ..	12	0	0
Pumpshoes	1	18	0	Coffee..	1	19	0
Silecias, 5 pieces ..	11	14	0	Silk Lutestrings ..	4	6	6
Marino, 5 pieces ..	9	2	0	12 firkins of butter ..	31	0	0
Table covers	2	0	0	Yellow soap	18	4	0
Bedquilts	3	12	6	Treacle	15	7	0
Buttons	6	15	6	410 lbs. Cheese ..	10	14	0
Boys Caps	7	17	6	America Baccon ..	0	13	0
Blankets	7	9	0	Brushes	11	16	9
Worsted & Yarn ..	11	5	11	Teas in cannisters ..	2	4	0
Hats	11	18	0	Shugar..	5	0	0
Silk Handkerchieves..	13	1	2	Corrans, &c.	6	4	6
Crape..	3	11	9	Handkerchieves ..	11	14	9

PART TWO

EARLY YEARS OF
CO-OPERATIVE INSURANCE
1867-1899

(i) Foundation of Co-operative Insurance Company

A fire destroyed a co-operative store at Tenby, South Wales, in April, 1865, with damage amounting to £200. The store was un-insured and the committee of the local Society issued an appeal for donations which was printed in the *Co-operator*.[1]

During the same month, James Borrowman, the Secretary of the Co-operative Society at Crosshouse in Ayrshire, wrote to the *Co-operator*:

> "There are many schemes for our mutual benefit fast ripening for a practical existence; in fact, they only require to be brought clearly before intelligent Co-operators to ensure their speedy adoption . . . In the matter of Fire Insurance, too, we might effect a considerable saving. Why pay between £1,000 and £2,000 per annum to swell the profits or cover the risks of associations with which we have little or nothing in common? As far as I am aware, we have had only one sufferer

[1] See *Co-operator*, 5 April, 1865, for the appeal from Tenby, and the ensuing circular distributed to other co-operative societies: " Under the circumstances, we have determined to appeal to our brother Co-operators throughout the country for aid; and will be grateful for the smallest sum as a donation, or will thankfully accept any sum in the shape of a loan, to be repaid before any of the members receive interest on their shares, or dividends on their purchases; and the Committee are sanguine of getting the cordial support of their fellow-workmen throughout the kingdom in their strait . . . "

In 1861, there had been a great fire in Tooley Street, London. (See paper read before Insurance Institute of London on 1 December, 1930, by P. E. Ridley.) The loss of property involved in the Tooley Street fire has been estimated at various amounts between £1m. and £2m. The loss fell as a staggering blow upon insurance companies. It brought home to them the fact that it was not sufficient to be able to pay a reasonable return to shareholders and that it was absolutely necessary to create fire reserves to meet abnormal losses which inevitably occur from time to time. On 27 February, 1849, a paper had been read before the Institution of Civil Engineers entitled " On Fireproof Buildings." The author of the paper regretted the passing of the older moderate-sized buildings with sub-stantial wooden floors which had given timely notice to the firemen of failure, a condition which did not exist in the case of "fireproof" buildings. It was explained that the intensity of a fire and the difficulties of extinguishing it depended, other things being equal, on the cubic capacity of the building.

After the Tooley Street fire, the insurance companies decided to give up their fire brigades, and in February, 1862, the House of Commons appointed a select committee to inquire into the existing state of legislation and of the protection of life and property against fire in the Metropolis. The insurance offices suggested to the Government the adoption of the Manchester scheme (Manchester Police Regulations Act 7 & 8 Victoria c 40) whereby the Corporation maintained out of the police rate the staff or plant of the fire brigade service but assessed rateably upon all parties concerned as proprietors of property damaged by fire, the expenses specifically incurred in putting out each conflagration. Where the property was insured the expenses were incurred rateably by the offices concerned according to their several interests; where uninsured they were borne by the proprietors. The Metropolitan Fire Brigade Act, which came into force from 1866, placed the duty of extinguishing fires and protecting life and property upon the Metro-politan Board of Works.

from fire. Co-operative stores ought to insure each other, and so have a mutual fire insurance of our own. Smaller premiums would suffice, as little or no expenses would be incurred and the profits would be all our own. We want, too, a Co-operative Sick and Funeral Society, with Rochdale as a centre and other stores as agencies: thus the management would cost the merest fraction of the money lifted, showing a happy contrast to those gigantic humbugs whose working expenses are covered by the modest sum of from 7d. to 10½d. for each 1s. collected."

There is nothing unique in these observations of Borrowman. He was one of a long line of co-operators who had seen weaknesses and gaps in the Movement, and had sought support for their views in the columns of the co-operative journals since the 1821 *Economist*. Wholesale agencies, co-operative production, equitable labour exchanges, annual congresses and a central board for the Co-operative Movement, all had been sounded in the first instance through published correspondence. The Co-operative Movement was always larger and more varied than its corporate intelligence — it is a commonplace to provide evidence that dividend on purchases was a feature of a number of retail societies long before Rochdale; similarly, James Borrowman was singularly mistaken in believing that the Co-operative Movement had suffered only one fire. His remarks on the expense ratios of industrial assurance offices were pertinent and somewhat acid; they are also surprising, and indicate that criticism of the collecting societies must have been more widespread than one would have thought during the 1860s.

On 15 May, 1865, Borrowman wrote again to the *Co-operator* with more specific proposals in mind. The letter was headed " Co-operative Fire Insurance."

" Since writing to you on the subject of a Co-operative Mutual Fire Insurance Society, I have given the matter some thought, and now venture to suggest a plan which I think might be acted on at once; if each store willing to join in this movement would send its name and address to the *Co-operator*, for insertion monthly, until such time as they are all published, and then a list of them to be published annually in the *Co-operator*. When forwarding their names, if already assured, they will send last receipt for premium paid; if not, a line signed by a deputation from two of the nearest stores, stating whether they consider the amount of insurance just and no extra risk attached; and then the stores so insured shall pay their premiums into their respective sinking funds. In the event of a fire, a deputation from the two nearest stores to determine the value of the goods destroyed. In case of a dispute as to the amount of damage done, three arbitrators to be chosen, whose decision shall be final and binding; say, for England, Henry Pitman[1] and Abraham Greenwood;[2] and for Scotland, Alexander Campbell.[3] The sum required to cover damage done in the event of a fire, to be raised by a levy of so much per £100 insured by each store; for example — say total amount insured by the various stores is £300,000; amount awarded for damage done by fire, £300; this would require about 2s. per £100 insured. A store insured for (say) £400, would pay as their share 8s.; one insured for £1,500 in the same ratio, 30s. The plan is simple, the saving would be very great to co-operative societies in the aggregate and is well worth their consideration."

It will be seen that Borrowman was advocating individual sinking funds to be kept by each participating retail society, also a levy which could not be determined until fire damage had been assessed. He did not appreciate that insurance is the substitution of a premium, certain in level and fixed for a term, in place of the onus of unpredictable risk and consequential loss or damage. A levy would reduce the incidence of loss for any one party, but a predetermined and regularly subscribed premium would not be possible.

There is no mention of fire surveys, appliances or precautions. Moreover, although the assessors, as fellow-co-operators, might have some knowledge of stock and property valuation, they would hardly possess the skills required for arbitration of insurance claims. Nevertheless, James Borrowman had shown up the vulnerability of many

[1] *Pitman, Henry*, 1826–1909. Co-operator, stenographer, vegetarian, anti-vaccinator. Younger brother of Sir Isaac Pitman. He was a reporter for the *Manchester Guardian* and he assisted with the publication of the *Co-operator* in 1860 (the journal generally referred to as the *Manchester Co-operator*). For 40 years he was the official reporter at Co-operative Congresses.

[2] *Greenwood, Abraham*, 1824–1911. Born at Rochdale. Son of blanket manufacturer. Joined Rochdale Pioneers in 1846, and was soon elected to its Management Committee. Promoter of *Co-operative News* and for 25 years Chairman of Newspaper Society.

[3] *Campbell, Alexander*, 1796–1870. A pioneer in the Co-operative and Trade Union movements in Scotland. Participated in the Community experiment at Orbiston, Lanarkshire (1826–1828). Ardent disciple of Robert Owen.

co-operative stores, and he was not above driving home his point in a further letter in the *Co-operator* of 15 June, 1865:

"I see a store at Tenby has suffered by fire to the amount of £200. Unfortunately, it was not insured, and so the loss falls entirely on the members. Misfortunes such as these ought to stimulate stores to take some united action in this matter, such as proposed in the *Co-operator* of 15 May."

A response came from the Hull Co-operative Provident Company which stated:

"I am instructed by our directors to inform Mr. Borrowman, through you, that they fully coincide with the views which he put forward in the May *Co-operator* on Co-operative Fire Insurance; and, further, to say that they are willing to take action in the matter at any time when a sufficient number of stores have given in their approval. Our insurance at present is for £1,500 . . ."

A month later Shepton Mallet Society wrote:

"We consider the plan named in the *Co-operator* in reference to a Co-operative Insurance Society a good one, and are willing to become connected with it; you may therefore, in making out the list as named in the paper, insert our society; it is but a small one; the value of goods in stock is about £100 at which we are anxious to be insured."

This is the first occasion when the title Co-operative Insurance Society appeared in print. Three societies, Bradford-on-Avon, Dukinfield, and Tenby, all uninsured against fire hazard, acknowledged donations in aid of their recent fire losses.

Correspondence signed W.C. (presumably William Cooper)[1] appeared in the September, 1865 issue of the *Co-operator*

"the idea of forming a 'Co-operative Insurance Society' is a good one, and should commend itself to the earnest consideration of all co-operative societies. I would suggest that a list be opened to ascertain how many societies would join, and (if practicable) have the list printed in the *Co-operator* with suggestions and remarks on the formation and management of the society or company, from the various stores. Your correspondent 'Spectator' is quite right in saying that the

---

[1] *Cooper, William,* 1822–1868. One of the 28 founders of the Rochdale Pioneers' Society in 1844. He served as cashier for the Pioneers' for 24 years until his death. Much of the preparatory work in establishing the CWS in 1863 was steered by Cooper.

present system of insurance is costly, and tends to keep up an extravagant expenditure for clerks, agents, printing, advertising, stately edifices, etc. An Insurance Company on the co-operative principle could be worked at much less expense, and the insurers would be the gainers. Let the subject be well considered, and some action taken in the matter. Invite discussion, or rather the opinions of co-operators, and we shall soon see the thing desired an accomplished fact."

On 7 April, 1866, a conference was held in Glasgow, and a meeting of thirty-five delegates representing Scottish Co-operative societies considered a proposal for the setting up of a wholesale agency " to entertain the question of a Mutual Co-operative Fire and Plate Glass Window Insurance Association." Borrowman presided, but the conference resolved " that no further steps be taken in the matter of Insurance until the English Co-operative Conference Committee publish the result of their deliberation thereon." Shortly afterwards, the Rochdale Pioneers' Society took up the suggestion of James Borrowman, and printed a circular "to be sent to the various societies asking them a number of questions as to whether their property is insured? Whether buildings or floating stock? To what amount? The rate of payment for such insurance, etc.? " William Cooper wrote in support

> " it was decided by the committee to recommend £1 per member for each society, to be a foundation or capital to guarantee payment in case of fire to insurers. The capital to be paid at one shilling on each share, and the rest, or a portion of it, in calls, as required. The next meeting will take place after I have received a letter and a draft bill of some amendments to the Industrial and Provident Societies Act 1862, from E. V. Neale, Esq., which it is proposed to bring before Parliament, whether in this session or not I cannot say until after another committee, and probably a conference meeting."

The following notice appeared in the *Co-operator*, March, 1867:

> " Those societies that have not yet answered the questions contained in the form sent to them relating to Insurance, are requested to do so at their earliest convenience, and address the same to Mr. William Cooper, Secretary, 115 Oldham Road, Rochdale — societies wishing to pay the farthing per member towards the conference objects, may do so in stamps, post office order, or cheque, payable to Mr. Cooper."

Abraham Greenwood   *William Cooper*

A conference of delegates from interested Co-operative societies was held on Good Friday, 19 April, 1867, at Downing Street Store, Ardwick, Manchester, with the principal item on the agenda the subject of rules for a proposed Co-operative Insurance Company Limited — the business of insurance could not then be legally undertaken by an Industrial and Provident Society. Ninety-eight delegates attended the conference, representing 65 societies, mostly within 100 miles of Manchester. Abraham Greenwood took the chair, and printed returns were laid before the delegates giving particulars respecting the insurances of 151 societies. The total amount of property insured by the societies who had completed the questionnaire was £271,765, and the premiums thereon were £651 1s. 10½d., whilst the total fire damage had been £970 12s. 7d., of which £789 12s. 7d. had been caused in 1864, £30 in 1861, £1 in 1860, and £150 for dates not specified. Some societies had taken out fire insurance cover for periods of up to 20 years; Rochdale Society, for example, had been insured for 22 years without having made a claim upon their insurers.[1] Hence it was not possible to make an exact correlation between annual premiums and fire losses, as premiums increased *pari passu* with property owned by the Co-operative societies. However, there was an average of £4 insured property for each of the 69,641 members of the 151 societies which had submitted returns, so that each society

---

[1] The stock-in-trade of the Nottingham Co-operative Society was insured in May, 1867, with the General Life and Fire Assurance Company at a valuation of £1,600. See F. W. Leeman, *Co-operation in Nottingham* (1963), p.28.

E. Vansittart Neale   Charles Howarth

willing to guarantee that sum per member would provide more than
adequate cover "but a much less guarantee will be sufficient as the
premiums will cover the average losses each year, and leave a
surplus."[1]

Yet a fund would have to be held in reserve to cover a
possible extraordinary loss: "For this purpose £1 for each member
in the society joining the projected Co-operative Insurance Company
Limited would probably be ample to meet all contingencies." The
delegates unanimously agreed to form a Co-operative Insurance
Association. Reading and consideration of the draft Memorandum
and Articles of Association of the Co-operative Insurance Company
for incorporation under the Joint Stock Companies Act of 1862, was
then undertaken.[2]

[1] There is a reference in C. R. Fay, *Great Britain from Adam Smith to Present Day*
(4th edit. 1937), p 416, to the formation of the CIS in 1867: "Let the article be
sold through the Movement if it is not yet made by it, and insured through it
if it is not yet sold or made by it."

[2] The objects of the Co-operative Insurance Company were stated "To be not only
to insure the property but the lives of members, and to guarantee the honesty of
servants, etc. The property of non-members would also be insured." There was
considerable discussion upon the 51 clauses composing the Articles of Association.
It was explained that though the second clause specified that "the registered office
of the company shall be in England," this being the required legal wording, it
did not preclude the opening of sub-offices in Scotland and Ireland. Any co-operative society of 100 members joining the company would have to guarantee not
less than £5, and the proportionate guarantee for a greater number of members,
and to be allotted shares at the rate of one to every four members. The profits
were to be divided amongst the guaranteed members of the company.

It was estimated that there were at least 500 Co-operative societies contributing a total sum of several thousand pounds annually for insurance in 1867: " Moreover it is evident from the balance sheets of insurance companies that they make very large profits on their business."

The Company was duly registered on 29 August, 1867. Details of premium calculations were to be worked out by members of a committee. The *Co-operator* of 1 November, 1867, announced:

"We wish to call attention to the fact that the first meeting of the Co-operative Insurance Company Limited, will be held in the Mechanics' Institution, David Street, Manchester,[1] on Saturday, 16 November, 1867, at 6 p.m. when the directors of the Company will be elected and other important business transacted. As this is the first meeting of the Company since its incorporation, a full attendance of delegates is desirable. All co-operative societies are invited to send delegates. Societies that have not received circulars of invitation, with form of application for shares, and the Articles of Association, can obtain the same from Mr. William Cooper, 115 Oldham Road, Rochdale."

[1] The Mechanics' Institution, David Street, was the second Mechanics' Institute in Manchester and was opened in 1857. David Street was subsequently re-named Princess Street and the original building housed, until 1966, the main premises of the Manchester College of Commerce.

At the inaugural meeting it was resolved that the registered office was to be in Rochdale and that there were to be seven directors — James Percival and James Dyson of Manchester, John Hilton of Middleton, William Cooper of Rochdale, Charles Howarth of Heywood, Edmund Robinson of Hulme, John Potts of Rochdale, and that William Cooper was to act as the Secretary.[1] The second meeting was held on 10 December, 1867, in the Oldham News Room of the Rochdale Equitable Pioneers' Society and it was resolved that "the Secretary write according to the suggestion of E. Vansittart Neale, Esq. to N. B. Bouber for forms of books and other necessary papers." The rates of the Western Insurance Company were to be used as a basis for quotation for fire policies. John Potts and William Cooper were then asked to seek the consent of the Pioneers' Committee for the use of the Society's central or other offices for the Co-operative Insurance Company. Various formalities were undertaken on 26 December, 1867, and officials appointed. Councillor Smithies,[2] of Bolton, was requested to act as Treasurer; Abraham Greenwood to become Manager; and "Mr. Zackary Mellor, the Town Clerk of Rochdale be desired to become the Solicitor to the Company." Number 2 committee room in the new central store, Toad Lane, Rochdale, was to be the head office of the Co-operative Insurance Company. One guinea was forwarded to the Western Insurance Company for forms and papers, and it was decided that the Manchester and Liverpool District Bank should be the official bankers for the Company. (The bank account was later transferred to the North of England Co-operative Wholesale Society in 1872.) In January, 1868, the directors were concerned with supplying a design for a Company seal. The first intimation that business should be sought was an instruction "that the Secretary see Mr. John Fothergall as to the form for insuring corn mills." Later in the month, the Secretary was further asked to write to Walter Morrison, a member of Parliament sympathetic to co-operation, for a copy of the report of the Select Committee

---

[1] *Percival, James*, 1833–1895. One of founders of Manchester and Salford Equitable Society. Became treasurer of CWS in 1868 and later accountant and auditor.
Dyson, James, 1823–1902. Silk hatter. Original member of CWS. First Chairman Amalgamated Union of Co-operative Employees.

Hilton, John, 1824–1890. One of founders of Middleton and Tonge Co-operative Society. Original member of CWS.

Howarth, Charles, 1818–1868. Rochdale cotton mill worker. Rules for Rochdale Pioneers' Society mainly drawn up by Howarth. Original member of CWS.

[2] *Smithies, James*, 1819–1869. Born at Huddersfield. Became a wool-stapler in Rochdale. An original member of CWS.

on Fire Insurance companies.[1]   A design for a policy heading was adopted and 500 policies were to be printed,[2] together with 700 circulars to be sent out to co-operative societies.

The first items of fire insurance business came in February, 1868, when the stock-in-trade of the North of England Wholesale Society to the amount of £1,000 " at a like rate to that they are now paying " was accepted. Kendal Equitable Industrial Co-operative Society was also insured to the extent of £800 stock-in-trade at 2s. per cent and buildings £400 at 1s. per cent. £200 stock-in-trade of Shepshed Co-operative Society was also accepted at 2s. per cent. Subsequent meetings of directors in February and March were more fitfully attended. On 7 March, a quorum could not be achieved, and it was resolved " that the absentees from the directors' meetings be written to know if they intend to hold their offices in this Company." The mandate had some effect on attendance at the ensuing meeting — 28 April — when six of the seven directors were present.

Proposals considered in April, 1868, from ten co-operative societies[3] included one for £4,000 on a new building at Upper Medlock Street store, Manchester. Prestwich Co-operative Society was insured for £400 for shop and cottages at 2s. per cent premium, but a policy granted to the Bathgate Society in Scotland on buildings and stock was quoted at 2s. 6d. per cent for the bakehouse " in consideration of bakehouse being apportioned their insurance." Enquiries were to be made regarding reinsurance in other companies; and two of the directors were to sign policies written out by the Secretary, and examined by Abraham Greenwood, the Manager. A branch store of the Oldham Co-operative Society was insured, " but that further enquiry be made about the drapery and grocery stocks and the rates now paid to them on this stock. That the floating stock be insured for £500 at the same rate as they now pay." Most of the early business was local, but during May, 1868, £300 was insured on premises of the Belfast Workingmen's Co-operative Society at 2s. per cent, and advice was sought from E. Vansittart Neale on reinsurance with non-tariff offices. In July, the Over Darwen Society was insured for £5,600 on its central store and stocks; half of this amount was

---

[1] See Footnote, above p.20.

[2] There was a heavy tax on fire policies, but the Gladstone budget of 1865 reduced the tax to one penny per policy per year.

[3] The first Scottish society to insure with the Co-operative Insurance Co. was Bathgate Society and not Crosshouse Society, for which James Borrowman was Secretary.

reinsured with the English Insurance Company. Capital funds of the newly-formed Company were to be deposited in the bank, but £50 was to be on call to purchase shares in the Rochdale Co-operative Land and Building Company Limited.[1] Directors' expenses were to be met by allowing them second class railway fares if they travelled from a distance. Enquiries having been made regarding the Oldham store, an offer was made to insure the stock for £1,000 at 3s. per cent premium. The Rochdale Pioneers' Society gave wholehearted support to the Company by bringing in over £8,300 of business, including "fixtures, board rooms, meeting rooms, library and books and newsroom" for £1,000; a butcher's shop in Toad Lane, "also the slaughter house, stabling live and dead and other stock" for £1,000.

A first advertisement for the Company appeared in the *Co-operator* on 4 July, 1868, giving the registered offices as Pioneers' Buildings, Toad Lane, Rochdale:

"This Company is established for the insurance of co-operative societies, on the principle of mutuality. After providing for policy liabilities and expenses of management the profit will be divided equally between shareholders, investments and insurances effected. The directors beg to call the attention of committees of co-operative societies who have not yet insured their property, as well as those whose policies are about to expire, to the claims of the Co-operative Insurance Company to their assistance in developing another formation of co-operative enterprise. A large number of shares are already taken up and policies issued covering property to a considerable amount."[2]

A first call of 5s. on each share was made in February, 1868, and in May, 1870, the capital was increased from £1,200 to £4,800 in £1 shares with a call of 4s. on each share.[3] The share-capital structure

---

[1] "Mr. Smithies of Rochdale said the Pioneers had a separate Building Company with a subscribed capital of £4,000, and they had built 37 cottages. They had power not only to build cottages, but to buy and sell land, make bricks and do almost anything. The Pioneers' Society found one-half the capital and the bulk of the members belong to the Equitable Society." *Co-operator*, 15 May, 1867.

[2] "The Co-operative Fire, Life and Guarantee Insurance Company was projected in London in 1867, with a proposed capital of £12,000. Mr. Abraham Greenwood and Mr. William Cooper were two of the promoters." C. Walford, *Insurance Encyclopaedia*, Volume 2, 1873. There is also a reference in Walford to a "Co-operative Fire Assurance Association": "This Company was registered in 1869, but does not appear to have been entered upon business."

[3] The directors of the North of England Wholesale Society had become empowered to take shares in the Co-operative Insurance Company at their half-yearly meeting on 16 November, 1867, at the Manchester Mechanics' Institution — see *Co-operator*, 2 December, 1867.

Fire destroys Co-operative Store at Tenby

Meeting of the Founders

I hereby certify that the rates of contributions shown in the several preceding Tables (to each of which my signature is attached) include a loading or equivalent provision for commissions and expenses, as under. —

Tables 1. 2. 3 and 5. 22½ per cent on each rate of contribution.

Table 4 . . 10 per cent on each rate of contribution, and an equivalent during the term of payment for the same amount of expense (excluding commission) as is contained in the loading declared for Tables 1. 2. 3 and 5 and a further provision for half this last amount after the payments have ceased and for the remainder of the Member's life.

Tables 6. 7. 8. 9 and 10.— 15 per cent on each rate of contribution until the pension falls in, and an equivalent for 5 per cent on each contribution after the pension has fallen in and for the remainder of the Member's life.

Tables 11. 12 and 13. 20 per cent on each rate of contribution.

And I further certify that, in my opinion, the net rates of contribution, after giving proper effect to the deductions representing these loadings and provisions, may be fairly and safely adopted for the purposes of the Co-operative Friendly Society, according to the Rules and Regulations thereof as in force at this date.

Lond'. Prov'. Law Ass' Soc'y   Ralph P. Hardy   Actuary
24 Fleet St: London
19th Oct. 1878   Actuary authorized by the Treasury to certify annuities.

The undersigned members of the Co-operative Friendly Society, in proof that the foregoing Rules and Tables have been adopted for the Regulation of the Co-operative Friendly Society, thereunto attach their ~~names~~ signatures.

John Allan

William Pannell

William Foster

Titus Hall,

Wm H Hill

Thomas Wilberforce.

Thomas Wood

Edwd Vansittart Neale Secretary

Certification of Rules of the Co-operative
Friendly Society, 1878

James Odgers

of the Company was such that each Society-member guaranteed £5 and held allotted shares at the rate of one share to every four individual members of the Society concerned. The Articles of Association were altered to incorporate this amendment in November, 1870.

The first annual meeting of the Co-operative Insurance Company, attended by about 60 representatives, was held at the Union Chambers, Dickenson Street, Manchester, on 6 February, 1869. The Chairman stated that the premium rates charged were usually those at which insurances had previously been effected in other offices; that inspection of fire risks had not taken place, nor did the funds so far warrant the directors incurring the expense. In discussion, it was asked why an offer of business from a co-operative manufacturing company's works had been declined. The chairman replied that they insured only ordinary co-operative stores, and that in the case mentioned special reasons connected with the lighting and stoves made it an undesirable risk to accept. Another delegate urged the importance of appointing a practical man to act as inspector of proposals.

The first financial statement of the Company was made up to 1 October, 1868, after scarcely four months of active business. The directors considered that an early opportunity should be taken to develop fidelity insurance on behalf of the servants of co-operative societies. They also looked forward to the Company becoming a permanent co-operative institution and to an extension of its business operations — £444 had been received on share calls, and this almost matched the balance in bank of £424, but it was evident that such a sum was extremely inadequate to represent the risks that were being undertaken. A greater guarantee than that represented by the called-up share capital was necessary. A delegate enquired whether the sum in the bank could be lent to co-operative societies at 5 per cent interest — for which there were many opportunities. Before confidence could be created, he argued, more capital would have to be provided. The chairman explained that out of 151 societies that had submitted returns to Mr. Cooper, as willing to join the Company, only 36 had actually done so. He believed that possibly a quarter of the premiums, if not one-half, could be returned. Profits were to be divided, half upon capital subscribed and half upon the amount paid in premiums.

In an issue of the *Co-operator*, published after the report of the annual meeting of the Company, there appeared a reference to life assurance in an advertisement for the Victoria Assurance Society of London: " The mutual principle of operating this assurance society," it was reported, entitled members to the whole of the profits, "and thus in the matter of life assurance ensures to them the benefits of the co-operative system." A postscript stated "by a special application of the profits, policies become payable during the lifetime of the assured.[1] The Co-operative Insurance Company does not assure individual lives."

Enquiries were made during February, 1869, concerning fire tariff associations, and a sub-committee was delegated to investigate the possibilities of undertaking fidelity guarantee insurance. The sub-committee recommended that the policies and forms of the European Assurance Company should be adopted. The first guarantee policy was approved in April and issued in June.

A fire claim from the Rochdale Pioneers was settled, after investigation, for £5 17s. on 24 August, 1869. £600 was withdrawn from the bank account in October, 1869, and three loans each of £200 were made to the Rochdale Pioneers, the Rochdale Corn Mill and the Rochdale Manufacturing Society. Auditors' fees for two years amounting to £1 were paid in January, 1870.

The second annual meeting of the Co-operative Insurance Company took place on 5 February, 1870, and passed the resolution "that in the opinion of this meeting, the great risks resulting from the storage of paraffin oil renders it inadvisable to issue policies of insurance to societies who store or sell such oil on their premises." Samuel Stott,[2] the Treasurer who had taken over on the death of James Smithies, resigned, and J. R. Shepherd was elected in his place. William Cooper had died in December, 1868, and Abraham Howard[3] took over as the new Secretary. It was agreed that past and present directors were to be paid two shillings for each meeting attended. The Secretary was presented with £10 for services rendered, and the Manager was to receive £4.[4] The salary of the Secretary was later fixed at £20 per year, and that of the General Manager was to be £2 per year. Share lists were opened in October, 1870, to individuals, and business could be accepted from persons other than co-operative societies.

In a paper read to the Co-operative Congress on 11 April, 1871,

[1] Presumably an oblique reference to a system of ' with-profits ' policies.
[2] *Stott, Samuel*, 1824–1897. First president of the Rochdale Corn Mill.
[3] *Howard, Abraham*, 1830–1906. Early member and sometime president of Rochdale Pioneers' Society. Became first President of Liverpool Co-operative Society.
[4] See letter from Mrs. S. M. Evans, April, 1965 (Mr. R. E. Evans of Finchley CIS office is the eldest living relative of Abraham Greenwood). "I have often listened to the tales of Grandpa Greenwood and laughed over his being the first General Manager of the CIS at the ' large ' figure of £8 (sic) per annum."

Howard stated that the first policy was issued on 21 February, 1868. He mentioned to delegates that the Company wished to begin life assurance business, but the action of Parliament had set this in abeyance. The first fidelity guarantee policy had been issued on 25 June, 1869, and by the end of September, 1870, the total cover of guarantee policies was £6,100. The advantage of fidelity guarantee business was explained, in that it compelled the appointment of trustworthy persons and therefore confirmed the judgment of the selection made. The Co-operative Insurance Company in undertaking this class of risk had charged premiums similar to those charged by other companies, both in the fire and guarantee departments. The rules were so amended that persons or societies who supplied the business would have one-third of the profits divided according to the amount of premium paid, whether they were members of the Company or not. Another third was to be divided amongst the members in proportion to the amount of their guarantee and the shares taken together; the remaining third was to be undivided and become a reserve fund — which was not to be appropriated except in cases of actual deficiency — until it was equal in amount to 5 per cent of the whole policies in force. In 1870, the shareholding membership had been thrown open to individuals, and the directors were prepared to grant insurance on private property as well as on Co-operative properties. It was stated that no further call beyond 4s. a share would be made, except under circumstances of necessity, but interest and profits would be carried to account of shares until they were fully paid-up. Interest at the rate of 5 per cent was to be credited to share capital and the apportionment of profits was to be made every five years. The guarantee of £5 per member was in addition to, and independent of, the number of shares taken up. In the subsequent discussion at the 1871 Congress, William Pare,[1] the veteran Co-operator, recommended that a change should be made in the name of the Company, and that it should be called the Co-operative Insurance and Guarantee Society. He thought that this would make it better known as the society that guaranteed the honesty of co-operative servants, and he further suggested that no servants should be employed by any co-operative society who were not so guaranteed. G. J. Holyoake asked whether the Company intended to

[1] *Pare William*, 1805–1873. A leading Owenite, William Pare was appointed first Registrar of Births, Marriages and Deaths of Birmingham District in 1837. He was for a time Acting Governor of the Owenite Co-operative Community at Queenwood, Hampshire. Pare was a successful businessman and wrote extensively on co-operation and currency reform.

confine its fire business to co-operative societies. If this could be extended to non-co-operative property, he thought that he could help them to a good many insurances. William Pare also would be prepared to insure some of his own personal property with the Company if this were possible. A Mr. McInnes of Glasgow said that at the time the Company was established, he recommended that it should be founded on a broader basis, and regretted that there was a legal restriction on societies in Scotland becoming associated with the Company. He knew that there were a few societies in Scotland insured with the Company, but he also knew that if there was any impediment to the payment of these policies, the Scottish societies would have no legal standing in their local courts. There were three registrars — one for England, one for Scotland and one for Ireland — and unless an insurance office was registered with the appropriate registrar, there was no legal claim. Lloyd Jones, another survivor from the heroic days of co-operation, contended that the Co-operative Insurance Company might take their capital from any person and they might effect insurances with whoever came forward. He did not see why the Company should limit its business to co-operators. It was the duty of co-operative societies to insure in their own Company, but only 150 had done so out of 600 or 700: "Cottage property could also be insured, and it was the least risky and most profitable." John Hilton, a director, did not think that the Society had risen so rapidly as it ought to have done, and co-operative societies had not offered to insure with the Company to the extent that they ought to have done. The slowness of growth of the Company was referred to by another delegate, but he was of the opinion that things should not grow too rapidly. He felt more satisfied when he knew that the whole of its expenses had been covered during the last year out of the interest on its accumulated capital. Lloyd Jones drew up the following resolution

"that this Congress approves the principle and objects of the Co-operative Insurance Company and recommends the various co-operative societies and their members to take shares, and also to insure in this Company; and that the delegates present pledge themselves to do their best for the promotion of this object."

John Butcher, Secretary of Banbury Society, indicated that co-operators could pay their premiums out of their dividends. It was pointed out that the total value of the buildings and fixtures belonging to the various co-operative societies throughout the country amounted to £1,750,000, but the total value insured through the Co-operative Insurance Company was only £140,000. However, all the servants of the Wholesale Society were guaranteed by the Company. William Pare warned that great care should be taken in the life assurance branch business: " But all the care that was necessary to be taken was to go to a first-rate actuary and get him to lay down life tables, based upon the best information that could possibly be had." Henry Pitman thought that the Insurance Company would become more popular " if it were known that the lives of unvaccinated persons would have preference, as being less risky than the lives of the vaccinated." At any rate, he hoped " that no questions would be asked, or objections raised on this ground, as was the case with certain doctor-ridden and exclusive offices." Reference was made to an attempt by the Scottish societies to form an insurance society, but the registrar had refused to certify the rules.

The chairman urged that persons should be appointed in each town for the purpose of bringing business to the Company, and be paid by commission. Abraham Howard replied that this was the first week that the business of the Company had been opened to the general public, and one reason why it did not make more rapid progress was that at the beginning the basis of the share capital was very low, and that they could not push the business until they could guarantee the payment of all claims that might be made upon them.

It came to the notice of the directors in April, 1871, that paraffin was being stored in adjoining premises to the Rochdale Pioneers. Chester-le-Street Society also enquired concerning insurance and stated that they kept paraffin and gun-powder — the insurance was declined.

In May, 1871, a sub-committee was appointed to consider the possibility of employing agents, and Lloyd Jones agreed to look out for suitable agents in the course of his lecture tours. In August, 1871, it was minuted " that agents be immediately appointed in various co-operative centres."

Several changes took place amongst the office holders during October. Abraham Howard resigned as Secretary, and became Treasurer in place of J. R. Shepherd. T. Wood became the new Secretary. Howard reported in the same month on the fire at Charlton Branch of the Hebden Bridge Society, and it was resolved to make a written request to the Society to make a careful inventory of salvage.

The advisability of removing the Head Office of the Company to Manchester had been discussed early in 1871.[1] Terms were agreed with the North of England CWS for the use of their office and board room at an annual rental of £5 from July, 1871.

Fire insurance was accepted on behalf of James Borrowman in November, 1871, for £400 at 2s. per cent. A guarantee bond was also undertaken on his behalf to the Scottish Co-operative Wholesale Society for £800 at 40s. per cent, " subject to answers from one of the referees who have not yet replied being satisfactory." James Borrowman purchased twenty shares of the Company in July, 1872.

The possibility of opening branches of the CIC was investigated from March, 1872. Shortly afterwards, the Scottish Co-operative Wholesale Society was approached and appointed as an agent of the Company. The terms were 5 per cent on cash received as premiums and a similar commission on all share deposits received through their agency. At the annual meeting in the following February, the Scottish agents reported that they did not anticipate much business, as the vast majority of co-operative stores in Scotland stocked paraffin oil and also used it for lighting. The meeting decided to amend the regulation concerning the insurance of premises in which oil was kept, and agreed to consider whether, under certain conditions, it would waive the embargo on such cover. A sub-committee was appointed to consider the advisability of appointing a permanent Secretary — the existing Secretary had been paid £30 for a year's service, the Manager £4, and the Treasurer £1.

James Odgers, then assistant secretary to the Central Co-operative Board, was appointed Secretary to the Company on 18 March, 1873.[2] His office was later to be termed General Manager, and he was the first in a line of but four general managers, who were to control the

---

[1] It is not known exactly when the first insurance company was established in Manchester, but as long ago as 1771, a local fire office — the Manchester Fire Office — was in operation. Three independent engineering insurance companies still have their head offices in Manchester — the British Engine Boiler and Electrical, the National Boiler, and the Vulcan Boiler. The National Motor (formed by a group of local tradesmen known as the Manchester and National Horse Owners' Union), the Federated Employers', and the Methodist also have their head offices in Manchester.

Manchester also pioneered in the field of insurance education. In 1873, James Robb, Manager of the Northern, and his associates, decided there should be more contact between local insurance managers in Manchester. They formed an association with membership originally restricted to senior representatives of the tariff offices. Other cities followed the example of Manchester and established local Insurance Institutes and these were eventually associated in a Federation from 1897, which became the Chartered Insurance Institute in 1912.

[2] In May, 1873, Thomas Wood, the Secretary to the CIC, retired.

destiny of the Company over the first century of its existence. Odgers' initial salary was fixed at 10 per cent commission on all fire insurance premiums, and 5 per cent on guarantee premiums and on share deposits received, but it was conceded that he should draw 30s. weekly on account of commission, receiving the balance at the end of the current year. There is no evidence that Odgers had any previous knowledge of insurance procedure when he joined the Co-operative Insurance Company. Beatrice Webb was to meet him in 1889, after he had gained 16 years' experience, and she commented — " Odgers is a positivist, an enthusiast who gave up a salary of £200 per year to become a co-operative employee at £1 per week inspired by J. S. Mill's chapter on Co-operation."[1]

She added these impressions of his character :

> " He is without humour and without push or striking ability. But he is one of those men who makes the backbone of great movements through steadfastness and integrity of character. 'Where shall we find the moral impulse wherewith to inspire the Co-operative Movement? Profit sharing is played out' is his constant meditation."

[1] Beatrice Webb, *My Apprenticeship* (1938 Penguin edit.), Volume 2, p.410.

One of the first tasks given to the new Secretary was an instruction to write to E. O. Greening[1] to enquire whether feeding stuffs, manures and oil cakes were especially inflammable or liable to spontaneous combustion. Odgers was soon engaged in visiting and inspecting premises in the Manchester area. In September, his railway fares to Todmorden and Blackburn were reimbursed — Blackburn Co-operative Society was advised to use fire screens at two of their branches. Fire insurance at Shepshed Co-operative Society premises was accepted, subject to the proviso that if paraffin was the proximate cause of any fire, the loss would not be made good. Odgers claimed 4s. 8d. for bed and meals at Leicester. A proposal from the CWS Shoe Works at Leicester was declined, until they agreed to remove their joiners' shop from the ground floor. The remuneration of the Manager was increased from £4 to £6 for the year's service 1872 to 1873, and Odgers' weekly salary was to be raised by 5s. to 35s. with commission payable quarterly or half-yearly.

In 1873 the CIC applied for membership of the CWS and paid the necessary deposit.

In the same year, the CWS transferred £2,000 from its reserve fund to form the nucleus of an insurance fund

> " and from this time the Society undertook a considerable portion of its own insurance risks, including buildings, stocks, outlying stocks, steamships, goods-in-transit by sea, and the guarantee of its own servants. There have been further sums transferred from the reserve amounting to £4,000 and with the premiums charged to the insurance fund, the fund now amounts to £22,812."[2]

It should be noted however that when the CWS Trade Insurance Fund was formed, many of the trade risks to be covered were not acceptable to the CIC. In 1898, the CWS rules were extended to enable the Trade Insurance Fund to include all insurance except life. The CWS also instituted a Co-operative House Building Scheme.[3]

A letter from Leicester enquired whether the Company would undertake life assurance with limits not exceeding £10 for members of the proposed Co-operative Sick and Mutual Burial Society;

---

[1] *Greening, Edward Owen, 1836-1923.* Ardent Co-operator. Deeply interested in Co-operative horticulture. Played a prominent part in the formation of the International Co-operative Alliance, and following William Pare, was a keen advocate for a Co-operative College.

[2] P. Redfern, *New History of CWS* (1938), p.405.

[3] See *CWS 21st Anniversary Pamphlet* (1884).

Coatbridge Co-operative Society wondered whether plate glass insurance could be undertaken — it was resolved not to extend the scope of business to include either of these forms of cover. In December, 1873, the Co-operative Wholesale Society decided to take up an agency for the CIC in London, in addition to the one already held at Newcastle, on the terms of 5 per cent on premiums and share deposits received.

A deficiency claim concerning a treasurer of the Ancient Order of Foresters "appeared to turn on the point whether his omission to keep the cash received on account of the funds of the Court separate from his personal and trading moneys was a criminal act." (July, 1873.) It was resolved to write to the Ancient Order of Foresters stating that as no criminal defalcation was incurred, the CIC could not be held liable to meet the claim.

The cover period of fire policies was discussed, and it was decided not to issue policies for any period less than three months, and that the pro-rata annual premium be increased by 10 per cent for a cover period of nine months, 20 per cent for six months, and 40 per cent for three months. The Secretary was instructed to write to any reputable insurance office, such as the Equitable and the Royal to ascertain their terms for reinsurance business.

An executive committee of four — the Chairman, Manager, Treasurer, and one other — was empowered to fix rates of premium for fire and guarantee business from March, 1873, " accepting such as they may deem necessary should be submitted to the directors' meeting." Oldham Society was permitted under their fire policy to substitute a large iron dish on which their warming stove stood, for a flagstone.

The 1872 Co-operative Congress had debated a proposal for an insurance guarantee system to provide co-operative societies with credit on preferential terms, but it was argued that the effect of guarantee arrangements might be to encourage societies to be less cautious in their dealings. E. O. Greening did not accept the contention that insurance tended to diminish responsibility, and in illustration he referred to a plan carried out in Sweden and Norway, where " since the municipalities had taxed the citizens to pay the cost of fires, they had diminished to a great extent, and very few buildings were now destroyed, and in some cases payments were made to the citizens from the equalisation of this rate." He then suggested that the Wholesale Society and other retail societies should form a central committee with each society making itself liable for a given amount — a scheme akin to the original proposals of James Borrowman. A resolution was moved and seconded by E. Vansittart Neale :

> "That the Central Board be requested to collect statistics with a view to test the practicability of establishing a system of mutual guarantee amongst co-operative societies; to collect the opinions of the various societies on the subject; and to enter into negotiations with the Co-operative Insurance Society[1] and the Wholesale Society for the practical working out of the plan."

The resolution was adopted "nearly unanimously," but there is no evidence that any further action was taken to set up a system of credit guarantee for the Co-operative Movement as a whole.

A full-page advertisement for the Co-operative Insurance Company appeared in the 1872 Co-operative Congress Report. Head Office was now at 1 Balloon Street, Manchester, and the Scottish office was housed at the Scottish Co-operative Wholesale Society, 15 Madeira Street, Glasgow. The business of life assurance, it was announced, would be commenced as soon as the Company could comply with statutory requirements. Proposals for fire insurance or guarantee bonds were invited either from co-operative societies or individuals, and the share list was open to societies or individuals. The advertisement referred to the overreaching of many earlier co-operative ventures and the vulnerability of funds of friendly societies: "The utmost economy has been used in the management of the Company hitherto, and the directors intend to continue the same policy." In a return, submitted to Congress, no less than 139 Co-operative societies were noted as having no insurance cover whatsoever.

The annual Report for 1872 had shown that there had been only one fire loss during the year — Hebden Bridge Co-operative Society had made a claim, which was paid, for £62 4s. 4d. The total profit realised since the commencement of business by the Company was £617 6s. 11½d. According to rules, profit distribution was to be made after five years of operation, but although this was the fifth year, profits were not to be distributed until 1874, "as business had not been properly established." Shares to the extent of 6,468 (4s. called-up) had been subscribed, which was an increase of 2,252 over the

---

[1] It should be noted that throughout this early period there is a strong tendency to refer to the Co-operative Insurance Company as the Co-operative Insurance Society.

previous year. The year's interest on investment amounted to £88 3s. 11d. and interest on shares and bank commission £64 10s. 2d. The number of fire policies in 1871 was 152, with a value of £140,515; in 1872 the number rose to 216, with a value of £196,943.[1]

Between 1872 and 1873, the business transacted doubled. In 1873 the total sum insured was £287,822 on a share capital of £9,494. The advance, though rapid

> " is not commensurate with the requirements of the Co-operative Movement. There are at present only 40 shareholding societies, whilst the number now existing in the United Kingdom is probably about 1,500, comprising 400,000 members. If these societies were also shareholders in the Company, its guaranteed capital would thus be increased to the amount of £80,000. Subscribed capital to an amount less than that figure would enable the Company to extend its business and to make the necessary deposit of Government securities to commence life assurance."

At the Sixth Annual General Meeting held in 1874, delegates from twenty-six societies and eight individual shareholders attended, all of whom were representatives from Lancashire and Yorkshire, with the exception of one from London.

The Hebden Bridge delegate complained that he had to pay 6d. more premium with the Co-operative Insurance Company than with a previous office. Another delegate drew attention to the Secretary's salary of £73 9s., and asked whether it was not rather large compared with business done. A Minute of the Board was then read fixing the payment of the Secretary by commission. The Chairman explained — up to 10 April, 1873, office work had been done by a part-time Secretary, but the increase in business made it necessary to appoint a permanent Secretary to keep the books, to travel, and to inspect property. Another delegate pondered why the £1,000 kept in current account at the bank was not invested. The Treasurer explained that this balance was kept in order to pay claims immediately.

James Odgers read a paper at the Airedale Co-operative Conference in June, 1874, imploring retail societies not to relax their efforts to

---

[1] To place the size of the early CIC in perspective, an estimate of total inland fire insurance cover in 1872 was given as £1,900m. Shipping insurance was estimated at £800m. and life policies with bonuses at £300m., " making a total of liability to insurers, and of benefit to insured equal in amount to £3,000m. sterling — a sum nearly four times the whole national debt."

Andrew Kirkwood, *Lectures on Insurance and Industrial Law* (January, 1874) pamphlet in Library of Chartered Insurance Institute.

prevent fires after taking out insurance — for every fire was a destruction of Co-operative wealth, and it was therefore important that in all cases of special risk, appliances should be made available in readiness for emergencies. He then pointed out that co-operative societies offered an immense field for an economical scheme of life assurance and annuity business in which the profits would go to the policy-holders after providing a sufficient reserve fund. Each co-operative store should set up a life assurance department, or even a sick benefit fund, he added, in parenthesis. He referred to the dissipation of time and money in the meetings of friendly societies held in public houses. If a life department were added to each co-operative store, the members could either pay their premiums when they were at the store, or transfer a portion from their quarterly dividend. Accident business was contemplated:

> " This department of insurance being undertaken by societies in their united capacity, would occasion a much greater interest on their part in questions of sanitary and social reform; for the members would then know that all improvements made in these directions would add to the stability of their own institutions by the increased length of life resulting from conditions more conducive to health and happiness."

Odgers reported on the capital structure: the number of share-holding societies by September, 1873, was 51, and there were also 20 individual shareholders. Being registered under the Companies Act of 1862, individual members were not restricted to holding 200 shares only — but they were only allowed one vote irrespective of the number of shares held. Representation of societies was based on the rules of the CWS which allowed one delegate for the first 100 members and one extra for every additional 200 for whom shares had been taken up, in the proportion laid down.

The premium of fire policies for 1873 amounted to £368 on 371 policies. The number of fidelity guarantee policies in force was then 111, amounting to £20,910, on which £392 had been paid as premium during the year, making the premium income for guarantee business higher than that for fire. Only 144 societies were insured with the Company; the amount of their fire policies and their premiums being only one-sixth of the total amount of insurances of Co-operative societies in England and Wales as given in the Registrar's returns for 1872. Odgers admitted that the fire and guarantee department having been established for six years had shown slow progress, but the claims ratio had been less than eight per cent over the period. He suggested that one reason for this was that the Company had not received sufficient attention at co-operative conferences, and a further probable reason was that profits were only to be divided every five years, although interest at 5 per cent was credited annually to share capital on account of profits accumulating.

What were the criteria for investment of funds? Investment was to be restricted to easily convertible securities — security being the priority. With this proviso, funds were to be so invested as to promote the interests of the insured. In the fire and guarantee departments nearly all the business was with retail stores; accordingly, the larger portion of funds received from policyholders was deposited with the Co-operative Wholesale Society, and was used for business in the same manner as it would be if paid directly to the CWS by the local societies, instead of through the Company. In order to increase the taking up of the Company's shares, Odgers appealed to the retail societies to transfer part of their trade balances from the Wholesale Society to the Company — the shares would receive five per cent interest and would entitle societies to participate in profits.

An advertisement for the Company in the 1874 Congress Report, noted that Scottish office had transferred to Paisley Road, Glasgow, the Newcastle office was at Pudding Chare, and the London office at 118 Minories. All three offices were housed in premises of the Co-operative Wholesale Societies. A first notice of an individual agency was given — " Agent John Butcher, West End Shoe Works, Leicester." The directors were now being drawn from a much wider area than Manchester — a Mr. Allen from Glasgow, Titus Hall from Bradford, and W. Allott from Heckmondwike; and an important policy-maker for the future of the Co-operative Insurance Company — William Barnett from Macclesfield. The Company had transferred its banking account to the Co-operative Wholesale Society. This 1874 advertisement gave as the first object of the Company a portent for the future: " The object of this Company is to retain the profit on the insurance business in the hands of those who insure." The guarantee policies were being issued under two forms of cover. In the fire department, " co-operative stores, manufacturers, houses, cottages, fixtures, furniture, goods and merchandise are insured against loss or damage by fire; and from the care taken by the survey of risks and otherwise, only the most moderate premiums are required." Fire losses caused by lightning and explosions of gas were also covered.

The advertisement intimated that life assurance would be commenced as soon as members subscribed the requisite amount of capital. The manager was instructed to see E. Vansittart Neale as to the legality of commencing life assurance without making a deposit of £20,000 and also the possibility of insuring under the Friendly Societies Acts. Neale gave his opinion, confirmed by Thomas Hughes, that the section of the Life Assurance Act of 1870 requiring a deposit in Government securities before commencing life business, applied to the establishment of the *business* more than to the establishment of the Company. The directors turned to the alternative of investigating whether life assurance for the Co-operative Movement could be provided under the Friendly Societies Acts. A correspondent to the *Co-operative News* suggested that life assurance should be undertaken by a new co-operative assurance company which should issue policies for £5 and upwards, and also provide sickness and accident cover. Its agency system should be similar to that of the Prudential. James Odgers hastened to reply in the following issue of the *Co-operative News* that life assurance had been a dead letter, as previously to the passing of the Life Assurance Companies Act of 1870, the Co-operative Insurance Company had not issued life policies, and therefore was precluded from doing so until it had accumulated £20,000 as a statutory deposit. Early in 1874, E. Vansittart Neale advised that it would be illegal for the Co-operative Insurance Company to guarantee honesty of servants to private employers.

During March, 1874, an offer of marine business was declined ("proposals of Agricultural and Horticultural Association of London for fire policy on nitrate of soda and floating policy on manures in various docks; and an offer of all their marine insurance business was declined with thanks.") An account was paid in July to the Royal Insurance Company "for our share of expenses of extinguishing fire at Paisley Co-operative Society on 20 January, 1874, amount £6 7s. be paid." A fire policy of £1,000 was written for the Amalgamated Carpenters and Joiners Society at 2s. per cent. Retail societies were continually exhorted to improve their fire precautions. Failsworth Society were notified that the stove pipes in their central store were in contact with woodwork, and Manchester and Salford Society were warned about their store in Downing Street, Ardwick, "where the arrangements for heating irons used in the shoemakers' workroom were more hazardous than when the policy was issued." A fire policy for £500 2s. 6d. was taken out during November, 1874, on behalf of G. J. Holyoake.[1] In order to further guarantee business, the directors resolved that premiums should be reduced, but there should be a minimum of 10s. per cent. A letter from the Rochdale Pioneers' Society was received stating that another company had offered to guarantee a Mr. Rigg's fidelity for £100 at £13 10s. first premium, and £12 10s. for renewal — "it was resolved that we agree to issue a policy on same terms." £1,000 was withdrawn from the CWS and investment received more attention — £300 was invested in the Equitable Co-operative Permanent Benefit Building Society, and £750 each in the Albert Mill Company and the Heckmondwike Manufacturing Company.

Retail Co-operative societies were urged to take up shares in the CIC. It was pointed out that societies could hold any number of shares, but not less than ten in their corporate capacity.

Reinsurance business was extended cautiously. Early in 1874 it was minuted

"that with a view to offering co-operative societies greater facilities for insurance in companies in which we have confidence when the risks they offer are such as we are unable to undertake, an agency business be commenced and the terms of the Alliance, the British and Foreign Life and Fire Assurance Company be agreed to."

Such business was already being conducted with the Equitable and the Royal, but the Alliance informed the CIC that in order not to violate their rules

"it would be necessary for our agency account to appear in their books in the name of an individual. It was agreed with the consent of J. Smith, Assistant Secretary of the Central Co-operative Board that he be appointed our nominal agent of the Alliance Life and Fire Assurance Company."

In reply to a query, the Board stated that it did not wish to open an agency in Bristol. Apparently, the CIC was satisfied with the business it was gaining from local retail societies — for instance, in August, 1874, the Halifax Industrial Co-operative Society insured all their 23 branch shops with the CIC. By the end of the year, however, the directors were again prepared to consider appointing agents at a commission to extend business, "especially the insurance of cottage

[1] Holyoake, George Jacob, 1817–1906. Owenite Social Missionary. Imprisoned 1842. Founder-editor of The Reasoner, a Secularist journal. Extensive writer and lecturer on Co-operation and social reform. First historian of the Co-operative Movement See History of Co-operation (1875–79).

property." The Secretary also suggested that a commission of 15 per cent fire and 5 per cent for guarantee business be allowed to co-operative societies who were acting as agents, but the proposal was adjourned.

The journal *The Insurance Record* was subscribed to from March, 1874. During the summer, the Report of the Royal Commission on Friendly Societies was published, and the CIC Board especially noted the 44th clause which recommended " that the Law be amended so as to enable companies to carry on legally the business of industrial assurance within the same limits and subject to the same restrictions as friendly societies." In September, the CIC Board passed the resolution

> " that adoption of any scheme for commencing life insurance business be deferred until the Friendly Society Bill has been introduced into Parliament next year; that a scheme be then drawn up, based upon the provisions of the said Bill, and submitted to the Board for consideration."

The Board congratulated itself that the continuing immunity from serious loss would spread confidence. It was calculated that the entire losses of the Company during the first seven years of its existence, which amounted to £329 16s. 6d., was only 10 per cent of aggregate premiums paid. Two-thirds of the aggregate premiums of the Company from its commencement, less its losses during the same period, was to be retained in the Fire and Guarantee account as an accumulated insurance fund for future eventualities, and the balance transferred to the profit and loss account. Valuation of assets and liabilities was to take place at the end of each year, and in the event of the valuation showing a surplus, it was proposed to pay out dividend as advisable. The first division of profits was to be made in 1875. Members' interest and dividend was to be added to the account of share capital, and no interest or dividend was to be paid out until shares were fully paid-up.

The pressure of business during 1874 was eating into the lunch break of Odgers, who found it inconvenient to take one-and-a-half hours in the middle of the day; he proposed he should postpone dinner until after business and leave at 5 p.m. instead of 6 p.m. In January, 1875, the Board received a letter from Odgers stating that an opening had occurred which he desired to seize and being uncertain whether he should need to leave immediately or not until September, he wished to give the longest possible notice to the Board of his intention to resign. By March, Odgers intimated that he wished to be allowed to withdraw his notice, and the Board agreed to his request.

The Leicester Industrial Elastic Web Manufacturing Society submitted a claim to meet the cost of damage by water as a result of fire. The storage of combustible material was a constant source of anxiety to the CIC. Fire cover was normally quoted at 2s. 6d. per cent " if paraffin removed to outbuilding; 3s. 6d. per cent if kept in cellar." A fire occurred later in the year at Dewsbury. The Secretary carried out the normal procedure followed by fire salvage officers before the fire claim was paid. Several months later, it was noted that a more adequate water supply was available in Dewsbury as a consequence of the fire and it was therefore possible to reduce the level of premiums charged to branch stores. Terms of cover generally were being delineated more clearly; for instance, the Carnforth Society were informed that their risk would be declined unless they conformed to conditions as to the sale and storage of gunpowder. The rate quoted for the Rochdale Cornmill warehouse was to be increased from 10s. to 13s. per cent " in consequence of the increased risk by four additional pairs of stones in mill adjoining, and that half the amount of policy be reinsured." Fire cover for cottages in Rochdale to the total value of £6,580 was accepted in March, 1875; in the following month, the CWS Shoe Works at Leicester was accepted for £6,150 at 5s. per cent.

The Rochdale Pioneers applied for 236 additional shares in March, 1875. James Borrowman's name appeared in the minute book of the CIC in April, 1875, as he had applied for cancellation of the 25 shares standing to his credit. The balance of the Company's current account with the CWS was then £1,100. £500 was transferred to a deposit account, and a loan to the Equitable Co-operative Permanent Benefit Building Society was increased to £500 in June, 1875, but an application from the Lincoln Land and Building Society for an advance was not approved "as the amount of loss by Dewsbury fire reduced our funds on deposit and current account to a sum which should be immediately available." Ten mortgagors from the Equitable Co-operative Permanent Building Society were insured at 1s. 6d. per cent on mortgages ranging from £500 to £1,500. The Board "recommended to appoint as an individual agent — H. Pumphrey, Secretary of Lewes Co-operative Society, of a Co-operative Benefit Building Society there, and Honorary Secretary to the Southern District of Central Board." A policy decision on income tax was made: "That in our return to the income tax commissioners the profits for 1874 be stated as the interest carried to the credit of shareholders and one-fifth of the balance of profit accrued during the seven years of the Company's existence."

Commission of 15 per cent on fire business was to be allowed to agents, including Co-operative societies acting as agents on property other than their own, and to secretaries of building societies. Reinsurance business was further expanded — Bedlington Co-operative Society was insured for £6,000, £2,000 retained at 3s. per cent, £2,000 reinsured with the North British and Mercantile Insurance Company, and £2,000 with The Equitable Fire Insurance Company. In April, 1875, the Secretary was asked to prepare "instructions to agents" which were culled from those of the North British and Mercantile, the Alliance, the Norwich, and the Provident Fire offices; one hundred copies were printed "and type left standing." James Odgers was granted ten days' holiday in August, and it was noted that in October he claimed expenses for visits to Bury, Lancaster, Galgate, Morecambe, Carnforth and Nottingham. He was instructed to submit a return of each class of policy renewed or replaced, and a similar return for policies not renewed. In November, 1875, the Secretary stated "that he thought it might pay to have a youth to assist in the office, and enquired whether his own remuneration, being by commission, was intended to include that of all assistance required in the office, and if so, whether he was to engage or how otherwise." The reply was soon forthcoming: "It was resolved that said commission includes all office wages and that the Secretary has power to engage subject to the approval of the directors."

During 1875, there was a general reduction in the terms quoted for guarantee policies. The question of floating policies for guarantee business was also raised.

Consideration of life assurance was adjourned in September, 1875, and the Secretary was asked to obtain Vansittart Neale's opinion " as to whether this Company and a friendly society could be so united as to prevent a rupture between the two at a future time." Neale replied that no society registered under the Friendly Societies Act could be definitely combined with co-operative insurance, except by limiting its benefits to the members of the Company, which he thought would destroy the likelihood of success of life assurance.

Fire insurance cover up to £4,000 on common risks could be entertained provided it could be sub-divided into not less than ten portions; £2,000 was the limit on an equivalent risk if not sub-divided. Premium rates of 1s. 6d. per cent were to be quoted on common risks of £4,000, and a graduated premium rose to 10s. 6d. per cent as a maximum. Any risks on mills or factories or any other special risks were to be made only through chief office.

The Manager was instructed to adopt new methods for checking policies to ensure that they corresponded with the particulars on the proposals rather than certifying they were correct copies of the Secretary's entries in the policy book. The Board further decided that it was in order to delegate responsibility to the Secretary and Manager jointly for the acceptance of proposals of a routine nature. The directors reserved the right to decide the rates to be quoted for proposals requiring detailed consideration.

Twenty-two replies were received to 820 circulars distributed to local societies concerning the possible extension of business to life assurance and the formation of a Co-operative Friendly Society. Only three societies were prepared to assist with the latter venture, and of these societies, two declined to advance any capital. The Manchester and Salford Society fully supported the foundation of a Friendly Society, but the Rochdale Pioneers wished to discuss the proposals further. E. O. Greening, on behalf of the Agricultural and Horticultural Society, was in favour of life business, which he thought should be undertaken under the Companies Act so as to have no restrictions, " but states that while the directors prefer to invest funds in joint stock companies rather than helping London or Southern objects, he cannot hold out any prospect of money from the South." Notwithstanding these rebuffs, the Secretary, with Vansittart Neale's assistance, was to prepare a scheme for co-operative life assurance, "and use all reasonable means to procure suitable tables." It must be pointed out, however, that these tables were to be used for a Co-operative Friendly Society rather than for ordinary or industrial life assurance. Rules for the proposed Co-operative Friendly Society were finally approved in August, 1876, but without any practical outcome.

In January, 1876, James Odgers received a balance of salary for the previous 15 months—£10 0s. 4d. He also received £33 6s. 10d. commission on reinsurance and agency premiums. The Secretary thought it would be necessary to employ a fire risk surveyor to report on special risks — other offices would then be more ready to guarantee risks which had previously been surveyed. Due attention was paid to fire precautions: "That the book on fire protection by Captain Shaw of London Fire Brigade be purchased for the Company as soon as it is published." An advertisement for an efficient clerk was inserted in the *Co-operative News*, and James Barlow, of Eccles, was appointed at 32s. 6d. per week. Attention was paid to methods of extending business. It was concluded that personal application for insurance quotations were best made to the Board of Directors, or to co-operative societies, but the time had arrived when risks should be considered which had hitherto been declined on account of their high rates. A co-operative society was permitted to make half a pound of shoemaker's wax at any one time in a room having a flagged floor; but Lincoln Society was notified that no liability would be entertained for loss from a haystack fire resulting from natural overheating. The CWS Soap Works at Durham smelted tallow; hence the rate would be increased from 7s. 6d. to 10s. 6d. per cent. Proposals from theatres "and any similar class of risk" were to be declined, but Ramsbottom Society, having agreed not to allow scenic or theatrical representation, could have a reduced rate on their new building from 4s. to 2s. 6d. per cent. The methods of business undertaken by other offices was closely examined and often copied. In cases where other companies allowed commission to policyholders "this Company follows suit," hence 7½ per cent was allowed to Springhead Spinning Company. H. F. Webb, previously an agent for the Royal Liver Friendly Society, was engaged. In December, 1876, a firm of insurance brokers was appointed agents. In the same month, the rate for the CWS warehouse in Garden Street, Manchester, was reduced from 8s. 6d. to 4s. per cent — "the rate charged by London and Lancashire Fire Office." No dividend was to be paid for the year ended 1875. Profits of £372 1s. were to go instead to the insurance fund.

Business undertaken outside the Co-operative Movement was growing. In August, 1876, £500 was retained on fire insurance of a chemical works at Sankey Bridge, Warrington. Scales of premium allowances were laid down in cases where premises concerned had fire appliances:— steam fire-engine — 10 per cent; manual fire-engine — 5 per cent; fire-plugs—up to 2½ per cent. A letter was received from Ernest Jones, a recently appointed agent for the Fire Department, who asked for 20 per cent commission instead of 17 per cent to enable him to pay ordinary commission to his sub-agents and to reimburse himself for fire surveys — the request was declined. Further proposals from Jones were declined for cotton mills and warehouses, chemical works and woollen mills. Other agents continued to be appointed, including "a master of the endowed school, Calverton, Notts." A loan to the Union Land and Building Society at 6 per cent was made, provided that the "directors of that society give personal bond to this Company for the amount and that our investment in the Rochdale District Co-operative Cornmill be withdrawn." Publicity received some attention; the CIC agreed "that 7s., half the cost of printing 1,000 slip adverts on this company incurred by John McKay — our Paisley agent, be allowed him."

On 27 June, 1876, James Odgers was re-styled Manager, at a yearly salary of £150 with travelling expenses. He had been asked previously whether he would prefer general management and outdoor work, or whether he would restrict himself to internal office work, should another clerk or surveyor be appointed. Abraham Greenwood had previously tendered his resignation as Managing Director. This position had been held by him since the formation of the Company. Several months later, Abraham Howard of Rochdale, the Treasurer of the CIC, also resigned. The Manager informed the Board that the directors and manager of the Hecla Insurance Company had made away with the assets of the company, leaving the policyholders without security. It was resolved that the two policies insured through the agency of the CIC on behalf of the Hecla were to be transferred to another office and the premium for the unexpired time paid by the CIC.

At the Co-operative Congress held in 1876, criticism was made of the CIC for not being more enterprising. One delegate deprecated that the Company was not willing to accept fire business for cotton mills. Abraham Greenwood replied that the Board was not lacking in initiative; they had appealed to the co-operative societies for capital

51

as a basis for accepting higher and riskier business, but the societies had not responded adequately.

An application was received during February, 1876, from the National Industrial Life Assurance and General Deposit and Advance Company, for the directors of the CIC to take it over, but the offer was declined. At the annual general meeting of the Company held in March, the takeover proposals were referred to:

> "An old-established life assurance company doing a very small business offered to transfer its powers to us in order that we might carry on the business as a company without being subject to the limitations imposed by the Friendly Society Act and without the necessity of depositing the £20,000. We have declined this offer, preferring to be entirely free from any previous liabilities and believing that a Society registered under the Friendly Society Act recently passed permitting insurances to the extent of £200 and annuities would answer our purposes for a considerable length of time."

There was an increase of 60 per cent in fire business sums assured during the year 1874/1875 — £433,694 to £696,313. Delegates at the annual general meeting were also notified that the CIC was prepared to extend fire insurance business to every class of risk except theatres. Previously, cover had been restricted to premises of co-operative stores. All amounts at risk in excess of £2,000 on any one property were reinsured — many with European offices.

The registered office of the CIC was removed to City Buildings, Corporation Street, Manchester, on 6 March, 1877.

City Buildings, Manchester

(ii) *Life Assurance Proposals and the Fire Tariff.*

Vansittart Neale read a paper, early in 1877, on the scheme for a
Co-operative Friendly Society, which had been approved in principle,
as a means of providing against sickness and death and for endowing
children. He pointed out that the life tables were to be calculated on
rates given in the report by the actuarial committee appointed under
the Friendly Societies Act of 1875. No member was to be liable for
any call beyond the contribution fixed by these tables except for the
local expenses of running his own branch. James Odgers explained,
at a conference in the same year, that insurance was a branch of
business which differed from both distribution and production. He
pointed out that in cases where co-operative societies had become
agents of the Company, they were less effective than individual agents.
He suggested that each co-operative society should form a small committee to deal wholly with insurance, and the society concerned
should invite individual members to act as personal canvassers. He
also proposed that the lodge meetings of the new Co-operative
Friendly Society should be held in co-operative stores, and not in
public houses, as was the case with the majority of friendly societies.
At a meeting to decide on the arrangements for launching the
Co-operative Friendly Society, the chairman regretted the coldness
on the part of societies to the venture, seeing that the delegates
authorised the directors 15 months previously to prepare rules for
the proposed society; these rules had been drawn up very carefully
by Vansittart Neale with the assistance of Abraham Howard and
Abraham Greenwood. Vansittart Neale then moved the resolution:

> " That as the number of members comprising co-operative
> societies in the United Kingdom is sufficiently large to justify
> them in taking steps for the mutual assurance in cases of any
> contingency to human life or health capable of computation
> by way of average, a society be established to transact all
> classes of life assurance permitted by the Friendly Society Act."

The justification for the society being formed under the Friendly
Society Act was the painful experience acquired by the failure of the
Albert and European insurance companies. The resolution was
carried, and a further resolution received unanimous approval for the
scheme as proposed by the CIC directors for

> " a society with local branches separately responsible for
> sickness insurance in the first instance but having a provision
> for the formation of the central guarantee fund for the security

of all branches and a central body for undertaking life assurance, endowment and annuities. Each branch being constituted an agency for the central assurances."

Rochdale delegates explained that they already had a sick scheme in operation. Halifax complained about the non-acceptance of insurance for the Halifax Flour Mill. Odgers replied that this was a class of business not acceptable to the CIC, and he had been told that it had been placed with another office. In the event, Odgers had unwittingly avoided a considerable drain on funds, for in 1886, the Halifax Flour Mill was burned down.[1]

The wage of G. H. Horrocks, an office clerk at the CIC, was increased from 10s. to 12s. weekly in February, 1877. Harris, the fire surveyor, had been offered an appointment with another office, and in October, 1877, a John Hilton of Middleton was appointed " travelling representative " at a salary of £78 a year with travelling expenses. Ten shillings and sixpence was paid in June, 1877, for the purchase of a book on *Law of Fire Insurance and Fire Surveys*. It was also minuted that " all parts of the *Insurance Encyclopaedia* be obtained." It was agreed not to advertise in the *Post Magazine* as " results to be anticipated do not justify the cost." An advertisement was inserted in Holyoake's *History of Co-operation* at a charge of two guineas. Holyoake was also taken to task: " That Mr. Holyoake be informed that as we gave no instructions for the insertion of advertisements in *Secular Review* and no advantage appears to have resulted, we decline to pay for them." Small payments to the *Manchester Examiner* and the *Leeds Mercury* were also made during 1877, presumably for advertisements.

Quotations for fire business were being related more and more to the tariff rates. A letter was sent to the Rochdale Co-operative Corn Mill stating that as their rate was 7s. 9d. per cent less than the tariff, no further reduction could be made, despite their adoption of fire-extinguishing appliances. Procedure adopted by another office was emulated: " That in fixing the rates for risks classified under special tariffs we adopt the practice of the Equitable and Mutual Fire Office and quote 5 per cent less than the tariff — the premium being then subject to our deductions for appliances." Growing reinsurance business was

---

[1] " . . . after depression followed fire. In 1886, on Thursday, 26 August, about half-past six in the evening, Mr. Horsley one of the Society's men looking up casually from the outside at the screening mill was startled by the sight, on the second storey of one of the upright screens on fire. In a flour mill fire grows swiftly . . . The damage was £7,000 . . . Needless to add the whole was insured; and the insurance company paid up amiably."
Jubilee History of Halifax Flour Society Ltd. 1847 to 1897, p. 102.

being accepted from other offices: " We take £1,500 of the Consolidated Fire Office's policy for £5,000 on Hollin Bank Mill, Blackburn." The Belfast Fire Office agreed to accept reinsurance business from the CIC, and no objection was raised to surveys being made by their staff until the CIC could appoint its own. A further £1,100 on Roebuck's cotton mill at Oldham was taken from the Northern Counties Fire Office.

Fire claims were being investigated with increasing thoroughness — for instance that of the Blaydon Society in October, 1877, involved a sum of £600. The claim was admitted, " but the extra £5 for lasts be not admitted — the lasts belonging to fixed stock not insured under our policy . . . " The rate for the CWS premises in Garden Street, Manchester, was reduced to 7s. 6d. per cent " on condition that glue in workshop be heated by steam . . . "

At the end of 1877, it was agreed to reinsure portions of the risk of the Northern Counties of England Fire Office, and that part of these risks would be marine insurance. Almost immediately, the CIC was called upon to meet its obligations. In February, 1878, there was a total loss of a ship carrying coals from Sunderland to Singapore, with the CIC liable to one-third of £1,325. Later in the year, Vansittart

Neale proposed that use should be made of a marine risk index. There were further marine losses. In April, 1878, a vessel sank on a voyage to Bombay at a net cost to the CIC of £566 13s. 4d. In the following month, an agreement was made with the Northern Counties office that the maximum cover undertaken by the CIC would be £200, at 1s. 6d. per cent. A treaty for guarantee of portions of risks accepted by French fire insurance companies, and of French business of English offices, was to be reinsured with the Northern Counties office. A heavy payment to the Consolidated Fire Office of £890 was made on account of a fire at Hulme, Manchester, in June, 1878. By September, 1878, it was decided that all foreign business should be declined, except by way of guarantee of foreign companies. The manager submitted a statement of fire guarantee business from its commencement in November, 1876, to October, 1878, showing a net loss. The Manager did, however, point out: " It was considered that the excessive losses represent only the fluctuation to which insurance business is liable, but at present no reason exists for ceasing to transact this guarantee business." Reinsurance business was also being conducted with a Berlin office who took " all our risks we offer on condition we give them preference over all other companies." The CIC contemplated a merger in December, 1878, with the Consolidated Fire Office.

Prompt payment of premiums by agents was not being enforced and the Manager was empowered to restrict the issue of policies or renewal receipts in cases where the previous month's amount had not been paid. John Hilton, the "travelling representative", was instructed " to visit the towns and villages in the immediate neighbourhood of Manchester with the object of obtaining proposals for insurance from societies, companies, building societies and private firms and also applications for shares." The Manager was also instructed to approach trade union branch secretaries to act as agents.

A sub-committee was appointed, early in 1878, to investigate the possibility of acquiring more office space for the Company. In the meantime, advertisements were inserted in the *Co-operative News,* the *Manchester Guardian* and the *Post Magazine* for an additional clerk. James Lowe, of London Assurance, was engaged at £100 per year. Later in the year, John Hilton was appointed superintendent of the agents. James Lowe's salary was to be increased to £150 from January, 1879, " provided he agrees to wait for at least one year from that date." James Odgers also received an increase, bringing his salary to £175 per year, and clerks Barlow and Horrocks were to be paid 36s. and 15s. per week respectively. "Beautifying" the office cost £6 2s.; two chairs were purchased for £1 6s., together with a safe and stand, and a spring balance " for weighing letters, etc." It was agreed by the Co-operative Newspaper Society that the CIC was to tenant 9 and 10 City Buildings, Manchester, at £52 yearly, and to vacate its existing office.

The amount in the deposit account of the CIC was increased to £5,000 by transfer from current account. Approval was given to the Manager to issue policies at premiums of 5s. or under without previous reference to directors.

A Risk Book containing a record of all property insured by the CIC in Scotland was to be kept at the SCWS offices, and the SCWS were allowed to issue cover notes as required. A Mr. McCulloch of the Union Fire Office, Glasgow, was appointed to survey risks.

At the tenth annual meeting of the Company held in February, 1878, it was noted that the amount of fire insurance business in force in 1876 was more than £1m. The premiums in 1876 were £1,725; in 1877, £3,928 — an increase of 127 per cent. The fire losses in 1877 were 42 per cent of premiums — this was 18 per cent less than the average specially provided for by the Articles of Association. During the previous year, several individual agents had been appointed, but some of them were not bringing in a satisfactory amount of business. It was noted that a number of co-operative societies had mortgages on house property, hence it would be quite legitimate for officials of local societies to insist that the property concerned be insured through the CIC. Proceedings for setting up of the proposed Co-operative Friendly Society were becoming most protracted. Twelve meetings had been held but " owing to the complication in connection with the tables, registration had not been effected." The travelling representative had been appointed to further the business of the Friendly Society, but the delay in receipt of the tables had prevented the CIC from availing itself of his services.

Attention of members was drawn to the fact that when the CIC insured co-operative premises, no surveyor's fees were paid, but when they provided cover for other property, a competent fire surveyor had to be employed. Local societies were pressed to put all their business with the CIC leaving the Company to reinsure the amount that could not be carried. The remuneration of the directors from the formation of the CIC had been 2s. for each meeting attended; the fee was raised to 4s. from 1878.

Doubts were raised early in 1879 over the wisdom of continuing to reinsure business received from other offices. Several losses had occurred in quick succession on one of the treaties in March, 1877, before any premium had been received, and the extent of the business after one year had not been sufficient to recoup these losses. During 1878, five companies reinsured portions of their surplus risks with the

CIC. On one of these risks, a heavy loss was sustained in the great fire at Hulme, already referred to, two-thirds of which was due to short water supply. Much of the reinsurance business submitted to the CIC was precarious and diminishing by the end of 1878. One company had gone into liquidation, another was doubtful, and two others were transferring business from the CIC — presumably because of the small amount of its share capital. The CIC realised that its slender capital structure was handicapping any extension of business. No profits had been divided except on one occasion, and " as the smallness of our capital and competition with other offices compels us in many cases to accept lower rates thus reducing our chances of making large profits as was originally hoped for . . the formation of adequate reserves is a prime necessity . . ." Any further distribution of profits above 6 per cent on paid-up capital would be postponed until these reserves had been built up to adequate proportions.

Delegates were told at the annual general meeting in 1879 that the Friendly Society had still not yet been registered. The rules had been sent back from the Registrar for alteration of name to Co-operative Assurance Friendly Society.

Claims during the previous year had been particularly numerous, mostly on reinsurance, and this business was therefore to be discontinued.[1] A delegate at a Co-operative Conference held in December, 1879, was dissatisfied to find that the CIC was following the rating of other companies. " Why," he asked, " should they follow tariff and not stand on their own bottom ? "

Agents who had done little business were written to " asking them to use more energy." It was decided to pay Hilton, the travelling representative, solely on commission. Internal office matters were attended to: " That unused lock taken from door of previous office be sold to the Manager for 5s. . . . One of T. H. Taylor's copying processes be obtained." Surveying expenses at Birmingham, Newcastle and London were paid. A notice was sent to the Union Land and Building Company:

" That if they do not present their next balance sheet in such a form (containing cash and trade accounts) as will enable people ordinarily conversant with accounts to appreciate the

[1] The marine treaty with the Northern Counties office was cancelled from 30 June, 1879, and reinsurance arrangements for fire with the same office were cancelled during August, 1879. An application for appointment as an agent in Paris was declined in February, 1879, and in the same month the French reinsurance treaty was cancelled.

position of the company, we shall not feel justified in allowing our loan of £500 to remain invested with them."

The CIC was becoming sufficiently confident of its own business methods to take others to task. The Manchester District Unitarian Sunday School Union was to be allowed to use the tables of the Co-operative Assurance Friendly Society when copyrighted, " on condition that they print by permission of said Society."

A major policy decision was made during September, 1879, in connection with the difficulties of obtaining reinsurance cover. The CIC now felt it desirable to seek membership of the Fire Offices Committee[1] " with a view to obtain greater facilities for the re-insurance of our surplus amounts and greater security for our policy-holders . . ." The Manager wrote to a number of small tariff offices; in each case the amount subscribed and paid-up was double that of the Co-operative. If admitted to the fire offices tariff, the CIC would be the smallest tariff office. The CIC was notified that no new members of the Fire Offices Committee would be allowed to give concessions to their policyholders, and the Secretary of the Northern branch of the Fire Offices Committee said that the paid-up capital of any member should be at least £20,000 for security of payment on any loss. (A point in favour of the CIC was that the share capital was increasing as rapidly as its direct business.) The matter of membership was considered at the London meeting of the Fire Offices Committee on 7 November, 1879, which decided to levy a yearly subscription of £12 on the CIC for membership of the FOC.

Delegates at the annual general meeting in 1880 were told that the rules of the Co-operative Friendly Society had been approved, but due to the depressed state of trade in the country, the CIC did not think it advisable to ask societies to subscribe the necessary capital to pay the initial expenses. Nor did the CIC feel justified in assuming

---

[1] Cf. H. E. Raynes, *A History of British Insurance* (1948). The forerunners of fire tariffs came into existence in England before 1858 through *ad hoc* agreements amongst companies, but it was not until 1858 that the Association of British Fire Offices was formed, later changing its title to Fire Offices Committee in 1868. There were also associations of manufacturers for mutual assurance. In 1869, one was formed in Manchester known as the Cotton Spinners Mutual Fire Insurance Association. In this case, the particular complaint of the mill owners was that the companies were not giving discounts in premium when fire extinguishing appliances were installed.

Automatic sprinklers were first installed in this country in 1885. The invention was an American one and had been in use for some years there before Mather and Platt of Manchester manufactured sprinklers after acquiring the patent rights. It was introduced first into cotton mills, and the non-tariff companies — of which the Cotton Spinners Mutual, mentioned above, was one — gave a discount of 20 per cent, afterwards increased to 30 per cent, in mills where they were installed.

responsibility, having already paid out nearly £90 for expenses:

" We therefore had the rules stereotyped and now hold the plates. We do not feel justified in recommending that any further steps be taken in the matter otherwise than in union with the ten other societies who have appointed one representative each and who, with a representative of the Company. form a committee of management."

The number of societies in England and Wales insured with the CIC in 1880 was 390, and in Scotland 62. At that time the total number of registered societies in England and Wales was 955, and in Scotland 218, " leaving 721 societies not insured by us, many not insured at all." It was the larger societies who were shareholders and also policyholders with the CIC. The CWS, Rochdale, and Halifax societies held nearly one-third of the shares.

It was necessary to amend the Articles of Association of the Company in 1880 to enable admission to the Fire Offices Committee as participation of policyholders in the profits of an office was contrary to the rules of the FOC. The usual condition of admittance that the company concerned had to have a paid-up capital of £20,000 was waived in the case of the CIC, which was admitted with a capital of £10,000. It was indicated that the CIC would have to raise rates a little in connection with societies where paraffin oil was stored. Abraham Howard of Rochdale commented that some years previously they had looked upon the FOC with horror as a combination for increasing the prices of insurance. He still thought the proposals were contrary to the principles on which the CIC had started business. Another delegate thought that the proposal to discontinue profits to policyholders was objectionable, but the chairman explained that to circumvent this the local societies were to receive commission on their own business. It was queried whether there were no successful offices outside the tariff, to which the chairman replied that nearly every month some of the non-tariff companies failed, whilst it was very rare indeed that a tariff office did so.

At a further meeting, it was pointed out that owners of mills and other buildings had thought that some concessions should be made on their insurances, and as the tariff offices did not agree, the mill owners had set up their own insurance companies. Many of these companies had come to grief, and another was in such an unsatisfactory condition that the CIC had to discontinue business with it:

" We were, therefore, experiencing some difficulty in

placing our surplus risks satisfactorily and had been obliged in some cases to give them to foreign offices whom we did not know much about. The Directors, therefore, came to the conclusion that it would be an advantage to join the tariff association to enable them to place their risks with safe companies."

Later, a set of tariffs was placed in the custody of the Manager at his private residence " subject to the proviso that if he leaves our employment before Lady Day next he must return them." The FOC finally agreed to admit the CIC on 11 May, 1880. On the instigation of the FOC, the Manager decided to reinstate the rule that agents were not to divide their commission with policyholders.

Vansittart Neale supported the tariff move; he pointed out that the CIC often found that the whole year's premium was swallowed up in losses, and it would be the same with all other offices who limited the area of their operation. It had been stated that in joining the tariff, the hands of the CIC would be tied, but he argued that the CIC was already restricted to accepting business at the rates of non-tariff offices, who were forced to accept the lowest rates to get any business at all. With restricted opportunities for reinsurance, the CIC could not handle the potential business of Co-operative societies adequately; they could not, for instance, take the full risk that the Wholesale Society offered them. The CIC had discontinued accepting reinsurances from other companies, thus relinquishing the greater portion of the premiums received on extra-hazardous risks. The FOC rules regarding distribution of profits would hardly distort CIC policy; profits had only been divided once in the history of the Company and the amount was barely 8d. in the pound.

The delegates at the annual meeting in 1881 were told: " We deem it expedient to restrict our insurances in future to those risks which are amongst the best of their kind." Unfortunately the figures for the previous year did not coincide with these aspirations. Fire losses were 100 per cent of premium income (fidelity losses were merely 9.2 per cent). The heaviest fire loss was in respect of a cotton spinning concern at Bolton at a cost of £1,417. Odgers admitted some deficiency in surveying the Bolton risk.

Odgers defended the adoption of the fire tariff on grounds of expediency at the Co-operative Congress held in 1881. He contended that the CIC was still a Co-operative Company, as nearly 19,000 shares were held by Co-operative societies, and only about 500 by individuals. It was possible for the Company to become more perfectly co-operative if the societies would hold shares in proportion to their business and become agents in their corporate capacity. E. O. Greening was antagonistic. It was an unfortunate change to convert what was in effect a Co-operative society into a joint-stock concern; " and it was an indication of the unfortunate spirit which appeared to prevail in establishments at Manchester — a desire above all things for com-mercial and monetary success." It was no answer to say that the door was open to all societies; some societies were too poor to take shares and yet they required to be insured. " By abolishing the system of bonus upon insurance they put it in the power of the large societies of exploiting the small societies, and were drifting towards another of the great insurance monopolies which were rapidly becoming viewed by the public as great nuisances." E. O. Greening returned to the fray in the following year. He felt he could not urge the claims of the CIC, when it was no longer Co-operative. Odgers remonstrated that the decision to enter the tariff had been made a year previously with only two dissentients. Indeed, the change made very little difference to the policyholders, because most of the business consisted of Co-operative stores and private dwelling houses. The shops tariff, under which stores were rated, was a very elastic one, and did not specify the additional rates to be charged for different elements of risk, except where mineral oils were stocked. For most descriptions of property there were no tariffs. The number of Co-operative risks rateable under tariffs specifying the rate for each element of risk was very small indeed, and of these corn mills were the most important, but it was common knowledge that the rates applicable to large corn mills were inadequate, therefore it would be unwise to charge lower rates, even if the Company had not become a member of the FOC. By being a member, the surplus amounts could be reinsured with thoroughly-sound offices and the proportion of loss to each would be less. By spreading the risks, lower rates could be charged than would be possible otherwise, thus the new course pursued by the Company was in one sense Co-operative. Lloyd Jones objected to the inference that the opinion of Congress was not likely to have much effect on the CIC, and Odgers conceded that the decision over tariff might be reconsidered, but at the present time it did not appear likely that it would be altered. Vansittart Neale, who had been one of the Directors at the time of the change, com-mented " the Company was conducted under the conditions indispens-able for success, and to the greatest advantage of the insurers. This explanation was given two years ago and he thought it was wasting time to bring the subject up again."

In September, 1882, the Manager was instructed to ascertain which non-tariff offices would be prepared to guarantee surplus amounts. He subsequently reported in November that he had written to 14 English companies, six representatives in London of Foreign companies, and the head offices of 30 French and 17 American companies. The response was hardly encouraging. Eight English companies had declined to accept CIC business; all the Foreign companies except one had given up accepting non-tariff reinsurances, or had joined the tariff owing to heavy losses suffered by these Foreign companies in guaranteeing English non-tariff business. Nevertheless, during the 1880s the CIC had increasing connections with Foreign offices. During the years 1880 and 1881, accounts were paid to Magdeburg Fire Office, Jakor Insurance Company, the German-Swiss Reinsurance Company, Azienda Insurance Company, La Confiance, Generali, the Union Insurance Company of Berlin and the Berlin Cologne Fire Insurance Office. Offers were received from the Equitable Fire Office to guarantee up to £15,000 on Co-operative stores. The Mutual Insurance Office would be willing to accept CIC reinsurance, subject to the Company joining the proposed Union of non-tariff offices. "Thus," concluded Odgers, "five out of six parties I wrote to in London could not help if we retired from the tariff. Also a resolution of the Fire Offices Committee prohibited persons from representing tariff and non-tariff offices at the same time." In 1884, a new corn mill tariff was issued by the FOC and provision in the shops tariff required a new minimum rate of 6s. per cent for drapery in establishments employing 50 workers, and 8s. 6d. per cent in cases where drapery and grocery were combined. James Odgers was asked to visit the FOC to seek a concession and to protest against these rates.

Strenuous efforts were made to increase the subscribed share capital to £10,000. Appeals were made to the larger societies to pay up their share capital in full. Vansittart Neale and Odgers acted as a deputation to the CWS Finance Committee to seek temporary overdrafts for the CIC of £20,000 when required. The CWS Bank agreed to provide this financial accommodation, but " on a condition which would prevent CIC from availing itself of the offer."

It was becoming a fixed policy for the clerks in the office to be paid an annual increase in salary. Barlow was being paid 44s. per week by the beginning of 1882. The wages of Horrocks were increased

63

from 21s. to 25s. in January, 1883, and the Manager was empowered to engage an office boy at not more than 7s. 6d. By 1884, Mason, the office boy, was receiving 10s. per week, Horrocks 28s. and Barlow 47s. In May, 1884, W. Backhouse intimated that he would leave the office.[1] R. H. Fitton was appointed at a wage of 7s. 6d., together with a James Evans at 15s. per week. By January, 1885, there were five clerks in the office of the CIC — Barlow, Horrocks, Mason, Fitton and Evans.

Agents were supplied by chief office with addressed letters and envelopes for remitting. Any agent who had not brought in any business during 1880 was to be dismissed. In October, 1881, advertisements appeared in the *Manchester Guardian* and *Leeds Mercury* over a period of one month for new agents. It had been noted at the end of the 1870s that business brought in by those agents who had worked for other insurance offices was the type of business in which the most serious losses occurred. The Board therefore decided to cease appointing agents who also acted for other Companies. By February, 1883, there were 104 individual agents, but policies with a total premium income of £919 were submitted from 24 of these agents, and only £231 through the remaining 80; eight agents had not done any business since appointed. Advertisements were also inserted in 1880 for part-time surveyors to be appointed in London, Bristol, Birmingham, Newcastle and Glasgow. In August, 1880, two surveyors working for other tariff offices agreed to supply press copies of any surveys they had on risks in which the CIC was interested, and they agreed to be at the service of the CIC in rating any difficult risks, for a yearly fee of £30. This arrangement was on a trial basis for six months, but was eventually terminated, and a substitute arrangement was made of paying them a fixed fee for right to refer to the questions of risk and rating, with an additional fee for each copy of plans, reports and surveys done expressly for the Company. The CIC continued to learn on the job. A Minute of November, 1882, instructed that "Nine copies of Beerbohn's *Commercial Trade List* be obtained containing information re corn mill fires and a copy sent to each member of the Board." In the same month, a subscription for a copy of the *Fire Underwriters Companion* was paid. Five thousand copies of the Manager's *Suggestions*

---

[1] Walter Backhouse, previously employed by the North British and Mercantile Insurance Company, had been appointed as fire clerk at £100 a year from August, 1880: " It being understood that if he remains with us, it be raised to £110 — 1882; £130 — 1883; £150 — 1884."

re Fire Risks on Co-operative Stores were printed and circulated in 1884, in which it was pointed out *inter alia* that tapers in metal cases should be used for lighting gas lamps, or failing these, " Clark's patent electric lighter." Issues of the *Insurance News* were purchased from October, 1884. A reference volume of seemingly considerable expense (five guineas) was acquired—"with the object of classifying our premiums and losses as soon as practicable on the best method, a copy of Mr. Glover's work entitled *Compilation of Fire Insurance Statistics, etc.* be obtained." Harris's *Fire Insurance Dictionary* was purchased at one guinea in 1885.

Fire risks which could only be taken at a rate in excess of 42s. per cent were declined from 1880, except when they formed part of an insurance at a generally lower rate. In 1881, fire risks at rates above 21s. per cent were to be refused, unless the premises were owned by local Co-operative societies, or proposed through their agency. In a reply to the Central London Fire Office in June, 1884, the CIC thought that the Central London fire rates were excessive, but the CIC agreed that higher rates should be charged for large stores, and that it would adopt higher minimum rates for all renewals and new business and there would be a doubling of the limit on all Co-operative stores as follows: in cases where value of buildings and contents under £5,000 — 2s. 6d. per cent; £5,000 to £10,000 — 3s. per cent; £10,000 to £15,000 — 3s. 6d. per cent; £25,000 to £30,000 — 5s. per cent. A heavy loss occurred in February, 1881, when £1,165 was paid as a result of an india-rubber fire at Salford. In October, 1881, another heavy loss was met on a Leeds corn mill where the total claim was £8,500. Other expenses included " men assisting (not fire brigade), £6 10s. Leeds Constabulary Brigade £16 15s. 4d., Liverpool London and Globe Brigade £14 9s., Sun Brigade £5 10s. 6d., Emanuel and Son Brigade £5 10s. 6d." At that time, the Manchester Fire Brigade was being paid something over £12 per year by the CIC, but the CIC did not consider it worth while paying £2 yearly for monthly reports on fires to the Northern Offices Committee of the FOC. A proposal for £1,000 on Lewis's store, Market Street, Manchester, and for £2,500, " being 1/63rd part of total insurance on Dobson and Barlow's Works, Bolton," was accepted.

At the 1884 annual meeting, a director referred to fire losses and stated that at one time Co-operative stores were classified as good risks, but latterly many insurance offices had classified them as very heavy risks, and had, in some instances, declined them altogether. This was due, in his opinion, to losses through assistants throwing down matches, and beam ends being often inserted into the flues. In the first five-year period 1867–72, the losses were £68; between 1872 and 1877, £1,951; 1877 and 1882, £8,744; and since 1882, £4,016. The average fire loss borne by an insurance office should not exceed 60 per cent, but during the previous year the CIC losses were 73 per cent.

A refinement was incorporated into the fidelity provisions in 1881: " That as an experiment we adopt the plan of the Provident Clerks and General Guarantee Assurance of requiring the person on whose behalf the policy is applied for, to execute an agreement to indemnify the Company in case of loss by embezzlement before issuing policy." A new form of policy was introduced in 1882 for insuring certain amounts on each of a specified number of employees of any one Society. Premiums for policies of more than £100 on any one individual were to be 1s. less for every additional £100 insured, in each case subject to limitations that no insurance against loss by embezzlement however large could be affected for a less premium than two-thirds of the previous rate. The existing plan of allowing cumulative reductions according to length of employment and number of persons guaranteed to the same Society was to be abolished with certain exceptions. From July, 1883, fidelity policies were extended to cover larceny, but were to exclude all other criminal acts or defaults. In September, 1885, a resolution was made: " That form, now submitted, of fidelity policy for persons employed by Government be adopted subject to such compensation and improvement — suggested by Mr. Neale and the Manager — as will be accepted by the Board of Trade."

As a result of joining the FOC, the 5 per cent allowance to share-holding Societies holding CIC policies was discontinued and share-holding agents were allowed commission on their own fire insurance as well as on other insurances conducted through their agency.

The lack of any firm policy on investment by the CIC is indicated by a Minute of June, 1880, " The question how best to use our invested capital be deferred . . . "[1] In 1882, a loan of £500 to the Co-operative

[1] The possibility of participating in the Post Office annuity scheme was proposed in 1881: " Directors of the CIC with a view to enabling the members of the society to obtain the best securities at the lowest prices authorised an enquiry to by made of the Government authority in London, whether a co-operative society or the Co-operative Insurance Company could be appointed agents for the National Life Assurance Annuity Department. They received a reply that by the Act of Parliament under which the business was undertaken does not permit of appointing agents or any parties other than the Post Office officials."

Permanent Building Society was withdrawn. A notice was received from the Rochdale Pioneers in May, 1883, that they wished to reduce their interest payments from 5 per cent to 3½ per cent on a loan from the CIC, and a similar request was received from the Co-operative Printing Society.

A new type of security came into the possession of the CIC from September, 1880, when it was agreed to accept from the Union Land and Building Company the transfer of a row of houses in Bates Street, Longsight, Manchester. The title to this property was passed to the CIC on the cancellation of a loan of £500 to the Land Company. The Manager was instructed to examine the houses and have repairs and " beautifying " carried out with a view to letting the houses as early as possible. The property was insured from £1,200 from April, 1881. The CIC, having to act as landlord, had to meet the commitments of property management — new wallpaper " at not more than 1s. per piece " was to be allowed to one of the tenants; poor rates had to be paid and repair bills met; Mrs. Buchanan's kitchen was not to be re-papered until she had paid arrears of rent. In October, 1884, the inspector of nuisances to Rusholme Local Board of Health had to be informed that the drains of the houses in Bates Street were constructed in accordance with the requests of his Board. Mortgage loans were made in April, 1885, for £2,600 on houses at Hazel Grove and Longsight in Manchester.

Advertising received attention. Samples of show cards and almanacs were inspected in November, 1881, and it was resolved " that 1,000 in same style as that of the Victoria Fire Office be prepared, except that the Arms of England, Scotland and Ireland be substituted for the Queen's head . . ."

The question of profit-sharing was a live issue in the Co-operative Movement in the early 1880s, but the CIC was lukewarm; so much so that the Co-operative Congress of 1882 passed a resolution " That it be a request from this Congress to the Insurance Company to reconsider their decision respecting the Co-operative distribution of their surplus profits." During 1883, the CIC directors received instructions: " Each director present at Congress do his best to prove thoroughly co-operative character of the Company if that is assailed." A reference was made at Congress to a Reverend D. T. Whitt, who, in a recent sermon, had spoken of life assurance as follows: " Some of you are making a great swosh in life and after a while you die leaving your family as beggars and will expect Ministers of the Gospel to come and lie about your excellences. If you send for me I tell you what my text will be — ' He that provideth not for his own household is an infidel '."

In February, 1882, it was resolved that the Company's investment in the Co-operative Assurance Friendly Society was to be treated as a donation. A special meeting was called in June 1882, to decide whether to extend the time within which £250 had to be subscribed by Co-operative societies and individuals towards the establishment of a Co-operative Assurance Friendly Society as a condition of the Company itself lending £50, or alternatively whether the CIC should repay the subscriptions received and decline any further action. In July, 1882, a special meeting agreed to the Co-operative Friendly Society being wound up and foundation subscriptions and loans were to be returned to subscribers.[1] An instrument of dissolution was drawn up and registered in October, 1882. On the demise of the Co-operative Assurance Friendly Society,[2] the CIC was forced to consider the question of undertaking life assurance business on its own initiative,

[1] *Co-operative Assurance Friendly Society* (Receipts and Expenditure to 1882).

Receipts

						£	s.	d.
Subscriptions from 28 societies and nine individuals		..				55	10	0
Loans from two societies	..	..	..	..		13	16	0
Bank Interest..	..	..	..	..		0	10	2
Donation from CIC..	..	..	..	..		7	13	2
Balance	..	..	..	..		69	11	2
				Total	..	147	0	6

Payments

						£	s.	d.
Deposits in Bank	..	..	..	..		69	6	0
Book Rules	..	..	..	..		7	6	0
Subscriptions and loans repaid		..	..	..		69	6	0
Bank cheques..	..	..	..	..		0	3	3
Bank commission	..	..	..	..		0	1	9
Postage	..	..	..	..		0	5	2
Advertising dissolution	..	..	..	..		0	12	4
				Total	..	147	0	6

[2] Canon W. L. Blackley outlined an interesting scheme for compulsory national insurance in a pamphlet " Thrift and Independence " (1884). He also explained his scheme before a committee of the House of Commons on National Provident Insurance in 1885. The main points of his scheme were that every individual should contribute £10 to a national sick fund out of which a pension of 4s. per week was payable from 70 years of age onwards and a sickness benefit of 8s. per week. The fund would be paid into and distributed through the Post Office. It would take in the whole nation, rich and poor alike. The £10 was to be collected by the employer having deducted it from wages of men between 18 and 21 years of age. With other people of means, the £10 would be collected through taxes. J. M. Baernreither, *English Associations of Working Men* (1889). See also Blackley's article " National Insurance " in *Nineteenth Century*, November, 1878.

and not as a co-operative venture for the Movement as a whole. In September, 1885, the Manager was " to enquire terms a Manchester actuary would do work preliminary to Life Department being set up."

The Co-operative Insurance Company still restricted its policies to fire and fidelity insurance. This showed a proper sense of priorities, for the Co-operative Movement in acquiring more premises, stock and capital resources for manufacturing, processing and selling its goods, did not pay sufficient attention to the insurable risks of property ownership and personal fidelity hazards of its staff. Both fire and fidelity risks were consequences of the inadequacies in the day-to-day management of co-operative organisations — poorly constructed premises, often extremely vulnerable to fire hazards, coupled with inexperienced staff and sketchy methods of stock control,[1] probably no worse than comparable conditions and practices in retailing and manufacturing generally, but at least the Co-operative Movement had the opportunity to seek collective information and begin to set its own house in order, as far as fire and fidelity insurance was concerned, through the Co-operative Insurance Company.[2]

Any other form of insurance cover for co-operators in the form of life assurance or friendly society sickness and incapacity benefit, would have to compete with other industrial life offices and collecting societies with growing national coverage, already including members of co-operative societies. The Co-operative Insurance Company wisely thought fit to proceed on a narrow, specialist front, without too much hindrance from other companies who would not have, in any case, direct knowledge of co-operative store practice, premises or staffing. Successful underwriting of a limited range of risks would enable the Company to gain a certain amount of expertise which would make possible an extension to other branches of insurance. " There is no doubt whatever that the difference between a society which began operations and failed, and another which survived, lay

[1] See for instance the experience in 1887 of the Lawrence Hill Branch of Bristol Co-operative Society. A loss was sustained by the Society, despite a large turn-over — " A chartered accountant was called in and he quickly diagnosed the complaint, the result being that the storekeeper was arrested on the charge of stealing the Society's goods." E. Jackson, *A Study in Democracy. An Account of the Rise and Progress of Industrial Co-operation in Bristol* (1911) p.197.

[2] Bolton Co-operative Society became a member of the Co-operative Insurance Company as early as 1867, but in 1889, the Bolton Society set up its own insurance fund which grew over the years so that by the early twentieth century it was self-insuring many of its shops and cottages and also undertaking part of the fidelity insurance of its staff.

almost entirely in the ability or otherwise to control the heavy expenses which were the inevitable concomitant of expansion."[1]

Thomas Hughes and Vansittart Neale edited a *Manual for Co-operators* in 1881, which included advice on surety. The authors explained the guarantee to a society that its storekeeper would carry out his agreement could be given by a bond with one or more sureties in addition to the storekeeper himself. A better plan, it was argued, was to induce the storekeeper to deposit with the society a sum made applicable to meet any claim as to leakage, as well as any losses from fraudulent acts " Against these last however, societies may guard by fidelity guarantee policies which are issued by the Co-operative Insurance Company as well as by other guarantee companies." But those policies were limited to cases of dishonesty; they did not extend to losses arising from carelessness.

(iii) *Friendly Societies*

The common ground in the nineteenth century between the Co-operative Movement and social insurance was the Friendly Society. Any form of self-help which would insure against pauperism was laudable in the eyes of the Establishment during the early nineteenth century; moreover, the Co-operative and the Friendly Society movements were favourably received because they eschewed any form of political agitation or party allegiance. In a recent historical study of the friendly societies, it is written :

> " The Friendly Society Movement, as it developed between 1815 and 1875, sprang from the efforts of those who became members and it owed comparatively little to outsiders. In this respect it might be compared with the trade unions or the co-operatives, both of which grew as a result of energy and determination shown by the members they served. These three movements represent, in a sense, the ways in which those without political power sought to protect themselves in an increasingly industrialised society."[2]

Legislative control and protection, originally devised for friendly societies, also came to the assistance of struggling co-operative societies and associations — Robert Owen's Association of All Classes of All Nations was registered under the Friendly Societies Act of 1834. Indeed, it has been asserted that Edwin Chadwick took the centralised administration of that Act as a model for the New Poor Law of 1834

[1] C. Clegg, *History of Refuge Assurance Company* (1958), p.26.
[2] P. H. J. H. Gosden, *Development of Friendly Societies in England 1815 to 1875* (Manchester, 1959), p.7.

(Chadwick had drafted in 1828, *An Essay on the Means of Insurance Against the Casualties of Sickness, Decreptitude and Mortality*, in which he argued that the Government had bounden duty to provide the community with the means to defend itself, at least expense, against the evil consequences arising from sickness and death — for which statistics were required. Chadwick urged that the wealthy classes should support the lower orders by encouraging the setting up of soundly-based provident institutions.)

As early as 1803, a Poor Law return had estimated 704,350 members of friendly societies — already a far larger membership than any other form of working-class organisation. Under the Industrial and Provident Societies Act of 1852, all provisions of friendly societies continued to apply equally to co-operative societies, except where the Act stated otherwise. But the friendly society movement spread earlier and faster than co-operation, and in the case of the larger fraternities — often with a firmer financial basis. The Oddfellows had founded their first lodge in Manchester in 1810. Apart from the national orders of the Oddfellows and Foresters, there were numerous local and particularist friendly societies and burial clubs.[1] In all, the membership of the 14 varieties of friendly society analysed by the Royal Commission on Friendly Societies in 1874 was estimated at four million, which far exceeded the members of co-operative organisations, even allowing for double-counting, as individuals were often members of several friendly societies.

The early life offices and friendly societies gathered and assessed statistical data on sickness and mortality experience of the working classes.[2]

---

[1] A list of 19 local Manchester Burial societies founded between 1818 and 1863, with 110,734 members and £41,491 funds was submitted to the Royal Commission on Friendly Societies in 1874 by Assistant Commissioner Stanley.

[2] The Carlisle Life Table was "a wonderful instance of the ingenuity of an actuary in deducing a generally-accepted law of mortality from the most meagre data." The actuary in question was Joseph Milne who based his table on observations of Bills of Mortality of a Dr. Heysham between 1779 and 1787 in Carlisle. The sample only included a total number of deaths above infancy of 1,149. Northampton life tables were compiled by Dr. Price on the Parish of All Saints, Northampton, 1735 to 1780. He assumed a stationary population, as the baptisms equalled the number of deaths, consequently the rate of mortality was exaggerated. Government annuities which were sold at the end of the eighteenth century were based on the Northampton life tables with this built-in overestimated mortality. The country lost £2m. before the rates were changed. The English Life Tables widely used by insurance offices were based on the censuses of population 1841 and 1851. Both of these censuses suffered from the defect that the population was not broken down into classes. The Actuaries Table, 1837, called the "Old Experience Table," was adopted by sixteen English offices and one Scottish Office. The New Experience Table was drawn up in 1863 and used by twenty English offices.
See A. Kirkwood, *Lectures on Insurance and Industrial Law* (1874).

The Manchester Unity of Oddfellows had a customary benefit in 1845 of 10s. sick pay, £10 death benefit for members, and £6 to £10 on death of wife. Some lodges were charging 4d., others 5d. and 6d. weekly. Contributions were not graduated according to age. There were many lapsed members, and often if funds were exhausted a levy was made. In other cases, a friendly society lacking funds lapsed its sickness benefit, and members were restricted to burial money. Ageing populations of members, with no influx of young replacements, and no age-specific premiums, bore heavily on funds of the societies.

The Manchester Unity of Oddfellows listed over 72,000 members in 1863 within Lancashire and Cheshire alone, but " No person shall be admitted above the age of forty years . . . "[1] Later, the industrial assurance companies were to use some of these data, after actuarial refinement, when they ventured into the area to compete with friendly society benefits.

It was the North West region which from the mid-nineteenth century also became the centre of a new form of friendly society — the collecting society — with a national coverage and providing employment to full-time agents. The Royal Liver Friendly Society had 600,000 members, and the Liverpool Victoria Society 200,000 members, by 1875. Both had quickly achieved a nationwide coverage. Collecting societies owed their strong appeal to the dread of a pauper funeral which haunted the working-class breadwinner.

> ". . . and how exceedingly advantageous, philanthropic, and cheap is this scheme of life assurance! It is within the reach of the very poorest man or woman, who have starved and pinched and worked, to save the pennies that are to carry him or her by the Parliamentary train to a new scheme of labour, to behold friends and relatives to revive fading associations, or to find a quiet resting place far away from the smoky, busy, wearying, vicious town, in the hamlet where they first saw the light of Heaven — where they hope, life's fitful fever over, to close their eyes in peace and to sleep their long last sleep in the little churchyard, over the grassy mounds of which they gambolled in childhood, the bricklayer on the housetop, the machinist, the captain and mates and seamen voyaging across the surging

[1] Taken from bye-laws for Manchester District of National Independent Order of Oddfellows, 30 July, 1867.

waves of the ocean, may, one and all, at the cost of a very
moderate outlay, receive, in the event of an accident, a liberal
compensation for loss of time, and the payment of a heavy sum
to their wives or relatives in event of death."[1]

The collecting societies had grown out of the local burial clubs that
had been common since the eighteenth century and before.[2] The
local sick and burial societies in the Manchester district did not however
receive much commendation in the report of the Royal Commission on
Friendly Societies 1874: " These appear to be generally worse conducted than the pure burial societies and tend to merge into the latter
class."[3]

The specific allowance for funerals provided by the friendly societies
during the 1870s varied between three pounds and ten pounds. The
burial societies provided sums towards interment which were frequently larger than those of the friendly societies. In 1850, an Act had
been passed that no sum should be insured on the death of a child
under ten years of age, beyond the sum actually incurred for funeral
expenses, and this was not to exceed three pounds. From 1858, no
money was to be payable on a child's death without a certificate

[1] J. Brokenshir, *Practical Directions for Life Assurance Agency* (3rd edit., 1858),
pp.62–63.

[2] F. M. Eden, *Observations on Friendly Societies* (1797), gives a prospectus of a London
burial society:
" A favourable opportunity now offers to anyone, of either sex, who would
wish to be buried in a genteel manner, by paying 1s. entrance and 2d. per week
for the benefit of the stock. Members to enter above 14 and under 60 years of age,
if approved of, and to be free in six months from the date of entrance. The deceased
to be furnished with the following articles: a strong elm coffin covered with a
superfine black, and furnished with two rows, all round, close drove, with best
black japanned nails, and adorned with rich ornamental drops, a handsome plate
of inscription, angel above the plate and flower beneath, and four pairs of handsome
handles, with wrought gripes (sic). The coffin to be well-pitched, lined and
ruffled with crepe, a handsome crepe shroud, cap and pillow. For use, a handsome
velvet pall, three gentlemen's cloaks, three crepe hat bands, three hoods and scarves
and six pairs of gloves, two porters equipped to attend the funeral, a man to attend
the same with band and gloves; also the burial fees paid if not exceeding one
guinea."
Edwin Chadwick estimated the cost of funerals in 1839 as 13s. per head for
pauper funerals in London, £5 for artisans, and for tradesmen up to £50.
See *Supplemental Report on Interment in Towns* (1843).

[3] There was, for instance, an Equity and Economical Reformed Penny Club for the
Interment of the Dead, which held its first meeting at the Boathouse, Oldfield
Road, Salford. The rolls of members were deposited but the secretary devised a
forged certificate for submission to the Registrar.

signed by a doctor stating the probable cause of death. Rumours still circulated of ghoulish practices.[1]

All in all, it would have been unwise during the early years of its life for the Co-operative Insurance Company to have broken into the market providing burial money for the working classes. The existing ramifications and affiliations were extremely widespread, and many of the co-operators must have been members of one or more of the friendly or collecting societies.

(iv) Life Assurance

The term "industrial assurance" is a misnomer. Through a historical accident, the word "industrial," which appeared in the title of two small and unnoticed insurance offices in the mid-nineteenth century, was given a connotation which became embodied in a legal definition in the Life Assurance Companies Act of 1870. The germ of what became known as industrial assurance can be traced as far back as 1807, when a scheme for the establishment of "The Poor's Assurance Office" was the subject of a Parliamentary committee of inquiry. The assured parties entitled to benefit were to be those "who subsisted wholly or principally by the wages of their labour." Commissioners were to be appointed, and the Post Office was to provide the administration. Insufficient support was forthcoming and the plan was shelved. Apparently, the first appearance of "Industrial" in the title of a life assurance company was the Industrial and General founded in 1849.[2]

Given the growing demand for life assurance and the uncertainties of legal protection, it was hardly surprising that some insurance offices engaged in dubious practices. The failure of the Albert Life Assurance Company in 1869, which came as a great shock to the

---

[1] See Edwin Chadwick's address to the Social Science Association in 1865: "I had some years ago to make enquiries in relation to the operation of the lowest class of insurance and in connection with provisions for the destitute, those by means of sick clubs and burial societies . . . I put forth in my reports a part of the evidence disclosed to me, showing that the practice of secret murders, and the neglect of children, had taken root, and was spreading for the sake of the burial money . . ."

[2] The Industrial and General Company is not referred to in *The History of Industrial Assurance* by Dermot Morrah. This Company was taken over by the newly-formed Peoples Provident in 1855, and this latter Company was eventually wound up in 1872 in connection with the European Life Assurance Company bankruptcy. It is more usual to trace the origin of industrial life assurance to the British Industry Life Assurance Company of 1852. This Company made rapid progress, and in 1860 it was amalgamated with the Prudential which, six years previously, commenced the issue of industrial policies. Although the Prudential soon became, and remained, the largest provider of industrial assurance, many of the collecting societies lapsed their sickness benefits and became in effect industrial assurance companies, although legally registered as friendly societies.

public, was mainly due to overreaching takeovers of other offices; the parent company had been founded in 1838, and had absorbed twenty-six other offices during the ensuing thirty years.[1] In the same year of 1869, investigations were made into the working of the European Life Assurance Company, which finally collapsed in 1872. From 1870, all subsequently-established life offices were required to deposit a statutory £20,000 with the Court of Chancery, and show life funds separately from other funds.

Much information on early industrial assurance practice came to light in the reports of the Royal Commission of Friendly Societies, particularly in the 4th Report, published in 1874. Evidence was given that many burial societies were synonymous with industrial assurance: "No-one who has reflected upon friendly societies on the one hand and Life Insurance Associations on the other, can fail to have observed that the Burial Society is the connecting link between them." The Commissioners recommended that the law relating to burial societies and industrial assurance should be assimilated, although their terms of reference were purely in relation to friendly societies

> "but in pursuing it (the inquiry) we have found ourselves
> constantly in presence of the fact that a business almost or even
> precisely similar to that of burial societies established under the
> Friendly Society Acts was carried on by a class of bodies regis-
> tered under the Company Acts; that the keenest competitions
> often existed between the two classes of bodies; that the same
> methods were followed; the same complaints urged by in-
> dividuals against both."[2]

[1] See William T. Thomson, *Present Position of Life Assurance Interests of Great Britain* (Edinburgh, 1852).
The total sum of life assurance at the end of 1851 was £150m. Eighty-two of the offices existing in 1851 had been established between 1840 and 1850. Thompson suggested that all offices should pay a certain sum in Government funds to the registrar, that there should be a Government auditor to assist the registrar and the Board of Trade should be empowered to suspend operation of companies whose management was tending towards insolvency. There were also articles in the Assurance Magazine during 1851–52 advocating that deposits with the Board of Trade and the production of proper accounts should be made.
During 1851 to 1855, no fewer than 92 life offices were established. Seventy-nine had an average life of less than five years. A select committee was set up to inquire into assurance associations in 1853, and it found that many of them were fraudulent. However, no legislation was passed until 1870.

[2] Times and attitudes change. Defoe wrote at the end of the seventeenth century — "Insuring of life I cannot admire. I shall say nothing to it, but that in Italy, where stabbing and poisoning is so much the vogue, something may be said for it." Defoe was of course wrong, as it is only where human life is fairly secure that life assurance can flourish. It is indeed modern capitalism more than anything else to which we owe the growth of insurance. See *Essay upon Projects* (1697).

The Commissioners pondered whether there could be reform of burial societies as well as friendly societies without an investigation into industrial assurance. Evidence was received from a number of industrial assurance companies, but the Commission directly examined only one such office — the Prudential. The collectors of the small weekly premiums called at the homes of the insured and they were "the pivot of the whole system." In the local societies, the collector was generally engaged on a part-time capacity after normal working hours. But in the general societies, they were full-time, "and they require of course a higher remuneration." Lapsing of policies was too prevalent. "The general burial societies in many cases absolutely maintain themselves by their lapses," commented the Commissioners in the 1874 Report. Sham companies were set up which existed only in the collectors' round books. The Report made adverse comments on the readiness with which insurance staff and policyholders were transferred between offices, and the Commissioners concluded " on the whole our opinion is decidedly adverse to this form of society (the General Collecting Burial Society)."

The Royal Commission recommended that the insurance of lives of infants under three years of age should be prohibited, and in due course, the Friendly Societies Act of 1875 limited the insurance of lives under ten years of age to £10, and for children under five to £6. After 1875, the purely life assurance aspect came to dominate the work of the larger collecting societies.

The growing success of industrial assurance *vis à vis* the burial clubs and some of the early friendly societies was dependent on many factors, including more careful selection of lives, supervision of field methods, together with more attention to internal administration — the ratio of management expenses to premium income remained high in the 1870s, fell gradually during the 1880s and 1890s, but even at the turn of the century, the average remained as high as 50 per cent. Over the period 1880 to 1900, premium income increased fourfold, and the funds of industrial assurance offices multiplied by twelve.

The industrial assurance offices were providing a professional service that was dearly bought by the masses, but which was the counterpart of the ordinary life cover for more prosperous policyholders, and could hardly have been provided by any other means — the Gladstonian state scheme based on the sale of annuities and endowments through the Post Office was a protracted failure as it had no agents to collect premiums and to act as mentors to the policyholders.

The individual members of the national friendly collecting societies had no say in the internal affairs of their societies — a situation which contrasted with the affiliated orders such as the Oddfellows and Foresters whose administration was a most suitable training ground for an increasingly articulate working class.

(v) CIC and Ordinary Life Assurance from 1886

At a board meeting in July, 1885, the opinion of a J. H. Theobald of Lincoln's Inn on the Assurance Companies Act 1870, was read:

> "In my opinion Section 3 of the Life Assurance Companies Act does not apply to this Company. 'Established' as used in the section, is, I think, equivalent to 'incorporated' and as the Company was incorporated before the Act, Section 3 does not apply. Section 7 seems to me to show conclusively that 'established' does not mean merely 'existing' as so to read it in that section would result in an absurdity. The Company can therefore commence life business without making a deposit of £20,000. If the Company carries on life assurance it will be within the definition clause in Section 2 and the provisions of Sections 5 and 7 and subsequent sections relating to the accounts, will apply."

Mr. Prest, an actuary, undertook to supply an original set of six life tables in December, 1885 — for the insurance of £100 at death, the premiums payable during the whole life; with premiums ceasing at various ages up to 65; for the insurance of joint lives; and for the insurance of £100 on attaining the age of 60 or prior death. Together with tables of surrender values applicable, a fee of 21 guineas was offered and accepted. The calculations were based on the Manchester Unity of Oddfellows' Experience (1866 to 1870), with 3 per cent interest.

The annual general meeting of February 1886, resolved that "life insurance be undertaken by the Company and that profits of the life department shall belong exclusively to the life policyholders." It will be remembered that on the foundation of the CIC, the Articles of Association of the Company gave as one of its objects the insurance of lives of members of Co-operative societies exclusively. The CIC received a second countervailing legal opinion that as the Company had not insured any lives before 1870, it would not be allowed to do so unless the statutory deposit of £20,000 was made in Government securities. The Co-operative Friendly Society had been established to

77

circumvent this onus, but as noted previously, the Co-operative societies were not prepared to advance the capital required, and the project had been given up. It was proposed that *all* policyholders should participate in the profits of the life department, and that the policyholders should not be divided into two classes, one participating and the other not.

The profits in the fire and fidelity departments had not been divided amongst the policyholders, but had been wholly retained as a reserve. The annual general meeting of 1886, however, passed the momentous resolution that was to help determine the character of all future co-operative insurance business: " We recommend that the shareholders forfeit any rights they may have to the profits of the fire department and agree that they shall belong exclusively to the policyholders."

Local Co-operative societies were urged to provide facilities for the payment of premiums out of dividends:

> " and thus to increase the profitableness of the business by diminishing the heavy charge occasioned by the cost of collecting a mass of small payments, which in some other insurance societies makes insurance for the poorer classes more than 50 per cent dearer than it is for the richer classes."

In reply to a question, E. Vansittart Neale said, that in the event of the first counsel's opinion being wrong, in that the Company would not have the power to undertake life assurance without complying with the Act of 1870, the policies issued would be valid, but the directors might be liable for penalties for having issued them. To prevent lapses and forfeitures, the surrender value of life policies, not kept in force by payment of premiums, was to be secured independently of any application by the policyholder to the CIC. On application, a policyholder could have his policy held in force as long as the surrender value was sufficient to pay the premiums and compound interest thereon. Further, he could have the surrender value treated as a premium for a fully paid-up policy for a reduced amount, or alternatively he could take the surrender value in cash. No policies were to be issued for a premium of less than five shillings a year, nor for a sum less than £25[1] (suicide within one year of the issue of the policy would forfeit the policy). The CIC agreed to meet medical fees and revenue stamps, and in May, 1886, a Dr. Glasscott was appointed chief medical officer.

[1] In the Life Department, the sum insured had been fixed at a minimum of £25 in order not to compete with the friendly societies.

A delegate at the Co-operative Congress commented that the CIC should insure as low as £5; "£25 was too high for a man with a family earning only 24s. per week." E. O. Greening supported the new venture of life assurance businesss in that all profits of the life department should belong to the assured. The *Insurance News* of 15 June, 1886, also commented favourably on the progress of the CIC

"... the Co-operative, though small is thoroughly sound and respectable and in its own quite unobtrusive way is now doing a safe and improving business. There is no reason why possessing such a connection as it does, the Co-operative should not prove successful in this new department. Arrangements have been made so that the life funds are to be kept quite distinct and they will not be held liable for any other engagements of the Company."

The Actuary's life tables were incorporated in a prospectus which also showed the relative advantage of life assurance and the investment of money at 3 per cent compound interest. Tables were given of surrender values — one for fully paid-up policies, and the other for policies with periodical premiums. In June, 1886, an advertisement appeared for a life insurance clerk " who will qualify himself to become an actuary." Several applicants were interviewed, and S. P. Leah was appointed at 17s. 6d. per week. Another post was created for a superintendent of agents, and F. A. Williams was appointed at 50s. per week, which was to be increased to 60s. if results were deemed satisfactory by June, 1887.

The Board Meeting held on 13 July, 1886, resolved " that policies be issued in accordance with this day's list of proposals, including one for £150 on the life of the Prince of Wales, if he is a member of a co-operative society." At that meeting it was agreed that on quinquennial valuations the directors could apportion any part not exceeding four-fifths of any surplus shown amongst the life policyholders.

Proof of age was required for life policies, but it was conceded that " parallel of latitude north of which the Insured may travel and reside be altered from 35° to 30°." To safeguard its own geographical knowledge, the office purchased *Bacon's Atlas* for 35s.

In December, 1886, it was minuted: " That each Co-operative society whether agent for the Company or not, be invited to recommend to the Company one or more industrial agents likely to secure life and fire insurance business which societies as corporate agents would be unlikely to obtain."

Fire losses had been heavy for the financial year 1885–86. The main causes of the increase were defective construction of buildings, inserting beams into chimneys, and hearth stones insecurely fixed or broken. Gas lights too near either woodwork or goods were also a contributory cause, as was the throwing down of unspent matches. The Alliance Office discontinued granting reinsurance facilities to the CIC, as it maintained that no profit could be made from insurance of Co-operative stores at the low level of rates prevailing. The CIC would not agree to increase the rates, but did agree "to be more systematic in charging additional rates for other elements of risk than mere increase of size . . ." New terms of commission were laid down for the SCWS in March, 1886: 5 per cent on premiums for all fire business other than on co-operative property; 15 per cent on first premium for fidelity of own servants; 15 per cent for all other fire policies except tariff risks. A portion of insurance on the Liverpool Exhibition Buildings and contents was accepted at FOC rates in March, 1886.

The increasing amount of clerical work at chief office necessitated that a decision should be made regarding the growing bulk of correspondence filing. It was decided that letters older than six years should be destroyed. Five hundred copies of agents' instructions were printed, and it was minuted that where special canvassing representatives had to walk three or more miles each way in order to visit a committee of a local co-operative society, they were to be allowed 2s. 6d. in addition to the usual fee.

By the end of 1886, 28 life policies had been issued for a total sum assured of £2,350 and a total premium income of £118 5s. 8d. Early in 1887, a policy was issued "subject in the case of the insurance on the Manager's life, to confirmation, after receipt of medical officer's report." F. Austen Williams canvassed the CWS employees for life business. Full commission rates were granted and the Manager urged the CWS to collect premiums. At a conference in March, 1887, Odgers read a paper on life assurance, and in discussion, the Rochdale delegate thought that the Company had made a big mistake in not entering the field of life assurance from its formation in 1867. Judge Hughes (Thomas Hughes)[1] attended a conference in 1888, and expressed his astonishment at "the miserable appearance of the returns of the Insurance Company, a society nominally, at least, supported

[1] Thomas Hughes (the author of *Tom Brown's Schooldays*) was a member of the Hebden Bridge Manufacturing Society.

by the whole body of co-operators." It was most painful for him to learn that the whole amount paid in life premiums during the year 1887 was £613, and he trusted that in future years a more cordial support would be tendered to the Company by co-operators. E. Vansittart Neale stated that if the Company took £10,000 on a single risk it would be a gambling transaction, because their reserve capital was insufficient to justify them in running such a risk. The Company went as far as they possibly could; to go further would endanger both the Company and the insured. A delegate pointed out the losses in the fidelity department, which had been incurred during the previous year, had reflected great discredit on the Co-operative Movement. He thought it was due to "insufficient remuneration of the employees." Hodgson Pratt, the Registrar of Friendly and Provident societies, thought it important to consider the relative advantages of joining an insurance company supported by the State and one supported by the Co-operative Movement. The first object should be security, and that was more effectively secured by the State than by any private concern. He considered " that if the advantages of insuring with the Co-operative Society were not greater than the advantages of insuring with the State, he should prefer to insure with the State."— presumably Hodgson Pratt was referring to the annuity scheme administered by the Post Office.

The question of teetotalism was raised in August, 1887: " That all questions as to whether profits of insuring teetotallers shall be divided separately from other policyholders, be postponed, but that books be so kept that if, eventually it should be decided, there would be no difficulty in doing so."

The share capital was increased in 1887 to £50,000. Dividend of 6 per cent on called-up share capital and 5 per cent on capital credited in excess of calls was agreed from 1887, but in 1888, the dividend on excess call capital was reduced from 5 per cent to 4 per cent. The principle of distinguishing between guarantors and shareholders was incorporated in amendments to the Articles of Association. Members of the Company were to be any persons or societies admitted by Directors. As a general rule not more than 1,000 shares could be allotted to any one shareholder.

Other offices began competing with the CIC in offering life assurance to co-operative members. One such office was willing to insure co-operative members for sums of £50 and upwards for weekly premiums a little over 1/52nd of annual premiums. Each

81

Co-operative society was either to collect premiums weekly or to deduct them from dividend and then to pay the proceeds, less 5 per cent to the insurance company every three months. The CIC retaliated:

> " That the proposed plan better be carried out in connection with this Company — the weekly premium to be 1/13th of our usual quarterly premium plus any fraction of 1d.— and that we will offer all necessary facilities for carrying it out, provided that the societies who adopt it will guarantee the full quarterly premiums to us, and the old agency commission to be allowed to them."

Directors agreed to attend quarterly conferences and visit committees of non-member Co-operative societies to induce them to join the CIC as shareholders and agents. William Barnett, the Chairman of the CIC since 1882, was to visit Macclesfield and Cheshire generally; E. Vansittart Neale, Rossendale and South Yorkshire.

A certain T. Briggs of York was appointed as an agent in July, 1888, and he enquired whether he might sell interest-in-book if he removed or gave up his agency. The CIC Board resolved

> " that the Company be no party to a sale of such interest, and that the directors decline to pledge the Company to transfer the business of one agent to another; preferring that if, or when, an application for such a transfer is made, it shall be dealt with on its merits — the Company retaining its liberty, on discontinuance of an agency, to renew the policies without the mediation of an agent or to make the most satisfactory arrangement it can for their renewal through another or other agents."

Advertisements for agents in Manchester, Rochdale, Oldham, Stalybridge, appeared in the *Co-operative News* in October, 1888. During 1888, 109 life policies were issued for a total sum insured of £9,025.

A publication of the leading fire offices commented on the CIC:

> " It has stood the test of time, has been economically managed, and consequently holds accumulative reserve funds to meet extraordinary claims or claims greater in extent than those hitherto experienced by itself and fire offices generally, after providing for every liability on current risk it has a surplus profit reserve of considerably more than a year's premium income, consequently very few offices in this respect have achieved its stability."

Annual returns were required by the Metropolitan Board of Works on fire insurance business in the London area. By 1886, the amount of fire business covered by the CIC in London was over £200,000. New limits for fire business were raised to £3,000 in November, 1887, for Co-operative stores, churches, schools and private dwellings. A small fire claim was received in 1888, from E. Vansittart Neale of Bisham Abbey, for £4 13s. 6d. There was also a fire claim of £200 submitted by the Civil Service Supply Stores of London, in December, 1888. A fire occurred in the northern branch premises of the Rochdale Equitable Society in March, 1889, with serious damage to buildings and contents not specifically mentioned in the policy. The assessor and insured agreed to terms: " But claim for books, pamphlets and the like be not entertained, but that loss on newsroom furniture, fixtures, etc., be paid out of unexhausted balance of insurance on fixtures and utensils in trade."

The CIC property in Bates Street continued to require attention; £100 was written off the value of these houses at the beginning of 1887, and an agent was appointed to collect rents. A notice was received from Manchester Corporation that ash-pits behind the houses were required to be drained.

Investment of life funds was now a further pre-occupation of the CIC Board, and the Manager was instructed to investigate and report on suitable securities in the market, after he had produced a classified list of investment portfolios of other insurance offices. Railway guaranteed stock and local authority mortgage loans were much favoured by the CIC during this period. (£800 of Lancashire and Yorkshire Railway guaranteed stock at 6 per cent was purchased in September, 1887.) The Manager sent to each director a short list of half-a-dozen suitable investments for selection — the directors were to decide from time to time how much to invest and in what class of security, and were then to leave the stockbroker to do the best for them, " but brokers should be instructed to buy only when investment would produce the rate of interest specified in the instruction." In May, 1888, the range of investments was broadened so that " our investments through stockbrokers be not only in railway guaranteed stock and Corporation stocks, but also in high class railway preference shares." The Manager was also authorised to purchase up to £1,000 nominal value in any one investment transaction. £1,700 was invested in railway preference stock during May, 1888, and later in the same year, £1,000 of London, Brighton and South Coast Railway 5 per

83

cent stock. Other avenues of investment were investigated — it was reported in May, 1889, that some good chief rents were available for sale in Macclesfield and the Manager was instructed to bid not exceeding £2,000 at 25 years' purchase. The CIC Board agreed to contribute £50 in relief of distress caused by a railway accident in Armagh, in July, 1889. (The previously highest donation had been £20 to the E. Vansittart Neale scholarship fund in 1887.) One of the directors of the CIC requested an advance on the security of a house; the advance was granted on the deposit of collateral security. A loan on the life policy of James Odgers was also agreed to, subject to an assurance from Mr. Prest, the actuary, that the reserve value of the policy exceeded the loan. An application from the Lincoln Co-operative Land and Building Society for a loan on security of houses in course of erection was declined.

Precautions were taken to ensure that transcription of policies should be correct, and the Manager recommended " the carbon paper process as a precaution for writing and issuing policies upon forms bound together in a book . . . " Wages of the eight office staff were increased in February, 1888, including Rugen, the office boy, whose wage was increased to five shillings.

The first life claim after three years of life business was received in September, 1889, on the death of a John Clare of Mossley, insured under policy No. 63 for £25.

Questions were raised and answered concerning foreign commitments. In September, 1888, the Brisbane Co-operative Society was informed that the CIC was not prepared to appoint overseas agents,

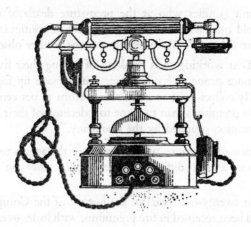

and W. C. Knox of Kansas was advised " that at present we are not disposed to invest in securities outside Great Britain."

The CIC agreed to subscribe to a scheme for Co-operative telephones " should a minimum number of 1,000 users join the association to constitute an exchange; the annual rental not to exceed £5 per annum for each exchange wire and telephone, and £1 per annum for each private office or workhouse telephone." (Only one exchange line was required by the CIC). A first typewriter was purchased in 1890, and a telephone installed in 1892. (The first ledger posting machine was not installed until 1926.)

Mr. Prest was asked to prepare life tables for insurance of £100 payable in ten years from date of entry or previous death. He advised that the quinquennial valuation to be undertaken in December, 1890, should be conducted by an actuary of high standing. Edwin Justican, F.I.A., was duly appointed at a fee of £26 to undertake the Life Department valuation and to certify all schedules required by the Life Assurance Companies Act. The Actuary was informed that the profits were to be divided solely amongst those policyholders, whose premiums, accumulated at 4 per cent compound interest, amounted to the sum insured under their policies, and that all policies of the Company were of the participating class.

During the years 1887 to 1890, a considerable proportion of the policies issued in the Life Department was on the lives of agents and shareholders. In view of the slow progress of life business, a conference of shareholders and agents was held in 1890 to discuss methods of promoting life assurance business: " The chief difficulties are the newness to working men of the idea of making provision by insurance for wives and families who at the premature death of the bread-winner would otherwise be left destitute and of continuing with its provision for old age." More telling was the further observation:

> " That working men thinking of having their lives insured are more prone to having their minds made up for them by weekly collectors at an extra charge from 15 per cent upwards on the premiums than to come to a decision of their own upon information supplied by the Company."

The newness of insurance work to most of the agents recruited by the CIC was also a difficulty which could only be overcome with time.

In the first twenty-one years of the history of the Company, over £63,000 had been received in fire premiums, with losses over £34,000, equal to a claims rate of 54 per cent. Fidelity premiums received during the same period were £10,700 and the claims £5,300, a rate of just under 50 per cent. At the end of the first seven years, there were 71 Co-operative society shareholders; in the second seven years, there were 180 societies with a paid-up capital of £10,500; and in the third period ending 1889, there were 287 societies holding shares with a paid-up capital of £12,600.

Attention was drawn during 1890 to the benefits obtainable by yearly, half-yearly and quarterly payments of life premiums. There was also discussion of the obstacles to an increase in fire and fidelity insurance, especially in Scotland. Miller, the CIC representative from Scotland, pointed out that one of the difficulties in furthering quarterly and periodic premium collection was the number and the persistence of the agents of other companies selling weekly business.

The outcome of the first quinquennial valuation showed that the life fund on 31 December, 1890 was £3,427, and the net liability under all policies in force was £2,602, making a surplus of £824 — " no part of the surplus is for dividend, but will be carried forward for future division with the life policyholders." However, in the Life Department, 125 local Co-operative societies had only sent in two proposals in five years. In Airedale, 12 agents serviced 11 life policies, in Dewsbury, nine agents dealt with 11 policies, and in Huddersfield, nine agents with 17 life policies. An agent complained of the difficulties of getting a proposal accepted — unlike agents of other insurance offices, they had to make exhaustive enquiries and obtain much confirmation from witnesses; other companies would insure children, for instance, at an earlier age, and policyholders could pay weekly.

Odgers submitted a memorandum on life assurance by weekly or monthly payments, but this was adjourned for discussion for a further twelve months. In October, 1891, a solicitor was once more instructed to see if the Company's Memorandum of Association could be so altered as to remove the existing restriction on life and fidelity business without having to deposit the £20,000 with the Board of Trade. The answer was satisfactory, and amendments were incorporated to enable the insurance of lives of members of Co-operative societies or their relatives, and to substitute the word " member " for " shareholder."

Notice was brought to the directors of a new scheme of the Sun Life Office for insuring under certain conditions without medical examination, and it was resolved that the matter should be considered by the CIC in March, 1890, when the limit on CIC life policies was £500. The subject of child life assurance was again brought to the fore at the end of 1892. Legal opinion held that the limitation imposed by the Friendly Societies Act on the sums payable on death of children did not apply to the CIC, and the Chief Registrar of Industrial and Provident Societies advised the CIC in 1893, that conversion of the Company into a Society would enable continuance of its power to conduct life business without the requisite £20,000 deposit, but any extension of objects in the Life Department would be subject to the interpretation of the Life Assurance Act of 1870 by the Board of Trade. If the Company continued to issue policies to individuals, it could not be exempted from income tax, unless each policyholder was allowed to become a shareholder.

The CIC was critical of those local Co-operative societies who paid inadequate wages to employees in positions of trust. A proposal was declined in October, 1890, for two vanmen employed by Exeter Co-operative Society, as the CIC felt that the wage was not sufficient for the risk. Hence in May, 1891, it was minuted: " Policies in accordance with today's lists acceptable except fidelity proposal in name of Charlotte Mills employed at 8s. per week by the Sheffield Co-operative Society to manage their crockery department." Another society was written to, reiterating the opinion of the CIC Board that the wages paid by the Society to its manager were not commensurate with his responsibilities.

By the end of March, 1891, the subscribed share capital of the CIC was £47,400, leaving only £2,600 of the nominal capital of £50,000 unsubscribed. All 50,000 shares were allocated by 1892. The number of fire policies in force in 1889 was 19,971, in 1890 — 24,162; sums assured under fire policies in 1889 — £4,593,655, in 1890 — £5,074,750. Life policies in force in 1889 numbered 263, in 1890 — 327; Life sums assured in 1889 — £23,675, in 1890 — £29,400. Fidelity policies in 1889 numbered 1,038, in 1890 — 1,121, with sums insured in 1889 — £109,925 and £120,800 in 1890.

In a reply to a query regarding the commencement of industrial assurance, Odgers pointed out that the working expenses of the Prudential in 1892 were 43 per cent whereas those of the CIC were 13 per cent.

E. Vansittart Neale, who had been a director of the CIC for many years, intimated that he would resign in 1892. It was agreed that he should leave the Company with " some form of acknowledgment." This took the form of a solid silver casket with a parchment scroll enclosed " with decorations and Mr. Neale's portrait in bas relief, his coat of arms enamelled, the Company's coat of arms and an inscription thereon . . . "

The presentation address to E. Vansittart Neale stated:

" Holding the position of General Secretary and Legal Adviser to the Co-operative Union during all the 16 years of your connection with this Company as director — the offices of both institutions being in the same building — you were always accessible; and the occasions on which difficulties were referred to you were very numerous.

With your previous experience as a director of an insurance company, and with your legal knowledge, you were always able to find ways out of these difficulties; and your aid was always given most willingly, and regardless of your own convenience.

Invaluable were your services in 1877, 1878 and 1879 in drafting the rules and forms for the Co-operative Assurance Friendly Society, which it was proposed to establish in the time of uncertainty whether life insurance might legally be undertaken by the Company. Although the scheme was finally abandoned it prepared the way for the establishment of the Life Department in 1886 . . . We refer last to the foresight and sound judgment displayed by you and the founders of the Company in 1867, in so framing its constitution as to permit a continuous increase in the number of members without necessarily increasing the capital; a wise method of combining

a growing representation of the mutual interests of co-operative
societies as policyholders with the primary financial responsibility of the shareholders . . . "

The address was dated May, 1892, and was signed by William
Barnett and James Odgers and all the directors of the Co-operative
Insurance Company.

E. Vansittart Neale replied from Bisham Abbey

" the Company has now reached a position, where we may
I trust, consider its future to be assured. It is a sincere satisfaction to me, to have in any degree contributed to the growth
of an institution, which will I believe promote with increasing
success, the important object of giving to co-operative societies
as collective bodies, and to their members individually, that
security against fire, fraud and the chances of mortality which
it was formed to provide . . . E. Vansittart Neale."

Miss Beatrice Potter (Mrs. Sidney Webb) attended the Co-operative
Congress of 1892, held in Rochdale, and she passed some comments on
Northern enterprise that were most perceptive. She queried whether
Lancashire people were keeping their place in the forefront of progress,
especially in the matter of national education.[1] Beatrice Potter
was often tempted to wonder whether we should always be able to
say that what Lancashire thought today England would think
tomorrow, or whether the time would not come when we should
have to say that what England had attained today, Lancashire, hope-
lessly handicapped by lack of physical vigour and intellectual strength,
would be painfully struggling after tomorrow.

[1] *Co-operative Congress Report*, 1892, pp.128-129.
" Twenty years ago, education was carried on by private enterprise. In 1870 it was
decided to make education a great national co-operative undertaking. In some
respects Lancashire and Rochdale were not quite so forward in this matter as the
South country. The local schoolboards have power to fix the standard at which
children shall go to work. The Parliamentary returns show that whereas Oldham,
Bolton and Leeds fixed upon Standard Six, Rochdale could not afford its little ones
more schooling that was meant by Standard Five. Rochdale children had not a
fair start in life, because mothers went to the factory while their children were still
in the cradle. At ten years old the Rochdale child was 1½ inches shorter, and 5 lb.
lighter than the ordinary national schoolchild. Then it went to the factory at ten
instead of waiting till 12, and during the interval it grew 3½ inches less and weighed
11 lb. less than the ordinary schoolchild . . . This was a rather serious state of things.
People might say that these things were worse 40 years ago; but we must remember
that all through England things have changed. Forty years ago the people of
Lancashire had a monopoly of education, largely owing to zealous dissenting
ministers having established a voluntary system of education, while the South
country and London were in utter darkness. But this had all been altered, there
was now a splendid system of education in the South, and a high standard of learn-
ing was insisted on before children went to work."

G. J. Holyoake attended the annual meeting of the CIC in 1892, and queried when the Company was going to be put on a proper co-operative basis so that the profits, if any, could be carried to the credit of the consumers — he saw nothing co-operative about the Company as it was then constituted. A conference, held in Leicester in October, 1892, ventilated some of the problems being faced by the agents of the Company — not only was the ground completely covered by industrial assurance companies, but these companies also allowed reduced scales for those who paid monthly or quarterly or half-yearly. Many policyholders, it was said, would willingly take out insurance if they could draw their own insurance money — endowment insurance was gaining ground rapidly. In reply to a question whether a special rate could be applied to a teetotaller, it was said all the death claims experience of the CIC since the formation of the Life Department had in fact related to teetotallers. Moreover, it was not correct to say that only members of Co-operative societies could be insured; they could also insure anyone connected with trade, friendly societies or joint-stock societies. James Odgers replied that when the rates for the Life Department were first drawn up, it was decided to charge much less than was usually charged for participating policies. Other companies had two scales of rates, one for " without profits " and the one for " with profits." The CIC rates were half-way between the two. A writer in 1893 stressed the importance of canvassing and said that there should be more superintendence of agents. James Odgers replied to another critic who supported weekly collection of premiums:

> " It is not likely that we can undertake the weekly collection of premiums all over the country by personal agents without the total expense being in excess of 40 per cent, but whether it could or not, the adoption by the Company of the weekly collection of premiums would involve the sacrifice of the facilities for the economy offered by Co-operative stores organisations and would set up a vested interest opposed to economy."

The limitations of the office accommodation were being severely felt by 1890. It was resolved in August " that gas lights in this office be so altered as to give less heat and foul air." The Manager reported in December 1891, that the safe in the large office was becoming damaged by wear and tear, and that the number of policy books was becoming too great for the available accommodation. The Manager was instructed to investigate the possibility of acquiring new offices, and in February, 1893, the Co-operative Newspaper Society agreed to rent to the CIC the second storey of their new building opposite Manchester Grammar School in Long Millgate. The new offices in Long Millgate were occupied early in 1894, but the Co-operative Newspaper Society would not allow a CIC sign on the outside wall of their building hence the Company compromised by having their windows lettered.

In October, 1890, it was re-affirmed that " proposals for fire insurance from Jews and foreigners be not entertained except in cases where we are offered shares of large insurances chiefly effected with other good tariff offices." There is no evidence that the CIC conducted racial discrimination in considering insurance proposals. Presumably these groups in general inhabited premises more liable to outbreaks of fire than those of other policyholders.[1]

The CIC remained hesitant about accepting business from cornmills. In August, 1891, a policy for £3,000 on Dunstan cornmill was accepted, provided the liability of the CIC was restricted to a rateable share not exceeding 1/25th on the loss under each item " and that if this condition is not accepted by the Co-operative Wholesale Society, the insurance be declined." The Manager issued each autumn a circular concerning fire hazards in Co-operative stores. The limit on fire insurance was raised from £4,000 to £5,000 in July, 1894, on premises of Co-operative societies where the CIC was the sole insurer. A higher limit of £8,000 was authorised when other companies insured at least £15,000, " with an addition of £2,000 in each case when there is constant water supply, a steam fire engine and a rate-supported fire brigade."

Further investments were made in railway preference stock in 1890, and £1,000 worth of 3½ per cent Huddersfield Corporation stock, redeemable in 1934, was purchased. In the same year, £2,000 was invested in Manchester Ship Canal mortgage debenture 4 per cent

[1] The first insurance proposal from a Jewish person was not accepted until 1912.

91

stock. North Staffordshire Railway 4½ per cent debenture stock was purchased in 1891 for £1,800. Five shares of £10 each in the Mutual Telephone Company were applied for in 1890, but by 1892, the shares had to be exchanged for £40 cash from the liquidator. In 1894, a loan of £3,000 at 3 per cent was made to Manchester Corporation. A further £3,000 was invested in the same stock later in the year and £3,000 in Great Eastern Railway Company preference stock.

The CIC proceeded cautiously on the extension of mortgage business. In July, 1891, a Mr. Smith of Sparkbrook, Birmingham, was informed that his kind of property was not in keeping and that "we should prefer not to advance money on building so distant from here as Birmingham." An offer was made for chief rents in the Didsbury and Crumpsall districts of Manchester in 1892, but an application from the Southern Co-operative Provident Benefit Building Society for a loan was declined in May, 1893. In December, 1894, £1,550 was lent at 4 per cent on mortgage on the site of 17 houses in London Road, Manchester. The CIC was also dealing with matters of property maintenance — a notice had been received from Manchester Corporation in July requiring Bates Street to be sewered so that water closets could be installed in the Company's houses.

The Manager was instructed to apportion each item of expense as accurately as possible between the three departments of Fire, Life and Fidelity. He was further instructed "to carry direct from Expenses Account to Profit and Loss Account as propagandist expenses any excess of expenses in Life Department over the loading in the premiums." He was to charge to the Life account for expenses a sum not exceeding the difference between commission and loading. The stock of Leah, the Life clerk, rose in 1894. Prest, the Actuary, had died, and it was minuted "that after the comparison of Mr. Leah's figures with those prepared by Mr. Prest for the end of this month, the checking hitherto done by Mr. Prest be discontinued." Any special calculations required for the Life Department were to be referred to the new Actuary, Mr. Justican.

An application was made for 400 shares in the Scottish Co-operative Wholesale Society in March, 1891. During May of the same year, it was resolved to invest £2,000 in the SCWS at 4¼ per cent, and that the CIC should undertake to provide the SCWS with printing business. The need to extend business in Scotland was considered in March, 1893. By October, the CIC was admitting that it could not obtain sufficient information from agents for the correct rating of risks under the local Glasgow and Paisley tariff, and that it would be impossible to survey other risks in Scotland without sending a fire surveyor from Manchester, or alternatively appointing a clerk to be stationed at Glasgow. The SCWS agreed to an annual sum of £5 10s. for the use of a desk in their office, and Albert Burgess was transferred from Manchester to Glasgow as the first clerk to be based in Scotland. Ultimately, he became the first manager when a Branch was established in Glasgow. Of the 250 Co-operative societies in Scotland at the time, only 104 had any connections with the CIC. Life business in Scotland was also very poor, only £88 premium was collected in 1893.

The CIC continued to turn its face against foreign connections. In September, 1891, a proposal from the London and Lisbon Cork Wood Company to insure property in Portugal was declined.

Two directors were paid £3 12s. each for signing policies during 1893. William Barnett surrendered his Life policy No. 77 for £16 13s. in April, 1894. By March, 1893, the number of office clerks had risen to ten. The salary of the Manager was raised to £500 per year from January, 1892, and a proposal on his life for £325 payable at 60 or previous death was accepted with five years added to the ordinary rate and the usual commission deducted. The telephone subscription was increased from £5 to £10 " to enable us to use the National Telephone System."

A notice was received in June, 1893, from the Fire Offices Committee of proposed new rates for 49 classes of risk hitherto non-tariff, and new rates for shops employing not more than 50 assistants. The CIC requested exemption of small Co-operative stores from the new rates. It further requested that biscuit, bread, bakery and clothing

manufacturing, fancy goods, and furniture stores, should be exempted, otherwise the CIC would consider having to withdraw from the Fire Offices Committee. Early in 1894, this request was rescinded, and the CIC merely claimed exemption for Co-operative stores employing under 50 assistants. The Fire Offices Committee complied with this request and agreed to exempt from the extra 2s. 6d. rate such-styled " combination of trades " shops. In July, 1894, FOC shop rates were further increased for medium and large stores, and the Manager, " instead of giving notice of a claim to exempt this Company from charging new rates only in cases of stores employing not more than 15, has given notice claiming exemption for all Co-operative stores whatsoever from the new rates." It was further resolved on 31 July, 1894

> " that as hitherto, the smaller stores be rated independently
> of the tariff; that where other offices are interested with us in
> the insurance of larger retail co-operative stores, the new rates
> be charged if equitable . . . but that where other offices are not
> co-insurers . . . such policies be undisturbed and remain at the
> old rates and subject to the old conditions."

"Workmen had not given life asurance the attention it deserved," commented William Barnett, the Chairman of the CIC in 1895. He pointed out the marked difference in premiums and expenses between industrial life and ordinary life offices. He thought that working men should save the excessive costs by adopting ordinary life assurance: " It is the principle of co-operation to do away with the middleman's profits, what a paradox that working people have to pay 30 per cent more for life assurance than the middle and upper classes." Though co-operators were largely working-class, the CIC preferred to adopt the methods of the ordinary life offices and thereby enable members to receive 25 per cent more insurance cover for their premiums than if the CIC had employed collectors of weekly premiums. Working men, it was asserted, were better able to insure owing to reductions in the cost of living. Barnett calculated that a certain basket of articles which would have cost £111 in 1874, could be bought in 1895 for £65; moreover a sum of £91m. had been deposited at the Post Office during the year and only £81m. withdrawn — most of the balance might well have been used for life assurance and annuities.

Statistics of fire losses were presented for the year 1895. Sooty chimneys, swinging gas brackets, explosions, supposed incendiarism, and " an over-heated poultice," were given as a selection of proximate causes.

In 1896, the quinquennial life valuation showed profits on premiums collected of 22½ per cent, and the Actuary felt that all interested in the welfare of the CIC should be congratulated on the achievement of a healthy financial position and surplus. At the 1896 annual conference an agent raised the issue that more business would be done if profits were divided — presumably amongst the agents. Another delegate queried whether the Local Government Board had ceased to recognise Co-operative policies with regard to fidelity insurance. It was explained that for a time the CIC policies had been accepted through an over-sight as the Company's Memorandum of Association did not allow the issue of such policies to bodies that were not Co-operative " and as the Government declined to class itself as a Co-operative society the policies had to be dropped."

A policyholder wrote to the *Co-operative News* in November, 1896, complaining that

> " in all our stores anyone can easily become a member and members control the management. I have been a customer (a policyholder) for ten years but I cannot become a member, that is a shareholder, and I have no voice directly or indirectly in the management. How directors are appointed and what salaries they and the manager gets I have no idea, I have never seen a balance sheet . . . "

Odgers replied that the Company, when formed, was a federation of Co-operative societies without any individual members, but after three years the directors had thought " as the correspondent thinks now, " that if individuals were to be insured, they should be allowed to become members. From that time until 1891, the share lists were opened both to societies and individuals, and at the end of 1891, there were 102 personal shareholders and 305 societies holding £50,000 of shares. It had to be admitted that private shareholders, who were not policyholders, were not desirable members, but they could not be forcibly expelled and paid off. Hence the policy of the directors for some years had been to facilitate the gradual disappearance of individual members, and so return in course of time to the original federal constitution.

In October, 1895, the Institute of Actuaries' Healthy Male Table was substituted for the Manchester Unity of Oddfellows' Experience (1866 to 1870) as the premium basis for all new proposals for life assurance. The current charge for expenses to the Life Department was to be 12½ per cent gross of the annual premiums from the end of 1895. The Actuary was instructed to prepare new child endowment tables and double endowments, viz.; £100 at the end of the period, and £50 on previous death. Justican also calculated a formula for surrender values. The rates of mortality assumed for children's lives were to be the Carlisle Experience Tables.

(vi) Social Conditions and Welfare in the North West

The CIC suffered for many years from a bad selection of lives; its experience was not untypical of the period and of other bodies providing some form of insurance cover for the working classes in the North: " It is this very high percentage of old lives in Lancashire and Yorkshire particularly which render the condition, financially, of these counties so unfavourable, as it is these lives, which, constantly claiming on the sick funds of the lodges, make such a large draw on the capital."[1]

It was estimated that each male child lost 39 per cent of its working life if born in the Manchester township during the 1880s:

> " Here are men and women entering the period of decline
> at an age when they ought scarcely to have passed the prime
> of life. And what is particularly distressing is the thought that
> although in some respects the local conditions of life have
> improved within the last half century, in other respects bad
> has become even worse."[2]

A contemporary observer commented: " the City of Manchester can only be compared to a gigantic hotbed of pestilential fermentation."[3]

It need hardly be emphasized that education was lacking for many children in the working-class districts of Manchester at the time of the foundation of the CIC. In the areas of Gaythorn and Knott Mill, only 53 per cent of the adults could read and 35 per cent could write,

---

[1] F. G. P. Meison, *The Manchester Unity of Oddfellows* (1869), p.21.
[2] Expectation of Life at Birth (1881 to 1890).

Males:	Manchester 28.78 years.
	England and Wales generally — 43.66
	Rural districts — 51.48
Females:	Manchester — 32.67
	England and Wales — 47.18
	Rural districts — 54.04

[Extracted from Life Tables compiled by Sir John Tatham and referred to in T. R. Marr, *Housing Conditions in Manchester and Salford* (1904).]

[3] James Whitehead, *Rate of Mortality in Manchester and other Manufacturing Towns* (1864).

Of the 733 children enumerated between the ages of three and fourteen, 46 per cent attended school, 42 per cent were neither at school nor work, and 12 per cent were at work.[1]

It is impossible to avoid consideration of the relationship between friendly societies and the Poor Law during the nineteenth century when investigating social conditions of the labouring classes. Both types of institution administered relief in sickness and old age;[2] both provided funeral expenses and medical attention. The overlap of services was dealt with in the 4th Report of the Royal Commission on Friendly Societies 1874, in which it was estimated that the friendly societies were saving Poor Law relief funds to the extent of £2m. yearly. Even as late as 1907, the majority of people on outdoor relief in Liverpool were members of burial clubs.[3] A pressing call on funeral money drawn by the poor was to replenish their wardrobes.

[1] In January, 1868, the districts of Gaythorn and Knott Mill were visited by T. R. Wilkinson, who read a paper on the findings to the Manchester Statistical Society.

[2] *Royal Commission on Poor Laws* (1909)
Evidence given by Miss J. S. Thorburn, member of Select Vestry of Liverpool, on 14 January, 1907.

[3] Evidence of N. Raw, visiting Medical Superintendent, Mill Road Infirmary, Liverpool. *Ibid.*

"Except in the case of mourning out of club money, and a very rare pair of boots, none of our out-relief women seem ever to buy clothes. They are always given by someone."[1]

(vii) *Fin De Siècle: A New Society*

A fidelity policy of £100 for a Co-operative society secretary was agreed to in January, 1895

> "subject to member of committee counting the balance of cash and checking bank pass-book monthly, and subject to publication at least once yearly showing amounts of share loan capital to credit of each member. If society not agreeable to latter condition an extra 3s. per cent to be charged."

More surprisingly, it was resolved in March, 1896, "that regimental and garrison canteens be treated as Co-operative societies for the purpose of fidelity guarantee." — the minutes refer to the Manager having interviewed a Captain F. S. Garratt of 6th Dragoon Guards at Preston. On the other hand, if it was found that the Burnley Weavers Society was unregistered and without legal power to prosecute defaulters, "their two proposals be declined." In May, 1896, the Manager reported that during the previous seven years the Company had received in premiums for fidelity guarantee £7,500 —

---

[1] Defoe had suggested in the seventeenth century that the monarch should be the general insurer for the whole of British overseas trade. He also suggested unemployment insurance for seamen, with a 50 per cent cover for 14 per cent contributions. There should be social insurance for sickness, accident, disablement, old age, funeral expenses and survivors' insurance. Defoe proposed pension offices for all artisans under 50 years of age, with an annual premium of 4s., with a conditional right to indemnification in cash, but with a preference for indemnification in kind, e.g., medical services. There would be compulsion on local authorities to refuse relief to the uninsured.

See *Essay on Projects* (1697).

The National Health Insurance Act of 1911 preserved the contact of the poor with friendly society benefits, but could not preserve the spirit of association through which the early friendly societies had grown to strength. Under the 1911 Act, private companies undertaking industrial assurance were associated in the scheme provided they set up non-profit-making mutual insurance branches. By 1925, nearly 50 per cent of insured persons were affiliated to these "industrial" approved societies. The Health Insurance Section of the CWS, which was formed in July, 1912, included 220,000 such members in 1,300 agencies by 1926. Each approved society made its own periodic valuations. If there was a surplus, then a scheme for additional benefits could be submitted to the insurance commissioners (likewise a deficit). Hence there was considerable diversity in the scale of benefits available. On transfer of members between societies the transfer value went with the member — subject to the consent of the vacating society. This ruling protected societies with poor benefits from wholesale cessation of members. Under the Unemployment Insurance Act 1920, industries could contract-out of the NHI scheme, industry by industry. In fact only two did — banking and insurance. Subsequently, economic conditions in the 1920s discouraged other industries from following their example and further contracting-out was withdrawn from 1927.

most of which was for general managers, secretaries, treasurers and cashiers. As the loss ratio was only 22 per cent, the Manager drew up a sample tariff to cheapen guarantees for shopmen and branch managers, with additional premiums where greater opportunities for misappropriation were open.

In many cases the CIC gave a generous interpretation of losses by fire. For instance, an explosion in a gas engine belonging to the Derby Co-operative Society caused damage for which the CIC was not legally liable — but the Company agreed to make an ex-gratia payment to cover half the loss (September, 1895).

The Company's eight houses in Bates Street continued to cause concern, but an offer of £1,200 for the properties was declined. The CIC wrote to their agents " expressing our dissatisfaction that they should have allowed our property to have become so badly deteriorated." Repairs were duly carried out, and by May, 1895, the houses were " in fairly good condition " except for division walls between the yards which were to be reconstructed by the Manchester and Salford Equitable Society.

Applications for mortgage advances continued to be treated with extreme care. A request for an advance of £2,700 on a warehouse in High Street, Manchester, in August, 1895, was not granted as the premises had a narrow frontage, accommodated a number of sub-tenants, and included wooden partitions, with altogether a quarter of the total area occupied by staircases. A policy decision was announced in August, 1895, that " we are not prepared to lend money on mortgage of property subject to a chief rent exceeding one-sixth of the gross rental." By the end of the year, the Company was lending at 4 per cent, sums not exceeding 80 per cent of net value of new property. Early in 1896, a Chiswick resident was informed that the Company was not prepared to lend money on property held only during a 99 years' lease.

Loans were made to local authorities in the Manchester area. It was minuted in 1895 that any sum not exceeding £5,000 could be advanced to Gorton Urban District Council. " Does the town clerk of Derby need cash? " it was queried in October, 1895, " we hear he does for a sewer scheme." Warrington Corporation was offered £4,000 for ten years, and a smaller sum to Burnley. Railway shares continued in favour. The Manager was empowered during the summer of 1895 to invest £3,000 in the Lancashire and Yorkshire

Railway, and a further £3,000 to the London Chatham and Dover or the Great Eastern. He could, in total, invest up to £7,000, including the above railway stock. The Company's stockbroker was instructed to invest a total of £5,000, but "if various investments, then the total investment in any one security, including present holding in it, must not exceed £5,000." The investment could be in one or more of the following: London and St. Katherine Docks, Surrey Commercial Docks and Tyne Commission Bonds; alternatively, the investment could be made in "any British Railway which, during the last year, has paid not less than 2½ per cent upon at least £2m. of ordinary shares . . ." The Scottish CWS notified the CIC that it would reduce interest on its loan of £2,000 from 4½ per cent to 3½ per cent from October, 1896. The CIC minuted: "We are not prepared to lend at less than 4 per cent for persons who are not life policyholders." A sum of nearly £5,000 was lent at just over 3 per cent repayable in instalments after sixteen years to the schoolboard of the Borough of Dumfries on the security of the school rates. Tyne Commission Bonds, to the extent of £2,300 were purchased in September, 1896, with further purchases of these securities in the following year.

It was decided in March, 1896, to distribute profits in proportion to each policyholder's interest or share in the common fund. A list of 58 bonus allocations to life policyholders was made in March, 1896. These bonuses were allocated when premiums received for such policies at 4 per cent amounted to the sums originally assured.

In view of the extension of business to Scotland, the director representing Scotland was to attend not only the annual meeting but also all board meetings.

Agencies of those persons who had brought in no new business for three consecutive years were cancelled from March, 1896. A request from the CIC agent at Halifax early in 1897, for a salary " so that he might devote all his time to our business," was received but declined. The office staff continued to increase. By 1895, the wages of Horrocks were £4 2s. and S. P. Leah £2 7s. Fifteen clerks received advances of wages in 1896.

It was learned in the summer of 1895, that the Fire Offices Committee was prepared to reduce shop tariffs. The support of the CIC was enlisted by the FOC in 1896, in opposition to a Parliamentary Bill which would enable the Land Commissioner to Scotland to recover from owners and occupiers of premises where fires occurred, half of the expenses of extinguishing such fires.

Pressure was brought to bear on the editors of co-operative journals: " It be a condition of paying for advertisements in Co-operative publications issued monthly or more frequently, that Co-operative life assurance, with special reference to this Company, be the subject of at least one leader per annum and one paragraph per quarter." (December, 1895). In the following year it was noted that

> " societies in whose records we advertise be informed of our regret to find that the income of business resulting therefrom is too small to justify, but that we should expect a better result, if, among their departmental notices in the records, they would include insurance and state from where proposal forms and information can be obtained."

Offers of foreign business were still regarded as unacceptable: " The application from the Christchurch Co-operative Society of New Zealand be declined on the grounds that we are not prepared to launch into colonial enterprise." (December, 1896.)

Manchester Corporation officials appeared to be somewhat incommunicado, and in February, 1896, the CIC subscribed to a petition sent to the Lord Mayor of Manchester, " requesting him to convene a public meeting to consider the provision of telephonic communication by the Corporation."

A request to undertake accident insurance was received early in 1897, and the Manager had to re-affirm that the Memorandum of Association would not allow the CIC to undertake such business.

F. A. Williams, the Superintendent of Agents, pointed out in 1898, that although the Company had been doing life business for only eleven years, it had been able to distribute a bonus amounting to almost

25 per cent of the premiums. Shareholders received none of the profits on life business, but those Co-operative societies that acted as agents received 15 per cent commission. James Odgers thought little headway would be made with life assurance until workers' wages were increased. The Fire Department was hit hard by claims for £3,000 in 1898, as a result of the Great Cripplegate fire in London where £2m. worth of property was destroyed. A delegate requested at the annual general meeting of 1898, that the expected number of deaths for the next year in the Life Department should be calculated, but the chairman explained that they would need at least 10,000 lives insured before any accurate forecast could be made.

In April, 1898, the Manager consulted the Company's solicitors regarding the best legal method of enabling a Co-operative society to effect a collective life assurance policy on all its members. Mr. Justican, the Actuary, also gave advice concerning the mode of undertaking such a contract with fewest restrictions and enabling claims to be met without probate.[1]

A circular was issued to all local Co-operative societies outlining the new scheme of collective assurance. The circular stated:

> " To enable Co-operative societies to save their members the difference of 31 per cent between the cost of industrial assurance and the cost of Co-operative ordinary business which is limited to 12½ per cent, the Directors of this Company have prepared a scheme of collective life assurance at ordinary rates. Each society adopting the scheme would remit quarterly, half-yearly or yearly as may be arranged, the premiums for insuring the whole number of their members, and the Company would pay to the share capital of each member on his death the sum insured by the agreement between this society and the Company. The society would supply to the Company a full list of all its members, giving their names, ages and respective numbers in its register."

No evidence of health was required, nor were there any limits of age. The Company would accept all the members of any local Co-operative society on the evidence of the first list of members. Subsequently, the local societies were to supply lists of new members containing corresponding particulars, with an additional statement on

[1] In the summer of 1898, a scheme of collective fire insurance was also drawn up to cover contents of private dwelling houses. The insurance cover was to follow the insured from house to house without endorsement so long as he was a member of the Co-operative society which paid the premium. The scheme remained a dead-letter.

their health. Eighty per cent of the full sum insured would be paid on the death of any new member declared unhealthy at entry. New members over 70 years of age would not be acceptable for insurance cover.

To enable societies to estimate the cost of this form of collective assurance to be covered by a small percentage of their profits, examples were given of the premiums payable per thousand members, showing different sums at death and at various specified ages taken to be the average of the aggregate body of members (for a sum insured of £3 at average age of 40, the annual premium per thousand members would be £92. For a sum of £10 insured, the yearly premium would be £328). Profits from participation in the scheme were to be divisible between supporting local societies after expenses of administration were met. Each society was to decide for itself whether non-purchasing members or members purchasing less than a specified amount each year should be included in the list of insured lives. A letter in the *Co-operative News* of 28 May, 1898, stated that the average yearly premium received by ten industrial life offices was 8s. 8d. for an average assurance of £9 12s. 4d. The collective premium for age 40 quoted by the CIC worked out at 6s. 2d. yearly. Considerable discussion took place regarding the proposed collective life scheme at the annual general meeting of 1898. A delegate could not see how the scheme could be worked out at the level of $12\frac{1}{2}$ per cent expenses. The chairman admitted as much. He thought that the directors should however receive credit for trying to solve the difficult problem, and he thought that they would not be satisfied until they were undertaking industrial life business in some way or other.

In the *Co-operative News* of 12 November, 1898, a correspondent pressed for the introduction of industrial life business in the Co-operative Movement, and in the following issue, James Odgers affirmed that the directors were in favour of such business, provided that the continued restriction on the Life Department to insurance of members of Co-operative societies and their relatives could be removed. To effect this would mean another special resolution to alter the objects of the Company, and another application to the High Court — unless as a result of enquiries then being made, it was found to be more advantageous to convert the Company into a Society by special resolution under the Industrial and Provident Societies Act, and so enable amendment to the objects of the Society. Enquiries were then made whether it would be necessary to deposit £20,000 as a result of establishing a Society *de novo*. A letter was received from the Board of Trade in December, 1898:

> "I am directed by the Board of Trade to acknowledge receipt of your letter of 11 ultimo enquiring whether the conversion of your Company into a Society under the Industrial and Provident Societies Act 1893, will be regarded as establishing of the Company within the meaning of the Life Assurance Companies' Act 1870. In reply I am to state that the Board are advised that as the Company is not within Section 3 of the last-mentioned Act its conversion into a Society under Section 55 of the Industrial and Provident Societies' Act would not thereby render it liable to the payment of £20,000 under the Assurance Companies' Act of 1870."

At an extraordinary general meeting held on 11 February 1899, the directors, having decided that instead of petitioning for enlarged powers of the Company it would be better to convert the Company into a Society, passed a special resolution for the conversion of the Company into a Society:

> "That the Co-operative Insurance Company Limited be converted into a Society by registration under the Industrial and Provident Societies' Act 1893 and for this purpose that the nominal value of the shares held by any member other than a registered society exceeding £200 be cancelled on such conversion and that the sum paid thereon be treated as capital paid in advance of calls in respect of the remaining shares held by any such member, the nominal value of whose shares shall then in no case exceed £200."

Such capital paid in advance was to be repayable. The Chairman went on to say that in recommending conversion, the directors were only doing what the promoters of the Company in 1867 would have wished to do if they had been able, but at the time, with the exception of the small assurance allowable under the Friendly Societies Act, the business of insurance could only be undertaken by companies registered under the Companies Act or incorporated by special Act of Parliament. Subsequently, amendments made from time to time in the Industrial and Provident Societies Act had at length given nearly as much freedom to a Society as could be obtained by a Company, the only important restriction being the limitation of interest of individuals and the shares of the society to £200, but no individual had held more than this stipulated maximum of £200.

104

The rules of the Co-operative Insurance Society were duly registered on 11 March, 1899, the date of the 31st and last annual general meeting of the Co-operative Insurance Company. After the meeting, a special resolution was carried to amend rules to enable the Society to carry on the business of insurance in all its branches, and the Chairman mentioned that it was likely that the Society would enter general accident business as soon as possible, but that the administration of the Employers' Liability Act had developed into " so many inconsistencies and awkwardnesses," that it would be desirable to have some further experience of its working. A eulogy appeared in the *Insurance News* of 20 May, 1899:

> " Fortunate almost beyond compare is the position of the Co-operative. In the first place it possesses one of the best and most remunerative fire businesses in the country, small perhaps but continuously and steadily growing and practically beyond the reach of competition. Every department is amply fortified financially but beyond the individual fund there is a general reserve fund, and the paid-up capital, the whole effect being that in proportion of its liability, the Co-operative is simply overflowing with wealth."

At the end of 1899, the principle was accepted that representation of Scotland and England should be in accordance with the relative proportion of insurance business contributed by the Society's shareholders, and it was therefore recommended that there should be an increase to nine members on the Board of Directors; two of the directors would represent Scotland.

A question was raised concerning the future position of local Co-operative societies as life assurance agencies. James Odgers explained that nine-tenths of the whole business was being done through individual agents. The CIS would not insist that societies should hand over all their business to individual agents, but these agents ought to be able to accept all the business that was forthcoming and not life business only.

The Manager was instructed to look into the question of the life assurance expense ratio to see if this could be reduced to 10 per cent. He was to enquire whether the charge levied on the Life Department could be reduced to that figure, and whether other companies limited charges to their Life departments at the expense of other departments. Odgers reported in July, 1899, that when adapting the Prudential industrial policy for use by the CIS he noticed that liability under the policy was limited to the fund of the industrial branch and to the share capital of the Company. It was resolved to follow the same system in the CIS for all branches of insurance when new policy forms were printed. Medical examination was waived in cases of assurance up to £20, but subject to the usual safeguards adopted by other industrial offices. Premiums would be collected weekly on these tables and personal agents only were to be employed in obtaining such business.

The maximum fire insurance cover had been raised in May, 1897, to £7,000; this limit was to relate to Co-operative buildings only where the CIC was the sole insurer. A proposal was considered in March, 1898, that the CWS should be offered the opportunity of accepting reinsurance business from the CIC. A similar offer was to be made to the Scottish Co-operative Wholesale Society. It was resolved however to defer the decision "pending enquiries as to the attitude of the CWS Committee on the insurance question." R. Holt of Rochdale, who had left the CIC Board in 1896, for "another sphere of Co-operative usefulness" — the CWS Board — reported back in April, 1898, that the CWS had no desire to insure Co-operative stores. It was therefore decided to adjourn the question of reinsurance with the Wholesale societies the resolution of which would have led to the withdrawal of the CIC from the tariff and from the FOC embargo on dividing profits with policyholders.

The Fire Offices Committee notified the CIS in July, 1899, that the CIS annual contribution was to be raised to £40, "but as the FOC had already exempted the Society from annual contributions to the expenses of the Wharf and Warehouses Committee and the Salvage Corporation and had so recently granted an important concession with regard to distribution of profits . . . it was advisable to refrain from objecting." A heavy fire loss was met in December, 1899, at Blaenavon, South Wales, for which the CIS share was £3,000. To expedite the settlement of minor fire claims, local directors could assess fire damage up to £10 outside Manchester and Glasgow from the beginning of 1900.

The extension of business in Scotland required additional staff to help Burgess at the Glasgow office, and it was agreed to appoint someone living in Glasgow to assist him from early 1897. The SCWS declined to accomodate the CIS within their main premises, but agreed to let accommodation in another building — previously a caretaker's house in Clarence Street, Glasgow. The office was one room at a yearly rental of £10.

The largest loan made by the CIC during this period was £7,000 to the Gorton Urban District Council at 3 per cent, repayable in equal instalments of capital and interest. In March, 1899, £2,000 of Birmingham Corporation 3½ per cent stock (redeemable 1946) at 117½ yielding £2 17s. 6d. per cent was purchased. Bolton Corporation agreed to accept an offer of £5,000 for a term of five to seven years. Warrington Corporation objected to the 3½ per cent demanded by the CIC over a fifty-year period and it was agreed to reduce interest to 3 per cent for a ten-year term. Mortgage advances continued to increase. In cases where sums lent on security of property were a large proportion of the value of the security, periodical repayments were to be at the rate of not less than 5 per cent per year of principal and interest. The directors were asked to survey mortgage proposals in rota. From December, 1897, applications for loans of under £100 on property were to be declined.

Personal sureties had not been required from local agents. But in July, 1899, it was decided that industrial assurance agents were to be insured by fidelity policies to the extent of £10 each. Odgers had been appointed Secretary of the CIS from March, 1899, and in October, he and the treasurer of the CIS were guaranteed for £1,000 each, and the accountant for £500. Horrocks became the first fire manager at a salary of £5 per week, and nineteen clerks received wage increases at the same time. By the summer of 1899, the office possessed typewriters and a " multiplying machine." The Secretary was subsequently empowered to advertise for a clerk to be concerned with accident business. James Clegg of Blackpool was appointed agent in September, 1898, and a selection of his first proposals are extant. John Jennings, also of Blackpool, was interviewed in April, 1899, and offered a wage of £4 10s. per week to organise the extension of industrial assurance business. Agents who had previously acted for ordinary life business only, were to be invited to canvass for industrial life, and were to receive 25 per cent commission on new business or renewals. Jennings took up his post as district representative in Bradford in May, 1899. The Bradford Provident Co-operative Society would not agree to rent a room to the CIS, and so Jennings was told to " do his best from his private dwelling house." A further six agents were appointed in June " for all branches including industrial business," also a clerk to keep the industrial accounts. The extension of industrial business brought associated problems of supervision and it was decided " that as a rule the appointment of industrial agents elsewhere than in districts where they can be supervised is discountenanced." The procedure for recruiting agents was that applicants recommended by the inspector of industrial agencies, if approved by the Secretary, could then be appointed by the inspector. In August, 1899, Jennings had to report a lack of industrial life business and he therefore suggested calling a conference of industrial agents.

In September, 1899, it was decided that expenses should be charged by weighting the annual premium income of departments as follows: Fire — 23½ per cent; Fidelity and Accident — 20 per cent (exclusive of commission allowed). For life policies the expenses were to be the difference between commission allowed and the following percentages: Ordinary Life — 12½ per cent; Industrial Life monthly — 30 per cent, weekly policies — 40 per cent. A sum of £3,000 had been appropriated from the Fire Department to establish the Industrial Life Department. The directors hoped that the expenditure would become a diminishing amount.

It had been decided not to undertake workmen's compensation insurance, in view of the legal uncertainty and absence of statistical experience; but personal accident business had been introduced from April, 1899, and burglary insurance was to be undertaken with a limit of £1,000 on any one risk.

The Board instructed F. A. Williams to proceed to Glasgow in July, 1899, and to introduce industrial business in Scotland. To support the move, it was agreed to appoint from October, 1899, a full-time agent in Glasgow, also one in Edinburgh and Perth at wages of 20s. weekly with commission. A special committee was appointed to meet monthly in Glasgow, to comprise two Scottish members and two others. A. Burgess was to be the secretary of the Scottish Committee, and from December, 1900, he was designated branch secretary at Glasgow. James Odgers reported in August 1900, that by the appointment of five full-time agents in Scotland and thirteen in England, additional clerks, Jennings as inspector, and other chargeable expenses, " the Society had already committed itself to an outlay in 1901, of about £1,800, against which could be set only the balance of loading after payment of commission. It was decided that the appointment of any other full-time agents be postponed sine die."

The Fire Offices Committee finally approved the division of profits exclusively among CIS policyholders in June, 1899. In such distribution, only the premiums paid in respect of the amounts retained by

108

the CIS were to be taken into consideration. The number of personal shareholders, then amounting to one hundred, and the number of shares held by them, namely 6,000 of £1 each, were not only *not* to be increased, but were to be reduced as opportunity occurred.

In September, 1899, CIS clerks, S. P. Leah and a Mr. Heincke, both passed with honours the examination of the Federation of Insurance Institutes.

It was reported in March, 1900, that there were in all 171 industrial life policies for a sum assured of £1,577, together with five accident policies. The Chairman stated that the CIS had decided to enter the industrial field — " as it was better to be insured in a system not the best than not to be insured at all." He commented that since entering the industrial field there had been a stimulation of ordinary life business. Having transformed the Company into a Society, the time had arrived when it was possible to pay a dividend of two shillings in the pound on fire and fidelity premiums received — £1,300 had been transferred for that purpose.

The *Insurance News* pointed out that 1899 was a year of heavy losses for insurance offices; increasing taxation in foreign countries had been one of the contributory factors. " Some of the largest and strongest companies had made no profit at all " commented the journal, hence " the Co-operative fire loss of 41 per cent and the fidelity ratio of 26 per cent . . . is abounding prosperity." All these features were evidence of the favourable conditions and efficiency of the management of the CIS: " The Co-operative, like some of the denominational offices is an eloquent testimony to the profitable result from the persistent and the unambitious cultivation of a special and camparatively limited sphere." A conference was held in November, 1900, in Glasgow, where James Odgers stated that 596 industrial life policies had been issued in Scotland during the previous nine months, but only one-third of these were on a weekly basis. A delegate emphasised that the Industrial Department would not become successful until door-to-door canvassing was adopted. At the time, there were 18 full-time agents actively canvassing for business. Full-time agents were paid by salary; spare-time agents by commission only.

Full-time district agents were appointed in such centres as Halifax, Huddersfield, Leeds, Burnley, and an assistant was engaged to help Jennings at Bradford. James Odgers was empowered to appoint additional district agents, the posts to be advertised at £1 per week with commission, or 35s. without commission. Remuneration for fire business was included in the salary of £1, but full rates of commission were allowed in other branches, subject to a reduction of wage by one shilling per week per quarter until finally extinguished. An applicant from Hamilton in Ayrshire offered his temporary services as a full-time agent " while the pit-shafts where he is employed are closed; it was resolved that we offer him £1 per week."

It became known to the CIS during 1900, that a tea company in conjunction with an insurance office was preparing to insure lives of customers — " if a man aged 50 next birthday purchased a ¼ lb. of tea each week he would be insured for three guineas at death " —a portent of many similar schemes with which the CIS had to contend in later years.

PART THREE

NEW PARTNERS

(i) 1900–1904

It was decided to close the Manchester office on 16 June, 1900, for a first annual picnic; a contribution of £10 from the funds of the Society was made, and the picnic party of 50 members visited the Dukeries. James Odgers was authorised to engage an additional clerk for the industrial life branch at a wage not exceeding £2, and another clerk "accustomed to shorthand and typewriting at a wage not exceeding £1 per week." Three more clerks were appointed in October, 1900, for the life, fire and accounts departments.[1] It was decided to appoint a fire surveyor for the South Midlands and London, based on Northampton. On 1 December, 1900, a certain E. Williams was taken on as a clerk — "six years' Refuge — engage him." By March, 1901, the office establishment was thirty. The salary of James Odgers was increased from £500 to £550, and his signature was lithographed for preprinting on policies. The first female clerk in the CIS was appointed to the Bradford office at 12s. per week in January, 1902. She was Miss Jennings, the daughter of the District Superintendent. A minute of 5 March, 1904, shows that a female clerk — Sarah Rawnsley — had been appointed to the Life Department in 1903 at a wage of 12s. per week. This was the first appointment of a female clerk at chief office.

[1] H. J. Butterworth was appointed as a shorthand-typist, self-taught (at work). "There were five typewriters in 1900 with a moving keyboard . . . Liverpool Branch stretched as far as Caernarvon, Bangor, Crewe, Isle of Man, Southport, Wigan, Warrington . . . There was often difficulty in Wales in connection with the language and sometimes one had to fetch in the local schoolmaster to translate . . . Shorthand was a key to promotion. Text books on insurance were rare. The Life Department was one desk in 1900. E. Beat was in charge of valuation section the forerunner to the Actuarial Department with the responsibility of yearly balancing of accounts. Beat was the first clerk in the valuation section under Leah . . ."

There was some liberalisation of the terms of life policies from this period. Combined annuity and endowment tables were devised in 1900 and the Actuary also prepared child endowment tables for sums payable at various ages up to 21 years for premiums of 2d. per week. Free paid-up policies in the industrial branch were to be issued after the first five years' premiums had been paid. Proposals on lives over 65 were to be accepted, but only where younger members of the same family or household were insured, and then only if such persons appeared more robust than the average, and with a further proviso that the premium was not to exceed 6d. weekly. It was decided not to reduce benefits for hazardous occupations, but with a reservation appended: " P.S. Enquire re policy of other offices." There still remained extra-hazardous risks on " publicans, pregnant women, nurses and others subject to infection or contagion, extra-hazardous chemical workers, grinders of tools and cutlery, tin miners."

Mortgage advances were made on houses in the London area at Wimbledon and Wandsworth. A borrower was allowed to deduct income tax from his loan interest as a special exception, and the CIS was to recover it from the Inland Revenue authorities, who authorised this procedure of income tax deductions from mortgage interest and enabled the CIS to adopt the system as a general policy. A request was received in October, 1901 from Ealing Tenants Limited for a loan of £3,150 upon a number of building plots. It was resolved that as a general ruling no loans were to be granted except to individual owners of property.

From 1900, the CIS set about searching for new head office premises. A Mr. Munday of Nottingham offered to sell a cottage property, hut and hoardings, situated in Pilgrim Street, Carter Street and Corporation Street, Manchester, with 15 years remaining of the lease for £1,800. Manchester Corporation intimated that erection of buildings would be allowed in Corporation Street on condition that the CIS would provide a suitable opening into Hanover Street. James Odgers obtained an interview with the land agent of Lord Ducie, the ground landlord, and the vendor agreed to a sale price of £1,550 in October, 1901. The CIS directors agreed: " We accept lease of 6s. per yard (rent per annum about £244) for the land." The CWS advised that they could not spare the CIS any more land in Manchester, and so the CIS took over a large room on the second floor of the Co-operative Newspaper Society in Long Millgate and negotiated with the Co-operative Union for extra accommodation in St. James Street from January, 1902. The property of the Co-operative Printing Society and adjacent sites in Corporation Street and Hanover Street were valued as a result of these overtures, and the CIS decided it would decline to offer £15,000 to the Printing Society, but would ask for first option if they should wish to sell. In January, 1902, it was minuted that " we do best to buy property in Carter, Redfern and Pilgrim Streets adjoining that recently purchased from Munday. Offer not more than £3,000."

A CIS office was opened at Newcastle-upon-Tyne in 1902, at a yearly rental of £18, and R. H. Fitton was appointed as branch manager. An application for an agency at Lisburn in Northern Ireland had been declined in November, 1900.

A Co-operative society wished to know at this time what was the largest amount that could be invested as share capital with the CIS. It was decided that the maximum allocation to any one shareholder should be 25 shares.

An association which was to endure over many years was formed in February, 1901 — an agency of the Vulcan Boiler Insurance Company to handle the boiler insurance business of the Co-operative Movement on behalf of the CIS.

War contingencies were also felt for the first time by the CIS during 1901. It was minuted: " If industrial policyholder at date of effecting policy has no intention to visit seat of war, but afterwards volunteers to serve country at war, his policy be endorsed cancelling the prohibition."

James Odgers was appointed as Manager *and* Secretary from February, 1902. James Darroch of Glasgow, aged 20, was to be paid 24s. weekly, and J. P. Jones of the Manchester office, aged 25, £2 weekly. At that time there were three clerks at the Glasgow office. A boy was engaged for the Newcastle office at 7s. 6d. and a " typewriter bought for him," in May, 1902. By 1903, there were 29 clerks in the Fire Department; eleven in the Life Department; two in the Accident Department (including J. P. Jones); seven in the Cash Department. Early in 1903, the first woman clerk resigned — the daughter of Jennings, the district inspector at Bradford. The Manager was empowered to engage an additional worker in the Fire Department to enable one of the existing clerks " to devote all his time to surveying risks with a view to fire prevention." S. P. Leah was promoted from chief clerk to Manager of the Life Department in January, 1904. F. A. Williams was nominated as Inspector of Agencies, and

James Barlow as Accountant. The total staff in 1904 was 50 clerks, in addition to seven "principal servants" — Mason, Barlow, Fitton, Burgess, Leah, Williams, Horrocks. James Barlow had the longest service; he had been appointed in 1877.

All full-time agents in Scotland were instructed to report to Burgess at Glasgow from February, 1902. James Odgers commented on the relative cost and efficiency of full-time and other agents, and it was decided in 1903 not to appoint any more industrial agents until the balance sheet had been prepared. The varied nature of the previous employment of agents is illustrated in the case of a C. R. Morgan of Cricklewood. He had determined to give up his employment as a railway goods guard and to devote all his time to canvassing and collecting insurance. The CIS engaged him in 1904, although for part of his time he acted as an agent for the Co-operative Building Society who reimbursed the CIS at the rate of 10s. per week. In all, 29 applications were received for a vacant post of full-time agent at Paisley at the end of 1904.

Problems of overlapping of functions persisted in Scotland. It had to be repeated at the end of 1904 that authority over persons employed by the CIS in Scotland was to be exercised through A. Burgess, and that all requests for surveys of Co-operative property in Scotland were to be sent to the Glasgow office, except in cases of extreme local urgency.

It was decided to consider an increase of the directors' committee from nine to ten from 1903, to allow an additional number to represent the northern division — North East England.

A fire occurred at the CWS warehouse in Newcastle in May, 1902. It was calculated that the total value at risk was £159,000 for which insurance cover was only £50,000. The CWS "own risk" was £109,000 and the estimated loss £95,000. Insurance offices paid over £34,000, leaving a net loss for the CWS Insurance fund of over £60,000.

A CIS director suggested the introduction of a scheme for granting loans for house purchase. After discussion, it was thought there was no urgency, and the subject was adjourned *sine die* 6 September, 1902. Another director reported a case of fidelity business having been lost through CIS enquiries being too searching, and conditions too strict. The Secretary was instructed to institute enquiries concerning the procedure of other offices.

A further loan was made to the CWS in April, 1902 — £3,000 at 3½ per cent. Investment in the National Telephone Company was increased from £25 to £50 in November, 1903. Long Eaton Co-operative Society sought a loan for building a branch, but the CIS was circumspect: " Before considering the matter the directors desire to see a copy of the latest balance sheet." After inspection of the accounts, it was decided to consider approval of the Long Eaton loan provided the Society had private dwellings which it could offer as security — the CIS would then be prepared to consider granting loans on these private properties. An enquiry from Bedlington was received in 1903, whether the CIS would lend, in each of three cases, £200 upon the security of houses and land worth only £240: " It was resolved that where coal mining is the chief industry not more than about two-thirds of the value be lent." Londonderry Co-operative Society requested a loan for their building department which they would then re-lend to their members. The CIS did not accede to this request, but was prepared to accept mortgage applications from individual members provided that arrangements could be made for plot surveys.

Manchester Corporation approved plans for the proposed erection of new offices for the CIS and consented to the closing of Pilgrim Street, provided that Carter Street be widened. T. Wood, a CIS director, mentioned that the CWS were the owners of the land on the opposite side of Carter Street, and he thought that the property thereon was condemned and would have to be demolished. He suggested that the CIS should offer their present property to the CWS in exchange for equal portions of the site fronting to Carter Street and Corporation Street, which he believed were preferential in terms of access to light.

Single premium ordinary life policies for sum assured of £25 were issued from 1905. An ordinary life office offered to sell its industrial branch, begun four years previously, to the CIS in August, 1905, but the offer was declined.

A donation of £100 was made to the endowment fund of the Manchester Consumption Hospital at Delamere, Cheshire, in 1903.

Care was taken to present the balance sheet and report of the CIS in the most favourable light — in 1902, it was resolved " that the para. on page 3 referring to depreciation of railway stocks be deleted. This adjustment could be incorporated as follows: ' On page 7 the amount of the reserve fund be reduced by £200, and that this amount be deducted from the value of railway stocks . . .' "

The most formative stage in the early history of the Co-operative Insurance Society fell during the years after 1899. Within this period the course of future development of the CIS was largely determined. In particular, the relationships between the CIS and the rest of the Co-operative Movement became more clearly defined from 1899. On the conversion of the CIC into a Society, it became possible to sell insurance to the community at large through the medium of industrial life policies, but the CIS remained ambivalent over the merits of industrial assurance, as it felt that the service was uneconomic and savoured of the capitalist system with its preponderance of middlemen interposing between producers and consumers. The expense of weekly collections would be heavy whether organised by a Co-operative insurance organisation or otherwise, hence the CIS devised the collective life scheme to avoid some of the dis-economies of industrial assurance. The collective life scheme was in essence a group life scheme, and it was through collective life assurance that the CIS made its most direct contact with the members of the Co-operative Movement. Previously, the relationships had been more directly with local Co-operative societies as agents for fire and fidelity business.

These years from 1899 were also to see the growing fusion between the CIS and the CWS — years which began in an atmosphere of mutual recrimination. The CWS contended that the CIS was unprogressive and lacking the resources necessary to undertake insurance service for the Co-operative Movement as a whole. The CIS retorted that it was the only body within the Movement that had the necessary expertise and experience to undertake professional insurance business. A conference was held in Newcastle in March, 1902, where William Barnett read a paper in which he stated that at first the CIS could only carry £1,000 on one risk, but in present cases they held as much as £8,000 on one risk. During the previous year there had been 565 fires which had involved a sum of £7,821, which was only 36 per cent of the premiums, whereas if they had taken some very risky buildings they would have had a liability of £20,000 or £30,000, and their accumulated premiums would in the case of fire have been entirely wiped out. Barnett believed that opinion had risen in some sections in the Northern area that the whole of the fire business of the Co-operative Movement should be insured by the CWS, so that none of the outside companies would benefit. He pointed out that the CIS had been prepared to do all the profitable business that had been insured within the Movement, but on the other hand they would be quite willing, in fact they had made proposals some years previously, that the CWS should reinsure with the CIS rather than with other companies. Industrial assurance business had been commenced, but the CIS admitted that heavy initial expenses had been incurred.[1]   A representative from the Sunderland Co-operative Society said his society had to insure to the extent of something like £50,000 for their central premises, but the CIS could only offer £8,000. In this sense the CIS was acting as a middleman for the other insurance offices. R. Smith, of Hartlepool,[2] argued that Co-operative societies should have some knowledge of the difference it would make to the premium charged if certain structural alterations were made; the CIS should advise local societies accordingly and thereby effect mutual saving. When there was such a large society as the Wholesale Society, he went on, so well adapted to undertake insurance business with agents throughout the various parts of the Movement, it was apparent that the CWS could readily provide insurance for the Movement at less cost than another society doing virtually the same business.

Barnett commented on fire limits. In his experience, bigger risks were not remunerative by themselves and he doubted whether it would be profitable for the CWS to undertake business which was not profitable to any other organisation. Reference had been made to the funds the CIS had invested, but no notice had been taken of the fact that the CIS had invested about £21,000 with the CWS and £7,000 with the Scottish CWS. The Hartelpool delegate seemed to hint that the Co-operative Insurance Society was a society outside the Co-operative Movement. There were in fact 476 Co-operative societies holding most of the shares in the CIS, whilst there were only 90 individual shareholders with a small and diminishing holding. The CIS Fire Department insured over £16m. of Co-operative property — and reinsurance was a common practice with other offices. The matter was as broad as it was long; by placing part of their risks with other offices, the CIS were able to return to Co-operative societies part of the 15 per cent commission which they received.

[1] A special meeting was called in 1904, to amend a rule so as to allow any surplus in the industrial or ordinary life branches to be applied towards reimbursement of the sums paid from profit and loss account for the establishment and extension of business in these branches. It has not been foreseen that a considerable expenditure in excess of the loading of the premiums would be necessary to establish and extend the industrial branch.

[2] R. Smith was Chief Clerk of the Hartlepools Co-operative Society. He drew up the rules of the Approved Section (Health) of the CWS and became its Manager in 1912.

Chief Office, Long Millgate,
Manchester

A group of young men on the steps of the
Long Millgate office

The chairman of the Newcastle Branch of the CWS criticised the CIS for having joined a ring, when as a rule the Co-operative Movement kept itself away from rings. But he concluded: " No organisation . . . laid itself out better for economical dealing with insurance interests than the CIS appeared to do . . . an institution which was practically a Movement itself." In summary, the debate was whether the Co-operative Movement could self-insure. It was obvious that CIS was not in a position to take the full risk, and the CWS with larger resources and acting as spokesman for the Movement wished to be more directly involved in insurance business for the Movement.

The first moves in devising a scheme for collective life assurance came when J. Dewar, the CIS director who had suggested the granting of loans for house purchase in 1902, proposed that the CIS should accept from Co-operative societies, premiums equal to a fixed annual sum per member for insurance in case of accident. The Actuary submitted rates for insuring such members, aged 18 to 65, in case of fatal accidents for 6d. annual premium to insure £5 upon accidental death, or other sums at 10s. per £100, irrespective of age or occupation. Subsequently, he made further calculations on this personal accident collective scheme. He took into consideration that a considerable number of Co-operative society members were women, and he therefore recommended 2s. per £100 for accidental death while travelling, and 5s. per £100 for death from any accident.

In the *Co-operative News* of 28 August, 1903, a correspondent commented on industrial life premium collection[1] and suggested that some form of collective life assurance should be adopted and a payment made quarterly out of dividend by each local society. The CIS received a letter in December, 1903, from a Mr. Strang of Grantham, who asked to be allowed to issue life policies to customers who would pay each premium in the inclusive price of a quarter of a pound of tea. The offer was declined.

A circular was sent out to Co-operative societies in January, 1904, concerning a fatal accident collective life scheme for Co-operative society members. A society could insure all its members, or only those whose purchases amounted to a minimum value. The annual premium for a £5 cover per year would be 2d per member.

An editorial in the *Co-operative News* of 6 February, 1904, referred to the earlier scheme for collective life assurance for Co-operative

---

[1] CIS Industrial life policies in force in 1903 has totalled 4,614 monthly policies, but only 237 weekly policies. Total industrial premiums on all policies amounted to £1,507.

members. James Odgers replied that before the CIS entered into industrial assurance, it had published a scheme for collective life assurance but the scheme had certain defects: the ages of the members had to be ascertained and societies did not welcome the task; the total premium payable was an aggregate of all the separate premiums which varied according to age, and any local society which effected the collective policy would have had to pay much more heavily for the insurance of its older members than for its younger members. There would have been no relation between a member's purchases, the level of his contribution to profits, and either his premiums or his assurance benefit. The scheme would have saved 30 per cent in premiums for the members as a whole, " yet it required on the part of the younger and more vigorous members a great subordination of their personal interest to the general good of the whole body of members than the committee of the society were prepared to recommend." As the scheme was not taken up, the CIS directors, with the consent of members, entered into industrial life assurance. Tables were so arranged as to offer facilities for saving the cost of collection by giving increased benefits if premiums were collected monthly instead of weekly, and further increased benefits when the collections were quarterly instead of monthly. In effect, Odgers was admitting that industrial assurance business, if this meant weekly collection of premium, was hardly being attempted — in 1903, there were 20 monthly policies for every single weekly policy. He concluded :

" The cost of extending this industrial business in the face of the keen and not always scrupulous competition of older offices, had been so heavy that the committee with great regret have to move very slowly and many societies were disappointed to find that their members are not yet canvassed by agents of the CIS. Fortunately, however, the members of a Co-operative society need no longer be debarred from the benefits of Co-operative life assurance, for although extensions on the usual lines must continue to be slow, a new method of collective life assurance . . . had been adopted by the Society. Thinking of the whole collective scheme and possible modifications in it, thinking also of the demand for some sort of sound assurance scheme which might be offered instead of unsound pension or assurance projects as a means of stimulating purchases at the store, Mr. William Barnett, Society Chairman, at length hit upon a plan of providing life assurance in proportion to purchases . . . The plan had been considered and approved by the

Actuary; not only was Mr. Barnett's scheme free from the defects of the original scheme, but it was anticipated that 5 per cent of the premiums would cover the expenses. By substituting the new scheme for the usual weekly collections, the members of all the Co-operative societies in the United Kingdom would save, on aggregate, £100,000 per annum, through each society effecting a collective life policy. It was expected that the adoption of the scheme would induce members to purchase more largely from their stores, and that the increase in business would be accompanied by a relative reduction in expenses. It was not suggested that members should drop their individual policies when they assured collectively; on the contrary, such policies should be treated as additional insurance which all who could afford should be encouraged to effect."

On 23 February, 1904, William Barnett's collective life assurance scheme was approved in principle, but the Actuary was to investigate "the practicability of so graduating the benefits as to reduce the disparity between the assurances at younger and older ages."

The final decision to set up the collective life scheme was made on 5 March, 1904:

"In consideration of a premium equal to 1d. per annum in respect of each pound of purchases by the members of a Co-operative society, the CIS will issue to such a society as trustees for its members a collective life policy assuring on the death of any member not exceeding 70 years of age within one year from the date of such payment of premium to his or her representative, the sum of £1 or fraction thereof for each £5 or fraction or part thereof purchased from such society by the deceased in the terms of one year ended on the date when the accounts forming the basis of the premium were closed. Subject to confirmation by Mr. Justican, our Actuary, the profits, if any, will be applied as follows: two-thirds to increase the benefits, first by providing benefits for members over 70 years of age, such benefits to be raised as soon as practicable to the same scale as for younger members, and second by equitable additions to the sums assured at all ages and one-third to a fluctuation fund for all societies whose members are collectively assured . . ."

In July, 1904, it was decided that any society showing a surplus under the collective life scheme could have the following offers: an increase in benefits at all ages; or at the greater ages; or a deduction of such surplus from the next collective life premium payable; or any combination of the three foregoing methods.

A three-year average of total purchases was to be applied to members between the ages of 16 and 70; after the age of 70 the average would be ten years, and the contract would be an annual one. Each society wishing to participate would simply send a cheque and a balance sheet showing the sales on which dividend had been paid and the members would get a penny per pound less in the rate of dividend — no enquiries regarding health would be made. The directors thought that there would be no increase in expenses to societies as the scheme would draw in new members. The scheme was slightly amended in September — where the age at death was 63 or more, then the number of years included in average was extended by one for every year over 63 until age 70. The first society to adopt the collective life scheme was Macclesfield, who paid a first premium of £230 to insure their 4,500 members. Another society joined the scheme, and within three days of paying their premium had submitted their first claim.

What was the general reaction of the Co-operative Movement to the collective life scheme? William Barnett had attended the Co-operative Congress in 1904, and had put forward the collective life scheme for the support of Congress, but as the votes for and against his resolution seemed to be equal, he decided to withdraw it. A conference held in London in July discussed the scheme and questions were raised whether the average could not be raised from ten to twenty years' purchase, also the possibility of issuing paid-up policies to those who had been members of a society for a considerable period. At a further conference held in Manchester in October, a CIS director stated that after placing something to reserves, any credit balance would go back to the society. Husbands or wives, as members of the collective scheme, would be treated as joint members. The Chairman and S. P. Leah extolled the collective life scheme to Halifax Co-operative Society; and Eastleigh Co-operative Society was informed apropos collective life, " that we [the CIS] will send a deputation on their paying half the rail fare plus five shillings."

It should be noted that all members over 70 years of age had to have at least ten years' membership before qualifying for benefit. Moreover, older members would reduce the total of their annual value of purchases compared with younger members — hence if the average had been based on three years' purchases rather than ten, the average would be low, but it would of course admit members of only three years' standing.

In January, 1905, a member demanded that the collective life scheme should be extended to cover more members of the family than spouses as joint members, and should provide an old age pension extension. S. P. Leah explained that any balance left to the credit of the societies could be applied to increasing the benefits of older members whose purchases had fallen below those made in earlier life.

What would happen if the claims under the collective life scheme exceeded the premiums? William Barnett deflected the question by saying that the CIS was in a very strong position, with investments of £100,000 and investment income of between £3,000 and £4,000 each year. By the annual meeting of 1905, seven societies had joined the collective life scheme, for which the premiums received were £1,027; 61 claims for £424 had been paid and the collective life fund was £561. It is significant that these figures were fast approaching those for the Industrial Life Department, where the premiums, for the year ended 1905, were £1,942 for 5,393 monthly policies and 227 weekly policies.

As late as 1904, the full list of insurance proposals received for all branches of business was read out at each directors' meeting. (In time, there would develop a need for decision-making to be delegated at various levels of seniority, but for many years, even after the first world war, directors continued to deal with minutiae.)

In 1905, it was laid down that 5 per cent of the collective life premiums should be deducted to meet expenses, and the balance distributed to societies in proportion to their respective contributions to the surplus. After one society had intimated that it wished to withdraw from the collective life scheme because it wished to devise its own scheme on a local basis, the Secretary of the CIS was instructed to ascertain whether a retail society could undertake collective life assurance, and if so, subject to what requirements. (September, 1905.) Only two societies made claims in 1906, in excess of 95 per cent of the premiums, leaving a surplus on the collective life account of £1,733 by the end of 1906. A manager of a local Co-operative society objected to the trouble of checking members' purchases for collective assurance claims. It was resolved to insert a clause in the collective life policies giving the CIS a right to check purchases on which the amount of claims was based. The Secretary recommended a limit of £30 on any one collective life claim, after a local society had gone into deficit during 1907.

In its early years, the collective life scheme was so highly regarded by the CIS management that it caused some diversion of resources from the furthering of industrial life business. It was minuted in November, 1907:

> "In this branch (collective life) we have no competition whatever to contend with. It is not only the cheapest branch of business to work, but it is the best advertisement we can have. It is a speciality which appeals not only to committees as a means of attracting members and trade, but to the members also as personally beneficial . . . by placing collective life assurance first in our propaganda . . . more rapid and more economical progress will be made."

To emphasize their faith in the scheme, the directors appointed a canvasser for collective life assurance in Liverpool for a period of six months during 1909. In the same year, a re-introduced scheme of collective fire assurance was devised but was later deferred.

Although the collective life scheme appeared to be successful in its statistics of growth, yet an increasing number of local Co-operative societies sought to introduce their own collective life schemes. The CIS again queried in August, 1909, whether these private schemes were legally possible without a £20,000 deposit to the Registrar.

In September, 1909, the Secretary was instructed to consider collective life assurance for Co-operative employees — the premium and benefits to be proportional to wages.

Long Millgate, Manchester, in the 1890's

(iii) *A New Building*

The limited office accommodation at Long Millgate became a pressing problem during the early years of the present century. (Extracts from title deeds are given below, showing early references to names of streets closely associated with Co-operation in Manchester.)[1] Subsequent to the negotiations previously referred to regarding a site for a new chief office, Manchester Corporation, in January, 1905, offered to sell to the CIS a piece of land at Ducie Bridge, at the corner of Corporation Street and Cheetham Hill Road, at £12 10s. 6d. per square yard, subject to a chief rent of £13 10s. The CIS agreed to purchase the site, and plans were prepared for a new chief office. The CWS queried whether the CIS would sell their existing office site in Corporation Street, but would not agree to the price stipulated by the CIS.

A limited architectural competition was arranged for the new building and the firm of Bradshaw and Gass of Bolton submitted the successful plan. The Secretary was instructed to consult them so as to reduce the decorative features of the building and to increase the light by squaring the tops of the windows. He was also to enquire if the walls could be raised to carry the roof storey, and so enable a similar storey to be added at some future time. The CWS expressed disappointment that they had not been included in the architectural competition. For the interim period during building operations,[2] the Co-operative Newspaper Society offered the CIS two additional rooms: " In view of extension of business in next two years it was resolved to become

---

[1] A Deed of 13 March, 1790, concerned a chief rent of £5 16s. 2d. per year on land on the south-east side and near the Long Mill Gate. " The land was bounded on the north-east side by land belonging to the poor of Manchester and on the south-west side and including 2½ yards within a new laid-out street of 10 yards wide called, or intended to be called ' Hanover Street.' The land north-east of Hanover Street belonged to the Manchester Free Grammar School." It is interesting to note that Balloon Street, Back Balloon Street, Back Hanover Street, Dantzic Street, are all referred to in the 1790 Deed. Balloon Street was so named to commemorate James Sadler of Oxford, who was the first Englishman to ascend in a balloon in 1784. He made two more ascents in 1785 from Manchester.
[For histories of Dantzic Street and Miller Street see pp. 268-9.]
See also Abstract of Title of " Properties in and near Miller Street," 8 October, 1902. The Abstract referred to a charity founded by Will of 7 May, 1621, of Edward Mayes of Manchester, Gentleman — concerning plots of land on south side of Miller Street. In 1920, the Board of Charity Commissioners sold the land to the CWS. The land was bounded by Miller Street, Corporation Street and Dantzic Street. See also Conveyance 10 August, 1959, to CIS of the fee simple of land bounded by Miller Street, Dantzic Street, Mayes Street, Amber Street and Back Mayes Street.
[2] " On the site of the 1908 office were cottages with an old lady who made currant cakes and ' dossers' wedges ' . . . " Interview with H. J. Butterworth.

tenant of one of them." (January, 1906.) The CIS directors showed a keen interest in following the progress of construction of their new building, and in February, 1906, it was suggested

> " that any director desiring to see the difference between a
> building all red and one part-red and part-grey terra-cotta,
> be requested to visit either the Central Hall of the Liverpool
> Wesleyan Mission, or the Wesleyan Church at Haulgh, Bolton,
> and compare it with any office building of the Prudential
> Assurance Company before the United Board Meeting on
> the 3 March."

The estimated cost of the new building, exclusive of furnishings and fitments, was £13,384 (7d. per cubic foot). Central heating was to be included together with mechanical ventilation and soundproof windows. Advice was received from the architect who stated that £1,500 would meet the extra cost of a four-storey rather than a three-storey building, but that if the erection of the fourth storey was deferred an additional cost of £450 would be incurred. He strongly advocated "red ruabon bricks and grey terra-cotta dressings." A four-storey edifice was decided upon and an estimate was given in May, 1906, that building operations would take 15 months. In all, 19 firms tendered to erect the building including Robert Carlyle, the CWS, W. Thorpe, and Gerrard of Swinton. Robert Carlyle of Old Trafford submitted the successful tender. The firms had previously erected a warehouse in Market Street, which the CIS Secretary inspected and found satisfactory. He also visited other premises constructed by the same builders, including Beswick Co-operative Society and Mill Street Fire Station, both in Manchester. Manchester Corporation approved the draft plans for the new building in July, 1906. In October, the CWS offered £2,500 for the leasehold site in the Corporation Street, Carter Street and Pilgrim Street area, and the offer was accepted by the CIS. Notice was given to the Co-operative Newspaper Society that the CIS would vacate the offices rented in Long Millgate at the end of September, 1908, as the formal opening of the new building was to take place during May, 1908. An orderly procedure at the official ceremony was to be safeguarded through the attendance of two commissionaires and two police officers. No intoxicating drinks were to be provided at the Society's expense. The Secretary, charged with embellishing the building for the occasion, reported back: " That as a silk flag would cost £8 8s. and quickly wear out, while a bunting flag would only cost £2 14s. 6d. and be durable, he had ordered a bunting flag." The removal of chief office from Long Millgate took place during August, 1908. Shortly afterwards, the lower part of the inside windows of the treasurer's office were frosted over " to prevent view of money from the street." Part of the basement, ground, third and fourth floors remained vacant. In 1909, two rooms were let to an advertising agency.

James Odgers received an increase in salary from £550 to £600 per year from May, 1905. In 1907, the Accident, Burglary and Fidelity Department was re-organised as the Accident Branch, which was also to include Employers' Liability. J. P. Jones was appointed manager of this new department. By June, 1908, there were 26 clerks in the Fire Department, 20 in Life, seven in Accident, two in Agency, seven in Accounts. The average wage in the Fire Department was £1 13s. 9d.; Life £1 12s. 3d.; Accident £1 10s. 2d.; Accounts £1 19s. 5d. A fire insurance clerk receiving a weekly wage of 48s. intimated that he would leave the CIS in September, 1908, for higher wages in a London insurance office. Subsequently, the Secretary was advised that he could be more liberal in the level of wages paid to higher grade clerks. The salary of James Odgers was again increased from £600 to £700 from 1909. At that time there were 15 branch office clerks, 11 of of whom received a rise in wages. The cost of clerical incompetence was shown in a minute of 1 May, 1909: " Resolved that Manager be instructed not to employ clerks who are not competent to earn the minimum rates adopted by the AUCE."

Discussion of interest-in-book was shelved at several conferences during the period. The CIS directors decided, however, from January, 1905 :

> " That when, in order to hand business over to another agent, this Society withdraws from an agent paid solely by commission, a considerable portion of special and/or industrial life business obtained by his own exertions, an allowance . . . of a sum not exceeding one year's commission be allowed to him."

By 1905, CIS branch offices had been opened at Glasgow, Edinburgh, Bradford and Newcastle. A telephone was installed at the Newcastle office at £7 10s. per year from the National Telephone Company from May, 1905. Discussion took place in the same year whether there should be a branch in London and a director to represent the southern section. A room on the second floor of the Baptist Church House, 4 Southampton Row, London, at a rental of £55 per year was obtained from October, 1905, and F. D. Rugen was appointed London

Branch manager at £3 10s. per week, plus an office boy. From the beginning of 1910, a house was rented in Red Lion Square as the London office of the CIS. The CWS was approached concerning possible accommodation at their Cardiff depot. They could not comply, " as they consider it advisable not to complicate matters by having other business transacted on the premises." In due course offices were acquired for a CIS Branch at 53 Queen Street, Cardiff.

An enquiry was addressed to each industrial agent in February, 1907, whether business would be helped or hindered by the withdrawal of weekly insurance policies. The consensus of replies from the agents was in favour of retaining the weekly policies, and the CIS Board resolved " to retain tables and accept business from those who cannot pay monthly." Later in the same month, there was some dissatisfaction expressed over the number of agents who had done little business. Nevertheless, nine full-time agents in England received increased wages from June, 1907—their areas were Leicester, Newcastle, Accrington, Leeds, London, Bedford, Bolton, Pendleton and Burnley. Any new agents were to make themselves conversant with collective life, fire, fidelity, workmen's compensation, and be capable of interviewing officials of Co-operative societies.

James Darroch was transferred from Glasgow to Edinburgh to be in charge of the office there from March, 1908, but the authority of Burgess was to extend over Darroch at Edinburgh — Burgess was termed " Manager for Scotland " instead of " Local Secretary." The growth of branch offices made it necessary to consider the question of devolution of work and responsibility from chief office to the branch offices from 1909.

Appended to the minute books of the period are directors' rotas which show details of their activities and representation on other Co-operative bodies. The directors represented the CIS at local district conferences, at meetings of the Co-operative Printing Society, the Co-operative Newspaper Society, the CWS, and the Scottish Local Board of CIS. They made many visits to local retail societies concerning collective life and conducted insurance business surveys as far afield as South Wales, Kent, London and North East England. Progressively from the years before the first world war, the minutes become less evocative, more formal, less informative, almost ritualistic, and giving the impression that they could have been composed before, and not after, the meetings that should have produced them. The introduction of the typewriter makes for clarity but not insight.

The limit on ordinary life cover was raised to £1,000 from December, 1906, and from 1908, advantages of life assurance cover were referred to in the prospectus for mortgage advances.

The CIS houses in Bates Street were earning 4⅜ per cent interest in 1905. At the end of 1905, the agents for the properties were instructed to obtain tenders for water closets in place of earth closets. In July, 1906, the CIS disposed of the eight houses for £1280. (An offer of £1,200 had been declined ten years previously.)

A loan of £4,000 was made to the Co-operative Permanent Building Society during 1905, on the security of their building in Red Lion Square, London. (Messrs. Barnett, Bamforth, Hepworth and Oliver surveyed it "without charge"); but a request from the Building Society for a list of individual shareholders of the CIS was declined in May, 1906. A loan of £3,000 was offered to the Scottish CWS in September, 1905, at 3½ per cent. Renewed loans were made to Warrington and Burnley Corporations for £4,000 and £1,500 for terms of five years at 3½ per cent. The Secretary mentioned the purchase of stock of several water boards as suitable investments — "but was instructed to submit a larger selection with fuller particulars." A £5,000 3 per cent loan to Bolton Corporation was renewed at 3½ per cent from mid-1906. A hospital board was offered a £2,000 loan at 3¾ per cent for thirty years from September, 1906. An application was received from T. Dobson in November, 1907: "On behalf of a cotton spinning company, for a loan of £40,000 coupled with assurance on lives of five directors was read and declined." In the same month, £10,000 was offered to Liverpool Corporation at 4½ per cent, but Liverpool was not prepared to pay such a high interest rate. In November, 1908, the town clerk of Newcastle asked for terms for a loan of sixty years; it was resolved that the period was too long. A sum of £1,000 was invested in the National Telephone Company 4 per cent stock from the beginning of 1909. A loan to Bolton of £3,000 was agreed to in June, 1909, repayable in equal instalments over 20 years; many long-term loans were repayable on a similar basis. Loans on the security of land or property were not to exceed one-third of the Society's total funds, reserves and paid-up capital from mid-1910.

At the annual general meeting of 1906, the number of directors was increased by two, in order to represent the midland and southern sections. The Actuary, Mr. Justican, was paid 150 guineas for the valuation carried out at the end of 1905. At the end of the financial year, " the auditors attended and reported their satisfaction with the way in which the accounts were kept, and their dissatisfaction with the room in which they work."

A fire claim for £250 from Sheerness Economical Co-operative Society for loss of agricultural produce was paid in full, despite the fact that the Society failed to comply with a condition of the policy — that no produce should be stacked within fifty yards of any chimney. This liberal interpretation of fire claims was quite usual.

Fire limits were raised in March, 1907, on the building or contents of Co-operative stores where there was no serious risk, and for increased sums where sub-divisions or fire appliances were effective. The maximum limit was £10,000 on any one risk. In June, 1907, the insurance on the Sunderland Co-operative central stores was increased from £7,500 to £10,000 as the premises were sprinklered. In the same month, another Co-operative society, Derby, decided to insure its members' private dwellings in respect of fire.

Group fidelity insurance was commenced in January, 1906, with the issue of a policy to cover the shopmen of Winnington Co-operative Society. The Co-operative Permanent Building Society asked for a quotation for a collective fidelity insurance for their agents, free from the obligation to prosecute as a condition of claim. It was resolved that, "if CPBS accept the obligation to prosecute, a quote will be made, but not otherwise." (30 March, 1907.) The CPBS complied with this condition and the CIS quoted £100 yearly premium for a floating fidelity policy of £500 to cover defalcations by each and all of the 180 agents for the CPBS in June, 1907. An application for a loan of several thousand pounds was made at the end of 1908, but as the CPBS required the loan merely on deposit and without any acceptable security, it was decided that no loan should be granted on such terms. The CPBS also requested a reduced rate of fire insurance on private dwelling in 1909, and the CIS agreed to reduce the minimum rate of insurance to 1s. 3d. per cent per year for such property.

At the annual general meeting held in March, 1907, 226 members attended from the five divisions of the CIS — Edinburgh, Newcastle, Leicester, London and Manchester. Rules were amended regarding the granting of annuities, and the admission of trade unions, building societies, and friendly societies as members. The directors were given the power to apportion any surplus of any department (other than Life) as they thought fit.

It was noted in May, 1907, that there was a proposal for the formation of an Accident Offices Association on the same lines as the Fire

Offices Committee, and that members of the FOC were required to become members of the proposed Accident Offices Association. The CIS agreed to quote AOA rates, but should other offices offer lower rates or premiums for Co-operative societies, the CIS would insist on claiming exemption from the AOA rates. The Accident Offices Association duly accepted the CIS for membership in July, 1907 — " with power of appointing Co-operative societies as agents, and to divide profits amongst shareholders."[1]

A number of policy decisions were made regarding extension of business at the end of 1907. It was minuted:

> " As the whole cost of extending special and industrial branches, except the various provision in premiums for office expenditure and commissions, had been paid out of the interest on accumulated funds in other branches than Life, it is reasonable and just that the expenditure on Life Department should as soon as practicable be restricted to its fair share of the sum available."

The programme for development would include the following considerations: concentration on the type of insurance required by Co-operative societies; systematic visits to local societies; local managers to control agents in their own area; North East Ireland to be added to the Scottish area; other outside areas to be visited by the agency inspector. But it was admitted that more staff would be required for local offices: " Both centrally and locally, therefore, increased expenditure will be incurred by the adoption of our recommendations. But we regard this as a necessary step to promote greater efficiency in increasing the premium income . . . "

An interesting case of coupon insurance occurred early in 1908. *The Railway Review*, representing the Amalgamated Society of Railway Servants, introduced a coupon for insuring the holder to the extent of £15 on death, but the periodical had received notice from the Board of Trade that a deposit of £20,000 would be required if they continued to print the coupon. The publishers of the periodical, King's Cross Publishing Company, asked the CIS to substitute its name and to pay the claims which would be reimbursed by the Company. The CIS agreed to enter into a legally binding agreement to that effect, and from 1909, made an annual charge to the

---

[1] As an example of an accident claim in 1909, the Secretary reported that a policy-holder sought compensation of two guineas due to ptomaine poisoning: " It was resolved that firm which supplied tainted salmon be asked to reimburse the amount." (Insurance against ptomaine poisoning had been offered for some time.)

publishing company of five pounds. In February, 1910, the CIS decided to issue its own coupon accident insurance. As only one society took out a fatal accidents policy for £5 per member at an annual premium of 1d. per member, the scheme had to be discontinued.

A scheme was prepared in March, 1908, to bring about the elimination of individual shareholders. Interest on share capital was to be reduced from 6 per cent to 5 per cent and individual shareholders were to receive 150 per cent of their paid-up capital if they would agree to cancel their shares. John Shillito, the last remaining individual shareholder in October, 1908, was asked to withdraw his shares, which he did in November.

A letter was received in 1908, from a Birmingham solicitor representing clients who were willing to purchase the CIS—the offer was declined. After a long interval, four more full-time agents were appointed in August, 1908. In the same month, it was resolved to set up a statistical department.

Doubts had been expressed at the annual general meeting in 1906, concerning the high fire rates being charged by the tariff offices. The CIS was, however, at pains to point out that as far as Co-operative business was concerned, the CIS was effectively non-tariff. In October, 1908, it was resolved that the Secretary should enquire at Lloyd's underwriters to ascertain the terms on which a reinsurance treaty with Lloyd's could be arranged. During November, 1908, G. Horrocks, the Fire Department Manager, interviewed a Lloyd's underwriter concerning a fire reinsurance treaty. Terms were agreed and it was decided to withdraw from the Fire Offices Committee and the Accident Offices Association. The Lloyd's reinsurance treaty terms were five or six times the amount of the CIS limit on any one risk and commission allowed to the CIS of 25 per cent of premiums — the CIS was pleased to accept this offer, as the usual rate of commission was only 20 per cent. The reinsurance treaty became operative from March, 1909, and within two months reinsurance had been effected under 28 policies for a total sum insured of £137,357. In July, 1909, the Secretary of the CIS asked the directors for advice concerning the meeting of heavy claims, pending the recovery of sums from Lloyd's. He was instructed to decline to notify policyholders regarding the extent of sums retained and reinsured, and he should refrain from mentioning specifically that these sums were reinsured with Lloyd's. By August, 1909, Lloyd's reinsurance sums on a total of £826,000 amounted to £450,000, and a year later, the sums reinsured amounted to over £1¼m.

Plate glass insurance was offered from the beginning of 1909, and G. Horrocks, the Fire Manager, was compensated for giving up his personal plate glass insurance agency on transfer of the business to the CIS. Insurance of third party risks was undertaken from November, 1908.

The Secretary reported in July, 1909, that when the pending Assurance Companies Bill was enacted, the CIS would have to deposit £20,000 and would have to carry the interest received on the investment of its insurance funds to the credit of those funds. It was resolved that pending the Bill becoming law and a full understanding of its effects on the CIS, no more full-time agents were to be appointed and no investments made, other than mortgages and loans to the CWS.

Joint action with the Royal Insurance Company was sought to prevent " the Royal Co-operative Friendly Society " being registered as a company with the name of " Royal Co-operative." The Royal Insurance Company duly reported that an injunction had been granted to refrain the Royal Co-operative Collecting Society from registering as a limited company with wider objects than life assurance.[1]

At a divisional meeting of the CIS held in Newcastle in April, 1910, a delegate complained that the amount of business done in the Industrial Department was showing an increase of merely £3 per week. Such a meagre result indicated that some special steps were needed for the development of industrial assurance business. By 1910, there were only 206 weekly policies and 8,600 monthly policies in force. (The 1910 figures for weekly policies were less than corresponding totals for 1903 — when there were 237 weekly policies.)

Shop assistants were protected by the provisions of the Workmen's Compensation Act, but the CIS noted that the experience of other insurance offices with regard to cover for shop assistants had been so irregular that no settled premiums for that class of worker were available. G. Horrocks explained that the CIS was insuring against accidents to employees through the agency of other companies. In February, 1907, it was agreed to deposit the requisite £20,000 and to commence workmen's compensation insurance. Between 2 February and 22 July, 1907, as many as 750 Co-operative societies took out workmen's compensation policies with the CIS. The matter of rates

---

[1] The Royal Co-operative Society retained its name until 1952, when it became the Stamford Mutual Insurance Company Ltd. From time to time over the years the earlier title had led to much confusion with the CIS.

for workmen's compensation insurance was raised in November, 1907.[1] J. P. Jones, Manager of the Accident Department, was asked if the CIS was prepared to insure employees in one department only. He replied:

"I am afraid we would refuse to insure one department only. It would happen that the Society which offered the one department would be the department with the heaviest risks."

"Then you have one rate?"

"No, we have a rate for butchers very different from drapers."

"Then what is the objection to taking one department at your different rates?"

The Chairman interjected — "There must be a reason why we won't take one department, but perhaps it's as well if you took it up with Manchester."

Up to 1907, only three societies in Scotland had taken up collective life policies. In all, 77,000 members of Co-operative societies were collectively insured by 1907. The total premium for the year amounted to nearly £8,000, over £3,350 more than in 1906. Eight hundred and five death claims had been paid for a total of £5,700. During 1910, there was great activity to push the collective life scheme and conferences were held throughout the country.

From January, 1906, the CIS agreed to pay one year's commission when the Society ordered transfer of business from one agent to another. It was further decided that although the CIS declined to affirm the principle of interest-in-book, it was prepared, without

[1] The Workmen's Compensation Act, 1906, applied to every Co-operative society as an employer. From February, 1907, the CIS insured the liabilities of Co-operative societies and others under the several Acts of Parliament which granted compensation or damages to workmen in employment.

109 Corporation Street

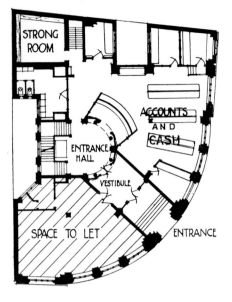

PLAN OF GROUND FLOOR.

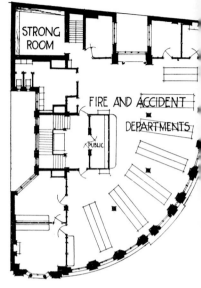

PLAN OF FIRST FLOOR.

Plans of 109 Corporation Street

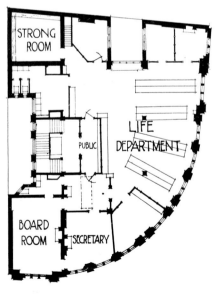

PLAN OF SECOND FLOOR.

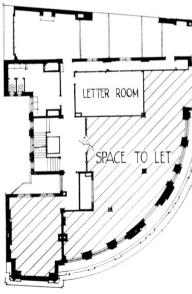

PLAN OF THIRD FLOOR.

William Barnett

prejudice, to consider a nomination by an agent of a successor to his agency. By March, 1906, the chairman stated that there were 500 part-time agents and 30 full-time agents in the employ of the CIS.

From the end of 1908, James Odgers was styled Manager for Scotland, in order to make it clear that his authority extended over James Darroch of Edinburgh office. In September, 1909, a special conference was held in Glasgow in connection with the opening of a new Glasgow office. Only half the Co-operative societies in Scotland at that time were members of the CIS, and William Barnett invited societies to become members on payment of a sovereign — they would then acquire five shares, four shillings paid-up, and full participation in all benefits as if they had 1,000 shares. William Barnett died as the result of an accident in September, 1909. He had been Chairman of the CIS for 28 years.[1]

At the end of 1909, the aggregate sum insured in the fire department after deducting reinsurances amounted to over £25m. The fire insurance fund stood at £92,000. The premiums for accident were £934, with claims £147; plate glass — £318, claims — £84; burglary — premiums £462, claims — £215; fidelity — premiums £2,802, claims — £1,069.

In May, 1910, James Darroch was transferred from Edinburgh to Glasgow office, and at the end of 1913, was appointed manager at Glasgow in succession to A. Burgess. A branch office was opened in Dublin in 1912.

[1] *Barnett, William*, 1830–1909. A bookbinder who served Macclesfield Equitable Provident Society from 1863 to his death; most of the time as Secretary and General Manager. Member CWS Committee 1874–1882.

(iv) Co-operative Controversy

Reference has previously been made to the first skirmish at Newcastle in 1902, in the campaign to bring the CIS more fully under the aegis of the CWS. The Northern agitators were not assuaged merely to raise the issue at Newcastle and in 1904, a conference of secretaries of Co-operative societies held at Stockton-on-Tees, received a proposal from T. Tweddell[1] of Hartlepool, a CWS director, and passed a resolution by a majority of one " that the time has arrived when the CWS should take into serious consideration the question of providing an insurance department, through which the risks of the Movement may be placed on a perfectly mutual basis." During November, a circular convening a southern section conference included the following proposal:

> " Seeing that the CIS was established in 1867 on behalf of the Annual Co-operative Conference, which then represented the whole Co-operative body as the Annual Congress now does, and noticing some recent expressions of doubt as to whether the insurance interests of Co-operative societies and their members are secured in the best way by the methods of the Insurance Society, it may be remitted to the Co-operative Union to take evidence and consider and report upon any defects and deficiencies and to make any recommendations which they may deem advisable in the interests of Co-operative societies and their members, such report and recommendations, if any, to be submitted to the Annual Congress."

At the ensuing Congress this resolution was passed, but no approach was made to the Co-operative Union to institute an investigation.

The Chairman of the CIS stated at the annual meeting held in April, 1905, that the CIS was doing business with 1,274 societies,[2]

---

[1] See letter from CIS District Manager of West Hartlepool office, 10 June, 1965 — " Tweddell was one of the founder members of the Hartlepools Co-operative Society. He was a J.P. and was Chairman of the Newcastle Branch of the CWS from 1893 to 1906 . . . Tweddell was Secretary of the Hartlepools Co-operative Society until he died 23 March, 1916."

[2] For an interesting example of self-insurance by a retail Co-operative society see Report of *Royal Commission on Poor Laws* (1909). Appendix LXVII (Evidence of J. W. Fawcett, Secretary Leeds Industrial Co-operative Society).
" It has a reserve fund, fire insurance fund, plate glass insurance fund, an accident insurance fund, amounting in all to £54,182." The statistics referred to the year ending 1905. Other figures showed investment in Co-operative and Municipal enterprise, etc., £191,000. Stock £208,000. Goods sold June 1905 to June, 1906, £1,500,000. There were also facilities for members to obtain dwelling houses by weekly payments — 756 dwellings sold at £197,000. The Leeds Society also advanced £201,000 on 907 dwellings not built by the Society.

but only 562 of these were members. He pointed out the advantages of membership: members received a dividend of 2s. in the pound on premiums which the Society retained as its sole risk, 15 per cent commission on their own business, and 6 per cent interest on share capital. There was a reserve fund in the Fire Department of £57,000, which was equivalent to more than two years' premiums.

At the Paisley Co-operative Congress in July, 1905, the future of the CIS was again discussed. At a further conference at Newcastle in the same month, the Chairman of the CIS reminded delegates that shareholders had incurred no risk for 37 years and had never been called upon to pay more than 4s. in the pound on called-up share capital. It has been quite remarkable that so many Co-operative societies had been so indifferent as not to join an institution that should encompass every society in the Kingdom; out of a premium income of £27,636 from fire insurance, only £10,890 came from Co-operative stores — the remainder was from outside sources. The CIS not only insured the whole of the business of the Co-operative stores, but they reinsured such business direct with other companies. At one time they had retained commission for doing so, but as the business improved, they offered even better terms to societies by returning most of the commission. The CIS took all the trouble, and of the 15 per cent commission which was gained, 10 per cent was returned to the local society. The total premium income of £10,890 from Co-operative stores was divided into three classes — small stores with not more than 20 people employed, stores between 20 and 50 employed, and stores in which more than 50 people were employed. In Class I there were 4,323 risks with a sum insured of £5,066,358 and premiums of £7,772 — most of these were not too large to be retained at the Co-operative Insurance Society's sole risk. In Class II there were 224 risks for sums assured of £671,891 with premiums of £1,703. In Class III there were 81 risks with sums assured of £305,087 with premiums of £1,415. The chairman calculated that there would be a balance of only £938 to provide for any total loss and for reserves in the 2nd and 3rd class after deducting commission, expenses, management and partial losses estimated at 35 per cent. "Throughout the whole of the turmoil his colleagues had exercised their discretion amongst very much prejudice and very much apathy, and for 31 years the premium of any one year had met the losses of that year."

Growing criticism of the CIS from within the Co-operative Movement broke surface again early in 1907. The Secretary of the CWS visited the CIS office, and stated that the question of the CWS undertaking insurance business was being pressed, and that as a first step the CWS would like an interview between their Finance Committee and a deputation from the CIS. In its turn, the CIS reiterated that it was prepared to reinsure excess fire risks with the CWS and SCWS jointly, and referred to a letter of September, 1898 to that effect. The main point at issue was that the growth of the Movement had meant erection of larger premises causing societies to go outside the Movement with the bulk of their insurance business. A conference of March, 1907 exhorted:

> " That the time has now come for a further development and extension of the facilities of insurance within the Co-operative Movement, and urges the CIS and the CWS to join in making more strenuous efforts to enable societies to do all their insurance business within the Movement so as to keep the funds from going to outside companies. Failing this the conference recommends that the CWS commence insurance in all branches."

Another meeting held at Middlesbrough in May, 1907, included a speech by Tweddell, in which he again expressed the opinion that the CWS should undertake all branches of insurance business. James Odgers and William Barnett inferred that the Middlesbrough conference was evidently intended to bring the subject prominently before the Co-operative Movement through its proposal that the subject of insurance should be included in the agenda for the next quarterly meeting of the CWS, at which the CIS was not invited to be present. Middlesbrough was the scene of yet another conference in November, 1907, with a paper read by R. Smith on " Insurance as it affects the Co-operative Movement." The speaker referred to the policy of the tariff offices and their tendency to absorb smaller companies, showing that since 1888, when there were 60 British companies, 32 had ceased to exist through absorption. Many of these amalgamations were harmful to the interests of the public and they were economically unsound. Smith added:

> " Why does not the whole of the Co-operative Insurance business find its way into Co-operative channels? If the Co-operative Insurance Society does not feel its way clear to take additional risks, and I can well understand its timidity in this matter, why should not the CWS be approached with a view to their enormous fire fund being put to some practical use? "

He then gave the following figures to show the relative scale of business of the CIS and the CWS Insurance Fund:

CIS Funds	..	..	..	£72,139
Sums Insured	..	..	..	£23,444,387
Proportion of Funds to property covered				.73d. per £
CWS Funds	..	..	..	£598,363
Sums Insured	..	..	..	£3,496,900
Proportion of Funds to property covered				41.06d. per £

" Thus," he commented, " the difference in the strength of the Wholesale fund is so marked that it is absurd to argue that the whole of the insurance business could not be done inside the Movement." He then outlined various schemes which might be suggested to meet the situation. A mutual insurance scheme could call upon local societies to make good losses in proportion to their own insurances. Alternatively, societies could form funds of their own and cover a proportion of their own risks. The CWS could do all the insurance business concerned through the establishment of a department for this work in the same way as the banking department, and it could invite societies to subscribe say 1 per cent of all their insurable interests and so begin concentrating cover for all risks in the Wholesale. He stressed that there should be no connection whatever with trusts or tariff rings.

Smith followed up his talk by a letter to the CIS directors pointing out that whereas the CIS during the previous four years had increased their premium income by 27 per cent, outside companies had increased their Co-operative connections by 64 per cent. A resolution was passed at the November Middlesbrough conference :

" That having regard to the enormous amount of Co-operative business going outside the Movement to private companies and the desirability of concentrating the whole of the Co-operative interest of the Movement under one central institution, the committee of the CWS be asked to receive a deputation appointed by this conference and urge upon them the necessity of taking up insurance business and thus keeping within the Movement itself the risks of societies which are now placed outside."

A deputation was nominated including R. Smith of West Hartlepool, W. Archer of Sunderland, E. J. Grey of Newcastle-upon-Tyne, J. W. King of Carlisle, and John Smith of Middlesbrough. The deputation reported back to a further conference of societies held at Newcastle-upon-Tyne on 11 January, 1908.

It had been pointed out to the CWS Finance Committee that the value of Co-operative property to be insured against fire risk was over £30m., the annual premium being roughly £70,000. The CWS fund, which was over £600,000, provided ample capital to guarantee the whole fire insurance business of the Movement and for some additional business of individual co-operators. The existing fire fund of the CWS, the deputation explained, had accumulated out of the profits made by retail societies, and the fund really belonged to the retail societies. It was not intended to ask the CWS to take only the surplus insurances, or for the whole of the insurance to be covered by the CWS and the CIS jointly, but that the CWS should undertake the whole of the business themselves — provided that the CIS was willing to be absorbed by the CWS. If the CIS was not willing, then the CWS would proceed without them. The January, 1908, conference at Newcastle passed the resolution :

"That this conference of Co-operative societies in the Northern section, having heard the report of the representatives appointed to interview the Wholesale Board re insurance, heartily endorse their attitude and resolve to re-appoint the deputation for the purpose of propagating an active campaign amongst societies until our objects be attained."

Mr. Oliver of Gateshead, a director of the CIS, wished to question the wisdom of such a proceeding. The whole matter he pointed out was under consideration by the CWS and the CIS, and a joint meeting was pending. A CIS minute noted tersely on 4 January, 1908, the receipt of a letter from the CWS and the SCWS inviting a CIS deputation to meet them: " It was resolved that, while agreeing to this, we ask the CWS to arrange for a shorthand report of the proceedings, of which each of the three parties should have a transcript, and that a joint report be made." At a meeting on 21 January, the CWS intimated that it wished to transfer all the CIS business to the two Wholesale societies, and did not wish to consider any working agreement. The CIS handed in a draft resolution that there should be a joint commission, and for there to be limits of united insurances mutually agreed. The increased business resulting from the action of the CWS and the SCWS should be apportioned to them, " reserving to the CIS the amount of its business in 1907, plus equitable share of increase." A reply was received from the CWS on 14 February, 1908, rejecting the CIS resolutions and reiterating that the most satisfactory course would be for the complete absorption of the CIS by the two Wholesale societies. The Northern agitators circulated Smith's paper to Co-operative societies, together with the report of the deputation appointed by the Middlesbrough conference. James Odgers commented that over the ten years 1897 to 1906, the gross premiums on reinsurance amounted to merely £100,000, whereas the total amount of losses recovered from outside offices by the CIS exceeded the amount of all net premiums paid to them. The retail societies therefore had this business done for them at less than cost price; the societies and the CIS also had the benefit of the commission. Odgers then explained that co-operators should not be taken in too gullibly by the scale of the CWS Insurance Fund. It was not the amount of the insurance fund, but the amount of premium income which was the standard by which the sum assured on any particular risk should be judged. For the CWS, or any other society, to undertake the insurance of the largest risks, was a departure from sound business and a step in the direction of gambling. If risks were to be placed on the insurance fund without correspondence to the amount of premium income, the logical conclusion would be to dispense with premiums altogether and keep up the amount of the fund by transfers from the profit on distributed business. Although the CWS agreed to adjourn voting on notice of motion concerning insurance at their March, 1908, meeting, a letter was received from Smith of West Hartlepool by W. W. T. Barnett of New Crompton, making the voting for him as candidate for the CWS Committee dependent on his attitude on the insurance question. The CIS Board resolved that this mode of electioneering in support of the agitation ought to be made public.

The CIS Board made further suggestions for an agreement with the two Wholesale societies in March, 1908: *Inter alia*, all branches of business undertaken by the CIS other than life business should be placed under the joint control of the CIS, CWS, and SCWS; that representation on the joint committee should be three-eights to the CIS, three-eighths to the CWS, and two-eighths to the SCWS, with the joint funds belonging to the societies in the same proportions. The two Wholesale societies could not agree to the proposals. On 19 May, 1908, a notice of amendment by the CIS to notices of motion from the Sunderland, Carlisle and other Co-operative societies was sent to the CWS :

" That in order to avoid competition with the CIS, which was established by the Co-operative Movement to transact its insurance business, the committee be instructed to propose a safe and equitable basis of working on which the two societies, united by a legal agreement, would act as one insurance organisation under joint management, without interfering with the constitutional autonomy of either . . . "

In June, 1908, the *Co-operative News* reported that the CWS directors wished to remind shareholders that the present proprietors of the CIS were the main shareholders with them or the SCWS and as such their interests were identical. The CWS directors agreed with the notice of motion from the Sunderland Society: " That the (CWS) Committee be directed to commence an insurance department for insuring risks of every description which may be lawfully undertaken."

At the Co-operative Congress in June, 1908, a J. Crocker of Leeds, moved the following resolution in the name of the Leeds Co-operative Society:

> " That in the event of the Co-operative Insurance Society Limited, the Co-operative Wholesale Society Limited, and the Scottish Co-operative Wholesale Society Limited, being unable to agree upon a joint method of carrying on the insurance business of the Co-operative Movement, they be invited respectively to report their differences to the Co-operative Union . . . "

He believed that insufficient consideration had been given to the proposal that such a highly technical subject as insurance demanded, and his Society wanted Congress to take some action towards getting the question sent back to the Co-operative Union so as to avoid any split in the Movement. John Shillito of the CWS said that he quite agreed that there was no more important question before Congress than that of insurance. He pointed out, however, that about thirty years previously, it had seemed that the CIS could not take over the insurable risks of the Wholesale Society. Therefore the CWS had to establish a fund of their own. That fund had grown so that at the present time it was three times more than the whole of the assets of the CIS. Mr. Wood of Burnley, a director of the CIS, said he thought the remarks of John Shillito showed that the question was too complex to be settled by Congress. He complained that the CIS had not had a fair and willing hearing, and that they were quite willing to abide by the decision of an independent tribunal. He had declared previously that the CIS did more than 75 per cent of the insurance offered by the Co-operative Movement. The statement had not been disproved by any independent body, and that being the case, the CIS did more of the insurance business of the Co-operative Movement than the Wholesale Society did of its general trade. Tweddell disclaimed being an agitator; it was eight years, he explained, since the matter was first taken up by the CWS regarding insurance, and since then discussions had been dragging slowly along; the reason was that they had been approached by the CIS to take over some of their risks, but the CWS could not possibly have taken the specific risks that had been offered to them. Tweddell pointed out that high premiums had been extracted from the Movement, and only once had any dividend been paid. At the CWS divisional meeting held in Newcastle on 13 June, 1908, the Sunderland resolution received 679 votes for, and 638 votes against. William Barnett explained that the CWS Insurance Fund over its life had lost £300,000, whereas the CIS had lost only £166,000; in addition, the latter had covered six times more property.

At the Manchester quarterly meeting of the CWS on 20 June, 1908, the insurance question was again raised. There was much discussion and ultimately the question was referred to the Co-operative Union for their decision. At the Birmingham Midland Section Conference, and also at the Northern Section Conference in July, 1908, Smith of Hartlepool re-read his paper on " Insurance as it affects the Co-operative Movement." An invitation was accepted from the SCWS in November, inviting the CIS to meet them and the CWS on the insurance question. Notwithstanding this move towards conciliation, circular letters were issued in February, 1909, by the Northern agitators to societies in the North West (a small committee had been formed previously to carry on the campaign in the Southern section).

In August, 1909, it was discovered that the CWS was offering fire insurance on dwelling houses at one shilling per cent; the CIS directors, in retaliation, resolved to " send our collective fire insurance circular to every co-operative society."[1] In the summer of 1910, the CWS issued an instruction to societies having overdrafts from the CWS banking department requiring them to insure their properties with the CWS insurance fund, and invited other societies to insure likewise. Many meetings were called by the CIS to enable societies to protest against the attitude of the CWS. It came to the notice of the CIS that a retail society received a letter from the CWS Board intimating that the granting of an overdraft would be subject to the condition that

[1] It was found that the Inland Revenue authorities required a 1d. stamp for every member insured under a collective policy and it was therefore decided to cancel the suggestion to circularise Co-operative societies concerning collective fire insurance.

deeds must be deposited and the subject matter insured with the CWS fund. In another case, the CWS tried to enforce a Welsh Co-operative society to transfer their insurance to the CWS because of an outstanding mortgage. The CIS decided that if the CWS called up the mortgage, the CIS would lend the necessary money. On 20 August, 1910, the *Co-operative News* stated:

> " The agitation in connection with co-operative insurance has now reached a grave stage and it is essential to the welfare of the Movement that something should be done as early as possible to bring it to a satisfactory conclusion. It is certain that the matter cannot be left where it is. It would appear to be the duty of every man who has any power in the Movement to do whatever he can to help forward the application of conciliatory measures."

On 18 February, 1911, special general meetings called by the CIS were held in Glasgow, Newcastle, Derby, London, Newport and Manchester, at which 492 societies were represented. Resolutions were passed, including the following: " That the directors be empowered to negotiate terms with the CWS and the SCWS for the transfer to them of the business of the CIS." The voting for the resolution was for 448, against 382, and as a result the CIS directors decided to communicate with the two Wholesales. A director of the CIS explained to a meeting on 25 February, 1911, in Manchester, that the Wholesale societies had no power to undertake life assurance, and their members could decline to adopt any alteration to their rules to obtain that power — the CWS had powers in their rules of 1898 to enter into all kinds of insurance business *except* Life. A leader in the *Co-operative News* of 4 March, 1911, felt that the question of insurance business of the Movement was being left in a most awkward position. Some delegates had agreed that the CWS could undertake the business on a larger scale and with more economy than had been effected by the CIS; others had pleaded the case of the CWS on the grounds that it was necessary to move in the direction of concentrating all Co-operative forces, especially in view of the increasing tendency at the time towards syndicalism. The outcome of voting at the special meetings called by the CIS showed that the biggest majorities were in favour of full absorption; there was also a large majority opinion against the CIS functioning as before.

At the annual general meeting of the CIS held on 1 April, 1911, Smith of Hartlepool, in reply to a criticism by the Chairman that his Society was not insured by the CIS, stated: " Your remarks may lead the societies to think that this Society was insuring with a cheaper and inferior institution. It is the Wholesale, which you will agree is a very safe institution, that we have our policies with."

In the *Co-operative News* of 27 May, 1911, a suggestion was put forward that a Co-operative Friendly Society should be formed in connection with the National Health Insurance Scheme. The Parliamentary Committee of the Co-operative Union suggested that there should be a joint Co-operative authority to act as an approved body under the National Insurance Act and the said Committee had no hesitation in indicating the English and Scottish Wholesale societies as the most suitable joint body for an approved friendly society. The CIS distributed a circular outlining the foundation and objects of the Society and maintaining that the CIS was the only society established by the Co-operative Movement for insurance purposes exclusively. It was equally evident that the CIS should launch the new sickness insurance scheme in its own name. The CIS directors consulted the Government department concerned and duly registered with the Chief Registrar of Friendly Societies an approved society under the title of The Co-operative Sickness Insurance Friendly Society in September, 1911.

On 9 November, 1911, the SCWS Board, on a majority vote, decided to ask the quarterly meeting of the CWS to empower the Board to negotiate with the CIS on the lines of *amalgamation*, but not as a takeover. The CWS could proceed without the SCWS, but they would require a three-quarters majority of the CIS share-holders. The suggestion from Scotland went unheeded; at the CWS divisional meeting held on 9 December, the CWS directors put forward the resolution — " That they may be empowered to negotiate with the CIS with a view to taking over their business." At the main CWS meeting in Manchester, a CIS amendment moved that a special committee of 15 persons be appointed to con-sider and report on the best way in which the business could be carried on to the benefit of the whole Movement. The vote taken for the CIS amendment was 184 for and 847 against. A special meeting was held to alter the rules of the CWS to enable it to undertake life assurance and to take advantage of the National Health Insurance Act. These resolutions were carried unanimously. In 1912, the CWS and the SCWS formed separate societies to administer national health insurance.

As a result of a meeting of a deputation with the finance committees of the two Wholesales, it was decided by the CIS directors in

June, 1912, to send voting papers to their shareholders asking the following question — " Do you authorise the directors to enter into negotiations for the transfer of the engagements of the CIS to the two Wholesales, the results to be communicated to the shareholders before acceptance? " The outcome of the voting was that 515 shareholders with 1,649 votes were for negotiations and 83 shareholders with 235 votes were against negotiations; Scottish shareholders from 56 societies with 202 votes said " yes," and 25 societies with 39 votes said " no."

On 19 July, 1912, the CIS, subject to acceptance or rejection by the shareholders, submitted terms:— that all persons employed by the CIS should be guaranteed employment by the Wholesale societies for at least five years, with status and remuneration equivalent to their present scale; that the services of James Odgers should be retained by the Wholesale societies in a similar capacity and that his present salary be paid for the remainder of his life; that each of the following officials — George Horrocks, Fire Manager; James Barlow, Accountant; James Mason, Treasurer; F. A. Williams; be given the option of retiring at any time on an annuity; that a sum of £130,000, together with the amount of paid-up capital at the time of the transfer, be paid. The Joint Finance Committee of the Wholesale Societies ultimately accepted these recommendations with an alteration from five years to three years in the case of employment protection, and a reduction in the amount of compensation from £130,000 to £120,000 — the business to be handed over on 1 January, 1913. Of the local Co-operative societies, 83 per cent had voted for the transfer of the CIS. An editorial in the *Co-operative News* said: " If we were asked why, we would say generally because the Movement prefers to lodge their faith in the power of the two Co-operative Wholesale

The 1913 Agreement

146

Societies." At a joint meeting of representatives of the Boards of the English and Scottish Wholesale societies and the CIS on 14 August, 1912, an amicable settlement was arrived at with regard to the take-over.[1]

At a shareholders' meeting held on 29 March, 1913, the auditor reported that the assets of the CIS were £406,000, an increase of £56,000 over the previous year. At the end of 1912, the share capital amounted to £53,775 and this was held by 988 societies, comprising an aggregate of 2,372,951 members. The total number of societies insured by the CIS in 1912 was 2,401. The aggregate sums insured, after deducting reinsurance, amounted to £33,440,376, being an increase of £1,614,091 over 1911. At the annual general meeting held on 29 March, 1913, it was decided that the CIS directors would receive on transfer two years' salary, the remainder of the £3,000 to be decided by vote. On 23 June, 1913, the agreement between the CIS and the Wholesale societies was signed and sealed. The signatures for the CIS were T. Wood and J. Dewar, directors, and James Odgers, Secretary. At the time of takeover there were 200 employees and the premium income was £200,000.

[1] The final terms of settlement between the CIS and the Wholesale Societies were —
(1) The Wholesale societies would undertake to fulfil all the engagements entered into and to discharge all liabilities of the CIS and to do all such things as may be necessary to obtain legal sanction of a transfer of such engagements in accordance with the provisions of the Insurance Companies Act 1909.
(2) That no greater percentage of the premiums for the renewal of life assurance policies issued by the CIS and in force at the 31 December, 1912, than were charged by the CIS for expenses and commission in the year 1911, shall be charged in future in respect of such policies.
(3) To employ for at least three years, unless guilty of misconduct, all persons employed at the date of the agreement and during that time the status and remunerations equivalent to the present to be reconsidered annually in relation to their ability and merits.
(4) To pay the salary of the Secretary and General Manager for the remainder of his life, on condition that from the date of agreement he is able to render at least three years' service to the Wholesale societies in such capacity as may be mutually agreed.
(5) To pay the CIS the sum of £120,000 together with the amount of the paid-up share capital at the time of the transfer, the sum to be distributed in the following manner:
  (a) to each shareholder a bonus of £2 10s. in respect of each £1 of share capital paid-up the balance to be apportioned as follows —
  (b) as members' dividend in proportion to the total amount of premiums other than the premiums received from shareholders in the nine years 1903 and 1911 inclusive. In addition to this the following payment is also to be made: to pay a sum equal to ten years' fees — £3,000 to the CIS directors, who will have to retire should the transfer be carried through, one-half—£1,500—to be apportioned to the relative number of years' service of the 13 directors respectively, the other £1,500 in equal 13ths disregarding length of service. The agreement was dated 14 August, 1912. (A large number of letters appeared in the Co-operative News criticising the large sum of money being paid to the directors in contrast to the staff, who were to receive nothing.)

On 3 October, 1913, a gathering of historic importance took place in the old CWS dining room, Balloon Street. The CIS directors and staff, together with the new chairman, John Shillito, and several directors and officials of the CWS attended. The function was to mark the final transfer of the business to the two Wholesales. Thomas Wood, the last Chairman of the old CIS, was in the chair at the commencement of the dinner, but vacated his seat to John Shillito halfway through the proceedings. On 24 October, the Scottish CWS entertained the Scottish staff and directors of the CIS. The first agents' annual conference under CWS auspices was held on 19 November, 1913.

Additional shares in the CIS were allotted in October, 1914 — 30,150 to the CWS and 16,075 to the SCWS, making a total of 80,000 to the CWS and 20,000 to the SCWS.

The campaign to bring the CIS under the aegis of the CWS had lasted a decade, and had been waged with the same intensity as any of the leading take-over bids in recent times. One would have expected a new CIS as a direct outcome of so protracted a struggle for management control, but in fact no widespread changes appear to have taken place. The only outward signs were changes in board membership, as directors were now appointed by the CWS and SCWS instead of by the retail societies; there was an opportunity to tidy up the capital position; and an official link was established by the appointment of the CWS Secretary as Secretary of the CIS.[1] But in matters of policy and organisation relating to the actual business of insurance there was no change. The CIS continued to function as it had done before the take-over, and the new Board accepted the sound underwriting practices which had been adopted by their predecessors. Perhaps no other business take-over has had such little effect on the coalesced unit.[2] The CIS, in 1913, was of course unaware that in a few years it would become involved in another take-over bid with far-reaching effects on its second half century of growth.

[1] The secretarial link lasted until 1952, when on the retirement of Sir Arthur Macdonald, it was recognised that the arrangement was quite impracticable.

[2] But see A. M. Carr Saunders *et.al.*, *Consumers' Co-operation in Great Britain* (1938), pp.173-4, for a different interpretation:
"The history of Co-operative insurance is of some interest, because it supports the claim of the Wholesale societies that all services, other than retail distribution can be more efficiently organised under their control than by specialized societies. While it was a separate and independent society, the CIS was far from enterprising; under the control of the Wholesale societies, it has made rapid progress."

(v) *The War Years*

The outbreak of war in August, 1914, did not have any immediate drastic effects on the CIS. It was agreed to cover war risks under existing life policies without extra premium, or extra charge in respect of new policies assured for sums less than £25, and that £100 was to be the maximum cover to include war risk under new policies. With fire policies, it was agreed to cover risks of loss by bombardment from the sea and "explosives from the air, etc." at 3s. per cent. In cases where the Manager was satisfied that distress caused by war was a bona-fide reason for non-payment of premiums on a life policy issued on or before the declaration of war, the policy was to be held in force for the duration of hostilities and for six months afterwards, subject to an accruing debt in the premiums due. The arrears were to be interest-free for the war period but afterwards were to be charged at 4 per cent. By the end of 1914, the total war claims paid under life policies amounted to 43 for a total of £241 18s. Arrears had increased in proportion to the monthly debit, but not to the extent that had been expected. The Courts (Emergency Powers) Act, 1914, stipulated that all life assurance effected before 4 August, 1912, for sums not exceeding £25, could not be treated as lapsed by non-payment of premiums without the authority of the Courts (there was a fear that war would bring widespread poverty).

G. Horrocks, the manager of the Fire Department, resigned in 1915, and Mr. F. Street, chief clerk of the department, replaced him. A surveyor for sprinklered installations was engaged in 1914, also a fire surveyor, at the same salary as the Fire Department manager was subsequently to receive in 1916 — £350 per year.

The total establishment of full-time agents at the commencement of war in 1914 was 32 in England and 18 in Scotland. It had been agreed in 1913 to appoint one agent for each retail society whose members assured collectively exceeded 10,000.

In 1915, the CIS agreed to insure against risk of damage by aircraft, but only at a greater distance than 15 miles inland from the coast, at rates varying according to circumstances, to be not less than 2s. per cent at the greatest distance. No further insurance in respect of war risk was to be accepted in areas where the CIS already insured £100,000 or more on property in any one town. In July, 1915, an agreement was drawn up between the Government and the CIS making the Society an agent, in common with other offices, for State insurance against loss by bombardment or by aircraft. The CIS was to cease to issue policies on its own fund for war risks.

The question was raised regarding the re-engagement of military conscientious objectors on discharge from prison, and in October, 1916, the CIS agreed to re-employ them provided there was no legal objection. From 1917, the CIS followed the practice of the leading life offices, by declining, during the remainder of the war period, to issue policies assuring the lives of persons called up for national service. In the event of death of an assured on active service abroad, the total premiums were to be returned. In connection with the collective life scheme, the condition that claims were to be based on the value of purchases made in the last year of life was not to be insisted upon for those in the armed forces.

The CIS responded to the need to raise national funds. Early in 1917, £250,000 of gilt-edged securities were converted into new war loans.

By the end of the war, Chief Office accommodation which had been ample previously was becoming exceedingly cramped. In the Fire Department, in September, 1919, the desks were lengthened and placed close together " providing accommodation for at least 50 more clerks." A war bonus of 25 per cent for those earning up to £2 per week had been increased to 35 per cent in the summer of 1917.[1] Those earning over £200 per year were to receive bonus of 15 per cent, but these advances did not apply to employees on active service. The bonus was further increased at the end of 1918, and again in 1919, for those on the lowest scale of wages. It was noted that as a general principle, men returning from the forces were to be reinstated in similar positions to those they had previously occupied, provided they were still capable of carrying out equivalent duties.[2]

Personal accident policies were issued from January, 1918, for " Trade Union delegates to France on a rate of £1 per cent on capital amount of insurance . . . and that the insurance should not be operative whilst the Insured is within 20 miles of the firing line."

[1] The war bonuses were paid to chief office, branch and district staff, and also to agents paid partly by wage and partly by commission, as well as full-time agents paid by commission only. The first war bonus was paid in March, 1915 — 15 per cent on wages of £2 per week and under. An optimistic minute noted " this is to be reviewed at termination of war."

[2] H. T. Fitzgerald, a serving member of the CIS chief office staff, was delayed in his demobilization and his father asked J. R. Clynes to intervene on his son's behalf. J. R. Clynes wrote (extant copy of letter in possession of the late Mr. Fitzgerald) to Winston Churchill, then War Secretary, and within several weeks, Fitzgerald was on his way to England for demobilization.

(vi) *The Planet Friendly Assurance Collecting Society*

Several of the men prominent in the early Labour Movement in Birmingham at the beginning of the present century formed their own friendly collecting society. They planned to use insurance as an evangelizing agent for their political views, but they were also seeking jobs for unemployed workers who, they claimed, had been victimized through participation in trade union agitation. The first meeting of the promoting committee for the envisaged Planet Society was held at Hallams Works, Fursley Street, Birmingham, on 17 May, 1905. It was decided to approach the Independent Labour Party for an advance of £50, and also to invite them to nominate a representative on to the Planet committee. In the event of the ILP not agreeing to advance the money required, it was decided that a £50 loan from the Birmingham City and Suburban Money Society should be taken up in order to meet the initial cost. The following reply was received from ILP headquarters and was signed by Phillip Snowden:

> " I put your letter of the 19 May, before the NAC, and I am asked to inform you that they regret being unable to see their way to advance you the loan or take part in any organisa-tion in your venture. If you carry forward your project you have our best wishes."

T. Hallam agreed to act as one of the bonds for the new society, and the secretary was instructed to write to a Councillor A. Hunt, to act as the other bond. Councillor Hunt replied — " I agree, only don't expect me to do any work: utterly impossible for some time to come."

Despite this financial setback, the Society was duly registered on 16 November, 1905, under the Friendly Societies Act of 1895, and the registered offices were fixed at 12 Barnets Road, Saltley, Birmingham. The first officials were J. Beard, Chairman; J. Simpson, Secretary; F. Spires, Treasurer. The trustees were H. D. Hallam, Councillor A. Hunt, and Tom Groom (who had been on the staff of Robert Blatchford's Socialist Weekly, *The Clarion*). Councillor George Titt, who subsequently became a Lord Mayor of Manchester, was another of the early supporters of the Planet. The first agencies were part-time in Birmingham, the Potteries and in Glasgow. The Secretary's salary was fixed at one shilling per week. A further loan of £50 was sought from the Birmingham Money Society. Soon after registration of the Society it was reported that there were ten agents. The balance of the insurance fund was something over £3 with a deficit of £4 10s. in the management fund, and outstanding liabilities of over £15.

152

against this, there was a stock of stationery. Management expenses were calculated as 25 per cent of the premium income. It was agreed to appoint a full-time agent at a salary of 10s. weekly for thirteen weeks provided that he obtained an average of 2s. of new business weekly.[1] By December, there were 454 members and the annual rate of premium income was £250. Early in 1906, it was agreed to engage a clerk for one day each week at 5s. to assist the Secretary whose salary had increased to 30s. per week. By March, 1906, ten district offices had opened, but in June, " a long time was spent in considering the financial position of the Society, and it was agreed that steps must be taken at once to reduce the management expenses." In September, it was decided to reduce the Secretary's weekly salary to 20s. and to dispense with the clerk. The period of stringency passed, and early in 1907, it was reported that there were over five thousand members with a premium income of over £3,000.[2]

The Planet was soon in dispute with the Pioneer Insurance Company over the transfer of business and appointment of that company's agents by the Planet. It was proposed to form a Planet fire insurance society in February, 1908, but there was no further record of this venture. Reference was made that the Co-operative Insurance Society had written to the Planet quoting rates for workmen's compensation insurance, but another company had bettered the CIS rates.

A special meeting was held in November, 1908, when it was agreed to form a Planet Mutual Insurance Society for the purpose of carrying on the business of insurance in all classes except life and workmen's compensation, and for the new society to be registered as a Co-operative Society under the Industrial and Provident Societies

[1] A CIS agent who had experience of the Planet in the years before the first world war has recently commented: " When I heard about the Planet I wrote them applying for an agency. I was then working for the Pearl Assurance Company in North Wales and earning roughly about 30s. per week. The Planet answered my application by asking me to meet one of their district managers for an interview . . . He explained to me that the only way I could start to work for them was to begin on a blank book, that is to say to start from scratch. They were prepared to pay me £1 per week for six weeks only. Then it would mean living on the com- mission, etc., on such business as I obtained. I had to refuse this offer, but told them that I would like to help in any way. I was prepared to do testing of lives in the area and indeed subsequently did so . . . This service I did without any pay or expenses . . . The district in which I lived was practically bereft of socialists so that it would have been very difficult to obtain business for the Planet."

[2] The Accounts for 1906 showed that although the annual rate of premium income was £3,135, the actual premiums collected were only £1,573. Claims expenditure was £184 19s. 4d. and there was a balance of merely £66 3s. 5d. in the manage- ment fund account at the end of the year. Entries in the fund account and balance sheet were calculated to the nearest farthing.

Act. The Planet Mutual Insurance Society requested the CIS to accept its excess insurances on special terms of commission in 1912, but the application was declined.

The Planet chief office staff worked under a strict regimen. A clerk had his application for a salary revision put back for three months as he had not improved his handwriting. Clerks losing more than two hours per month had time stopped from their holiday allowance, and persistent late-comers were not to be granted an increase in salary. To reduce management expenses, district managers of the Planet were asked to agree to a reduction in salaries of 2s. 6d. weekly. An offer of amalgamation with the Royal Liver was declined in 1910. Further difficulties arose with the management fund, which had given trouble for some time, and a deficiency had to be guaranteed by several committee members for sums ranging from £50 to £350. The Registrar instructed the committee to levy all the members of the Society. He declined to register the transfer of the London Counties Friendly Society to the Planet in August, 1910, and asked why proceedings had not been taken against the trustees for misuse of the benefit fund in aid of the management fund.

In 1912, it was agreed to form a separate society under the National Health Act, to be called the Planet State Insurance Friendly Society. The title was subsequently altered with the word " State " deleted and " Approved " substituted.

Just before the outbreak of the first world war, the secretary of the Planet Society wrote a vitriolic letter to the editor of the *Insurance Mail*. Several articles had appeared in that journal on the controversial subject of transfer of agents' business. J. Simpson admitted that the Planet had taken " odd shillings and pence here and there from other offices," but countered this by arguing that the block system of collecting premiums was a far greater danger to the livelihood of insurance men: " I calculate that, if the block system be adopted by all the offices it will mean that the services of not less — and probably more — than 30,000 full-time agents will be dispensed with." He then added somewhat histrionically:

> " We believe, rightly or wrongly, that we have a message for the people, especially the working people, and we will carry that message right into every working-class home in Britain. We are Socialists. We believe that the root cause of all the evil and wrong in the World is Capitalism. Capitalism is the dragon we are out to slay."

Early in 1915, the Planet sent the following resolution to the Chancellor of the Exchequer :

"The committee of the Planet are of the opinion that the scales of separation allowance, pensions and disablement benefits now in force for soldiers, sailors, are altogether inadequate and support the scales put forward by the War Emergency Workers' National Committee, believing that no person maimed in the country's service nor his dependants should be paid less than £1 per week, with 3s. 6d. for each child."

A new head office for the Planet in Corporation Street, Birmingham, was purchased in 1915, at a cost of £7,000. The CIS was invited to quote for insuring the new office, but another insurance company gained the business. In May, 1916, the valuer reported a deficiency of £7,800 in the Planet sickness fund; in the life and endowment sections there was a small surplus of over £500. The total premium income for 1915 had been £39,000, an increase of 22½ per cent over the previous year; but much of the increased business was of doubtful worth. It was obvious that the Planet was overreaching itself, and in June, 1916, a deputation visited the CIS chief office to discuss possible amalgamation. In the following month, the Planet wrote to the CWS querying whether the CIS Board would be prepared to consider representation of policyholders on its committee of management. The deputation from the Planet put forward the plea that their method of representation was more democratic than was the case with the CIS. This was denied, and the CIS pointed out that they were a fire and general office as well as a life office, and that other classes of the insured were as much entitled as life policyholders to representation. The Planet stressed that they had not sent their deputation to sell the Planet, nor to ask the CIS to come to their rescue; rather they were seeking a unity of democratic working-class forces, and not a takeover. They considered that the value of their assets was £45,000 or the equivalent of one year's premium income, and that compensation should be paid to the Planet committee, trustees and officials for their past services, also to district managers, agents and junior office staff. The chief officials and heads of departments should be reinstated in positions of equal remuneration; likewise all district managers and agents were to be safeguarded. It was calculated that a sum of £10,000 would be sufficient for these compensation arrangements and that a similar sum would be sufficient for the purpose of raising the policy benefits in cases where existing CIS tables did not provide for such an increase.

The Planet deputation insisted that interest-in-book should be safe-guarded for Planet agents. On 1st September, 1916, the following table of growth of the Planet Society was issued :—

Year	Members	Premium Income £	Fund £
1905	469	258	25
1910	25,682	10,557	5,047
1915	83,723	39,382	21,393

On 1 September, 1916, the Planet had 40 district managers, and 400 agents. The annual premium income was £45,000 with a fund of £25,000. Other bodies associated with the parent Society included the Planet Mutual Company with an annual premium income of £680, share capital of £720, and assets of £1,250; and the Planet Approved Friendly Society with 7,113 male members, 3,117 female members and investments of £4,400. The pros and cons of amalgamation were then listed: amalgamation would eliminate competition between two societies having mutual aims; it would also increase the possibilities of Co-operative insurance as opposed to capitalistic insurance. On the other hand, there was sentimental regret at the loss of individuality of the Planet, and that the constitution of the CIS did not permit direct control by policyholders.

The Registrar of Friendly Societies suggested that the best method of transferring commitments to the CIS would be for the Planet to undergo dissolution, and for the instrument of dissolution to contain a provision for the taking over of Planet liabilities and assets by the CIS. At a conference of Planet delegates held during May, 1917, the agreement to amalgamate with the CIS was approved. The dissolution of the Planet was advertised in the *Birmingham Gazette* of 26 July, 1918, and during the three months after the registration of dissolution, provision was made for the Planet to continue to issue policies under a CIS guarantee. In August, the trustees of the Planet were instructed to sign the formal agreement and 91 per cent of members accordingly agreed to the transfer. Those members of the committee and trustees of the Planet who were not to become employees of the CIS, were asked to offer their services as an advisory committee in case of any dispute in connection with the transfer arrangements.

The CIS countered an early request from the Planet that they should be paid £40,000 as a going concern, by suggesting that the figure of £40,000 should be subject to actuarial valuation. The CIS further proposed that the £10,000 that was to be earmarked for compensation should be deleted and replaced by two-ninths of purchase money, with the balance of purchase money to be expended on extension of business. The Planet then moved that all district managers and agents should be given the same liberty of action for political and public work as they then enjoyed. This was agreed. The Planet amended their earlier terms and now wanted all CIS agents to have guaranteed interest-in-book on the same terms as that of the Planet, but the CIS recommended that interest-in-book be confined to Planet agents. Aggressive canvassing did not stop short of the right of transfer of business from other competing concerns, and the Planet wanted reasonable facilities to be given to agents to complete transfers.

The final agreement was as follows :
"That the value of the Society as a business concern is equal to one year's premium at the present rate, subject to the amount of life business consisting of sound assets being shown by an independent actuarial valuation to be equal to five-ninths of the year's premium income, any excess or deficiency to be added or deducted from the purchase money."

A policy statement was issued on structure of the CIS :
"The object is to develop every section of the business with security, efficiency and economy, giving precedence to collective life and industrial business. For the development of the industrial section we adopt the simple, direct and effective methods of the Planet. The district managers will appoint part-time agents and introduce full-time ones, but the latter not to be appointed without the previous sanction of the committee, except in cases of urgency when the agency manager may appoint. In our definition of a district, we have already discriminated between industrial agents, who do all classes of business and will be controlled by the district manager, and ordinary agents who do every class of business except industrial and will deal with chief and branch offices."

A letter in the *Co-operative News* of 25 May, 1918, from a "well-wisher," stated that few triumphs were an unmixed blessing and the recent amalgamation of the Planet with the CIS was no exception.

The motives behind take-over bids are legion. Probably the urge to expand and so to control a larger section of the market is the most common factor. Some mergers are to acquire new resources which may be predominantly top managerial talent, but the take-over of the

Planet is probably unique in that the motive there was to acquire a work-force to enable the CIS to develop industrial assurance market opportunities after years of indifferent success with previous CIS methods.

The absorption of the Planet into the CIS brought a ready-made field force of full-time agents larger than that of the parent CIS; but the Planet agents, although predominant in numbers, did not capture the CIS. Planet consciousness was more apparent at Chief Office where personalities such as Simpson, who became Agency Manager for the CIS, sometimes ruffled his new colleagues with Planet ideas and methods. The terms of compensation to the Planet officials and their reinstatement in the CIS were certainly generous. Although the financial structure of the Planet at the time of the take-over was insecure, it must be noted that the Planet had only come into existence some years after the CIS had introduced industrial assurance, but had grown much more rapidly than the CIS in providing this form of cover. The CIS, with this new contingent of industrial agents, had to give wholehearted support to the pursuit of industrial business. Previously, it had been of two minds in that collective life was thought of as an alternative, albeit a more economic alternative, to industrial assurance. The Planet also brought an infusion of agency enthusiasm. Planet agents had interest-in-book and this right was safeguarded in their case. It was therefore apparent that the CIS would have to consider the extension of this concession to its other agents.

The CIS had always prided itself on the fact that it was on somewhat higher level than other industrial assurance companies. Whilst other offices concentrated on weekly business, the CIS proudly emphasized that the bulk of its business was for longer intervals of premium payment, and that even in industrial business it encouraged its clients to pay monthly or quarterly and so obtain greater benefits. But with the advent of the Planet the scene had changed. The new agents had been taken on with a new scale of commission which made it necessary for them to give special attention to weekly premiums: "This is no encouragement, in fact great discouragement, for the agents to press the superior advantages of quarterly premiums," commented a letter in the *Co-operative News*. "Is it worthwhile buying a Planet income at the expense of co-operative principles?" Simpson replied:

> "Whatever your correspondent may know about the Co-operative Insurance Society, he knows nothing about the Planet or his intention is merely to discredit by false and misleading statements. It is not true that the fusion of the Planet with the

158

CIS means any sacrifice of principle or the introduction of a new scale of commission or of any new practice. The CIS has conducted industrial business for a longer period than the Planet has been in existence. The Planet is not purely industrial and its ordinary branch business is proportionately larger than that of any similarly-constituted office. Nobody criticises the housewife for purchasing bacon by the pound instead of by the flitch. Yet every meddling fool fancies he has a duty to perform in exposing the thriftless system of industrial assurance. No camouflage about the principles will obscure the fact that the great mass of co-operators go outside the Movement to purchase their life assurance although the CIS has been catering for them since 1886."

From November, 1918 to September, 1919, eight ex-Planet agents were promoted to district managers, making 43 district managers who had served with the Planet. In all, 49 CIS agents and superintendents were also promoted to district managers, together with six outside persons who had not had previous service with either the Planet or the CIS, making a total of 98 district managers employed by the CIS by September, 1919. The headquarters of the Planet Society at Birmingham were purchased by the Workers' Union, but two small rooms were retained for use by the CIS.

At the Co-operative Congress in 1919, it was suggested that CIS agents might be used to spread the benefits of Co-operation. One delegate objected that the CIS employed men as agents who might or might not be co-operators.

It was decided in September, 1919, that a charge of $7\frac{1}{2}$ per cent be levied on all loans to agents for purchase of interest-in-book. The agents were to repay the loan and interest within five years. On 17 January, 1920, an article in the *Co-operative News* stated that a great deal of unrest was becoming manifest amongst the agents of the late Planet Society since amalgamation due to the anomalies of agents working under different conditions and at different levels of remuneration. The Planet agents had interest-in-book and the CIS agents had not. If the CIS did not believe in book-interest, why did it take the Planet over? In July, 1920, the principle of interest-in-book was admitted, but no interest was to be granted on business already on the books, except that of Planet agents.

W. Worthington, assistant actuary of the Royal Insurance Company, undertook the CIS valuation at the end of 1920, and the valuation of the Planet Society business up to the end of 1919. The Planet valuation was submitted by the Actuary in June, 1920. After deduction of the £5,601 deficiency on the management fund, the net amount of Planet funds on the valuation date was taken as £62,595. The expense ratio of the Planet Society had been extremely heavy. In 1913, the rate was 57.7 per cent, and by 1916–18 the rate was still almost 50 per cent. There was fairly clear evidence that there had been extravagance in management, combined with acquisition of new business out of all proportion to renewals. Fortunately, claims experience had been low during the early years of the Planet but the effects were beginning to be felt by the CIS during 1920. The basis of valuation adopted by the Planet nowhere approached the stringency of the CIS. The Planet transacted a large amount of business under ordinary and special sections with guaranteed reversionary bonuses, but the loading addition to premiums to accommodate these bonuses was totally inadequate.

The final figure for the cost of transfer in connection with the Planet Society, including compensation fees, legal expenses and stamp duty, amounting in all to £13,500, was taken from the general reserve fund in the CIS balance sheet for 1920.[1]

[1] Donovan Rains (CIS, 1913–1963) remembered the taking-over of the Planet — "One windy day, their H. O. records were dumped in the front entrance of 109 Corporation Street like a load of manure." The loose proposals blew away down Corporation Street and for several months people brought in mud-splattered documents with demands for a small reward.

PART FOUR

THE 1920s

(i) *Immediate Post-War Developments*

A review of organisation was made by the CIS Directors in August, 1919, with the aim of national coverage and with publicity to be steered towards the working and lower-middle classes. It was noted that to achieve an effective organisation, it would have to cover the whole of Great Britain. Districts were to be grouped in areas, each with an inspector or divisional superintendent over local district managers. Whilst it was desirable to pay particular attention to industrial centres, argued the agency manager, it would be a great mistake to ignore less thickly populated areas on the assumption that such districts could not be made profitable. Many important towns were not yet opened as separate districts, but had agents working either directly under head office or from the nearest branch or district office. Simpson pointed out that one serious difficulty was the delay that occurred before an agent could be appointed.

The respective powers of district and branch managers were also discussed.[1] Branch managers were to have supervision of all district managers, superintendents and agents, and to deal with all business from Co-operative and agricultural societies in the areas under their control.

The agency manager complained that chief office and the branches could not deal adequately with industrial life business testing. In effect, he was campaigning for the agents to be responsible to the district offices. Nor did he agree with the payment of fixed salaries to full-time agents. In 1920, the General Manager explained that it would not be a wise plan to appoint large numbers of agents directly under chief office or branch office control, unless an experienced industrial life inspector was involved who could frequently visit the agents and test the business. The General Manager considered that it would be better to concentrate on large industrial districts, and the agency manager was instructed to prepare lists of districts suitable for expansion.

James Odgers had retired on 31 May, 1919, after serving the Society as a full-time chief official since 1873.[2] When he joined the CIC he was the only full-time employee; when he left there was an indoor

---

[1] The branch managers in 1919 were: J. W. Robertshaw, Nottingham; R. H. Fitton, Newcastle; J. Clayton, Bradford; J. Darroch, Glasgow; J. C. Sykes, Cardiff; E. Knowles, Dublin; H. Evans, Birmingham; F. D. Rugen, London.

[2] James Odgers entered the Co-operative Movement through the Plymouth Co-operative Society when he was about 24 years of age, and he thereafter served 15 years on their Board. In 1872, he became clerk to the Co-operative Union, then known as the Central Co-operative Board.

staff of nearly 400. He was due to retire at the end of 1914, and the CIS Board, towards the end of 1913, appointed a Mr. Lintot as an understudy, with the understanding that he would take over as General Manager. Lintot was, however, called up for service shortly before war was declared, and although it has been claimed that he was offered the Fire Department on his demobilization, he declined the offer and left the CIS for another position. Odgers died in April, 1923.[1] J. P. Jones, Manager of the Accident Department, was appointed to replace Odgers as General Manager. J. P. Jones, then aged 42, had been in the service of the CIS since 1899.

An agreement was entered into with the Vulcan Boiler and General Insurance Company in 1919. The CIS was to issue its own policies on engineering risks, but the whole liability was to be carried by the Vulcan Boiler Company, who would be responsible for the fulfilment of engineering services. It was in connection with boiler insurance during the period 1870–1900 that modern third party insurance came into existence. From 1896, motor cars or horseless carriages began to appear on British roads. The Vulcan Boiler Company had undertaken to insure such vehicles in the same year, but very little was done by that Company to develop this line of insurance until 1912, when the Vulcan introduced a motor insurance scheme which was unique in that premiums were calculated on a mileage basis.[2]

A report by the General Manager on the situation in Ireland was drawn up in April, 1920, in which he stated that there was a general demand among the agricultural Co-operative societies for an Irish CIS. The General Manager could not prevail on CIS staff to transfer to Dublin, and he suggested that for the present the CIS should take no steps to carry out an extensive development in Ireland, although the Dublin Branch manager had recommended that the CIS should open an office at Belfast. In the same month in which the report of the General Manager was issued, a branch of a Co-operative creamery was burnt down: " In view of numerous disturbances in Ireland, the Society, as a precaution, was instructed to lodge a claim against the authorities under the Malicious Injuries Act." At the end of 1920, Tralee Co-operative Society, being in an area under martial law, was asked

---

[1] James Odgers' father was a doctor in Manchester. " Mr. Odgers would have made an excellent headmaster, just, fair, and stern." When Mr. Odgers went to London on CIS business he travelled second-class, with Sainsbury's sandwiches, travelling rug and foot-warmer. (Interview with H. J. Butterworth.)

[2] See W. H. Chaloner, *The History of 100 Years of Engineering and Insurance 1859–1959* (1959).
Also W. H. Chaloner, *National Boiler 1864–1964* (1964), pp.19, 58.

whether it woud be desirable to terminate its collective life contract with the CIS. It was resolved, however, to keep the scheme in operation. Later in the same year, another Co-operative agricultural society had its premises destroyed by fire. Many enquiries were received from Co-operative societies in 1921 for terms for insuring risks against fire and other damage arising from riots and civil commotions " including malicious damage by Sinn Feiners and other evilly disposed persons." The amounts involved were very large, and the SCWS and the Trade Insurance Department of the CWS were written to regarding reinsurance, but as both Wholesale societies declined to accept the risks, the proposals were reinsured with Lloyd's.

During 1921, there were numerous outbreaks of farm fires in the Manchester area, so much so that the Oldham Equitable Society threatened to take away all their CIS business if the request for cover for malicious damage was declined. It was claimed that the damage to farms was not the result of riots or civil commotion, " but incendiarism by persons who may be acting from political motives." These risks had not been included in the normal CIS fire policy, but it was agreed to accept them from March, 1921.

Many of the CIS agents in the years after the first world war were recruited from unemployed workers[1] from other industries, or from the ranks of those on strike. " We were a mixed bunch in those days. We had many skilled craftsmen whose chance of a job in their own trade had dwindled to nil. Quite a few ex-policemen (after the police strike, 1919) . . . "[2] It was also reported that the CIS Liverpool district office was receiving every possible assistance from the Liverpool Co-operative Society and had the solid support of trade unionists in 1920.

Some indication of the quality of the accommodation occupied by the new district offices can be given from the example of Blyth district in March, 1920, where the local Co-operative society was prepared to provide office accommodation at a rent of 2s. 6d. per week. It has

[1] John Braddock, the husband of Mrs. Bessie Braddock, M.P., was appointed a full-time agent at Liverpool Central District in November, 1926, and retired in July, 1957, aged 65. He was given leave-of-absence for one year from June, 1955, when he was appointed leader of Liverpool City Council. (He was chairman and member of 24 City Council committees or sub-committees.) He had been unemployed before joining the CIS. Previously he had been in the building trade. In 1932, he was found guilty of inciting a riot during an unemployment demonstration and an application was made by his wife to continue the agency during her husband's imprisonment. Mr. Braddock subsequently appealed against his conviction, and the conviction was quashed.

[2] letter from T. S. Sargent, 13 July, 1965. (ex-agent Liverpool Office).

been said that J. Simpson claimed that he only granted a basic 5s. weekly rental for district offices. (The Glasgow branch manager secured an office consisting of a shop on a ground floor for Glasgow East district at a yearly rental of £15.) In many cases, however, the districts were being run from the homes or parlours of the local managers. During 1919, over 60 new offices had been opened and 300 agents appointed but not all districts were an unqualified success. It was strongly recommended that in 1920 no new districts were to be opened except in exceptional cases and that efforts were to be devoted to consolidation of existing ones. Attention was to be devoted to large industrial centres where there were progressive Co-operative societies. The agency manager stressed the importance of industrial life business — the majority of people to whom the CIS could appeal were in receipt of weekly wages and " to cater for such clientele we are bound to accept premiums by weekly payments." An insurance office which could cope with industrial business could also deal efficiently with ordinary life, fire and general business. He claimed that by the summer of 1920, all industrial areas were covered more or less effectively, although many districts took in too large an area for effective future development. Army units were visited by CIS agents from 1920 and permission was secured in the Salisbury Plain area for agents to have access to the large military camps there. Advertising also receiving attention: CIS placards appeared on the railway stations at Blackpool from the spring of 1920.

James Darroch, Glasgow branch manager, reported to the CIS agency manager in December, 1920, that many old CIS men were disappointed at not receiving promotion, but he admitted that many of them were not industrial agents. The agency manager snorted: " If agents in Scotland want consideration, they must justify it with results." He did not consider it sound policy to limit any appointment in Scotland to Scotsmen, or to persons actually resident in Scotland.

It was decided to advertise for a full-time Actuary in July, 1920. The CIS was to seek a young man, " preferably one who has passed his intermediate examination." A report by the life manager stated that it would be necessary to make annual valuations after the quin-quennial valuation in 1920. H. Cox was appointed as the first full-time Actuary in November, 1920, and he got down to business very quickly. By February, 1921, he had investigated the staffing of his department, and he pointed out that 21 clerks were not required. The majority of these employees were recommended for transfer to other departments.

In July, 1920, it was reported that two clerks, J. L. Nuttall and M. Oldham, had passed the examinations held by the Chartered Insurance Institute. In November, 1921, members of the CIS staff were invited to submit schemes to promote efficiency and better management methods. Money awards were to be made for the best papers in order of merit. There is no evidence of any successful outcome of the proposals.

In March, 1921, the agency manager reported that the CIS was employing over 700 agents, but needed 5,000. It was impossible for him to supervise all the outdoor staff from chief office, and it was agreed to place all agents under the direct supervision of district managers, who were to report to branch managers, in turn responsible to the agency manager. The Actuary reported in June, 1921, that although £200,000 had been spent on development during the previous two years, yet to be fully operational on a national basis with a representative in every important town and village, the CIS would require about 12,000 agents. It was noted that the Prudential employed 17,000 agents. The Actuary thought that the CIS was not likely to be fully developed for at least 20 years after 1921, and in consequence, the whole of the country would not be covered by agents before competition from other proprietary offices became severe. He pondered whether the CIS could utilize its special connection with the local retail Co-operative societies to expand its business in towns and villages where the CIS was not fully represented by full-time agents.

The CIS had suffered considerable depreciation of securities during the war period and excessive mortality claims due to the influenza epidemic. During 1919 and 1920, however, the CIS invested £700,000 with the Wholesale societies. In 1913, the total premium income had been £250,000; in 1918, it was just over half a million pounds; and in 1920, £1,384,000.

In 1914, there had been 50 full-time agents; by 1921, there were over 700. Rapid growth and new directions brought problems of staff relations; for instance the organisation sponsored by district managers — the District Managers' Fraternal Association — resented supervision by branch managers, who were men experienced in fire and general business rather than industrial life. An enquiry had been received from a trade union in 1916, to ascertain whether CIS staff were members of a trade union. A reply was sent that the CIS neither required employees to join either a trade union or a Co-operative Society, nor did the CIS interfere with their doing so.

The General Manager referred in 1920 to the salaries of female employees, then numbering 200, the majority of whom had been engaged at rates of pay which they had themselves suggested, and which had been in advance of what they had hitherto obtained elsewhere for a similar class of work. A number of members of chief office staff joined the Guild of Insurance Officials in 1920.[1] The entire staff at London Branch joined in a body. The CIS agents on their part supported the Amalgamated Union of Co-operative Employees. A claim was submitted from the AUCE in September, 1920, for interest-in-book to be granted to all agents, and a minimum wage for full-time agents of £3 10s. per week. Terms offered by the CIS in October, 1920, were rejected by the Union. At the beginning of 1921, the AUCE amalgamated with the Warehouse and General Workers' Union, and the amalgamated body took the name of National Union of Distributive and Allied Workers (NUDAW), and submitted a claim for an increase in wages of CIS district office clerks. In September, 1921, the CIS followed the example of the CWS and resolved to cut wages by 10 per cent for a majority of the staff. In the same month, the Guild of Insurance Officials urged the CIS to reconsider the existing method of payment of staff at chief office and branches. The Guild suggested that staff should be classified into four grades, according to ability. Increased experience should be acknowledged by payment of a yearly increase in salary, subject to satisfactory reports. The Guild also recommended that there should be equal pay for males and females. The General Manager was unable to agree to the scales put forward by the Guild, but the Actuary commented in favour of a grading system for payment of salaries. Salaries were unfairly distributed. Before the age of 21, rewards were generous, but after 21, comparison was generally in favour of other insurance offices. This had the result of a leakage of trained staff to other offices with more progressive scales of salary. A new grading scheme and a revision of salaries which was planned to counteract these adverse tendencies was brought into force from the beginning of 1922.

(ii) Collective Life Assurance

By the beginning of 1914, 398 retail Co-operative societies were collectively insured. After the outbreak of war, a local society pointed out that many members had joined the armed forces, thereby reducing

---

[1] The National Union of Co-operative Officials was formed in 1917, itself an amalgamation of several bodies.

the spending power of households and level of insurance claims under the scheme. A request was therefore made that the scheme should be amended so that collective claims on the death of a soldier-member could be made up to what it would have been if the deceased had remained at home. By 1919, the surplus for distribution of the collective life scheme was £88,000. Although the scheme *in toto* was slowly developing, there were always many societies withdrawing from the scheme. In most cases, these societies were those with credit balances who felt that they were subsidising other societies. Many of the lapsing societies did not realise that in withdrawing from the scheme, they were running a risk of selection against themselves with the possibility of a run of claims causing serious loss. In certain societies there were many old lives on the books; in other societies it was suspected that purchases by young members in the household were being credited to older members. By 1919, the number of societies with debit balances amounted to 25 per cent of the total number assured; but it was noted that 88 of the societies concerned had shown credit balances in the preceding year. In 1920, detailed statistics of the operation of the collective life scheme showed that the average amount paid per claim in 1919 was £7 14s., at an average age at death of 59 years. The General Manager reported that the collective scheme would have to be treated as a whole, otherwise it would cease to be a collective scheme. If exceptions were to be made, or various rates quoted for various districts, it would introduce an element of instability.[1]

The CIS re-affirmed in October, 1919, its decision to confine its business to the United Kingdom, despite applications received from colonial Co-operative societies in connection with the collective life assurance scheme. The London Co-operative Society intimated that they proposed to discontinue membership of the collective life scheme at the end of 1920. They objected to losing the return on interest by having to pay premiums half-yearly in advance. Moreover, paid-out claims were refunded by the CIS at intervals with a considerable loss of interest on the money advanced. Above all, the London Society maintained they were contributing out of their credit balance towards losses sustained by other societies. As a result of these complaints, the General Manager of the CIS recommended that where a society

[1] The collective life scheme did in one instance influence the policy of a retail society. The Rochdale Equitable Pioneers' Society negotiated for amalgamation with the Rochdale Provident Society. The Pioneers felt that the chance of success of amalgamation would be improved if the members of the Provident Society were not to be collectively insured until they had been amalgamated with the Pioneers.

showed a consistently adverse record for a period of five years, their rate of contribution should be increased and the increase was to be based on the actual experience.

The collective life scheme was a good advertisement for the CIS, and many policyholders were attracted therefrom to other sections of CIS cover; but apart from this, little financial advantage was derived from the scheme, as profits were fully divided amongst the societies. On the other hand as the policies operated for a year at a time only the build-up of large reserves to meet future liabilities was not necessary, consequently a large retail Co-operative society could formulate and administer a private collective scheme with considerable success, provided that the age-distribution was satisfactory and general trade conditions remained prosperous.

The Life Manager pointed out that extending the collective scheme to include children's lives had shown negligible results; only four retail societies had taken out policies under the scheme. He further reported in July, 1921, that it had been suggested that the CIS might offer collective life assurance to several Canadian Co-operative societies who had applied.

By 1922, the collective life scheme was facing difficulties. There was an excess of claims and expenses over premiums of over £17,000. The purchasing power of members was seriously diminished due to a slump in trade and employment, and the CIS was paying claims based on purchases averaged over previous, more prosperous, years. It was feared that the CIS might have to amend the method of averaging, and base both the premiums and the claims on the previous year's trade only. In all, 43 societies had withdrawn from the scheme during the period 1904 to 1922. Out of the 1921 surplus, £50,000 was set aside for the estimated deficiency for the year 1922, as the rate of mortality (mainly caused by an epidemic of influenza) was showing a 50 per cent increase over the corresponding period in the previous year.

The Actuary reported, toward the end of 1923, that the scheme was showing an increased deficit, and it would be necessary to revise the scheme by offering two alternatives to members — to increase the premium from 1d. to 1⅛d. per £ based on sales (scheme 1); or to have benefits reduced by being based, either on three-year average purchases or one-year average purchases prior to death, whichever was the lower (scheme 2). In December, 1923, replies were received from 807 societies which were collectively assured; 498 societies agreed to adopt alternative scheme 1, and 294 societies opted for scheme 2; 15 societies indicated their intention to withdraw from the

169

scheme altogether. By the end of 1924, the collective life account was again in surplus, and from 1925, in the case of societies showing consistently unfavourable records, the Actuary was allowed to negotiate new contractual terms. The profit for the year ending 1924 under the scheme was over £27,000, but it was decided not to distribute any surplus. Certain societies with favourable experiences were not renewing their collective life contracts; many others were showing persistent debit balances. To help meet this contingency, it was proposed to reduce benefits for all unmarried members. There was also a continuing tendency on the part of some members of local societies to credit large purchases on old lives — to cure this abuse, benefits were reduced in certain societies for members aged over 65.

The collective life scheme suffered again from the ravages of an influenza epidemic during the winter of 1926-27. By May, 1927, over 2,600 influenza death claims had been made. The scheme showed a small surplus for 1927, but 12 more societies withdrew during the year, and premiums fell as a result of reduced retail sales during the latter half of the year, brought about by the General Strike and the subsequent coal dispute. Influenza recurred in 1929,[1] and the percentage of death claims to collections for the first six months of 1929, rose to 23.9 in the industrial branch, compared with 19.7 per cent for the corresponding period in 1928. Influenza claims under the collective life scheme during 1929 were over £60,000, leaving a surplus at the end of the year of only £15,900, compared with £75,000 for 1928.

A form of collective life scheme organised by a firm of multiple grocers was brought to the notice of the CIS in 1929. The contract was entered into with another insurance office and customers were to receive coupons for each 5s. of grocery purchases. The value of cover in event of death was to be five times the amount of the coupon during the three months before death. The insured had to be under 65 years of age, and the cover was for own life only, whereas the CIS was for the whole family; moreover members of Co-operative societies also received dividends on purchases.[2]

(iii) *Investment*

The CWS was asked by the CIS to look out for a suitable avenue of investment for £30,000 in October, 1913. Early in 1914, the CIS

---

[1] In 1929, it was queried whether sufficient attempts had been made by industrial life offices to investigate the cause of common colds.

[2] Group life assurance quotations for members of Co-operative societies, clubs, trade unions, were offered from 1921, and the Actuary also investigated the cost of a group life scheme for the clerical staff of the CIS, CWS and SCWS directors.

turned down a special loan request for £500 at 5 per cent from a Co-operative Garden Village Society. Several investments in short-term municipal loans continued to be made in 1914, and a number of water board stocks were included during the period, but quite apart from these holdings the CIS had accumulated £120,000 in a special deposit account with the CWS Bank by 1916. Investment in £100,000 of CWS development bonds was made at 6 per cent for a ten-year term in 1920 and 1921. The General Manager reported in 1922, that future investment policy should take into account that many of the existing investments were nearing redemption, and that in the future these funds should be re-invested for longer terms; these views were endorsed by the Manager of the CWS Bank, who recommended the purchase of longer-dated government, colonial and corporation stocks. As a result, investment of £20,000 was made in Australian Government 5 per cent stock (1935–1945) at 96 in April, 1922, and certain items of corporation stock were realised to enable suitable re-invest-ment of proceeds. By the end of 1921, investments in government securities had totalled £609,000 nominal value but in the following year, a considerable amount of war loan was sold — the Actuary reported in August, 1922, that the CIS had invested nearly £150,000 in National War Bonds in connection with life policies (by contract the policyholder on a certain date or previous death became entitled to receive a National War Bond).

Redemption of a batch of CWS development bonds took place from 1923, with the redemption price calculated on the assumption that 5 per cent interest only would be earned on re-investment of the proceeds during the period 1923–25. It was also agreed that a further batch of ten-year development bonds amounting in all to £133,000, for which the CIS had issued development bond policies were not to be redeemed before date of maturity. The CIS had urged the redemption of the bonds so that the Society could invest the proceeds in longer-dated redeemable securities.

Despite these transactions during the immediate post-war years, the CIS had still not reached the stage of realisation that an investment policy appropriate to an insurance office was required.

(iv) *Builders' Guilds*

An interesting post-war socio-economic development in which the CIS was partly involved from 1920 was the National Builders' Guild Movement.

The 1918 programme of the Labour Party had demanded "a steadily increasing participation of the organised workers", but in the event it was the slump in trade at the end of 1920 that provided a suitable situation for such demands in the form of guild socialist propaganda, mainly directed at workers in the building trades and in the Post Office. A large proportion of trade union leaders had joined the National Guilds League, but the most serious attempt to put guild socialist ideas into practice was made in the building industry. S.G. Hobson, a leading guildsman, and certain trade union officials from the Manchester area, decided in 1920 to establish a building guild. The attempt met with early success, large contracts for building houses were secured from the local authorities, and soon building guilds were set up in many towns.[1] A National Builders' Guild was established in 1921. In the summer of that year, the Higher Irlam Building Guild asked the CIS for a quotation for insurance of its member-workers under the Workmen's Compensation Act. The Guild also stated that the local council desired a policy fixed at £5,000 guaranteeing completion of a building contract undertaken by the Guild — the CIS quoted ordinary rates for workmen's compensation and for fire risks. The Taunton Building Guild also asked for and was quoted for similar risks. There was no reason, in the General Manager's opinion, why the CIS should not issue policies to building guilds; but the CIS solicitor doubted whether the guilds would be able to obtain the labour they required for completion of their contracts. The CIS subsequently agreed to guarantee the building guilds to a limit of 20 per cent of contract price. In effect, the insurance cover provided was a substitution for the money retained by a building owner against the contractor.

In January, 1921, the CIS authorised a bond for the Building Guild of Wigan, in respect of a contract to erect 135 dwelling houses, and in February, the Guild of Builders in London was appointed part-time agent to the CIS. A further guild bond was authorised by the CIS in connection with the building of 184 houses on the Tootal Estate at Weaste for Salford Corporation. In May, a letter was received from the Dun Loaghaire Committee of Guild of Builders concerning contracts on the same lines as those issued by the CIS to the Builders' Guilds in the Manchester area. The Irish Wholesale Agricultural Society agreed to associate themselves with the Builders' Guild in

[1] Branko Pribicevic, *The Shop Stewards' Movement and Workers Control 1910–1922* (1959), pp.9, 10.
See also S. T. Glass, *The Responsible Society: The Ideas of Guild Socialism* (1966).

Ireland, provided that future contracts would be based on the form of contract used by the Manchester Guilds, but the CIS would not enter into bonds or contracts between builders' guilds and other bodies, apart from public bodies and local authorities; for instance the CIS would not enter into a bond between the National Building Guild and the Nottingham and Burslem Co-operative societies in July: " We adhere to our previous decision to act only in connection with work for public bodies or local authorities." In October, 1921, a request was received from the Scottish region of the National Builders' Guild to grant a bond in connection with a contract with Dunfermline Town Council. The Manchester Committee of the National Building Guild contracted to construct 50 houses for Manchester Corporation in 1922, for which the CIS issued a covering bond. In all, several thousand houses were built by the guilds at lower prices than private contractors could tender. Ambitious plans for transforming the whole industry into a self-governing community were laid but soon came to grief. The short-lived success of the Building Guild Movement was due to the enormous demand for houses immediately after the war, and the favourable credit terms offered by the local authorities. When, in 1922, the Government radically restricted loans for housing, the guilds, without their own financial resources, quickly ran into difficulties.[1] Trade slump and Government policy, which was not fully in support of the guilds, also the weak organisation of the guilds themselves, hastened the process of disintegration. By the end of 1922, practically all of them had collapsed. An official receiver was appointed by the Court of Chancery in November, 1922; by that time the CIS had issued 14 contract guarantee bonds for a total of £282,000. Of the total amount, £210,000 had been reinsured, leaving a net retention of £72,000. (It has not been possible to trace the actual loss, if any, borne by the CIS.)

(v) *Valuation, New Business Problems, and the Parmoor Report*

Early in 1915, it was agreed to pay dividend on all classes of non-life insurance effected by Co-operative societies through their own account and not merely on fire and fidelity business. The practice of paying a uniform dividend year by year was to be abandoned, and any divisible surplus in the fire or general account was to be related to the previous years' business.

A quinquennial valuation of the Life Department was made at the

[1] Bribicevic, op. cit., p.10.

end of 1915. It was agreed that, in view of unsettled conditions arising out of the war, the surplus was to be carried to a suspense account, to be subsequently applied as the CIS Committee thought fit, and that interim bonuses were to be paid on all participating policies becoming claims during the five-yearly period 1916–1920.

Ten-year endowment assurance without medical examination was introduced in 1915 on lives not exceeding fifty years of age at entry with a limit of £100 on each policy, and on specially selected younger lives of up to £200.

The expense ratio for ordinary life assurance was fixed at 12 per cent from 1917 (this followed the practice of other offices). Life assurance progressed favourably during the latter years of the war. In 1917, 1,884 policies had been issued for a sum assured of £161,915. By 1919, there were 11,953 policies issued for sums assured of £982,771. The favourable figures continued during the period 1918–1920. The increase in ordinary life policies in 1920 over 1918, was 6,974, but the industrial increase over the same period was 71,288. Nevertheless, 42 districts showed industrial life collections of less than £10 weekly at the beginning of 1920. The CIS expense ratio for industrial life in 1918 was 43.3 per cent — including salaries, commission and other expenses; the claims ratio for industrial life policies in 1918 was 23.28 per cent, whereas the average for other offices was 40.64 per cent. (The CIS had a higher proportion of insurance on young lives). The quinquennial valuation for the period ending 1920 was on a $3\frac{1}{2}$ per cent basis to enable the CIS to benefit from a wider margin in consequence of the abnormal mortality experience during the foregoing period — the higher valuation basis would give a wider margin for loading in view of the heavier expenses the Society had been committed to, including the late Planet business which was to be treated as Co-operative business and valued accordingly.

The question of transfer of business arose in 1920 — the General Manager reported in April that a request had been received from the Lancashire and Cheshire County Fraternal Association of Life Assurance Officials for a deputation to meet the CIS Board to discuss the question of interference and transfer of interest from various offices connected with the Association.

Interest-in-book was also debated in 1920, and it was decided that in cases where an agent desired interest in existing debit, he would be required to purchase it from the CIS at an agreed figure. An agent with an interest-in-book was not easily persuaded to transfer himself and his business to another office, and he was naturally keener on obtaining new business and in preventing transfers and unavoidable lapses. The General Manager also contended that the purchaser pays for a connection which the seller has built up, and that this interest would not be injurious either to the CIS or its policyholders; indeed he was certain the rate of progress of the CIS would thereby be accelerated. The matter of interest-in-book had to some extent been brought to a head by the problem of transfer of business. In consequence of removal, it was frequently found necessary to transfer business from an agent who possessed interest-in-book, as an ex-Planet man, to one who had not been granted that right, with the result that the CIS was asked to purchase the interest. Refusal had caused much friction and unrest amongst the agents. Safeguards were adopted, viz: that a nominee for interest-in-book should be subject to the approval of the CIS Committee; an agent was not to be deprived of the right of nomination except for wilful dishonesty; an agent on resigning was to have the right to nominate any person as his successor subject to Committee approval; an agent was not to be allowed to acquire interest-in-book for the first 12 months of his agency. With regard to applications received from agents for the purchase of a portion of the industrial debit held by the CIS, it was agreed that the price was not to be less than 10 times the annual amount of debit. A deputation was received representing ex-Planet agents, who demanded that interest-in-book should be granted from the date of the acquisition of the Planet Society, instead of from 30 June, 1920. At that time, the CIS system of decreasing wage payment to agents took about $2\frac{1}{2}$ years to work out, whereas other offices usually paid fixed wages for say the first six months.

CIS agents in certain districts in 1920 were facing difficulties in obtaining business because of competition from other offices. The matter was referred to the Actuary, who reported against giving special terms to certain policyholders. However, he did feel that it was opportune to consider increasing the benefits paid under infants' policies — the benefits were raised from June, 1920. The existing rule of retaining as much business on lives aged 50 and under as on lives over 50 was retained, but from August, 1920, there was a reduction in benefits on older lives from age 55 and upwards, to enable some compensation to be made for the adverse mortality experience — about one-third of the industrial policies on the CIS books were on lives over 50 in 1920.

The national coal strike was causing arrears in industrial assurance premiums by March, 1920, so much so that it was recommended to extend the weekly premium lapse notices to policyholders with 13 weeks in arrears, and the monthly premium notices to four months in arrears. The Life Manager reported in October, 1920, that "if the coal strike persists it is likely to have a serious effect on the influx of new business in many districts." Unemployment mounted during the winter of 1920–21, and a large number of requests were received for extension of time granted for payment of premiums. It was agreed in April, 1921, that in genuine cases the period of arrears on industrial life policies could be extended for a further four weeks before issuing lapse notices. The CIS was adversely affected because the longer the period allowed for payment of premiums, the greater would be the number of cases in which healthy people would cease to pay, and the unhealthy would either pay or let their representatives pay, thereby causing selection against the CIS. The Actuary recommended that the negligible business from the special section life policies should be discontinued. The amount of such business being introduced was very small, and it was expensive, as each policy had to have individual attention each time a premium became payable. A PAYE system of ordinary life premiums was suggested by chief office staff in 1920, but the proposal was not approved.

Shortly after H. Cox was appointed Actuary, the Parmoor Committee on Industrial Assurance (set up in 1919) received evidence.[1] The investigation was mainly concerned with surrender values, free paid-up policies, consent to transfer, and related matters. The Committee recommended that payment to agents of procuration fees for new business should be prohibited, and there should be a minimum weekly wage based on a fixed collection per week, with a commission on all sums collected above that amount. The CIS Actuary considered that the recommendation would be disastrous to the Society, in view of the small debits of CIS agents. This recommendation was not adopted but other recommendations of the Parmoor Committee were incorporated in an Industrial Assurance Bill, Clause 4 of which stated that proposals were contained in the Bill for expenses in the industrial section of insurance offices to be limited to 40 per cent of *weekly* premiums, and 25 per cent of other industrial premiums. The CIS expense ratio for industrial assurance was not reduced below 40 per cent until 1925. In 1920, 30 per cent had been reserved from future premium income for expenses; the excess expenses were met (by 1925) from excess interest, profits on mortality experience, and allowances for new business.

[1] Lord Parmoor was a brother-in-law of Beatrice Webb.

The CIS thought that the provision of free paid-up policies and surrender values should be made operative immediately, and not have to wait five years as stipulated under the Industrial Assurance Bill. A further point of issue was that Clause 1 in the Bill did not appear to make any provision for industrial assurance business being carried out by a Society such as the CIS which was registered under the Industrial and Provident Societies Acts. The CIS was advised that its business would have to be conducted in accordance with the impending legislation and the provisions of the 1909 Assurance Companies Act; but late in 1921, the Government agreed that Industrial and Provident Societies had been inadvertently omitted from the new Bill and they would need to be included. The " limitation of expenses " clause was also amended so as to be operative from the financial year ending 1925 — the CIS had suggested that insufficient time was being allowed to bring this clause into operation, and had indeed suggested that the date should be 1925.

A. V. Alexander[1], then Secretary to the Parliamentary Committee of Co-operative Congress, reported that the Bill had passed the committee stage of the House of Lords, and would come up on the report stage on 1 March, 1923. He stated that as certain amendments tabled by Lord Parmoor had not been moved, the main fight would take place in the House of Commons. The General Manager of the CIS discussed the provisions of the new Bill with A. V. Alexander. Consideration of its clauses showed that practically all the recommendations of the CIS were incorporated, with the exception of the conditions under which individual policy transfers could take place between offices. The General Manager also saw the Chief Registrar of Friendly Societies concerning attestation of transfers, and the Government subsequently accepted the suggestion from the CIS concerning consent to notice of transfer that witnessing by a Justice of the Peace was not

[1] *Lord Alexander, 1885–1965*
    Created Viscount Alexander of Hillsborough in 1950, and received an Earldom in January, 1963. Son of a Somerset artisan and was born at Weston-super-Mare, 1885. In 1922 entered Parliament as Co-operative Party Member for Hillsborough division of Sheffield. His first office in MacDonald's Government of 1924, was Parliamentary Secretary to the Board of Trade. When MacDonald formed his second Government in 1929, A. V. Alexander was appointed to the Admiralty. On the formation of the war coalition Government and again in 1945, A. V. Alexander was first Lord of the Admiralty. Later, he was a member of a Cabinet mission (including Lord Pethwick-Lawrence and Sir Stafford Cripps) sent to resolve the constitutional deadlock in India. Soon after Alexander's return from India, Attlee created a Ministry of Defence, and Alexander became its first Minister. In 1950, A. V. Alexander was transferred to the House of Lords and the Chancellorship of the Duchy of Lancaster. In 1955, he became leader of the Labour Peers in the House. Lord Alexander died in January, 1965.

necessary. A. V. Alexander was largely responsible for lobbying the CIS case and getting the clause altered.

The Industrial Assurance Act of 1923 gave the Chief Registrar of Friendly Societies responsibility and supervision of all industrial assurance companies, and in this capacity he was to be known as the Industrial Assurance Commissioner. It was obligatory under the Act for all *bona fide* companies to deposit £20,000 in trustee securities with the Paymaster-General. The Act also strengthened the basis of valuation of life funds, and provided for the issue of free paid-up policies and the granting of surrender values, but the Act did not incorporate the "limitation of expenses" clause included in the Bill. The Assurance Companies Act of 1909 had restricted family insurance to a sum to provide funeral expenses of parent, grandparent, brother or sister, but the Act was abused by people who took out "own-life" policies, although they did not pay the premiums. Because the insured in these cases had then nominated or assigned the policy to the person who paid the premium, the 1923 Act stipulated that premiums on "own-life" policies were required to be paid by the proposer.

Life premium income for 1920 exceeded £1m, and was 50 per cent greater than 1919, and 150 per cent greater than 1918; the average sum assured had risen from £12 to £18 on each policy on industrial life, and from £70 to £90 on ordinary life. In July, 1921, the limit on whole life assurance was increased from £3,000 to £5,000 in selected cases who could pass a first-class medical. From October, 1921, the CIS had agreed to issue all industrial weekly premium policies with immediate full benefit. The Actuary recommended the introduction of a £2 per cent guaranteed bonus table in ordinary life, as the rate of bonus under the "with profits" and deferred tables had not been maintained. (Tables with a guaranteed bonus were being introduced by many offices and were thought likely to become popular in view of general bonus reduction.)

A fire reinsurance treaty had been entered into with a firm of Lloyd's brokers in 1910, but the CIS soon wished to retain much larger amounts, and a new treaty had been drawn up in December, 1913, limiting their reinsurers' acceptance to three times the CIS amount and allowing a commission of 20 per cent. The treaty expired in September, 1918. The General Manager reported in 1921 that the experience in connection with Co-operative fire risks had been adverse. The average losses based over the previous 10 years had been 75 per cent and, excluding sprinklered risks, had amounted to 82 per cent of premium income. In one year, losses on Co-operative stores had been equivalent to 102 per cent of premiums.

In 1921, it was agreed to provide a motor car for use by senior staff from CIS Chief Office. During 1920, £600 had been spent on railway fares within the Manchester region, which then included 38 district offices. The question was raised whether the CIS had on occasions placed the CWS Motor Department in competition with outside firms for motor repairs, but the CIS contended that where repairs had been dealt with by outside firms, the CWS had not been able to undertake the work involved.

A considerable amount of the business coming the way of the CIS during this period was abetted by advertising — " leaflets and posters which we are now issuing appealing to Co-operators, who have run into arrears with other companies and societies, to transfer their business to us, should have a very considerable effect if an agent is enterprising." (July, 1921.)

In the summer of 1921, a dispute, which arose over dismissal of certain district office staff, later led to strike action by district managers, agents and district office clerks. Many CIS districts remained loyal. The General Manager met a deputation of district managers and agents and resolved the cases of three district managers who had been given notice, with the result that one of the district managers concerned was to continue to hold his position until the end of the year when the matter would be reviewed.

Further increases of limits for policies without medical examination were made from 1922 — whole life assurance under age 50, a limit of £200, and over 50, £100; with the industrial and special sections for ages exceeding 50, the limit was raised to £75. During 1921, there was a reduction in the number of new ordinary life policies compared with 1920, doubtlessly due to the coal strike, the agents' strike, and the depressed state of trade.

Early in 1922, the CIS took over a small collecting society — The British Metal Trades and General Assurance Collecting Society, established in 1913. The premium income for 1921 was merely £6,000, but the bulk of the business was ordinary life. There were two full-time agents and two clerks. Both full-time agents were working in Wales, where the CIS was not then represented.

Ordinary life business was still declining in the early part of 1922. The total sum assured in force under ordinary life policies was £4m, although, as the Life Manager pointed out, there were 4 million Co-operators. The CIS had nearly 1,000 full-time agents, largely as a result of taking over the Planet, and many more part-time agents, whereas as recently as 1917 there had been only 100 full-time agents. Admittedly the economic climate was bleak, and unemployment was still heavy during 1922, but despite this situation, new branch offices were to be opened at Bristol and Southampton (Plymouth had been opened in 1919) and James Darroch was about to be transferred from Glasgow to take over the management of the London branch, otherwise in view of the lack of funds for development purposes, a general policy of consolidation and closing of unprogressive districts was followed during 1922. From July, 1922, the ordinary life and the small special section were amalgamated. Although there had been a heavy acquisition of new business in the industrial section, an equivalent increase in collections had not followed. The Actuary reported, at the end of 1922, that there would have to be a reduction in ordinary life bonuses. The burden of expenditure had grown during 1919-20 through increased activity in the procuration of new business, and the CIS therefore decided to pay a smaller rate of bonus to place funds in a more stable position. Efforts to encourage agents to introduce more ordinary life business had been made, but the emphasis had been confined to districts mainly under chief office supervision. The agents concerned had received a certain amount of technical instruction, and the Life Manager recommended that similar meetings ought to be held in other districts.

F. Austen Williams, the assistant secretary of the CIS, retired at the end of 1922.[1] On his retirement, he reminisced that when he joined the CIS there were few individual agents, as the Society had relied mainly on local Co-operative store agencies.

The CIS was successful, at the end of 1922, in obtaining from the Royal Arsenal Co-operative Society the whole of their fire insurance business, except that portion which had to be placed with outside companies owing to certain conditions in leases. The total sum assured concerned was £822,000.

Although few new CIS offices had been opened, the full-time agency staff was increased during 1922 by nearly 500, and the General Manager thought that the time had arrived when recruitment of agents should cease. The National Amalgamated Union of Life Assurance Workers,

[1] F. Austen Williams had joined the CIC in 1886 as superintendent of agents, having resigned as a CWS director. He had previously been a spare-time CIC agent at Reading from 1878.

which included many of the agents in other offices, had protested against the action of CIS agents taking business away from fellow trade-unionists, and decided to ask all their members to refrain from trading with Co-operative societies. NUDAW pressed the CIS to cease employing part-time agents, but the management argued that this was a counsel of perfection which was not possible to achieve — the existing ratio of full-time to part-time CIS agents at the time was about 40 per cent.

Administrative duties were becoming more strictly delineated in 1922. The Actuary was to be consulted on all matters of general policy of the Life Department — the valuation of 1922 was the first one to be completed solely by members of the CIS staff. The title of Life Manager was to be dispensed with, and three sections created, viz: Industrial Life, Ordinary Life Renewals and Accounts, Collective Life and Claims. The CIS Chief and Branch Offices Managers' Association wrote to the General Manager in August, 1922, and he replied that under no consideration was the CIS prepared to entertain any scheme of payment by results to the inside staff.

Complaints were received from Hartlepools Co-operative Society regarding the level of rates for plate glass insurance quoted by the CIS. The General Manager reported that the experience of plate glass insurance had been far from favourable, and it was due to this fact that for many years the CIS had declined to undertake such business, and had recommended Co-operative societies to form their own insurance funds.

The Agency Manager reported, in mid-1923, in connection with industrial assurance arrears: " If a line is drawn from Humber to Bristol Channel, it will be found that East and South of that line the claim rate is lower, collections higher and steadier than on the North and West of the line." There had been, over the years 1919 to 1923, a 637 per cent increase in industrial premiums, compared with a 45 per cent increase in ordinary life premiums — leading to an increase in premium income in 1924, which was greater than the progress of the Society during its first 50 years of existence, up to the taking-over of the Planet.

In 1924, the Actuary recommended a revision of all industrial life tables, with the withdrawal of some that were not suitable. The aim was to simplify business, and thereby reduce expense, and the Actuary also suggested that all policies in the industrial life branch should be declared as " with profits." At the end of 1925, a request was received for the granting of loans, within the cash surrender value, to holders of industrial policies. The loans were to be applied to reduce the arrears which had accrued owing to unemployment. During the late 1920s, the CIS, in exceptional cases, granted such loans, but in 1930, the Industrial Assurance Commissioner stated that such policies could not be held as security, and so no further applications were entertained.

In January, 1923, 13 per cent of trade union members in the country as a whole were unemployed. In the corresponding month of 1922, the figure had been as high as 16.8 per cent. The average annual unemployment for all workers in 1920 had been 2.9 per cent; it rose to 6.9 per cent in 1921, and by June, 1923, 1¼ million were unemployed, of whom 935,000 were men. The situation called for heroic measures, but some of the language used at CIS chief office was histrionic — " The capitalist-owned offices, with the monopolists and trusts, walk hand-in-hand grinding the bodies of the people . . ." (*CIS Review*, Volume 1, 1922).[1] Unemployment and insecurity did not create good insurance business prospects, and the CIS agents were warned in 1923 not to insure too high a proportion of hazardous lives: i.e., general labourers.

(vi) *Ireland*

Although Dublin office had been opened in 1912, no life business had been undertaken, and during the early 1920s there were requests from Belfast that the CIS should offer industrial life assurance business in Northern Ireland. The Ulster Agricultural Organisation Society, which was the equivalent of the Irish Agricultural Organisation Society in Eire, asked for similar arrangements for general insurance to those already in operation with the Southern body, whereby the CIS allowed the IAOS an overriding commission of 2½ per cent, provided they used all their efforts to induce affiliated societies to place insurance with the CIS. By 1923, it was reported that the CIS was exercising every care in the selection of risks in Ireland, and in all cases the policies bore a clause excluding liability in respect of claims due to malicious damage or arising from riot or civil commotion. Premium income had increased in 1920, largely due to increase in property values. Surprisingly, the unsettled nature of conditions in Southern Ireland from 1920 did not severely damage any class of insurance business — the greatest difficulty facing the CIS was the heavy cost of travelling, as business was scattered throughout Ireland.

[1] The *CIS Review*, a quarterly magazine for outdoor staff of the CIS, was launched in March, 1922.

The Nation at War, 1914

J. P. Jones

Nevertheless in a country torn by civil strife it is not surprising that the CIS was involved in settling claims for damage to property. For instance, early in 1923, the residence at Kilteragh of Sir Horace Plunkett, the Irish Co-operator, was partly blown up by mine and the assessors informed the insured that no claim could be made under the CIS fire policy. The Clare Co-operative Society made a claim for £500 under a fidelity policy in August, 1923; in addition to a cash deficiency, it appeared that there had been a considerable shortage of stock, and it was suspected that the Manager had been intimidated and compelled to supply goods "to irregular camp situated near to store."

The new Belfast office was opened in August, 1924, under super-vision of Dublin Branch. Within several years, the business of the Belfast office had grown sufficiently for it to be created a full Branch.

An interview held with officials of the Ministry of Industry and Com-merce in Dublin in May, 1925, with a view to the CIS undertaking life business in Southern Ireland, confirmed that a deposit of £20,000 was required from each insurance company or society not domiciled in Eire. The CIS, along with other offices, raised no objection to this requirement, but opposed the proposal that external companies should deposit securities to cover the actuarial value of life policies in Ireland. In 1928, the CIS complied, and deposited the requisite £20,000 of securities with the Accountant-General, Supreme Court of Judicature, Dublin Castle, to enable the conduct of life assurance business. Difficulties were also being faced with motor insurance business in Eire. Taxation was levied on new motor vehicle parts; there were limited facilities for repair work; and there was difficulty an supervision and inspection.[1] Fire business was also in difficulties, is generally speaking, districts outside towns were not equipped with fire brigades, and main water supplies were inadequate. The CIS committee minuted in October, 1928:

> " The establishment of a purely Irish organisation founded on
> Co-operative principles has been mentioned to our representa-
> tives, and the disposal of our business in the Free State at a
> reasonable figure to such an organisation might well prove the
> solution to what may prove to become a difficult problem."

[1] In 1928, the CIS secured the employers' liability insurance for the Irish Ford Motor Company works at Cork. The Ford plant was set up at Cork in 1917. It was the site of the first Ford tractor production plant in Europe. Henry Ford had suggested that Cork would be a good location for his main manufacturing centre in Europe. (The Manchester assembly plant at Trafford Park, opened as early as 1911, was always regarded as a temporary site.)
See M. Wilkins and F. E. Hill, *American Business Abroad: Ford on Six Continents* (Detroit 1964).

A CIS district agent for the Isle of Man was appointed in June, 1925, with the proviso that when the industrial debit reached a certain amount, he would be raised to the status of district manager.

The CIS was not prepared during the early 1920s to go further afield than the British Isles.

(vii) *The Cambridge Stamp Scheme*

The CIS management still showed prejudice against industrial assurance even after the first world war and the take-over of the Planet. Some of the CIS directors had not yet accepted the fact that despite the need for life assurance in every home, it was very rarely sought, and had almost invariably to be sold. They felt sure, as had their predecessors a generation earlier, that Co-operators were a race apart, and would take advantage of their membership of a retail society to by-pass collection of premiums by a full-time agent. In 1922, with this in mind, they established what became known as the Cambridge stamp scheme to reduce the cost of industrial assurance. The CIS Committee selected the Cambridge district for this pilot scheme, whereby policyholders could purchase stamps at the Co-operative branch stores, and hand in their stamp books every quarter, so that the stamps could be credited to their accounts as members of the local retail society. In September, 1923, the General Manager reported that the scheme had been in operation for eighteen months, and as far as administration was concerned had presented no difficulties, but the result of the eighteen months' hard work was an industrial debit of only £17. He ventured that there was not much likelihood of any further increase of business under the stamp scheme, as the CIS local representative had canvassed thoroughly every street in Cambridge, and had found that many people would not join the CIS scheme because they were unwilling to purchase their stamps at the local co-operative store, and preferred to pay their insurance premiums to an agent who called at the door. Further, it was found that under the scheme, owing to the books being collected once a quarter only, the rate of lapses was somewhat heavy; there was also great difficulty ensuring that the stamp books were handed in regularly. The result of the experiment was that the total value of stamps purchased was expended in salaries, commissions and payment of dividend to the policyholders. Canvassing for further members was discontinued, and existing members were allowed to retain their contracts and purchase their stamps at the local store. The scheme soon succumbed because of its inherent deficiences and idealistic conceptions of human nature (as did the Post Office life assurance scheme, somewhat later in 1928, after many years of indifferent success.) An extant premium receipt book of the Cambridge stamp scheme includes the following message: " Every penny paid to the CIS is worth 2d. to the Co-operative Movement. It is a penny we have secured for own use and a penny diverted from being used against us." And at the foot of one of the blank pages to which stamps were to be affixed is the message — " Stamp assurance means maximum benefits at a minimum cost."

(viii) *Mortgages and House Purchase*

In 1922, the outdoor staff of the CIS pressed for the introduction of a house purchase prospectus, as it was felt that this would lead to a large influx of new life and fire business. The General Manager also considered the question of combining life assurance with house purchase. The Actuary supported the preparation of a house purchase prospectus, because he felt that future advances would be demanded in a period " when house property valuations would be more stabilised in comparison to the immediate post-war period." At the time there were several hundred CIS mortgage loans totalling over £70,000, but the great majority of the loans had been taken out at the low rate of interest prevailing before the first world war, and it was agreed that future loans would bear a rate of interest of 5 per cent and policies to be issued under the proposed house purchase scheme would be eligible for an advance of up to 75 per cent of the certified value of the property concerned.

The House Purchase Scheme was introduced on 11 April, 1923. The original terms were that interest should be 5 per cent payable half-yearly with a maximum term of 25 years and maturity of the loan before the policyholder attained the age of 65. A full year's premium on each insurance policy involved was to be paid before a mortgage advance could be made. The maximum loan was to be £1,000, and loans were restricted to the purchase of dwelling houses for owner-occupation. In all cases, the property had to be insured with the Society against fire. By the end of 1923, 294 advances involving £110,516, with an average advance of £375 had been made. The total mortgages at that date, including those under the old and new scheme, were 633, comprised a total sum of £182,000. Early in 1924, the limit of advance under the scheme was increased from £1,000 to £2,000. There was an unlimited field for house purchase business — so much so that the amount of money invested under the scheme was thought to be excessive by the end of 1924, and it was therefore suggested that there should be a withdrawal of the scheme for loans on houses in course of erection. By the end of 1926, there were 4,405 mortgages totalling £1,659,000 on the books. In April, 1926, it had been agreed to continue to advance money under the scheme until the total amount reached a limit of £2¼m., and although the agreed limit was far in excess of the business undertaken, the house purchase scheme was temporarily suspended at the end of 1926, except for a certain class of loan to deferred policyholders.[1] The Actuary was concerned in the following year that house property values were falling. The scheme then remained in abeyance during 1927 and 1928, as the proportion of funds invested in house purchase property was still considered too high in relation to the Society's total funds. It was not until August, 1929, that the scheme was re-opened, with a maximum advance of two-thirds of " a conservative valuation" but in no circumstances were the amounts of mortgages to exceed £700. The valuations were to be made by CWS architects and the rate of interest was to be 5½ per cent. No loans were to be entertained on houses valued less than £400, nor were there to be loans for houses in areas " where industrial distress likely." Subsequently, the maximum loan was raised to 75 per cent of valuation in June, 1930, with a limit of £750.

The amount of life assurance business accruing under the re-opened house purchase scheme was not as great as had been anticipated. The CPBS, in January, 1931, agreed to supply the CIS with a list of mortgages which had been redeemed each month. This information was passed on to CIS district offices, to enable agents to secure continuance of fire insurance, and to canvass additional life and accident cover for householders. Between April, 1923, and June, 1931, 8,800 loans were granted in the house purchase scheme, amounting to a total of £3.2m. A request was received from the CPBS that the CIS should quote terms for a guarantee in respect of sums advanced on mortgage in excess of 75 per cent. (The CPBS had issued guarantee cover since 1925, but they had charged borrowers a fee instead of obtaining the guarantee from an insurance company.) The CPBS thought that in the economic climate prevailing in 1931, there would not

---

[1] It was held at the time that the withdrawal of the scheme in 1926 adversely affected ordinary branch business and that the scheme was withdrawn with inadequate notice.

be any appreciable reduction in house values — it was more likely that the value of property would rise due to the fact that building operations would probably be slowed down. The CIS entered into a mortgage guarantee scheme from 1932, because it thought it would lead to a further influx of ordinary life business. Later in 1932, the CIS was approached by a Co-operative society to provide guarantees on similar lines to those granted under the existing house purchase scheme with the CPBS. Guarantee policies were subsequently issued to Enfield Highway, Scunthorpe, and South Surburban Co-operative societies, and to the Hearts of Oak Benefit Society, in connection with private dwelling houses. CIS officials undertook property valuations from 1933, but in 1935, as CIS resources were fully utilized, it was recommended that surveys should be made by qualified valuers conversant with local conditions. It was pointed out that the Halifax Building Society had all its properties professionally valued. In the autumn of 1934, largely as a result of the tendency for the interest yield on investments to continue to fall, it was decided to lend at 5 per cent on the security of house property without life assurance, and up to 75 per cent of purchase price or valuation, but no action was taken due to the difficulty of deciding a suitable scale of remuneration for full-time agency staff. It was argued that to succeed, the CIS would have to advance up to 90 per cent and would have to sacrifice its existing connection with CPBS. It was suggested in April, 1935, that the CIS should establish its own building society, but it was pointed out that the formation of a building society would not benefit the CIS, as house purchase business already formed one-third of the ordinary life premium income, and investment for funds would be diverted to the building society. It was also possible that the erection of dwelling house property had reached its peak. Moreover, the intended building society would be in direct competition with the CPBS; a better policy would be to extend the existing house purchase scheme.

On the outbreak of war in September, 1939, the issue of immediate and deferred house purchase policies was stopped, but in December, 1939, the deferred house purchase scheme was re-opened, and in April, 1940, the immediate house purchase scheme was re-introduced.

In 1943, the General Manager considered that the house purchase scheme should be developed as widely as possible at the end of the war to maintain a reasonably high average rate of investment income.

When the CIS launched the house purchase scheme in 1923, its purpose had been two-fold — to develop the ordinary life business, and to offer policyholders the means whereby an insurance policy could be accepted as collateral security for a loan on house property. The yield was not at that time a pressing problem, but the position 20 years later was reversed. The House Purchase interest rate throughout the major period of the war was 5 per cent, and it was not until February, 1944, that interest was reduced to 4½ per cent. The maximum amount of loan at the beginning of 1940, had been £750; by 1944, it was £1,500. In the following year, interest was further reduced to 4 per cent, and valuations were to be 150 per cent of the "1939 value." In 1946, the maximum loan was again increased to £2,000, and 100 per cent loans could be made to sitting tenants. Interest rates and loan limits increased *pari passu* during the 1950s and 1960s. (The basis of "1939 valuation" was dispensed with from 1952.)

(ix) *Motor Business*

It has been said that the greatest single impetus to insurance was the internal combustion engine. Before 1914, motor premium income of the British offices was not published, but by 1931 (when the Board of Trade first separated motor insurance statistics from other departments) the annual premiums were £32m. By 1950, motor insurance had grown at such a pace that it could be regarded as a serious competitor to fire insurance in terms of premium income.

The first moves to offer specific insurances for the benefit of motorists took place in the closing years of the 19th century when the law of 1865, which required that every road locomotive must not exceed a speed of

4 m.p.h., and must be preceded at 100 yards by a man on foot carrying a red flag, was finally repealed. The new limit established by the Highways Act in 1896, was stepped up to 14 m.p.h., and the Motor Car Act of 1903, increased the speed limit to 20 m.p.h., but empowered local authorities to impose a limit of 10 m.p.h. within certain areas. It was natural that various forms of motor insurance should follow in the wake of the motorists' new-found freedoms, and in 1903, the Car and General Insurance Company was established for the sole purpose of underwriting motor business. The methods of rating were various, but pioneers in this field, among them Lloyd's of London and the Red Cross Company, soon established a principle of charging comprehensive premium rates on a basis of horse-power and value of the vehicle. By 1913, motor insurance business had become sufficiently well-established to be put on a tariff basis and various ratings standardized.

In the years immediately after the first world war, there was a rapid growth in motor insurance business conducted in the Accident Department of the CIS. The annual premium income reached £80,000 by 1922, and the Accident Manager recommended that negotiations be entered into for reinsurance arrangements. The Co-operative Wholesale Society manufactured " Bell " motor cars and lorries, and a motor cycle with the brand-name " Federation "— a 1922 CIS prospectus for insurance of the CWS-manufactured Federation motor cycles is extant.[1] The CIS followed the tariff offices in reducing premiums for commercial vehicles and motor charabanc insurance from the beginning of 1924. Advertisements were inserted in the motor press, and resulted in so much direct business that the agency commission saved more than covered the cost of the publicity.

Such was the growth of business that in 1924, the General Manager proposed that motor insurance should be run as an entirely separate department. This left workmen's compensation, burglary, fidelity, plate glass, livestock, and other incidental insurances to form the basis of a separate Accident Department; but the premium income achieved in motor business was more than equal to that of the other classes combined. In January, 1925, following the tariff offices, CIS rates for

[1] " I remember seeing ' Bell ' motor cars and motor lorries in Manchester in the mid-twenties. Very few of them were made. I think the only cars produced were used by the CWS themselves, and I think a few lorries were bought by local retail societies. They were made in Manchester by a small firm which was taken over by the CWS. The CWS bicycles and motor cycles were, I believe, produced by an entirely separate organisation in the Midlands."
Letter, G. L. Bateson, Deputy Manager, Motor Department, 14 July, 1965.

private vehicles were reduced, and the first special rates for the famous "Model T" Ford cars were agreed. (This interesting situation arose because the horse-power of that particular model (22.4 h.p.) was so high in relation to the value of the car that the premium would have been excessive.) In spite of the General Strike and chronic unemployment in 1926, motor business continued to flourish, stimulated to some extent by low premium rates, preferential commissions, and more directly by the rapidly increasing volume of vehicles on the road. Cars were becoming more sophisticated in design, so that the General Manager could report: "Up to two or three years ago a fairly large percentage of cars were laid up during the winter, but with the great improvement in the "all weather" protection afforded by modern cars, use in winter is undoubtedly increasing . . . "

This trend had an unfavourable influence on claims ratios and the new department was also forced to take note of the fact that the courts were awarding greater damages, a feature that was to continue until the present day.

W. Hesford was appointed Motor Manager from January, 1927, and a newly-created post of motor engineer for examining claims was advertised during that year and drew 460 applications. It was also during this period that the CIS "no claims bonus" system was revised on a cumulative basis, in preference to the previous flat rate deduction of 10 per cent.

By 1928, the CIS was noting, in conjunction with the tariff offices, that claims in connection with first-year drivers were exceptionally heavy. In the London area the claims ratio on CIS policies for 1928 was 90 per cent, and a special London area rating was put into effect in 1929, the first time this practice had been adopted for private motor insurance. In the interim, it was considered necessary to refuse motor or motor cycle proposals from anyone under 21 years of age in the London area whilst rates were being suitably revised; an action which earned a mild rebuke from the Ministry of Transport — the revision had been done in accord with several other offices, but the Ministry felt the matter should be "reconsidered." Clearly, some of the accidents concerned could be attributed to the increased performance of cars and to the increasing number of ageing vehicles.

By 1930, the premium income in the Society's motor department exceeded £500,000. Motor business of Co-operative societies was found to be profitable, and from 1930, there was a reduction in premium rates for such business.

Motor transport could also help in conducting insurance business. One of the early CWS Bell motor cars had been in use by CIS officials until 1923, when it had travelled more than 50,000 miles, and " cannot now be relied upon as it is frequently breaking down." The car was replaced, and a minute of October, 1927, almost repeated the request made four years previously: " The Manager reported this car purchased in 1923, is constantly breaking down. Resolved we dispose of car and purchase 12 h.p. Austin for £350." Nevertheless, in retrospect, it could be claimed that the Society had its money's worth. Obviously, the branch offices of the CIS would also benefit from motor transport — a minute of November, 1923, stated: " Recommend a light two-seater at a cost not exceeding £200 each be obtained for each branch." The request was still being made in June, 1924, and again in July, 1926. Cardiff Branch anticipated general approval, and a Morris Oxford was delivered there in June, 1926.

A Labour Government brought in the first Road Traffic Act in 1930. As motor insurance was not dealt with under the insurance legislation of 1909, it was legally possible for *anyone* to underwrite motor insurance. (Theoretically, the owner of one motor cycle could be insured by the owner of another cycle, and as a *quid pro quo* could provide the other party with an accommodation policy.) The new Act endorsed the system of reliance on statutory deposits (£15,000) which was now applied to motor insurance business. The level of deposit proved to be patently inadequate.

Although the Road Traffic Act of 1930 required compulsory Third Party insurance (motor cycle policies were required to include third party liability under the Road Traffic Act of 1934), the increase of 66 per cent in the number of CIS policies issued in 1931 did not match the increase in premium income, which rose by a mere £42,515 from £566,990 to £609,505 in 1930. Competition between offices was fierce, and many car owners, attempting economies, contented themselves with the minimum legal cover. In 1932, many policies lapsed owing to depression in trade, and the CIS Motor Department suffered a reduction in premium income of £50,000.

By 1936, there were 59 offices offering motor insurance in Great Britain, and the CIS was rated twelfth in terms of premium income. In the non-tariff group the Society was fourth, after the General Accident, the Zurich, and the Eagle Star.

(x) *Publicity and Investment Moves*

The General Manager reported in September, 1924, that advertising had been carried on for many years through the publications of the Co-operative Movement and also at agricultural shows (a publicity section had been established in 1921). He commented — " Apart from this, not much advertising was done."[1] By 1925, the total budgeted expenditure on press advertising had grown to the region of £7,000. For all forms of advertising during that year, £5,000 was allocated to the Motor Department, £5,000 to Fire, and £1,500 for general purposes. In 1928, the CIS took a full-page advertisement in the Daily Mail. The CIS was the first insurance office to have a Publicity Department with resources to produce its own material, without the need of an outside advertising agency.

A far-sighted part-time agent from Glasgow applied for permission to induce trade unions to take up group life assurance schemes through the CIS in January, 1923, but it was thought inopportune at the time — given the prevailing trade depression, and the meagre financial resources of the majority of trade unions. A group life assurance scheme was however introduced in 1924. It was advertised as being cheap, applicable to trade unions, clubs, and other organisations with at least 100 members in each group. Claims however were excessive, and the CIS feared that selection was being made against the Society, and so steps were taken to ensure exclusion of sub-standard lives from future groups.

Demands for the institution of a pension scheme for CIS staff were put forward from time to time. In 1921, it was decided that consideration of such a scheme should be postponed for a further period of five years. Many Co-operative societies asked for advice on the running of pension schemes at the time, and there were some personal enquiries for particulars of deferred annuity schemes. The possibility of a CIS pension scheme was again ventilated in October, 1927. A year later, in October, 1928, it was decided to introduce a pension scheme akin to that of CWS — with certain modifications.

A Life Assurance Scheme to provide for payment of the outstanding instalments under hire purchase agreements in event of the death of the purchaser was instituted from the beginning of 1925. Co-operative societies were circularised giving details and inviting them to take

[1] " My recollection of the first real attempt at advertising the CIS was by Mr. Leah prior to 1914. He spent hours making up adverts to put around matchboxes sold in Co-operative Society shops."
Letter of H. T. Fitzgerald, 8 July, 1965.

out policies, but few societies expressed any interest. In 1927, the CIS extended these arrangements to an independent hire-purchase company to cover all their contracts.

A new office in Kingsway was acquired for London Branch in 1923. The premises concerned stood on the site of what was formerly known as Clare Market, which had historical associations with Kingsway, and it was suggested that the building should be called Clare House. The property had an artesian well installed (which saved £250 yearly in water rate). In October, 1923, a letter was received from the valuation department of the London County Council intimating that the proposal to alter the existing name of West Africa House to Clare House was not considered desirable, as the property did not stand on what had been the estate of the Earl of Clare, and therefore would tend to create false history. The London Co-operative Society also wrote in December, 1924, protesting that the CIS had let the ground floor of Clare House to a retail hosier, who would necessarily be in competition with the Co-operative Movement. Despite these complaints, the name Clare House remained, and at the end of 1927 the General Electric Company (GEC) offered £70,000 to the CIS for the building. Alternative premises for the CIS at 40/42 Kingsway (designed by Sir Edwin Lutyens in 1910) were inspected,[1] and Clare House was eventually sold to the GEC for £90,750 in May, 1928.

The first moves in devising an investment policy were made in 1924. It was recommended in November, that a small investment sub-committee of two directors should be set up to consider the purchase and sale of securities, with advice from officials. (Reference has been made to the prevailing fears that the house purchase scheme was expanding so rapidly that there was a danger that it would soon absorb all invested funds of the Society.) The assets of the CIS at the end of 1923 were valued at just over £3m., and it was observed that "the problem of finding suitable investments is a very serious one." The CIS took note that other offices, during the early 1920s, had developed active investment policies with the effect that the bonuses of the offices concerned had been considerably increased. It was therefore thought necessary for the CIS to develop accordingly. Even so, the sub-committee set up was rather piecemeal, as it was considered feasible for each director to undertake a stint of service of a month or a fortnight on the investment sub-committee before making way for a

---

[1] One of the earlier tenants of 42 Kingsway was the Women's Suffrage League. A photograph in the London Museum shows suffragettes being escorted from the building on 30 April, 1913.

colleague. It was felt that the setting up of this sub-committee would be preferable to the previous arrangement, whereby investments were considered by officials, whose suggestions were then submitted to the main committee for a decision — often a time-wasting procedure. By February, 1926, the total value of investments covered by stock exchange quotation was £2.9m., of which £2.4m. represented redeemable securities, and £460,000 irredeemable. C. R. Fay, the social historian, commented at the time: " The assets of the CIS . . . are held, of course, in gilt-edged securities and are not in any way compromised by the trading fortunes of the Wholesale." Investments require constant supervision minuted the CIS Committee in March, 1926 — yet the investment of new money still remained under the supervision of a sub-committee whose activities, although deemed successful, were still restricted to monthly meetings, with no day-to-day surveillance of the market, except through reports from officials. The General Manager was asked to comment on CIS investment policy, at the same time furnishing comparisons with other companies, in the autumn of 1929. He listed recent purchases by the CIS of gilt-edged and industrial securities: Buenos Aires Great Southern Railway, Treasury Bills, and 5 per cent Conversion Loan 1944–1964. As a large part of the portfolio was gilt-edged, the rise in the bank rate in 1929 compelled the CIS to provide for heavy depreciation of most of its securities. A schedule of CIS investments held in April, 1930, included limited holdings of industrial stock, e.g., AEI (Associated Electrical Industries).

(xi)   *The General Strike*

The threat of a General Strike in 1926 induced the insurance offices to consider emergency arrangements. Sir Ernest Bain, acting on behalf of the Advisory Insurance Committee appointed by H. M Treasury, wrote to the CIS and other insurance companies, intimating that the tariff offices had agreed that, in the event of the Government deciding to carry all sabotage risks, the insurance companies would be willing to act on behalf of the Government in a similar manner to the course adopted in connection with aircraft risks during the first world war. The tariff offices had further agreed that they were prepared to extend comprehensive policies on private cars to include sabotage risks, even if the vehicles concerned were used in Government service by any licensed driver. The CIS largely complied with these suggestions. It was also decided to cover riot and civil commotion risks during the emergency. In the event, the General Strike was of such short duration (3–12 May) that the emergency measures were hardly applicable: as far as insurance was concerned, the lasting effects were arrears in industrial life premiums caused by the protracted coal strike and general economic stringency.

As early as 2 June, 1926, the continuing coal strike was seriously affecting CIS industrial life business and the earnings of some agents. Business which had fallen in arrears directly attributable to the strike was allowed to remain in force for the time being, and in cases where agents' earnings were drastically affected, a weekly advance could be made — the loans were to be free of interest, payable after the termination of the coal strike. By 26 June, collections in some mining areas were down to as low as 40 per cent, with a tendency to fall further still. The CIS agents in South Wales passed a resolution asking chief office to make up their earnings to what they were before the strike, viz: a minimum of £2 10s. In July, arrears of premiums were mounting steadily, and it was resolved that where policies were lapsed and re-entered, immediate full benefit was to be granted. This concession was to remain in force until the end of 1926, and if experience was satisfactory, arrangements were then to continue. Endowment assurance policies in arrears were to have the date of maturity extended.

In August, 1926, despite the coal strike, the volume of new business compared favourably with the corresponding period of the previous year. By December, however, arrears in the industrial life department had grown with the deepening industrial depression. The Actuary had stated, in November, that the coal dispute had affected adversely such a large number of societies that it was impossible to ignore its effect on the level of premium income of the collective life scheme for 1927. He referred to a comparable experience in 1922, when many societies had paid a considerably smaller premium than in 1921, as a result of a decline in sales during the coal dispute of that year. As many miners had not started work by March, 1927, and did not seem likely to do so for a considerable time, the CIS acceded to a request from the NUDAW that loans to agents in those areas drastically affected by unemployment should be extended. As late as April, 1927, policies could be kept in force and policyholders allowed time to pay off arrears by easy instalments. There was a large increase in the amount of surrenders in May, in both ordinary and industrial life policies. Although arrears of over £40,000 had been cancelled between November, 1926, and May, 1927, the Actuary had to report in the following October, that in order to clear accrued arrears, it had been decided to continue the special concessions. The scheme had been prematurely withdrawn at the end of June, 1927, despite the fact that considerable arrears still existed in some areas.

(xii) New Prospects

The question of undertaking marine insurance arose after an application was received for a part-time agency from the All-Russian Co-operative Organisation Society regarding insurance of goods at Russian and Continental ports. The CIS agreed to this proposal, but only for goods stored awaiting shipment, and not for insurance of property or life within Russia in view of the very unfavourable conditions prevailing at the time (the summer of 1923). Moreover, it was noted that insurance in Russia was a State monopoly, and English firms trading with the Russian company concerned were not prepared to accept the cover issued. It would therefore have been necessary to have made arrangements with Gostrakh, the national insurance organisation in Russia. Not until 1933 was marine insurance on an agency basis undertaken by the CIS with a view to building up an account to justify the establishment of a Marine Section.[1] (See page 217.)

In 1926, branch managers were pressing to introduce loss of profits insurance, which was eventually offered from the end of 1930. Few enquiries for this type of cover had been received from Co-operative societies, but the CIS had lost several sound non-Co-operative fire insurance proposals because it had declined to entertain profits risk.

The *Daily Herald* invited the CIS to cover an accident insurance coupon scheme for the benefit of its readers. The initial offer was declined by the CIS, but in 1929, the matter of raising finance for the development of the *Daily Herald*, in the event of the Labour Party coming into power, was raised. In the same year, coupon insurance was again discussed. General opinion amongst insurance offices at the time was that coupon business had resulted in heavy losses, and the majority of insurance companies undertaking it had treated such losses as advertising expenses. Negotiations between the CIS and the *Daily*

---

[1] In 1936 the CIS joined the Life Assurance Association in agreeing to insure persons engaged in civil aviation. Aviation insurance in Britain began about 1911. Aeroplanes were then uninsurable, but owners had been using Lloyd's for third party insurance. There were no aerodromes, and damage was caused to farm crops after forced landings; spectators also contributed by trampling down crops. At military trials on Salisbury Plain in 1912, a syndicate of Lloyd's agreed to cover a number of aircraft in the trials, but bad weather caused so many crashes, that insurance cover was withdrawn and the infant market for aviation insurance died. In 1919, the demand revived, but this time, Lloyd's underwriters and other companies formed a group, which, by 1929, had almost a monopoly of aviation insurance. During the 1930s, other companies started their own outside group, and reinsurance also developed.
See D. E. W. Gibb *Lloyd's of London* (1957) p.326.

Herald continued into 1930. The *Daily Herald* felt obliged to introduce coupon insurance, as similar schemes were offered by other leading newspapers — indeed the national dailies had come to an agreement to offer identical coupon schemes to readers, and the *Daily Herald* itself was a party to the agreement. In February, 1930, the CIS eventually agreed to pay claims on the coupon scheme as an agent for the *Daily Herald*. Further enquiries were made concerning financial backing — would the CIS be prepared to make a loan of £300,000 for development expenses for the newspaper? After careful review, the CIS agreed to grant the loan on the understanding that adequate security would be required, and wrote to Ernest Bevin accordingly. In August, 1930, the *Daily Herald* indicated that they had decided to manage on temporary financial accommodation and wished to postpone consideration of the long-dated loan.

(xiii) *Staff and Organisation*

The district managers and assistant district managers formed a new union in the summer of 1923 — the National Union of Co-operative Insurance Society Employees — which was resented by a deputation of CIS agents, as the new union was not, in their opinion, eligible for affiliation to the TUC.

Officials from the National Union of Distributive and Allied Workers (NUDAW) complained of loans for purchase of interest-in-book being declined to CIS agents who remained members of their Union rather than the National Union of Life Assurance Workers. The CIS had issued a circular letter requesting all employees to conform to a resolution of 1919, regarding compulsory trade union membership, and the CWS had issued a later instruction that all employees were required to join a trade union not later than 28 March, 1925, otherwise they would be dismissed from employment. This action again raised the issue whether a union could be recognised by the CIS without the union concerned being affiliated to the TUC.

The block system of allocation of agency areas which was extended in the early 1920s had advantages, but there were also serious disadvantages. Obviously, an individual block system for industrial debit would mean a high proportion of supervisors, which had never been the policy of the CIS. In effect, the CIS developed a small team system rather than an individual block system. This prevented an individual agent with a poor record from spoiling any territory for business. It meant that any one agent could collect in several block areas, for only in rural districts was there a strict delineation of boundaries. By July, 1924, approximately 35 per cent of the full-time agents were working on a modified block system, and the process of concentration was continuing through the exchange of business between agents. Efforts had been made during 1923, to train agents and district managers in connection with fire and accident business; ten fire and accident inspectors were appointed, also four travelling inspectors who were to work together in a group in new districts, assisting the agents in building up their business.

By the end of 1924, the outside staff included 154 district managers, 1,762 full-time agents, 760 part-time agents, eight industrial canvassing inspectors, and the ten general inspectors. There were 2,000 full-time agents by the end of 1925. Radical proposals for re-organisation of the CIS were considered in 1926. Chief office officials reported on the desirability or otherwise of abolishing branch offices. The consensus of opinion was that there should be no change in the duties of district managers, but that branch managers ought to be re-named divisional managers. The matter arose in connection with Cardiff Branch, where the CIS General Manager had suggested that a district manager should be appointed branch manager. Up to that time, no district manager had been promoted to take charge of a branch, although there had been several promotions to branch manager, either from other branches or chief office. An organisation sub-committee also suggested that the time had arrived when there should be an Assistant General Manager, together with a full-time Secretary. The Agency Manager was responsible for the efficient control of district office staffs and agents; in addition he was in charge of industrial life accounts. The branch managers supervised agencies of Co-operative societies and individual agents within the branch areas. Branch offices also dealt with claims not dealt with by district offices, e.g., fire and motor policies were written at the branches, and the branch managers paid periodical visits to districts in connection with their duties in supervising district managers. The Agency Manager thought that the recruitment procedure for branch managers from chief office or branch office staffs was unsatisfactory. He asserted that when a new branch manager was appointed, it was because he had proved himself to be a good clerical official or fire surveyor, and generally the new manager knew nothing about the work of the district office or the full-time agent.

Although industrial life premium income had increased to £1m. by the end of 1924, wide areas of the country were still not covered by the Society. The whole of Wales was still largely untouched, as far as industrial business was concerned. The total premium income increase in 1925 was £25,000 short of that achieved in 1924, and it was noted that other companies were increasing their strength in some rural areas, many of which were CIS deserts. From January to September, 1926, there was less new business than in the corresponding period of the previous year, and the premium increase in the industrial department was merely £6,300. During 1927, there was a more settled state of business and a substantial increase in industrial life premiums. The total increase in premium income for 1927 was £400,000, of which the industrial department claimed £313,000. This was a record; the highest figure previously had been £290,000 in 1923. Ordinary life business, however, continued to increase very slowly. The agents contended that bad trade, the restriction in the house purchase scheme, the low bonus rate, the changed policy of the CIS over the consolidation of agents' territories, and the heavier commission on industrial business, were the contributory factors explaining the low increase in ordinary life business. It was also argued that the CIS was over-cautious in the medical requirements for ordinary life proposals. By 1928, the CIS had grown to fifth in terms of premium income in size of companies undertaking industrial business. Premium income for industrial business rose to £2m. by 1929, and ordinary life to £735,000. The weekly collections in the Industrial Life Department in 1920 had been £2,800; by 1929 this had risen to £38,000.

Branch managers were instructed during the late 1920s, that development in mining areas, particularly South Wales and North-East England, should not be encouraged, but every effort should be made to consolidate the existing business in those areas. Attention was to be devoted to equipping district offices to enable business to be conducted with greater efficiency, rather than opening any new districts. The employment of clerks by district managers at their own expense was prohibited in 1928.

The matter of telephones for district offices was raised in 1926. Clients were surprised that they could not contact district offices by telephone; it was becoming more urgent than ever with the increase in fire, house purchase and general business, for office communications to be brought up to date. It was minuted that all districts with premium income exceeding £2,000 per year were to have a telephone.

A policy of encouraging greater development amongst better class life business prospects was pursued. A recommendation was made for the appointment, from 1931, of six divisional superintendents to devote their whole time to the supervision of district offices and the training of agency staff. They were to work independently of branch managers, who were to be mainly responsible for the servicing of the insurance needs of the retail societies in their areas, and for advising the district offices on matters relating to fire and general business. Additional ordinary life canvassing inspectors were also appointed in 1931.

At the end of 1930, chief office re-organisation was undertaken. Industrial Accounts was transferred to the Premium Accounts Department, and redundant clerks were transferred to assist in actuarial work. A new addressing machine and a ledger-posting machine were purchased. W. Worthington, the consultant Actuary (who was also Assistant Actuary of the Royal Insurance Company), stated in 1927 that he considered CIS management was understaffed at the top — too much work was borne by the General Manager. (Worthington's connection with the CIS dated from 1920. He had been called in following the take-over of the Planet. He was consulted again at the end of 1925, when he considered that the Society was in a thoroughly sound position.)

James Darroch was appointed to the newly-created post of Assistant General Manager in March, 1927. Early in 1928, T. Hills was selected from 394 applicants to succeed E. Lowe as Accountant. In June, 1928, a new full-time Actuary, B. Holgate, FIA, was appointed to replace H. Cox, who had accepted a position with another insurance office. Holgate, the first fully-qualified Actuary on the staff of the CIS, was to devote the whole of his time exclusively to the work of the Society. Two months later, Worthington died suddenly. In January, 1929, R. Dinnage was appointed to the actuarial staff; he became Assistant Actuary at the end of 1930, having secured the FIA Diploma.

Much of the increase of fire and accident business being secured during the mid-1920s was dealt with through brokers. From 1925, there were annual valuations, hence annual bonuses, as was the case with other Industrial/Ordinary insurance offices. In 1928, the limits for assurance of lives without medical examination were raised. (Yet despite the generally improved mortality experience in Britain during the 1920s, there had been no appreciable increase in expectation of life for males over the age of 50 during the preceding half-century 1871 to 1921, and little improvement since 1921.)[1]

1
		Expectation of Life		
		1921		1871
Males aged 40	..	28.43 years	..	(25.37)
Males aged 50	..	20.63 years	..	(19.28)
Males aged 60	..	13.82 years	..	(13.28)

Extracted from *New Scottish Life Table* (based on 1921 Census on Deaths, 1920–22).

With the spread of consumer hire-purchase arrangements during the 1920s, the Co-operative Movement developed its own clothing clubs, known as mutuality clubs. There was a suggestion that agents of the CIS should collect these clothing club moneys for local retail societies. A sample scheme was approved in Gillingham, and in December, 1926, it was resolved that CIS agents in England and Wales could undertake such work, subject to certain conditions. The number of CIS agents collecting for mutuality clothing clubs was reduced from 300 to under 100 in 1935, due to local societies appointing full-time representatives for that type of work, many of whom were recruited from redundant shop assistants.

(xiv)   CIS Business and CWS

The Trade Insurance Department of the CWS approached the CIS Accident Manager in 1924, with regard to the issue of bonds required by the Government in respect of Customs and Excise duties. Before that time, the bonds had been obtained from another insurance office.

The CWS affirmed in 1924, that they were endeavouring to induce the offices then holding CWS insurances to reciprocate by allowing the CIS to share in the business, but very few of the risks concerned were in effect placed with the CIS. The CWS, after discussion, promised that, wherever possible, they would give the CIS a line on larger risks in 1927. It was, however, pointed out that if the CIS had the placing of the total CWS fire risks, the CIS would be able to bring sufficient pressure on tariff companies to induce them to reciprocate.

From time to time, difficulties arose concerning fire salvage. The CWS notified the CIS in 1925, that a large department store was selling Wheatsheaf shoes manufactured by the CWS at prices considerably below cost. The stock was originally the property of the South Surburban Co-operative Society,[1] whose premises had suffered fire damage. It was resolved that the CIS should give an undertaking to the CWS that the question of disposal of fire stocks would be reported to the CIS Committee, and that fire salvage would not be sold on open market, unless Co-operative societies declined to purchase the goods in question. By 1927, there was increasing difficulty in expanding the Fire Department, as the CIS had secured practically all the

---

[1] As an indication of the fire business undertaken within the Metropolitan area by the CIS, the total value of property covered by the Society in 1927 was £6,444,000 (the corresponding total insurance cover by all offices was £2,142m., including six companies with cover of over £100m. each).

retail Co-operative societies' risks, and were thenceforth dependent for future business on outside sources. Efforts had been made to secure a share of large risks placed by brokers, but the results were poor.

In 1927, CIS diamond jubilee celebrations took place in a number of towns. The *Co-operative News* issued a special supplement on the CIS, and a short history was prepared by Messrs. Haslam and Brown. J. R. Clynes was invited to attend the Manchester celebrations which were not held until early 1929.

(xv) *Industrial Assurance and Friendly Societies Act* 1929

A case concerning the CIS was held before the Industrial Assurance Commissioner in 1927, in connection with transfer of business. Pending any amending legislation, the CIS was legally advised that it would have to refuse such business. The point at issue was that an agent had transferred business from a collecting society, without having complied with statutory requirements that a form of consent had to be completed by the proposer. The case was heard on 25 February, 1927, and a fine of £25 was levied on the CIS, and one of £5 on the agent.

In June, 1928, the matter of legal limits of industrial assurance for children arose in connection with a summons against the City of Glasgow Assurance Company who had issued a policy for more than £15 on a child under 10 years of age. It was claimed that this was in contravention of the Industrial Assurance Act of 1923. The industrial offices immediately ceased accepting insurance on lives of children for more than £15, and suggested an amending Bill for such policies. A. V. Alexander intimated to the CIS, in July, 1928, that the Government would only proceed with an amending Bill if no opposition were offered; if the CIS did anything to jeopardise the passing of the Bill, it would only strengthen the opposition. A meeting was held between A. V. Alexander and Sir Thomas Neill[1] in September, 1928, and as an outcome it was agreed that amending legislation was required with regard to children's assurance; but over the other outstanding question of transfer of business, Sir Thomas Neill suggested that the CIS should fall into line with the associated offices, who had agreed to respect each other's business. Representatives from the CIS and the Association of Industrial Assurance Companies met the Chancellor of the Exchequer, with A. V. Alexander

[1] *Sir Thomas Neill, 1856–1937.*
Sometime Chairman of Association of Industrial Assurance Companies and Chairman of National Amalgamated Approved Society, 1915–1936.

joining the deputation. The delegation reported that the Solicitor-General had agreed to recommend the Government to introduce an Indemnity Bill to regularize policies issued prior to the amending legislation. The ensuing Industrial Assurance and Friendly Societies Act of 1929 had the effect of preventing over-insurance on the lives of children under the age of 10 years, and made provision for minimum surrender values and paid-up policy values. The CIS Actuary reported that the existing level of procuration fees would make it impossible for the CIS to pay statutory surrender values, and that it would be necessary to negotiate with agents and district managers for a reduction in procuration fees. Surrender values and proportionate paid-up policies were to be available after one year only of paid premiums (under the 1923 Act it had been three years). These stipulations were to apply to ordinary life as well as to industrial life business.

(xvi) *Strikes* 1928–1931

For some time, the CIS had been endeavouring to define more clearly the area of each district in London. An agreement had been reached with NUDAW, but the London Area Council refused to accept the decision of the National Committee. The Fulham CIS agents called for strike action, and they had support from Hammersmith and Bethnal Green, but other CIS agents in London ignored incitements to strike.

In November, 1928, the CIS London agency staff, despite the fact that they were members of NUDAW, were informed that as their numbers were so small, the CIS management could not enter into a separate agreement with them — all NUDAW members were to realise that " they must recognise agreement entered into with the Union catering for 93 per cent of total staff." As a result, a limited strike took place in London, but soon collapsed.

A new CIS agency agreement was forwarded to NUDAW in April, 1929, with an intimation that the Industrial Assurance and Friendly Societies Act of 1929 ruled out any possibility of further consideration of the terms. Although the 1929 Act had made children's endowment assurance less profitable on the current rates, the CIS decided to continue such business provided that agents would accept somewhat lower terms, but the agents renewed their general claim for higher commission rates. The final issue narrowed to one of whether certain insurances should carry 12½ per cent commission to agents instead of the 10 per cent previously allowed. The Union decided against acceptance of the terms proposed, and in January, 1930, NUDAW gave notice to strike, as outstanding matters in respect of the new Agency Agreement had not been settled. The Lord Mayor of Manchester, the Minister of Labour, and the TUC, offered assistance in mediation.[1] The General Manager reported that 90 per cent of the agents were on strike, but that district officials had voted against strike action. An early settlement was reached in February, 1930, the terms of which included 10 per cent commission on endowment assurance business and guaranteed minimum earnings for agents of 50s. weekly. In August, industrial business was being retarded by continued unemployment and the effects of the agents' strike — it was held that the strike caused a fall-off of 30,000 proposals.

In December, 1930, over 100 agents in the London districts did not pay in, saying that they were on unofficial strike on account of a wrongful dismissal. It was decided to give legal notice of termination of engagement to the agents concerned — the notice to be withdrawn if they resumed work. Dismissal notices for 101 London agents in all went out from 24 December, 1930. By the end of January, 1931, the Agency Manager had secured sufficient men to replace those dismissed, and the premiums collected by the dismissed agents had been paid in. Some of the men concerned even co-operated with the CIS after being fired: " A number of men dismissed were assisting the newly-installed men to the fullest extent and using their endeavours to persuade policyholders to continue to pay premiums." This third strike had also taken place at the instigation of the London Area Council acting in anticipation of support by NUDAW — the first evidence of impending strike action had occurred on 22 December, 1930, when NUDAW issued instructions to agents to withhold their collections, and to hold themselves in readiness for a strike from 1 January, 1931. Over 90 per cent of the agents ignored the Union's instructions at a series of meetings. On 29 December, NUDAW issued a countermanding instruction that agents should continue to observe the terms of the existing agreement, and that they should pay in as usual during the week of 29 December. Notwithstanding the instruction the agents went on strike. Sir Walter Citrine asked the CIS Board to reveal the same spirit and fairness as had characterized them on other occasions, and accede to the NUDAW request for an early meeting. In effect, the January, 1931, strike was a fanning of the embers of the previous strike of January, 1930, for although the trouble had been apparently settled, and the agents informed that a

---

[1] The President of the TUC at the time was John Beard, who had worked as an insurance agent.

repetition would have serious consequences for them, a section of London agents had remained restive. The London agents' case in the strike of January, 1931, was that an agent had been wrongfully dismissed, purely on account of his age. The agent in question was aged 70 in May, 1930, and would have retired but for negotiations in the progress of the pension scheme, which allowed agents at the age of 70 to take part-time agencies and retain all business other than industrial, provided that they were able to give adequate attention to their agencies; further, a minimum pension of 5s. per week was to be paid to them. A request was received from NUDAW in April, 1931, that the dispute should be referred to the National Co-operative Conciliation Board, but the CIS Committee refused either to re-open the question of the dismissal of London agents, or to refer the matter to conciliation.

During the previous strike of January/February, 1930, although CIS district office staff were then members of NUDAW, they balloted and decided not to support the agents in their strike action. Following this decision, sections of outside staff, apart from agents, namely district officials, clerks and audit testers, decided to sever connection with NUDAW in June, 1930, and joined NUCISE.

Although NUCISE was deemed eligible for affiliation to the Trades Union Congress in 1931, it was not so accepted. Many CIS agents during the early 1930s were members of NAULAW, and others were in the T & GW Union and the NUGMW. The CIS recognised all three unions, also the Guild of Insurance Officials — whose status remained in doubt regarding TUC eligibility. Sir Walter Citrine wrote, in 1936, that the General Council of the TUC " now feel the Guild cannot be regarded as an Organisation complying with the CWS resolution." However, several months later, the TUC rescinded its decision, and restored the *status quo* of 1926, under which the Guild was recognised as a Union eligible for affiliation to Congress.

Industrial depression was prevalent during 1930. The increase in industrial life debit from January to June of that year was only £71,000, compared with £121,000 for the same period in 1929; the net increase in the Ordinary Life Department was £8,300, compared with £16,900. At the end of 1931, the notorious Means Test was introduced, with the right to investigate any credit, including dividend held by an individual member in any Co-operative society; but there was no statutory obligation on the part of Co-operative societies to divulge information, except at the request of the member — there was nothing to force the unemployed out of Co-operative membership. Despite the economic conditions during 1931,[1] the total premium income was £4,800,000, that is £300,000 more than 1930. At that time, the average earnings of CIS full-time agents was £3 19s. 3d.

[1] Memory traces of previous periods of economic slump tend to become ingrained in the social consciousness. The inter-war years were not ones of unrelieved and generalized economic distress. The "slump" from 1929 was one of rising sectional unemployment, but with real wages, productivity, and output, also showing rising indices.
See H. W. Richardson *Economic Recovery in Britain 1932-1939* (1967), and D. H. Aldcroft "Economic Growth in Britain in the Inter-War Years: A Re-Assessment." *Economic History Review* Vol.XX, No. 2, August, 1967.

PART FIVE

THE 1930s

(i) "Something to Think About"

Staff lectures were commenced at CIS chief office in 1931. James Darroch gave a talk on "Something to Think About" in which he suggested an interchange of indoor and outdoor staff. He also deplored the fact that there was too much specialization of young people within any one department. During 1932 and 1933, 23 lectures in all were given, with an average attendance of over 200. Mr. R. Dinnage lectured on life assurance, and argued that too much emphasis was being laid on endowment assurance purely as an investment plan. Short-term endowment policies could only be justified for house purchase; for providing funds for educating children; and for investment where life cover was not really required. With many CIS policies, there were rather too many small assurances by people who should have had long-period endowments in addition to protection for old age or a whole-life policy. B. Holgate pointed out that funeral expenses policies formed too high a proportion of industrial business. Every penny put into a policy on the life of a parent thereby diminished the sum which a married couple could afford to insure on the life of the husband. In general, husbands and fathers were much under-insured.[1]

In view of the unsettled state of business in the Irish Free State, the CIS ceased canvassing there in 1932, and allowed all existing policies to expire, with the exception of life business. A tentative offer was received from the new Ireland Assurance Company to take over the whole of the CIS business in Eire, but within several days of the proposed takeover, the offer was withdrawn. Following this fruitless effort to dispose of the business, policyholders were advised, at the end of 1932, that the CIS was not inviting renewal of policies. Eight clerks employed at the Dublin Branch were given dismissal notices, with an offer to consider applications from them for a transfer to chief office in Manchester. The Branch Manager, Mr. Murphy, received £250 as compensation for loss of office. Early in 1933, the National Employers' Mutual Assurance Company was approached by the CIS to take over its Free State business. The Company declined to take over the unexpired portion of risks, but was prepared to

[1] Holgate showed that during a representative week in 1933, the percentage of whole life policies concerned with men was 35, women 21, and parents 44; e.g. just over one-third of insurance premiums was for the cover of the breadwinner which was too low, and nearly half the premiums was for those over 50 years of age at entry. Two-thirds of premium should be on lives under 50; i.e., on own life. Of the 44 per cent concerned with parents, 30 per cent were effected by children, 10 per cent on children effected by parents, 4 per cent by other relations.

undertake the responsibility of administration until the expiry of existing CIS policies. The decision to discontinue business in the Irish Free State was not crucial to the future of the CIS — in all, it meant a loss of only £25,000 annual premiums — and in the light of present knowledge was probably a very wise decision.

From 1934, the driver of any motor car or other vehicle was required to possess a certificate of insurance approved by the Free State Government. The CIS, although it had ceased to accept business in Eire, still had a motor premium income of £15,000 in Northern Ireland, and all companies wishing to issue insurance certificates valid for Eire were required to deposit £15,000 with the Irish Government; the CIS agreed to make the requisite deposit.

(ii) *Funds and Interest Rates*

In terms of funds, the CIS rose to sixth place in rank order of industrial life companies; in terms of increase of business, the CIS was third during the year 1931. Its industrial assurance expense ratio of 37 per cent was sixth best out of 18 companies listed in the *Insurance Mail*, which commented that the CIS had grown five-fold during the decade 1922–1932, and was still growing fast; it was well-managed, its organisation was sound, and it was to be strongly recommended to the public.

Nevertheless, as with all financial institutions, the CIS was deeply involved in making adjustments to violent changes in national fiscal and monetary policy in 1931 and 1932.

At the beginning of 1931, it had been recommended that £20,000 should be set aside to form a reserve for interest equalisation until such time as " the market becomes more stable." By July, there was a report on the unfavourable conditions prevailing in certain sections of the stock exchange market which were having adverse effects on CIS investments. It was noted that the most unsatisfactory items in the CIS portfolio were Australian securities, British and foreign railway preference stocks, Cable and Wireless, and United Molasses holdings. The CIS Committee minuted in October, 1931 — " If prices do not recover very substantially before the end of the year, practically all life offices will have to face a state of affairs far worse than has ever been experienced." The alternatives facing the CIS in such a contingency were threefold — a postponement of valuation; a valuation of stock exchange securities at prices above market prices; a passing or reduction of bonus. The CIS was elected a member of a sub-committee of the Life Offices Association appointed to consider methods of dealing with the pressing question of falling security values, and the possibility was explored of approaching the Board of Trade for permission to value securities on the basis of market values at 31 December, 1930. The CIS dealt with its own problem by bringing into account the £20,000 interest equalisation reserve which, together with the full actual interest earned during 1931, made a yield for the year of £5 8s. 7d. per cent, a figure that compared favourably with previous years. In the valuation of the ordinary life section, the rate of interest for whole life contracts had been reduced in 1930 from 3½ per cent to 3 per cent. The deficiency in the investment reserve fund of just over £1m. at the end of 1931, was too large a sum to be met out of the year's profits — the situation could have been met and the bonus maintained only by weakening the valuation basis. Rather, the CIS met the deficiency by appropriations from the profit and loss account. The total depreciation of stock exchange securities at the end of 1931 was £1,294,000. By June, 1932, the figure had improved to £776,000 — but 1932 was not without problems for the CIS.

By mid-1932, with the introduction of a national cheap money policy, the prevailing 3½ per cent gross rate of interest on gilt-edged securities was the lowest for nineteen years. This rapid fall in the long-term rate of interest meant that short-term endowment assurance business could be encouraged. On the other hand, the low long-term rate of interest required higher rates of premium for deferred annuities, particularly at younger ages of entry. The Actuary reported that the collective life scheme was again suffering from falling retail prices. To help safeguard the scheme, the charge for administration was reduced from 3 per cent to 1½ per cent from the end of 1931.

With the fall in interest rates CIS holdings of stock exchange securities appreciated by £1,585,000 during 1932 — the pressing problem was now how to invest new money at a rate of interest which would enable the CIS to maintain its existing bonuses. One of the difficulties of a rapidly growing office such as the CIS was that its funds were increasing at a relatively rapid rate *pari passu* with growth of new business. Consequently, the money to be invested at the then existing low rates of interest was a bigger proportion of funds than was the case with other offices. (The era of cheap money, through its policy of lower interest rates, was influencing equity shares values. Insurance offices increased their holdings of industrial shares because of the low yield on gilt-edged securities. The "move into equities" also increased pressure from investors which in turn was a further influence leading to higher ordinary share prices.) The CIS investment sub-committee was increased to five members from March, 1933. Messrs. Judd, Pickup, Arnold, Riddle and Buchanan were to form the sub-committee, which was to meet once a month, with any two of the members empowered to act in an emergency — " provided they do not depart from prescribed policy of CIS Committee . . . " An early report of the investment sub-committee illustrated the broader scope of CIS investments when it referred to a greater proportion than usual of surplus funds being invested in debenture stocks, industrial preference shares, and shares of first-class utility companies, all of which were in Great Britain. In January, 1934, a proposition was entertained for investment of funds on the security of flats built in Glasgow by a private company and upon which Glasgow Corporation had issued loans at 5 per cent per year. The CIS agreed to invest the sum of £287,000 at 4 per cent for five years, subject to the continuance of Corporation housing subsidies.

John Mason, the treasurer of the CIS, completed 50 years' service in 1932. When he entered the CIC, the entire staff consisted of four members. He had seen annual premium income rise from £3,600 to £5m. Mason reminisced that chief office in 1883 was in City Buildings, Corporation Street, and occupied two small rooms; by 1933, chief office staff had grown to over 700. In the autumn of 1933, the *CIS Review* commented that soon there would be a cheerful blaze of neon lights on chief office building. " People travelling down Cheetham Hill Road will see the CIS set on high . . . The name of the Society is to be ' burned ' in red letters two feet high."

Sir Thomas Allen retired in April, 1933. For 22 years he had been a director of the CWS, and had been chairman of the CIS Committee since 1922, having been elected to the CIS Committee and the CWS Board in 1910. At the end of 1934, T. Hills, the CIS accountant, died. He had been co-author with R. Dinnage of the textbook *Industrial Assurance Organisation and Routine* (1933).

(iii)   *Cohen Committee and After*

The CIS submitted a memorandum in 1932 to the Departmental Committee on Industrial Assurance and to Assurances on the lives of Children under 10 years of age (The Cohen Committee).

The Cohen Committee considered the possibility of transferring all industrial assurance business to a public utility corporation which would have a statutory monopoly. The Committee also considered grouping of companies:

"In considering the new bodies which might be constituted . . . We except also, though unwillingly, because neither of them is conspicuous for economy, the Co-operative Insurance Society and the Salvation Army Assurance Society on account of their special associations." (Para.77)

A recommendation was also made that expenses of management should be required not to exceed a sum equal to 30 per cent of the total industrial assurance premiums.

Much can be gleaned from the evidence given before the Committee by CIS witnesses on 20 January, 1932. The evidence is worth quoting at length as it gives an insight into the policy of the CIS at this critical period of its growth.

The Cohen Committee noted that
"the capital . . . [of the CIS] is owned entirely by the two Co-operative Wholesale Societies and the dividend (which is limited to 5 per cent) is payable, at present, wholly out of the profits of the branches of the business other than life assurance, all the distributive profits of the industrial assurance fund going to the policyholders."

J. P. Jones, the General Manager of the CIS, gave evidence:

Question 3576
" . . . some years ago we tried to evolve a scheme whereby members of a Co-operative society would pay their insurance premiums from the accumulated dividend they had at the stores. Our idea was to endeavour to cultivate or induce policyholders to pay their premiums at longer intervals and thereby naturally be able to secure a better policy. We found in practice that it did not work satisfactorily."

Question 3590
"It is very remarkable that in the last ten years you have built up a premium income that represents about one eighth of the whole increase in industrial assurance premiums throughout all the offices in the period."

Question 3591
"Were they skilled agents or were they co-operative members who took to the work of agency and made themselves expert after their appointment?" — "In the main our agents have been taken from the mine, the plough, the workshop. Very rarely indeed have we appointed a man who has had experience with another office."

Question 3925 Mr. MacNaughton to B. Holgate.

"I see you say the surrender values under the Act of 1929, are too onerous for the offices?" Holgate — "Yes." (Holgate was asked whether he had any objection to a statutory provision for paying surrender values on policies which had been five years in force.)

Question 3928

Holgate: "It does seem to me rather unfair that the policy-holder surrendering should have a statutory cash payment which may have to be obtained by releasing securities at depreciated prices."

Question 3929

"Why have you changed your opinion since six months ago?" Holgate: "Because six months ago I did not anticipate that there would be anything like the present depreciation."

Question 3940 — Sir Alfred Watson to B. Holgate:

"Were you in the discussions which preceded the Act of 1929?" Holgate: "I was."

Question 3941

"I am rather impressed by the statement here that the free policy surrender values in that Act were imposed upon the industrial offices as a penalty. Do you think that is quite a correct way of putting it?" Holgate: "Frankly, yes."

Question 3979

Holgate replied on the experience of the CIS *vis-à-vis* other offices: "Our difficulty is that we are a young office, on the industrial side, and therefore the average duration of the policies is not very high. Until quite recent years not many of them would have acquired a surrender value, but the amount paid in surrender values is now going up rather rapidly."

Sir Benjamin Cohen, Chairman of the Committee, then questioned Holgate:

Question 4039

"Could you tell us, or could you find out how many policies have lapsed under a certain period, say, three months?" — "Not with any ease at all; it would need an absolutely new analysis."

Question 4040

"Do you yourselves not want to know how many lapses take place within three months?" — "No."

Question 4041

"I should have thought for the purpose of your business, you would want to know?"—"No. We do not require it at all."

Question 4042

"You keep no record of that?"—"We keep a record for valuation purposes of the way they lapse, but for accounting purposes we are solely concerned with seeing that we have received the premiums paid during the period."

J. P. Jones was further questioned on the scale of procuration fees paid to agents. He explained that they received 50 per cent for the first 40 weeks, and subsequently 25 per cent for weekly business, and 10 per cent or 15 per cent for monthly business.

Question 4063

"The agents get no share of the profits?"—"No share whatever."

B. Holgate also explained that the agents were members of a pension fund to which the CIS contributed 2½ per cent of the earnings of all employees over the age of 25.

J. P. Jones was then questioned:

Question 4072

"I am suggesting that they seem to me to be very well paid?"—"I wish we could get the agents to realise that."

Question 4073

"None of us think we are paid enough, that is human nature, but at any rate you pay them a sufficiently high scale to have enabled you to build up a business with astonishing success. The point I want to put to you is, having regard to the procuration fees, the commission and the superannuation contributions that are made for the agents, it seems to me they are, at any rate, paid substantially, and I should have thought the value of the business, whatever it was, belonged to the policyholders. I do not quite understand why the agents, at the time of retirement on a pension, should be able also to sell their books?" J. P. Jones—"It should not be overlooked that in granting interest-in-books to the agents, it was done for the specific purpose of assisting the Society in its early stages. If we had not granted book-interest probably we should have had to pay fairly high salaries, and I think, Sir, you will realise the value to a young office in its early days of a scheme of this kind. It is quite true the agents are well paid, but the question of book-interest is of no cost to the Society or to the policy-holders."

J. P. Jones continued in answer to *Question* 4074:

"Despite the fact that we are paying our agents highly remunerative terms, we are still able to give benefits which will compare with any other first-class office."

Question 4075 was then put to J. P. Jones:

"Yes, but then it may be there is a general level of extravagance throughout industrial assurance business that prevents everybody from giving the terms the policyholders might hope to get?"

J. P. Jones continued on the subject of interest-in-book:

"We have proved from experience that if a man has an interest in the business, as he has by putting some money into it, that man is usually a better servant of the office. It is to his interest that he should introduce only the best class of business, because when he comes to sell, if it is a bad type of business, he is going to lose on the sale. In allowing interest-in-book the Society gains a better servant — a man who is more likely to stick in his job . . . "

Question 4077

"Are you not a little afraid that agents who have a substantial monopoly interest in their books may through their organisations endeavour to control the management of the concern in their own interests?" — "No. That is impossible. Under our constitution the agents have no control whatever."

Question 4079

"It seems to me . . . that although this is a mutual society the existence of book-interest really makes it a share-owning concern, the shares being held by the agents . . . "[1]

---

[1] A Table was appended to the Report of the Cohen Committee showing analysis of new CIS Industrial Life business for three weeks commencing February, 1932. The total number of policies issued was 43,698 for a total weekly premium of £759 11s. 4d., and a total sum assured of £821,886. Of the total policies, 10,163 were endowment and 33,535 were whole-life. Of these 33,535 whole-life policies merely 5,622 were on *own* life; a much more substantial number of whole-life policies were taken out on life-of-another, particularly by parents, whereas with endowment policies the total number taken out by parents was almost the same number as own-life endowment policies. The number of husband and wife whole-life policies exceeded own-life policies. The average premium was revealing: for whole-life policies on own-life the average weekly premium was 4d; for whole-life taken out by parents the average premium was 2d., whereas with endowment own-life policies the weekly premium was 9d. In all, the memorandum submitted by the CIS to the Cohen Committee included 24 pages of evidence which took up the twelfth day of the meeting of the Committee on 20 January, 1932.

Sir Arnold Wilson and Professor Hermann Levy wrote in 1936, apropos the evidence of the Cohen Committee:

> "Four years have elapsed since the Cohen Report was published: It has never been specifically discussed in Parliament: The question has not figured in any party programme. The socialist groups of the Labour Party favour nationalization . . . They could not, however, carry with them the trade unions and the agents who value the control of the trade union approved societies: the Co-operative Societies, who spend considerable sums on political activities would strenuously oppose any legislation which weakens the approved societies connected with the movement or merge them into a state service."[1]

(iv) *Out of Depression*

The CIS has always eschewed political involvements — for instance the CIS Board in 1931 agreed with the recommendation of the General Manager that: " No quotation be given for the Co-operative Members of Parliament to provide benefits (at the rate of remuneration received as Members of Parliament) in the event of failing to secure re-election." But in 1936, it was agreed that for an annual premium of £10 per head, a payment of £200 could be made to unsuccessful Co-operative Party Parliamentary candidates.

On another occasion, the General Manager notified the Secretary of the TUC that he could not be expected to express an opinion on the nationalization of life assurance, as the subject was largely a political issue — reference had been made to the successful development by the Japanese Government of industrial assurance through the medium of the post office, but it was pointed out that industrial assurance was new to Japan, whereas in Britain it was a highly-developed industry; moreover Britain already had the equivalent of State supervision exercised through the powers of the Industrial Assurance Commissioner.

Payment of CIS ordinary life premiums by banker's order was introduced in 1931. Premium income increased by more than £500,000 in 1933, and was the second highest annual increase so far recorded in the history of the CIS. It was becoming evident that the national economy was recovering from the severe depression — the average weekly earnings of CIS full-time agents in 1934 were £4 13s. 8d.— but

[1] Sir Arnold Wilson and Hermann Levy, *Industrial Assurance — An Historical and Critical Study* (1937), pp.118–119.

the continuance of a cheap money policy was still causing problems for insurance investment managers.

Despite the constraints, the CIS received accolades in the *Insurance Mail* in 1934: " In last 11 years the Society has multiplied itself by over four times . . . no office in country with such a record . . . most progressive institution of its kind in the British Isles . . . CIS has magnificent agency organisation."

An accident occurred at premises of the United Co-operative Laundries Association in January, 1932, as a result of the collapse of a cast-iron tank holding 120 tons of boiling water. Two men were fatally scalded and 18 horses either killed or destroyed. The CIS admitted liability in respect of the two men concerned, but repudiated liability in respect of the horses and building. Appeals were submitted from the Association, conceding they had no legal claim, and as a result the CIS made an ex-gratia payment of £280.

Occasional complaints continued to be received during the 1930s from Co-operative societies concerning the sale of fire salvage of CWS branded goods by private persons. The General Manager reminded the societies that definite instructions had gone out to all fire loss assessors concerning the disposal of CWS or SCWS goods damaged by fire.

The rules of the CIS provided for the undertaking of all classes of insurance, but no marine risks had been entertained after the unfortunate experiences of the CIC in its early years. It was eventually decided to undertake such work on an agency basis from 1933, with a view to building up an account which would justify the establishment of a separate marine section.

It was during the 1930s that the CIS strengthened its ties with the international Co-operative Movement and entered more fully into reinsurance arrangements with independent offices. Offers of fire reinsurance were accepted from Belgian, German, and Swedish fire offices, and from more distant places including Trieste and Tokyo.

The continuance of low rates of interest into the mid-1930s made it necessary to revise rates on single premium policies and immediate annuities from 1935. At the end of 1934, the market value of stock exchange securities was £16,669,000, for which the book value was £14,572,000. Doubts were expressed whether the level of bonus could be maintained, given the existing rates of interest. The General Manager was to consider the question of taking up shares in " good industrial concerns " from March, 1935. The investment of surplus funds was constantly under consideration in 1935, but it was not always easy to secure a sufficient rate of interest on gilt-edged stock and, at the same time, to adhere to strict principles of security and provide a bonus for policyholders.

Contrary to the usual experience of insurance offices, the CIS during its development period had paid high rates of bonus. (Other offices during their early stages of growth had generally charged high premiums, or paid small bonuses in order to accumulate reserves.) In view of the "uncertain international situation" in 1936, the General Manager felt that it was desirable to leave surplus money to accumulate on current account in the CWS Bank. Investment in chief or ground rents was considered, also the possibility of extending the house purchase scheme by lending money on the security of house property without life assurance, but as previously noted, this proposal was not proceeded with.

Consideration was given in 1937 to a modification of the existing ruling that restricted investment to first-class redeemable stocks for redemption periods varying up to 40 years. In future, discretion was to be given to purchase on a limited scale securities of a less gilt-edged type — the CIS had accepted the advice of brokers that in the existing circumstances, the proportion of redeemable securities which, in 1937, was about 25 per cent of the CIS portfolio, should be gradually reduced to between 5 and 15 per cent. A statement was submitted illustrating how the funds of other leading offices were invested. This showed that the offices in question had a much higher proportion than the CIS funds in higher interest-yielding equity stocks. One of the larger insurance offices had heavy investments in property. A small but decisive step taken in the development of the CIS was an agreement in the summer of 1939, to invest a sum not exceeding £100,000 in industrial ordinary shares — a presage of post-war policy. Almost as though to underline the investment problems of the CIS, there was heavy depreciation of securities in 1939.

It was reported in 1935 that the Rochdale district office was too cramped for the amount of business undertaken, and suitable accommodation was offered and accepted in the central premises of the Rochdale Pioneers' Society — it will be remembered that the original office of the CIC in 1867, had been in the premises of the Pioneers' Society. Development in the north of Scotland was undertaken in 1935 — six full-time agencies were created for areas between Dornoch Firth and John O'Groats.

During the early 1930s complaints were made by agents and district office managers through their Unions concerning the administration of the national health insurance scheme. The CIS agents declined to carry out sick visits and they pointed out that other Approved societies had appointed experienced sick visitors; moreover it was legally binding for females to be visited by female sick visitors. CIS obligations were transferred to the CWS Health Insurance Section in 1936, and CIS responsibility for the administration of the National Health Insurance Scheme of the CWS finally ceased from June, 1937. The impasse had arisen through the CWS being empowered to provide national health insurance through the medium of Co-operative societies. Where the latter did not act, or having acted, desired to be relieved of their agencies, it had seemed appropriate to place the administration in the hands of the CIS, conveniently placed with its field force of agents and existing links with retail societies. The first complaints had been received as early as 1924 concerning the CWS arrangements, and an agreement had been reached whereby a local Co-operative society could request the CIS to act as local NHI agent. By 1929, the administration of the NHI business of 120 local societies was being handled by CIS agents.

Electrically-operated accounting machines were purchased in 1931, also a cheque-writing machine, but policies were still being hand-written as late as 1935, and continued to be so written for a number of years afterwards. An article in the CIS Review commented that policy writers could complete 400 industrial life policies each day. An all-electric typewriter was tested in 1936. By 1932, the automatic telephone system installed at chief office was seventeen years old, and was showing signs of deterioration. New batteries had recently been purchased in the hope that they would rejuvenate some of its lost efficiency, but the time had come, said the General Manager, when it was necessary to install a new switchboard.

The CIS occupied most of the accommodation of 111–113 Corporation Street, Manchester, as a tenant of the CWS. At the end of 1933, the CIS agreed to purchase the land and buildings. In 1938, the CIS sought additional accommodation for the use of chief office. Crown Buildings was purchased in Dantzic Street, and adjoining cottages were demolished. The CIS also investigated the possibility of erecting a replacement building for the Red Bank Ragged School, which occupied a site adjoining the CIS premises in Corporation Street.

Part-time agents at garages and estate agents, were contributing up to 25 per cent of new CIS motor business in the pre-war years. The CIS followed the tariff offices in offering concessions to private motorists who laid up their vehicles during the winter months.

Although there was a greater demand for motor insurance, this did not prevent a number of companies transacting motor insurance from going into liquidation during the pre-war years; and as the Road Traffic Act of 1930 did not make any provision for claims not capable of being met because of insolvency, many policyholders suffered. In 1936, the Board of Trade set up the Cassell Committee to report on the matter, and the Committee recommended the establishment of a central fund to which all companies undertaking motor insurance were to contribute, but no action was taken. In 1940, the Universal Insurance Company was wound up, and other companies were asked to assist. The Board of Trade approached the Accident Offices Association, but no individual office was prepared to take over the liabilities of the Universal. The Accident Offices Association did however support the Board of Trade recommendation of 1936 for the establishment of a central fund, and the suggestion of Montagu Norman, the Governor of the Bank of England, that the whole insurance industry should jointly meet the deficiency of the Universal Insurance Company. This suggestion was acceded to by the offices, with the CIS contributing £1,000 to the scheme of settlement.

A death benefit scheme was entered into with *Reynolds News* in 1936, whereby regular readers of that newspaper, who were also members of Co-operative societies collectively assured with the CIS, received a sum equivalent to one-third of the amount payable by the CIS under the collective life scheme. This payment was refunded by *Reynolds News*.

CIS business in Eire was finally terminated with the closure of the employers' liability account at the beginning of 1938, leaving a transfer of just over £600 to the CIS profit and loss account. There was some business in the Channel Islands before the outbreak of war, but it was very small — it amounted to less than 30s. per week and all the premiums were received by post.

The London Co-operative Society raised the question in 1938 whether the CWS directors were prepared to consider bringing the operations of the CIS more under the direct control of the share-holding societies of the CWS — i.e. a reversion to the pre-1913 position. The suggestion was not approved.

A CIS district manager was elected Lord Mayor of Bristol in 1938, and in the same year, CIS agents became Mayors of Smethwick and Colchester.

PART SIX

NEW HORIZONS

(i) War Years

The Prevention of Fraud (Investments) Act, 1939, raised the issue of the basis of operation of the CIS. The Act required Co-operative societies to satisfy the Registrar that they were *bona fide*, and in this connection the Registrar had laid down that a society which did not confine the major part of its trade to its members, or paid more than a moderate rate of interest on its share capital, was not a true Co-operative society. As no part of the surplus of the CIS went to its shareholders (members) other than as a fixed rate interest on share capital, the conditions of mutuality were deemed present, and thus the CIS could comply with the Act, which also stated that a society which was registered before 26 July, 1938, could stay on the register and could continue as an Industrial and Provident Society. As the alternative of conversion to a Company had no possible advantage to the CIS, it was agreed to continue to operate as an Industrial and Provident Society.

London branch office was finding it difficult to recruit suitable junior staff from 1939, as the CIS was having to contend with competition from other employers in the City of London, with the result that the CIS had to pay higher wages to attract young workers.

There were 12 female full-time agents employed by the CIS in 1938. In the case of agents called up for military service, wives who could attend to the business were offered temporary agency appointments. If somebody else had to be appointed, a fixed salary of between 50s. and 60s. was paid, with any balance of commission paid to the absent agent.

J. Simpson, the Agency Manager, retired in June, 1940, and was replaced by F. Butterworth, the assistant Agency Manager. During his retirement, Simpson acted as editor of the *Insurance Mail* and the *National Insurance Gazette* for the duration of the war.

The outbreak of war did at least encourage some streamlining of administration in the CIS, as was the case with other insurance offices and banks.[1] In July, 1940, in the interest of economy, the CIS Board gave the General Manager authority to approve certain measures without reporting them to the Board — such as the appointment of juniors, temporary staff, full and part-time agents, and the granting of loans to agents for purchase of interest-in-book.

---

[1] An example of the petty issues which were still being brought before the CIS Committee for resolution as recently as 1938, was a request submitted by two employees from Newcastle and Gateshead, to have leave of absence from 4 p.m. to attend a CWS male voice choir.

The CIS had been a party to a British Insurance Association agreement in 1937, whereby non-life risks of war or civil war were to be specifically excluded from all policies. The insurance offices noted that although the Government had accepted war risks during the first world war, it now considered this type of insurance outside its province. Shortly after the BIA agreement, 500 foreign insurance companies complied with the British insurance market in declining to accept war risks. A special scheme for the Co-operative Movement was suggested whereby the share and loan accounts of the CWS (which totalled over £84m. in 1938) could form a pool from which war claims involving the Co-operative Movement could be met. Each retail society in the scheme would contribute towards the claims in the proportion that the value of its own buildings and stock bore to the total value of Co-operative goods and premises.

Generally, industrial life policies in force before September, 1939, for sums not exceeding £50, on which two years' premiums had been paid, received protection against forfeiture on application by policyholders.[1] In order to encourage investment in Government loans, as was the case during the first world war, CIS policies were issued under which the sum assured was payable in war loan instead of cash. A. V. Alexander and the General Manager attended a Committee set up under Lord Weir in 1939, concerned with problems of compensation to owners of private property damaged through enemy action. The Government intimated in December, 1939, that compensation would be paid from public funds after the conclusion of hostilities. The wartime Government agreed to insure goods owned and held by them in the country and elsewhere against fire risks, but as a *quid pro quo* the Government insisted on a single organisation being formed with which it could transact insurance business. A management committee was thus set up consisting of representatives of the Government, the insurance offices, and Lloyd's: 75 per cent of the insurances were placed with insurance companies, and 25 per cent with Lloyd's; of the 75 per cent with the companies, 5 per cent was to be shared with non-tariff offices, of which the CIS proportion was ½ per cent. The CIS policies included limited cover against war risks under industrial and ordinary life cover, without payment of extra premium, from 1940.

By October, 1939, 62 life claims had been paid in respect of the

[1] The Industrial Assurance and Friendly Societies (Emergency Protection from Forfeiture) Act, 1940.

sinking of HMS *Courageous*. From the outbreak of hostilities war claims were excluded from collective life contracts. In 1941, agreement was sought for a modification of the collective life scheme, as the result of a request to deduct part of the sum assured in those cases where funeral arrangements were not carried out by the local Co-operative society. The peak year for surplus under the collective life scheme had been 1920, when £207,000 was distributed. Between 1923 and the end of 1940, total membership of the collective life scheme had dropped from a maximum of 980 to 786, but it should be noted that during the intervening period many societies had amalgamated or gone out of existence. In 1945, member-societies of the collective scheme represented only 3 per cent of total members of the Scottish Co-operative societies, compared with 36 per cent of the English and Welsh societies: nevertheless, the total number of persons insured under the collective life scheme increased until 1954, and premium income until 1962.

The early collapse of Belgium, France, and Norway caused CIS reinsurance treaties with eight European offices to be cancelled. In June, 1940, the district office at West Hartlepool was seriously damaged by enemy action. A heavy attack took place on Manchester on the night of 22 December, 1940, but neither the CIS Corporation Street premises nor Crown Buildings suffered serious damage, although it was feared that Crown Buildings might be lost due to a large-scale fire in the adjacent premises at Baxendales. It was found that fire-watching had insurance implications — the question was raised whether the more comprehensive fire precautions taken meant there was less risk of ordinary fire outbreaks, and several requests were made for a reduction in premiums. On the other hand, the imposition of purchase tax in 1940, made it desirable that Co-operative societies should increase their fire insurance on stocks, otherwise in the event of fire they would incur losses of tax already paid on stocks.

Swansea district office was entirely destroyed by bombing in March, 1941. Chief office supplied duplicate records of ordinary life, fire, accident and motor business to the local officials.[1] Agreement was reached with NUDAW for the payment to agents of one-fifth of a penny per entry for writing addresses on fire schedules, and two-thirds of a penny for re-writing industrial life record cards. It was estimated that the cost of replacing records in each of the bombed

[1] Bearer bonds deposited with the CWS Bank were photographed from 1940 as an added precaution of documentary evidence.

district offices was approximately £100. In the same month, Plymouth branch and district office was also completely destroyed by enemy action.[1] Hull district office was completely destroyed in May, 1941. Other CIS offices severely damaged during the course of the war included Bath, Exeter, and Canterbury. Arrangements were made with the Manchester and Salford and the Beswick Co-operative societies to provide the CIS with alternative accommodation should chief office be destroyed by enemy action. Evacuation caused more problems than merely the tracing of policyholders' addresses, which in itself was a most difficult problem — the earnings of agents in vulnerable areas were reduced, and they had to be given opportunities of transferring to vacant debits in other parts of the country. London branch office was evacuated to Hitchin in 1941.

By the autumn of 1941, 1,600 CIS staff were in the armed services and another 1,000 were on work of national importance. A stand-still agreement mainly relating to fire and accident business was reached between insurance offices in 1942 and accepted by the Board of Trade as being in sufficient compliance with the view of the Kennet Committee. (The Kennet Committee had recommended that offices should eliminate personnel engaged mainly in canvassing for new business.) Under the original schedule of reserved occupations, superintendents and district managers of industrial assurance companies, their clerical staffs, and certain other officials, were reserved at the age of 30 years. Insurance agency staff were not to be reserved. The Kennet Committee felt that 15 per cent of the men so deferred by June, 1942, could be spared without too much dislocation of service to policyholders. The Industrial Assurance Commissioner supported the policy of rationalization of staff, and urged fortnightly accounts for the duration of hostilities so that a full-time agent could collect two weekly debits, but insurance workers were strongly opposed to the proposal.

The CIS attained its 75th anniversary in 1942, unheralded except for a cable from the Swedish Co-operative Life Assurance Society conveying its congratulations.

---

[1] See letter from Miss A. A. Smale, 18 September, 1965.
"The raids on Plymouth became more and more severe. It was January, 1941. We had no windows, no gas, no electricity and no water. We managed to get a couple of oil heaters and work by the light of candles. However, in March of the same year our office was completely destroyed by enemy action, and everything was lost except one typewriter, a box of envelopes and a few reams of papers which had been kept in my house, just in case."

In December, 1942, James Darroch reported that the total loss by fire in Britain for each year since the outbreak of war *other than through enemy action*, had been greater than the average wastage for the ten years preceding the war. James Darroch became General Manager from February, 1943, and at the same time, R. Dinnage became Assistant General Manager.

Sir William Beveridge was Chairman and sole signatory of a monumental study of social security which was published in 1942 as *Social Insurance and Allied Services*, generally known as the Beveridge Report. Industrial assurance was included in the terms of reference, and Beveridge noted that the proportion of premiums used for purposes other than for the benefit of industrial life policyholders had fallen considerably during the course of the twentieth century, but the scale of diverted premiums remained excessive. He therefore suggested the setting up of an Industrial Assurance Board with a statutory monopoly of premium collection. The Board would take over and honour all existing policies of industrial assurance companies. It would employ, or compensate, the staffs and shareholders, and it would control all or part of the ordinary life business of industrial offices. The CIS Directors at that time were largely in agreement with the proposals. Indeed, the Beveridge Report made a number of favourable references to the progress and existing position, including the expense ratio, of the CIS.

The rising cost-of-living involved the CIS in a procession of wartime pay claims. CIS agents appealed against a pre-war decision not to extend interest-in-book to fire and general business, but the CIS Committee reminded agents that interest-in-book had been introduced at the take-over of the Planet, and that the fire and general business transacted by the Planet did not involve interest-in-book. (Loans of up to 75 per cent of purchase price of agents' books were entertained from 1938.) The Guild of Insurance Officials applied for a cost-of-living bonus at the end of 1938, which was not conceded, and in the following year, an application was submitted by NUDAW and other unions for the setting-up of conciliation machinery.[1] A demand for a war bonus for agents reached the dispute level in 1940, and the case was submitted to the National Arbitration Tribunal. NUDAW officials contended that the CIS had admitted the principle of war bonus by granting one to clerical and administrative staff, but the National Arbitration Tribunal award went against the agents'

---

[1] Lord Robens, present Chairman of the National Coal Board, was from 1935–1945 a NUDAW official in Manchester.

application. The management case submitted to the Tribunal was that it was imperative in wartime conditions to maintain strict economy; that minimum earnings of agents had increased by 15s. weekly since the beginning of the war; that average earnings of agents employed by the CIS were higher than those of other offices; that commissions and other fees had to be added to arrive at a true assessment of earnings; and finally, that the security of policyholders as well as agents was to be preserved by the financial stability of the Society. In 1943, the Arbitration Tribunal heard an appeal by district office clerks who were members of NUCISE for an increase in basic scales of wages — again the claim was not established.

From time to time, members of the armed forces reported killed were subsequently found to be prisoners-of-war. In the business of industrial assurance it is essential for claims to be paid promptly, and during the early war period, several cases occurred where incorrect claims were paid. District managers concerned were instructed to seek refunds, but the General Manager thought it was not worth the expense of taking legal action.

Claims for war damage to property were dealt with on a national basis by local committees of insurance officials who were responsible for their respective areas. The CIS, as with other insurance offices, seconded officials to serve on these local committees.

The operation of the war clause in the collective life scheme was suspended from the end of 1944, as civilian war claims had been comparatively light. The Government statement on social insurance relating to the proposed death grant provision was considered in 1944. The general feeling was that provided full employment was maintained, the proposals for death grant would not seriously restrict the field of business open to industrial life offices. Moreover, the Government scheme would neither affect CIS collective life nor ordinary life business.

The CIS followed the example of other offices in allowing cessation of premiums under whole life policies for policyholders attaining 80 years of age. War-time restrictions were not showing any adverse effects on prospects for CIS ordinary life business. Sums assured for new ordinary life business during 1941 amounted to £2.5m. compared with £1.5m. in the previous year; by 1943, the new sums in ordinary life had increased to £4.5m.

During 1940, the CIS had invested £2m. in Government stock, making the total holding of irredeemable stock approximately 20 per cent of invested funds. Local war weapons weeks were supported by the CIS. During 1942, the CIS stock exchange investments appreciated by over £900,000.

Although considerable re-organisation of the work of the CIS was undertaken during the war years, more especially at the district offices and agencies, in view of the number of staff called up for national service, the CIS agreed in January, 1944, to give provisional support to the recommendations of the Institute of Actuaries and the Chartered Insurance Institute for the provision of daytime study facilities for students. (At the outbreak of war there were approximately 100 employees at CIS chief office, and a further 100 at branch offices who were studying for the examination of the Chartered Insurance Institute, and 20 employees at chief office studying for Actuarial examinations.)[1]

At the end of 1944, the General Manager of the CIS submitted a report on post-war policy, and his recommendations included development of foreign business, aviation and marine insurance, and an investigation into CIS administration — in particular to resolve the already pressing debate over centralization or de-centralization of routine work. It was proposed to add to the number of divisional superintendents; to open up 21 new districts in the post-war period; and to extend CIS business in the dominions and colonies, the United States, and those European countries " where we are not interested at present." In March, 1944, a reinsurance agreement was drawn up with the Central China and India Trade and General Insurance Company — the first CIS treaty to be concerned with Asian countries.

Premium income in 1944 for ordinary life business was £2,270,000 (an increase of 14.73 per cent over 1943); collective life £671,000 (1.68 per cent); industrial business £8,664,000 (8.93 per cent); fire £519,000 (9.45 per cent); motor £540,000 (10.59 per cent) — total premium income of £13,150,000 (an increase of 9.72 per cent).

After the re-occupation of the Channel Islands, it came to light that representatives of other insurance offices, who remained in the Channel Islands during the German occupation, had formed a Central Industrial Life Assurance Fund, into which all premiums were paid, and from which claims, wages and expenses were paid. So far as the CIS could ascertain, no policyholders of the CIS had taken advantage of the fund.

From the outbreak of war in 1939, to 30 June, 1945, 33,918 CIS claims totalling £779,136 were paid in respect of deaths in the armed

---

[1] Merit increases had been awarded since 1928 to employees who were successful in the examinations of the Chartered Insurance Institute.

forces. In addition, 6,432 claims were in respect of civilian war deaths, involving a total payment of £129,222, and 659 through accidental death in the blackout, involving £9,881. In August, 1945, it was agreed to invest £3m. in Government Stock for Thanksgiving Week.

The average earnings of CIS agents had increased from £4 19s. 9d. in 1939, to £7 os. 11d. in 1944 but this increase of 40 per cent in nominal earnings should be set against a 50 per cent rise in the cost-of-living index for wage-earners between the years 1938 and 1944. Nor did the earnings of the insurance agents match those of wage-labour in general which rose 80 per cent on average.

At the end of 1944, the General Manager reported that considerable holdings of blocks of redeemable securities carrying high interest rates would mature in the near future. He reiterated that the investment policy of a life office should aim at a wide cover in sound securities, both as to class and redemption date. Since the outbreak of war, the CIS had confined its new investment to Government stock. It was therefore resolved to dispose of £750,000 of National War Bonds and other securities, and to re-invest the proceeds in Railway Stocks and 3½ per cent Conversion Loan from the end of 1944. A statement giving details of holdings in British railway securities was submitted early in 1945. It was reported that the post-war outlook for railways was a matter of considerable uncertainty, but the General Manager felt that there was no purpose in disposing of investments, "unless the Society proposes to adopt a more active investment policy re all investments." The share capital was increased from £26,250 to £52,500 by calling up an additional 5s. per share to comply with the Assurance Companies Act of 1946.

For many years, the Vulcan Boiler, the National Boiler, and the British Engine Boiler had shared the underwriting of the CIS boiler and engineering risks. In 1939, however, it had been recommended that steps be taken to enable the CIS to develop its own engineering section. These negotiations had to be suspended owing to the outbreak of war, and it was not until 1946 that the agreements with the tariff offices were cancelled. The CIS then entered into an arrangement with the Municipal Mutual Office, whereby the CIS was to issue engineering policies in its own name and reinsure the entire portfolio with the Municipal Mutual. This arrangement thus enabled the CIS to conduct engineering insurance from the beginning of 1947 on non-tariff lines.

Professor Levy (*vide* Wilson and Levy) proposed to the CIS in 1945, that as policies were issued as collateral security for house purchase loans, the CIS should also introduce a scheme to provide endowment policies for the specific purpose of promoting foreign travel. The General Manager wrote that the proposal would take the CIS outside the realms of legitimate insurance.

To combat any recurrence of the damage caused by the failure of the Universal Insurance Company (see page 220) a Motor Insurers' Bureau was set up in 1946 including tariff, non-tariff offices and Lloyd's. The main purpose was to establish a central fund so that compensation could be paid to victims of uninsured drivers. The CIS agreed to become a member.

The Policyholder quoted the CIS as top of its table for new business figures for 1946. *The Economist* also referred to the CIS as an office which " appears to have emerged as a leader of Life Assurance."

The balance sheet for 1949 showed an overdraft of £1½m. James Darroch, the General Manager, explained that this should not cause any embarrassment:

> " Some of our critics may endeavour to place a wrong interpretation upon it, but in actual fact it is due to a little bit of enterprise in anticipating the closing date of the 3 per cent Savings Bonds. We borrowed £2m. from the bank in order to purchase that amount of Savings Bonds before the issue was withdrawn, and the net result is that we shall benefit considerably in interest yield and will have cleared the overdraft by the time our balance sheet figures become public property."

A committee of inquiry made up of CIS officials was appointed by the General Manager in 1949, to investigate to what extent increased mechanisation at chief office would affect district office procedure, and whether any beneficial reorganisation could take place in district office methods. Evidence was submitted by district office and by chief office departments and the committee members also visited a number of other chief offices of insurance companies. In the preamble to the two volumes of evidence it was stated:

> " Our main concern is to provide the most simple and economical way for the handling of large premium increases, particularly in the ordinary life and general branches. These increases automatically mean a heavier burden to be borne by clerical staffs which cannot easily be met under the present conditions by an extension of staffs. The modern word is redeployment, and the way to ensure that our present staffs

J. Darroch

R. Dinnage

can cope adequately with the new demand is to submit existing procedure in all its phases to the closest possible scrutiny. Such an examination should be a continuous process and the concern of a small body of officials, without executive responsibility, able to present a balanced view on the best way to fulfil the varied requirements of our organisation . . . "

After what had been a rather hurried survey of several systems the members of the committee were satisfied that

" the machine has not yet been invented which will permit a substantial reduction being made in terms of personnel and yet retain that measure of efficiency built up during the past 25 or 30 years and which, with all its imperfections, will bear comparison with the organisations of most of our competitors."

The CIS was not in a position to anticipate the enormous advances about to be made in electronic computers. But the report does make an oblique reference to the future development of what became the Organisation and Methods Section.

(ii) Post-War Position

In the rank order of industrial life companies the CIS had reached eleventh place in terms of sums assured in 1925, and second by 1953.[1] In terms of total sums assured for life assurance (Ordinary and Industrial), 1913 to 1953, the CIS was ranked 63rd in 1913 (before the Planet take-over), 26th in 1937, and 7th in 1953. The CIS was the only industrial/ordinary office to improve its ranking between 1925 and 1953, when it moved from 0.6 per cent of the total of industrial life sums assured business in 1925, to 14.2 per cent in 1953.

The number of life assurance companies has remained fairly stable during the present century — unlike banking — but the volume of business done has increased steadily. Premium income of the CIS in ordinary life business increased by 4.4 per cent per year between the wars, and in the industrial branch by 3.7 per cent. The main feature of the growth of the insurance industry since the second world war has been the rapid development of pension scheme business, which has also been greatly stimulated by taxation concessions both to employer and employed. The post-war period has also included several important mergers and new groups in the insurance industry, but most of the rapidly-growing companies have grown by expansion of business rather than by absorption or association with other

[1] See J. Johnston and G. W. Murphy, " Growth of Life Assurance in United Kingdom since 1880," *Manchester School*, Volume 25, No. 2, May, 1957.

companies. There is also a tendency for the larger companies to have lower expense ratios. The total assets of British Life companies available for investment grew from £160m. in 1880 to over £3,500m. by the mid-1950s and £9,600m. a decade later.

(iii) Nationalization of Industrial Assurance

The distinction between life *insurance* and life *assurance* can be traced back to Charles Babbage in the early nineteenth century: " Assurance is a contract dependent upon the duration of life, which must either happen or fail. Insurance is a contract relating to any other uncertain event which may partly happen and partly fail."[1] In the Stamp Act of 1870, it was declared: " Insurance includes Assurance."

Industrial assurance in the mid-twentieth century is no longer accused of malpractice; indeed the term itself is becoming historical as offices now refer to their house-to-house collection of life assurance premiums as " Home Service " assurance. But in earlier years industrial assurance was vilified on grounds of social justice and economics. The controversy often descended into diatribes and polemics. At times, industrial assurance business was attacked by all three leading political parties, and became the subject of several Parliamentary committees of inquiry,[2] with subsequent legislation imposed to safeguard an unsuspecting public from hard selling and, at its worst, sharp practice on the part of industrial assurance offices. (To a certain extent, policyholders can only assess the worth of their insurance cover through competitive quotations, as few members of

[1] *Babbage, Charles, 1792–1871.* Mathematician who developed machine for calculating numerical tables. Also pioneer in punched card data processing. A Swedish " difference " machine on the lines of that designed by Babbage was used by Dr. Farr in constructing the *English Life Tables No. 3* in 1864. Babbage was an early writer on life assurance — see his *Comparative View of Various Institutions for the Assurance of Lives* (1828). He also acted as Actuary to the Protectors Life Assurance Company from 1824.

[2] See above pp.176–177, *Report of Board of Trade Committee on Industrial Life Assurance* (*The Parmoor Committee*) 1920.
The Committee referred to the difficulties of transfer of industrial assurance to the State. Lord Parmoor did not think the State could undertake this responsibility. In Appendix B " Industrial Assurance Companies and Collecting Societies " sub-heading " Statement of Premiums and Expenses 1912 to 1917 " 20 companies were listed with expense ratios expressed in precentages varying from City Life 60, Hearts of Oak 59, to London and Manchester 42.9 and Britannic 42.4. Twelve of the companies had a lower expense ratio than the CIS; The Prudential was 44.5, the Pearl 43.7, the Refuge 46.6. Of the collecting societies, the Liverpool Victoria was 44 and Royal Liver 39.5. The CIS is listed in the Appendix as an Industrial Assurance Company.

See above pp.211–216, *Report of Committee on Industrial Assurance and Assurance of Lives of Children under 10 years of age.* (*The Cohen Committee*) 1932.

the public are sufficiently conversant with actuarial science to make an objective assessment; and it is not uncommon for life policyholders to think they have been unfairly treated if they survive to pay more in premiums than the sum assured.) Certainly, there were excesses in the selling of industrial assurance in the early days, but progressively the policyholder has benefited from legislative protection which has often followed the precedents of the leading assurance offices. In such a technical matter as industrial assurance, successive Governments concerned with investigation and legislation often have had to rely on evidence and advice from the industrial offices themselves.

The main recurring criticism levelled against industrial assurance has been its high expense ratio in the collection of premiums from householders.[1] With the newly-founded industrial assurance companies it was difficult to accumulate adequate reserves whilst meeting the expenses of collection and the rapid expansion of branch offices. In time, the business of industrial assurance became more consolidated, the expense of conducting it was reduced, and stronger reserves were built up. Moreover, the gradually improving standards of living of wage-earners made possible the payment of larger premiums; hence many wage-earners from the end of the nineteenth century became attracted to endowment assurance rather than to whole life.

From an early stage, rather than impose controls, proposals were submitted for the full nationalization of industrial assurance.[2] The mortality experience of industrial life policyholders was generally adverse, and before the advent of health and unemployment insurance, the number of lapses in industrial assurance was large. From 1896, however, the insurance offices were legally obliged to serve a notice on policyholders before forfeiture of policies in arrears with premiums.

[1] The CIS ceased to issue weekly premium policies as from 1965.

[2] Sidney Webb, "Fabian Report on Industrial Assurance," *New Statesman*, 13 March, 1915.
" . . . the fact that industrial assurance enables a few hundred shareholders to derive colossal profits, a few thousand directors, managers and superior officials to draw large salaries . . . does not seem to us to justify the perpetuation of so wasteful a system . . . nor do we think the matter can be disposed of, as is some-times argued by the plea that industrial assurance is a matter of private concern . . . When the question is of service affecting nine-tenths of the whole wage earning class . . . the creation of a disciplined army of 100,000 able to exert great electoral influence in the State . . . we think it clear that public intervention is not only justified but imperatively required."
See J. G. Sinclair, *The Truth about Industrial Assurance* (1923); *The Return of the Rebel* (1929) [a novel about industrial assurance]; and *Evils of Industrial Assurance* (1932) [with a preface by Lord Snowden]. See also Lord Beveridge, *Voluntary Action* (1948), p.57.

Industrial assurance has been severely reprimanded on the ground that it has an excessive lapse rate,[1] caused mainly through overselling on the part of agents. Industrial assurance has also been criticised as an uneconomic service which has encouraged extravagance in funeral expenses.[2] It should however be made clear that a system of frequent collections at the homes of policyholders does not necessarily make industrial assurance more expensive to administer, merely because the premiums are physically collected. In terms of average cost per collection, industrial life premiums are often cheaper to collect than to transmit through the post or through banker's order. It is not the cost of the house-to-house collections which makes the expense higher in relation to premiums than is the case with ordinary life policies, but the much smaller amounts concerned on each payment of industrial premium.

The Assurance Companies Act of 1909 enforced the separation of ordinary and industrial business, and the Industrial Assurance Act of 1923 included: provisions for making substantial statutory deposits; separation of industrial assurance funds; administrative checks on transfers from one Society or Company to another; rules regarding amalgamation of offices, protection of policyholders; and the creation of the office of Industrial Assurance Commissioner. The nationalization of industrial life assurance was specifically referred to in the statements of policy approved by the Labour Party in October, 1928, and published under the title of "Labour and the Nation":

"The system of industrial life assurance needed to safeguard the worker against the risks confronting him and through which he too often today is shamelessly exploited . . . The Labour

[1] The Fabian Society investigation is worth noting on lapsing — "but if the social evil of lapsing is serious . . . it is all the more important that the average pecuniary loss of a lapse to the individual policyholder should not be exaggerated. The vast majority of the lapses occur where the total amount paid in premiums is very small, often only a few pence. It may, indeed, be literally nothing."

[2] See Herman Levy and Sir Arnold Wilson, *Burial Reform and Funeral Costs* (1935), p.60.
"It is frequently argued that its [industrial assurance] existence has, for practical purposes, solved the problem of burial to the working classes. Nothing could be more misleading. The commercial functioning of industrial assurance has nothing to do whatever with the actual costs of burials and funerals, interment or cremation, any substantial reduction of which might tend to restrict its business turnover. It is a very costly method of insurance with an average of 35 per cent or so, which has had no beneficial influence whatever either upon the economic and social aspects or upon the costs of the working man's funeral. It has no greater influence on these costs than a money lender on the way a client spends a loan."
The authors maintained: "It is frequently argued that industrial assurance has helped to reduce the costs of burial for the working classes. This is not true . . . It merely *enables* burial money and it has in many cases served to enhance expenditure of funerals." Ibid. p.58.

Party will vest their ownership in the nation and their administration in authorities acting on the nation's behalf."

A conference of the National Amalgamated Union of Life Assurance
Workers (NAULAW) in 1926 had supported measures for the
nationalization of industrial assurance, and the TUC in 1927 had
declared that: " In the opinion of this Congress the time is opportune
for an examination by the General Council and the unions concerned
into nationalization of industrial assurance and such other branches of
private and social insurance as can be associated successfully with it."
The National Federation of Insurance Workers contended *vis à vis*
the Labour Party that the insurance companies and the mass of workers
did not desire nationalization. It issued a memorandum in 1930, dis-
puting the assertion of the rival union that " Prudentialization meant
rationalization." The question of the nationalization of industrial life
assurance was not referred to in the 1929 election programme of the
Labour Party, and *The Policyholder*[1] argued that the proposal had never
been seriously considered either by policyholders or insurance staffs.

During the 1930s, Wilson and Levy looked to the CIS for support
in their literary campaign against industrial assurance:

" The Co-operative Insurance Society has made many attempts to
overcome the heavy cost of conducting industrial assurance, but it has
been compelled to follow the practice of the capitalist companies and
collect the premiums weekly or monthly with its resulting heavy
cost. It seems unlikely, therefore, that we can look to the Co-operative
Movement for any improvement in the present position: on the other
hand, those at the head of co-operative affairs in Great Britain must
be well aware of the true position and their support for any measures
of reform would be of great value, being based upon personal
experience."[2]

Although Beveridge included nationalization of industrial assurance
as one of the recommendations given in his *Full Employment in
a Free Society*,[3] he maintained that the main reason for doing so
was a desire to secure the services of outside staffs for his comprehensive scheme of social security. The ensuing Industrial Assurance and

[1] *The Policyholder*, 29 May, 1929.

[2] Levy and Wilson, *Industrial Assurance*, p.299 and N. Barou, *Co-operative Insurance*
(1936), p.70.
Barou noted that the CIS was the first consumer co-operative insurance organisation
to be founded out of 150 co-operative insurance institutions listed. Two agricultural insurance societies pre-dated the CIS — the Mutual Agricultural Company
in Denmark, 1812, and the Swiss Agricultural Society in 1862.

[3] The foundation of the Export Credits Guarantee Department of the Board of Trade
from 1919 was an early example of the State entering the insurance market.

Friendly Societies Act, 1948, amended the law relating to the collection of premiums for insurance against funeral expenses, but there was no hint at the time that the Labour Party had plans for full nationalization.

Ian Mikardo wrote a pamphlet in the spring of 1948, entitled *The Second Five Years — a Labour Programme for 1950*. In a section on nationalization of industry, he contended that the power of the privately-owned joint-stock banks with regard to the provision and control of credit was " anomalous and outdated." There was a high degree of operational redundancy in banking — " a profligate waste of premises, equipment and labour." The insurance companies were likewise castigated, but more severely, in that their operations were made needlessly expensive through a profusion of overlapping services. This overlapping was not nearly so serious in fire and accident insurance as in life assurance, and Ian Mikardo noted that

> " the case for nationalizing industrial assurance has been forcibly put on many occasions — notably in the Beveridge Report — and remains incontrovertible. Cost ratios are generally very high . . . The abuse is associated with over-selling and particularly the waste of labour and money involved in the high rate of lapses, have brought this system into wide disrepute."

He further commented that apart from the social insurance provisions already on the statute book, voluntary insurance was sought by many people and " it is highly desirable that they should be able to do so without having to bear inflated costs due to redundant machinery for selling and collection." A nationalized scheme would remove this redundancy and could cheapen the overhead costs of the service by combining it with some form of householder's comprehensive and ordinary life cover. Ian Mikardo envisaged new methods of selling and collection, " including the use of collecting stations in work places," which he noted had already been pioneered in the United States. As the distinction between ordinary and industrial assurance was a legal, and not a functional one, he argued that it would be impossible to effect an artificial separation which would leave either of the two branches in private hands. He noted that two-fifths of new ordinary life business was being acquired by industrial life agents and it would be uneconomic to divide a unified selling agency offering both types. Moreover, it was ordinary life business which provided companies with their major investment funds, and some of these larger companies had invested " not merely in gilt-edged securities but also in many types of commercial venture, not all of which are equally in the national interest." He concluded therefore that there was a "strong overall case for nationalizing as a whole the two life branches."

A meeting at Transport House was held on 18 January, 1949, attended by representatives of the General Council of the TUC and the Labour Party Policy Committee, together with representatives of unions catering for the insurance industry. The proceedings of the meeting were highly confidential, and in the words of one delegate: "We were requested to ensure that no inkling of the conclusions would be divulged to any but executive members." At the meeting,

> "a statement of the considered views and tentative recommendations of the Labour Party Committee was handed to each delegate and then read at rapid shorthand speed by the Assistant Secretary of the TUC, after which each memorandum was collected in order to prevent any unauthorised disclosure."[1]

James Griffiths, then Minister of National Insurance, went through the memorandum for the purpose of amplification. A delegate commented:

> "In order of preference the reasons given were firstly that by control vast sums would be made available for Government investment. These accumulated and increasing funds were social funds, subscribed by the public, largely from working-class pockets and it was indefensible that such accumulations should be left in private hands."[2]

Considerable reference was made to Wilson and Levy's book *Industrial Insurance*, "which was accepted as the result of a scientific inquiry into the industry." The first method to fuse control and ownership of industrial assurance was the possibility of the Ministry of National Insurance providing the benefits of existing industrial assurance through supplementary cover under the National Insurance Scheme. It was concluded that this would make many insurance workers redundant. The next consideration was whether to nationalize the whole of the insurance industry. The deterring feature in this case was foreign business. It was concluded that the risk of disturbance to foreign business, particularly with dollar resources in mind, was too great. There was the further possibility of taking over the whole of the life business of the industry, but it was noted that the

---

[1] Report of District Managers' Branch Conference NUCISE 24 April, 1949.
[2] President's Report. Ibid.

difficulty of division of business would militate against the proposal, as practically all offices transacting fire and general business also had considerable life business. This left the taking over of industrial life assurance only. But again there were difficulties. Some prominent industrial offices had extensive overseas connections and commitments in the field of general insurance. Practically all of them had ordinary life business which was expanding. As it would be too difficult in terms of administration to split the business of the industrial offices, they would have to be taken over as a whole. The final decision therefore was to take over the 14 industrial/ordinary life offices complete with all their existing connections of ordinary branch, fire and general insurance, inclusive of overseas business. The National Union of CIS Employees (a section of the Transport and General Workers Union) was the only union at the meeting to voice apprehension of these proposals: " It was our view that the promises made to staffs did not reconcile with the object to be achieved by public control." As far as the CIS was concerned, out of an expense ratio of under 31 per cent, 22 per cent was consumed in commission charges largely paid to agents.[1]

On 22 April, 1949, there was a further meeting of members of affiliated unions who were addressed by Herbert Morrison and James Griffiths. Herbert Morrison insisted that there would be neither socialization nor nationalization of industrial assurance. What would happen would be a conversion of the industry into a public service. But there would be no State departmental control, and industrial assurance workers would not be treated as civil servants. There would be established a business board which would be comprised of trade union representatives, " and those best fitted by knowledge, experience and professional attainment to administer efficiently." The speakers underlined the intention that the business of industrial assurance, in so far as the large and prosperous offices was concerned, was to become a public service. The small and less secure undertakings would be allowed to continue as before, despite the alleged evils of high expenses

[1] The question of expense ratios was also brought up at a subsequent meeting of CIS District Managers:

" Now when the Labour Party admit the necessity of domiciliary collection, they concede the argument justifying the existing expense ratio. Despite this it is affirmed that reduction of expenses and benefit of policyholders is the main objective. There is no answer to this problem; the promises and objectives conflict. We are of course told that the cessation of recruitment will serve to reduce staff and expenses. Fortified and guided by our knowledge of the business we know such a proposition is impracticable."

Report of CIS District Managers' Branch Conference 24 April, 1949,

and heavy lapses. Those members of the public who had entrusted their savings to these small societies were not to be protected, because it would not pay to incorporate them. There were to be 14 industrial offices, and in addition the Liverpool Victoria and the Royal Liver, to be taken over. The other collecting societies were to be left to operate unhindered.

The 50th anniversary jubilee celebration of the foundation of the Labour Party took place in 1949, and in the same year, the Labour Party produced a policy statement — *Labour Believes in Britain*. In the report of the annual conference of the Labour Party, Herbert Morrison, in referring to *Labour Believes in Britain*, wrote:

> " We have not made an abstract list of industries for social-
> ization. We have considered them in relation to the various
> parts of the programme in a natural way. For example, the
> proposals with regard to making industrial assurance into a
> public concern are made primarily on the basis of rounding off
> the social services and completing that great edifice . . . "

J. S. Worrall, a member of the Co-operative Party, retorted that the CIS was in effect a consumer organisation, as all profits were returned to its members; it provided a great social service, and the Labour Party was proposing to nationalize an already collectively-owned and democratically-controlled institution. He added: " What would be the effect of nationalizing this Insurance Society? It would mean that large insurance houses would be left under capitalist control whilst the Co-operative would be nationalized . . . " More pertinently, a request was put to the Labour Party Executive to withdraw indus-trial assurance from the election programme because " we have done no propaganda at all to educate the people as to exactly what we mean by the nationalization of industrial assurance . . . " The national-ization of cement, sugar, wholesale meat distribution, and water supplies, would be sufficient for the moment. A trade union delegate quoted the resolution of the 1926 Trade Union Congress that there should be an investigation by the General Council of the TUC into the question of the nationalization of industrial assurance. Moreover, the Labour Party Conference had said that no scheme would be satisfactory, unless it provided adequate minimum wages and joint control by those who administer and benefit from industrial assurance.

The USDAW Conference of 1949 passed a resolution in favour of nationalization: " And that the agency staff should have representa-tion and consultation at every level throughout the industry." A delegate from the National Union of Co-operative Insurance Society Employees at the 1949 Trade Union Congress commented:

"The insurance unions are sharply divided over nationalization. I have never known any issue which has raised so much doubt and anxiety. Although nationalization was accepted by Congress many years ago, in our submission, the proposals made by the Labour Party this year were rushed through too quickly, but if the Party had taken more trouble in preparing the ground, I think the response from the insurance unions would have been a happier one."

He argued that consultation should precede the takeover, but up to that time there had been no real consultation with the organised insurance workers. The Labour Party's proposals placed insurance agents in a very difficult position. There was a fear, especially amongst clerical and administrative staffs, that implementation of the proposals would mean large-scale dismissals, because it was maintained that one of the objects of nationalization was a reduction in the number of people employed in industry. The main objection levelled at the insurance industry in *Labour Believes in Britain* was that the constitution of the industry did not enable private profit to take second place to public interest. The political statement did not allow for the fact that the Co-operative Movement had never conducted insurance for the benefit of shareholders.

The Times of 6 and 7 June included two lengthy articles on industrial assurance. The Beveridge Report had stated that competition in industrial assurance did not result in the best offices driving their less efficient rivals off the market; competition therefore served no useful purpose. If the contention of the Beveridge Report was true, *The Times* article noted, "then the case for a State monopoly would depend essentially on the extent of the saving in costs to be expected from it." The article concluded — "Fresh Facts rather than fresh arguments are needed to see where the truth lies." The *News Chronicle* published a Gallup poll on the subject of industrial assurance on 8 June, 1949, showing that 50 per cent of adults in the country were paying premiums on industrial life policies, apart from a further 30 per cent of the population who had taken out ordinary life policies. The members of the public who were paying industrial assurance were asked for their views on whether their insurances were likely to be handled better or worse as a result of nationalization: 15 per cent said "better," 19 per cent "the same," 35 per cent "worse," and the remaining 31 per cent "didn't know." Of the general public, 84 per cent had heard of the possibility of the nationalization of industrial assurance, and of this 84 per cent, 22 per cent were in favour, and 39 per cent were against nationalization proposals. The vast majority of industrial policyholders regarded the general arrangements for collection of premium as satisfactory, 95 per cent making this reply.

An enquiry conducted by the Fabian Society amongst its branches showed that nearly all branch members agreed that it was necessary to consolidate existing nationalized industries and to extend nationalization to other industries, but the order of priority suggested differed widely from that adopted later by the Labour Party Executive and embodied in *Labour Believes in Britain*. Of the 39 Fabian Branches replying, 25 advocated nationalization of chemicals, 22 water supply, 13 commercial insurance, and 11 commercial banking. The list was certainly varied, but it would seem that industrial assurance, which the Labour Party was putting first, was thought of by only one-third of the Fabian branches. The *Manchester Guardian* commented: " This supports the generally-held view that the project is not particularly popular even among the most ardent socialists." A leader in *The Times* of 6 July, 1949, headed " Insurance and The State " commented: " In theory at any rate a State service could do for industrial assurance all that the Labour Party seems to expect on very much more slender grounds, of competitive State enterprise in other fields." It could, for instance, use all the machinery of State insurance and deduction from earnings to develop voluntary insurance to supplement the pensions and death benefits of the compulsory State Scheme. It could concentrate on benefits to be added to retirement and widows pensions rather than on small lump sums payable at death. Employers could be encouraged to deduct premiums from wages, along with other compulsory insurance contributions, and home visiting for collection of premiums could be severely restricted. Only if it turned out as a result of this practical test that the existing organisation of industrial assurance was too costly would there be any occasion for further action, and even then the corollary would be that to nationalize all offices doing industrial assurance would not be feasible; rather the State should restrict itself to a monopoly of all future business of a purely industrial character:

> " If this were done, the Prudential, the Pearl and the Co-operative Insurance Society, the three great institutions conducting assurance of nearly every description, probably could carry on independently, though they might have to combine with other offices to manage their closed industrial funds."

The case for nationalizing any branch of insurance, industrial or otherwise, had in no way been proved.

" As matters now stand," concluded *The Times* article, " the Labour Party is wide open to the accusation of wanting to use the shortcomings of industrial assurance as a pretext for taking control of the Prudential, the Pearl and the Co-operative with their massive business of all varieties at home and overseas, to the considerable detriment of national goodwill and the balance of payments."

" Sister Pru, Sister Pru, do you see anyone coming ? "

In December, 1949, a meeting took place between the Economic Committee of the TUC, the unions concerned with industrial assurance, and the Labour Party, to consider the Party's revised plans for incorporating industrial assurance in their general election programme. The basis for discussion at the December meeting was the resolution passed by the 1949 Trade Union Congress regarding consultation at all stages with accredited trade unions of insurance employees in connection with the nationalization proposals.

242

James Griffiths stated at that meeting the views of the National Executive of the Labour Party:

"I begin by laying this down as common ground and no Socialist can deny it: that a service designed to meet the contingencies and adversities of life ought not to be a service that gives profit to anybody. I therefore say that industrial assurance ought to be a public service. We have all said that. When the Beveridge Report was published and when the recommendation was made which we are seeking (in a slightly different form I agree) to implement, and was placed before this Conference, the Trade Union Congress and the Co-operative Congress, we all unanimously adopted it. We are not submitting a new policy to you. What we are seeking to do in this document is to outline how the policy agreed to by the Movement should be put into operation."

He then referred to the various committees of inquiry into industrial assurance, and mentioned the investigations of Sir Arnold Wilson, the Conservative member in the House of Commons during the 1930s. None of the investigations had given the system a clean bill of health.[1] James Griffiths added:

"When the Executive came to frame this statement, having already implemented all but this of the recommendations contained in the Beveridge Report, we came to the conclusion that in the next Parliament we ought to adopt Beveridge's recommendation which he called ' Change 23 '."

James Griffiths then outlined the usual criticisms of industrial assurance — the high cost of administration, the evil of over-selling, the high lapse rate. He quoted the Cohen Report: "Excessive competition with its almost feverish pressure for increase, is responsible for the principal defects of the business." Admitting that over the previous four years the lapse rate had declined, James Griffiths argued that the Labour Government, with its policy of full employment, had provided conditions appropriate for the expansion of insurance business.

[1] For an objective study of development of industrial assurance, see *Industrial Life Offices Jubilee — 1901 to 1951*. In 1900 the weekly debit of individual agents was often only £3 to £4 and the number of policies for £1 collected was about 100. Often the policyholders did not know which assurance office held his policy — he was merely "in Mr. Jones's club." Hence poaching was easy when an agent moved his office. In 1900 there was no profit-sharing on industrial policies. The average weekly premium on industrial life in 1901 was 2½d. By 1951 it had risen to 6d. Industrial assurance was involved in nine-tenths of the homes of workers and the average collection in 1951 from each home was 4s. 3d. per week. Average ratio of expenses, 1901, 43 per cent; 1950, 27.9 per cent. There were more agents in 1901 than 1950.

Insurance offices were investing *not their own shareholders' resources, but the money of the people:* " It is the bobs and half-crowns they collect and when money collected from the people is invested, that money ought to be publicly controlled and invested in the interests of the whole of the nation."

The Beveridge Report had recommended that an industrial assurance board should be set up which should take over all industrial assurance business and such part of the ordinary life business as was found convenient. James Griffiths conceded that he did not know why Beveridge had said that when you took over industrial assurance you should take over also such part of the ordinary life business as was found to be convenient,

> " but I will tell you why we arrived at in effect the same conclusion. We have sought the advice of the expert knowledge and experience available to us, and may I pay a warm, sincere tribute to the Co-operative Insurance Society and their officers for all the help and kindness they have given us in this matter?" (The inference of course was that the CIS had recommended this as a viable proposal.) " Everybody we have met has told us that there is no practical way of severing the industrial part from the other part of the business."

Hence the Executive decided that the companies and societies engaged in industrial assurance should be taken over as they stood. James Griffiths concluded:

> " Having become convinced — not quickly, not without thought, not without consideration, but indeed after years of consideration — that this ought to be a public service, we therefore commend it to you as being, in our view, the action which our Government ought to take in the future in this field."

Arthur Greenwood wrote an article on the subject in January, 1950.[1] He pointed out that in 1948, out of nearly 4½m. policies that came to an end, no fewer than 2½m. had lapsed. He quoted from *The Times:* " There would seem to be something wrong with a business in which, even in a period of full employment and steady earnings, no less than 58 per cent of the contracts discharged each year are broken by customers who have changed their minds." The concentration of financial and economic power in the hands of the proprietary companies had assumed immense and fearful proportions. They had control of over £1,000m. in their funds in the investment of which the policyholder who provided the money had no say.

[1] *Fact,* Volume 8, No. 1, January, 1950.

The view of Lord Beveridge was also referred to — that industrial assurance should be converted from a competitive sellers' business to a service controlled by consumers. The National Executive of the Labour Party therefore decided that the ends it had in mind could be best served by changing the character of the industrial assurance offices, and vesting ownership not in the hands of private shareholders but with the policyholders. An industrial assurance board would be set up, shareholders would be bought out, and ownership vested in policyholders, amongst whom all net surpluses would be distributed. It was admitted that there was nothing revolutionary in this proposal, as there were in existence a number of mutual offices, but it would enable the worst abuses of industrial assurance to be tackled. As it would be almost impossible to dissect a company's operations, the whole business of concerns which handled industrial assurance would be mutualized, including ordinary life assurance and other forms of insurance.

But Arthur Greenwood added:

"Investment of the funds of insurance companies will remain their own affair. The Government in pursuance of its full employment policy, will continue, as at present, to control capital investment by all financial institutions but this represents no change."

Agents' livelihoods would also be protected. They would remain the life blood of the industrial assurance service. They would be paid the full value of "book-interest", they would enjoy improved status, and would be freed from the more unpleasant pressures of intense competitive business.

In a further article, Arthur Greenwood dealt with the money the big insurance companies play with: "It is the policyholders' money — your money." He compared insurance with manufacturing industry, where the capital represented assets, and where the provision of these assets entitled the shareholder to a suitable share in the proceeds: "But no such case can be made out for the insurance companies which merely collect and pay out other people's money." The policy of the Labour Party would be to return the whole of the surplus to the policyholders. It is difficult to see the logic of this discrimination between insurance and other industry. Surely the customer purchasing the products of industry is providing some surplus that is ploughed back into the enterprise and finds its way into shareholders' pockets? To follow the proposals to their logical conclusion there should have been a recommendation that profits should be distributed to consumers

245

and shareholders in industry generally as well as in insurance. Arthur Greenwood also discounted the view that the insurance companies added to their income by wise investment. He retorted: "It's your money they invest not their own; therefore it should be your income they add to." The views of the Parmoor Committee of 1920, were quoted: "The share capital of industrial assurance companies exercises much less important functions than that of commercial or manufacturing undertakings . . ." Nor could Arthur Greenwood invalidate the fact that the collecting societies had a higher expense ratio for industrial assurance than the large proprietary offices. He concluded: "When all industrial assurance is on a mutual basis it should be possible to reduce costs per policy."

During 1950, the Labour Party adopted the new slogan of "mutualization" of industrial assurance rather than outright nationalization. At the annual Labour Party Conference in 1950, a Co-operative Party member referred to the policy statement, *Let us Face the Future*, in which it was stated that public interest was to come before private profit. The delegate contended that the proposals for "mutualization" outlined in Michael Young's pamphlet *The Future of Industrial Assurance* did not bear this out. It was not true that policyholders through "mutualization" would have a greater say in the insurance industry. Nor had any mandate been given by the Labour Party Conference to advocate a policy of "mutualization" — "No mention of it is made in *Labour and the New Society* and I have to ask for an assurance from the Government that 'mutualization' is not likely to be pushed forward without proper reference to Conference when the time comes."

The Co-operative Party Annual Conference of 1950, expressed its views on mutualization: "That this Conference shows its appreciation of the outcome of discussions with the Labour Party on industrial assurance and places on record the view that this might be a method of securing co-operative expression in other industries to be brought under public ownership."

In 1951, the Labour Party excluded from its election manifesto any reference either to nationalization or "mutualization" of insurance.

We must now turn to the discussions which took place between the CIS and the Labour Party from 1949 concerning nationalization proposals.

(iv) *Nationalization and the CIS — A Case Study in Communications*

The CIS General Committee passed a resolution on 8 December,

1942: "That we record that, in principle, we are in agreement with the proposals in the Beveridge Report, and on the understanding that they will be nationally applied and that adequate provision will be made for the protection of staffs."

The Co-operative Congress which met at Edinburgh in 1943, was dismayed at the lukewarm reception of the Beveridge Plan by the war-time Government. Congress strongly protested against attempts to dilute and postpone the plan for social security, and *inter alia* called for an immediate comprehensive plan of legislation designed to " convert industrial assurance into a national social service . . . "

In the spring of 1947, the CIS received a request for information from the Fabian Society in connection with an investigation which was being undertaken into the insurance industry:

> " There are some figures which we cannot get from commercial firms, and I [The Fabian Society] wondered whether you could supply them. For instance:
> (1) the present lapsing rate in industrial assurance
> (2) the proportion of general business you do [CIS] with business firms, and the proportion done with individuals."

The General Manager replied that a bald statement of lapse rate in industrial life assurance, even if it were known, would have to be treated with reserve. For instance, the operation of non-forfeiture clauses, and the fact that the surrender of the policy could be part of a transaction involving the issue of new policies, would have the effect of making any simple statement of the number of lapses of little practical value. Nor would it be possible to divide the policyholders of the CIS into the categories of business firms and individuals, as it would be impossible to determine the extent of overlap between the two classes.

A further letter from the Fabian Society, 11 July, 1947, referred to more general questions:

> (1) Whether ordinary life and industrial life business could be separated.
> (2) Whether the general business could be separated from life business.
> (3) General view on the future of the business.

Mr. C. E. Prater, a Director of the CIS, and Mr. B. Holgate, the CIS Actuary, met members of the Fabian Society, on 17 July, 1947. At the outset of the meeting, one of the members of the Fabian Society referred to the CIS " acceptance of the Beveridge recommendations regarding nationalization." Mr. Holgate explained that whilst the CIS had announced its support of the Beveridge Plan in principle, subject to certain safeguards, the nationalization of industrial assurance was not an essential part of that Plan: where the CIS differed from the other industrial assurance offices was in its acceptance of the death grant proposals, which the other offices actively resisted. The complete separation of life business into two entirely separate organisations would tend to increase costs, particularly if the business taken away was that on which the whole organisation had been constructed. Holgate said it was evident that some of the members of the Fabian Society attending the meeting were still thinking in terms of the abuses detailed in the 1920 Parmoor Report, and ignoring the improvements that had been brought about since that time.

Some months later, on 9 March, 1948, the Fabian Society sent the CIS General Manager a copy of the first part of their report, which was a survey of the insurance industry, but explained that the second part of the report (which would include the main recommendations for reform) was not yet complete:

"The whole report is being prepared for The National Executive of the Labour Party and, when it is completed, it will be their property. We have been very pleased to send those organisations like yourselves, who have been helping us with the information, a copy of Part 1, but it will be the Labour Party's responsibility whether they should circulate Part 2 or publish Parts 1 and 2 together."

Morgan Phillips, the Secretary of the Labour Party, had not received either part of the report by 18 March, 1948, and it was impossible for him to say whether any further action would be taken by the Labour Party on its receipt. (Part 1 of the Fabian Society Report contained a detailed survey of all classes of insurance, but only one recommendation.)

On 15 October, 1948, Michael Young, then Secretary of the Research Department of the Labour Party, first telephoned Mr. Dinnage, General Manager of the CIS, and subsequently confirmed by letter the formation of a sub-committee of the Labour Party to consider the forthcoming general election programme. He mentioned that the two members of the sub-committee were Herbert Morrison, and James Griffiths, the Minister of National Insurance. "What we much hope," said Michael Young, "is that you might be able to meet them at 4 p.m. on Friday, 22 October, at 11 Downing Street, to have a general and informal talk." Mr. Aneurin Davies and Mr. Dinnage went to the meeting and afterwards sent a memorandum setting out the considered views of the CIS Committee on a number of the points discussed and indicating some of the fallacies on which the Labour Party proposals were based. Mr. Young also asked for, and was supplied with, details on the strength of the agency force, breaking it down into age grouping, length of service, and rate of labour turnover.

Mr. Dinnage wrote Herbert Morrison requesting whether he would agree to meet CIS representatives again to enable them to amplify the memorandum which they had submitted on 10 November. Herbert Morrison intimated that the contents of the memorandum would determine whether he would see CIS representatives again, but there was no invitation forthcoming as late as the end of January, 1949. Michael Young eventually wrote on 4 February, acknowledging the usefulness of the memorandum, but saying he could not give any further information, as the discussions about insurance were still proceeding, and no decision had been taken: " However the matter is due to come up again at a forthcoming meeting of the Policy Committee. If after that discussion there are further points which Mr. Morrison and Mr. Griffiths and other members of the committee would like to put to you I will, if I may, write to you again."

Mr. Aneurin Davies and the General Manager had a further interview with James Griffiths and Michael Young on 9 March, 1949. James Griffiths intimated that after careful thought the Labour Party had come to the conclusion it would be impossible to split the industrialised business from other classes of business transacted by industrial/ordinary life offices. They had therefore turned their minds to the possibility of taking over the 14 industrial/ordinary offices and the two big collecting societies, the Royal Liver and the Liverpool Victoria, on lines similar to those proposed in respect of the steel industry. The idea was that each company would for the time being continue to operate independently, but the investment policies of the companies would be controlled by the Government. Further, the Government would look to a reduction in the number of agents and district offices, which they expected would lead to a considerable saving in expenses. James Griffiths conceded that the proposal had many difficulties to overcome, not least the necessity of safeguarding the agents' interests if the scheme was to gain their support, but he thought that the Government could look to a reduction in the number of agents and district offices as a source of considerable saving in expenses. On investment policy, Michael Young indicated that insurance funds ought to be used to develop new industries, and to support other industries in need of fresh capital. The CIS representatives pointed out that this would be a constraint on policyholders in the group of offices nationalized, as against policyholders in other offices, whose boards of directors would still be free to make such investments as they felt desirable and in what they considered to be the best interests of their policyholders. If either industrial or ordinary life assurance was to be nationalized, the Government would presumably take over the existing funds of insurance offices, including a large block of gilt-edged securities and industrial investments. The CIS discountenanced the view that insurance funds were invested to the disadvantage of the community. On the contrary, one of the reasons for members of the public taking out life assurance was their confidence in the investment services of insurance offices. The group proposed for nationalization would become one of the biggest motor insurers in the industry. If motor business was to be included in the takeover, the State might find it difficult to refuse to insure all types of business, with the result that the State might find itself insuring the worst risks, which would probably lead to abnormal losses and upward revision of rates. The CIS representatives referred to the statement made by Lord Beveridge in his Report, where having reviewed the whole matter of the setting up of an industrial assurance board, he had explained that the proposal was not an essential part of the plan for social security, nor was it the only possible solution of the problem of industrial assurance.[1] He had also stated that " the working out of this proposal would be an immense practical task to be confined to a special body with adequate powers and experience. The practical problems are numerous and intricate." At the meeting, James Griffiths indicated that a decision would have to be taken not later than 23 March, as the agreed Labour Party policy for the 1950 Election had to be issued not later than 31 March. He expressed his appreciation of the very helpful advice and for the frank discussion.

The General Manager of the CIS received a letter from Transport House on 1 April, seeking a meeting between members of the National Executive Committee of the Labour Party and representatives of the CIS to discuss further the question of industrial assurance, and the General Manager replied on 4 April apropos the Labour Party proposals: " We think it inadvisable at this stage that you should state that the Co-operative Movement supports them."

[1] The Industrial Assurance and Friendly Societies Act, 1948, limited the total amount which may be assured to any one proposer on the life of a parent and the step-parent or grandparent to £20. The Act also withdrew the right to issue policies on brothers and sisters, children and grandchildren, conferred by early Acts for the purpose of meeting funeral expenses.

The views held at the time by the various sections of CIS staff on the nationalization issue are interesting. The CIS agents were members of USDAW, and they largely supported nationalization proposals; the district managers and other staff attached to district offices were members of NUCISE, which had not at that time committed itself; the chief and branch office staffs were practically all members of the Guild of Insurance Officials, and as far as the Guild was concerned, there was no justification for the general statement by the Industrial Life Offices Association that the CIS employees supported nationalization — the Guild had in fact taken steps to have a disclaimer issued.

The CIS General Manager wrote to James Griffiths on 18 May, intimating that the CIS Committee " are opposed to the present proposals of the Labour Party with regard to nationalization . . . "

James Griffiths replied on 20 May, 1949:

" I was naturally very sorry to hear that your Committee had decided to oppose the present proposals of the Party about converting industrial assurance into a public service. I very much hope that in the course of further discussion it may be possible to find common ground, as the aims of the Labour Party and the Co-operative Movement are in essential principles the same."

The National Policy Committee of the Co-operative Union, together with the Chairman and General Manager of the CIS met representatives of the Labour Party, including Herbert Morrison, James Griffiths, Hugh Dalton, Harold Laski and Alice Bacon on 30 May, 1949, at 11 Downing Street.

James Griffiths argued that there were serious abuses in the conduct of industrial assurance business which could only be rectified by nationalization — Beveridge among others, had recommended such action. The Co-operative representatives pointed out to Mr. Griffiths that Beveridge had not stated that the nationalization of industrial assurance was essential to his scheme for social security but that if an Industrial Assurance Board was to be set up, its agency staff could also deal with Social Insurance schemes.

Mr. Dinnage pointed out that many of the abuses referred to by Mr. Griffiths were long since out-moded and that the current proposals were concerned mainly with insurance offices with high standards of management, whereas smaller and more expensively administered societies were to be left out of the nationalization proposals. It seemed obvious that the decision to nationalize could hardly have been taken on a matter of principle.

The Secretary of the Co-operative Union explained that if the proposals of the Labour Party were put into effect, the CIS would be taken over, and Co-operative industrial and life policyholders would lose the benefits of the non-profit-making basis of Co-operative enterprise in insurance. In addition, Co-operative societies would be unable to insure with the organisation which they had purposely created. He added: "Political reactions within the Co-operative Movement to any such proposals will be serious, and we should have no alternative but to encourage these if modification of the Party proposals is not affected." Herbert Morrison indicated the difficulty facing the Labour Party was that of withdrawing any of the proposals already made in their statement of draft policy.

The *Manchester Guardian* commented on 8 June, 1949, on the claim of the Co-operative Movement to be consulted more fully in the framing of Labour Party policy: "No unseemly public quarrel is intended, but there is no hiding the fact that the Co-operators believe the nationalization of insurance to be one of Mr. Aneurin Bevan's bright ideas which he has forced on a reluctant Executive." Labour proposals would drive all private insurance into the hands of those companies not to be nationalized, and it would be impossible to effect any real economy in the administration of industrial assurance without dismissing staff which the Labour proposals did not contemplate. The correspondent added: "The Co-operators believe also that they would earn the thanks of some members of the Executive if their pressure succeeded in modifying or postponing this nationalization project before the election programme is issued."

The nationalization proposals were defended passionately by James Griffiths at the Labour Party Conference in Blackpool in June, 1949. James Peddie[1] (a Director of the CIS) put the official case of the CIS. He asked for reconsideration of the proposal:

"Not because I reject the principle involved, but because it is obvious that the proposal has not had the detailed examination it deserves. It would be uneconomical to separate industrial from other classes of insurance business. Nationalization would be confined to 14 leading companies but omitted from the scheme the 134 small organisations which would be free to develop and compete against the nationalized body. It was ironical that the Co-operative Movement's non-profit-making insurance organisation would disappear under this scheme.

[1] Now Lord Peddie.

Although the interests of the insurance workers must be considered, the starting point in the consideration of the proposals should be the policyholder. The general field of insurance business has not to be nationalized because presumably it would be prejudicial to foreign business. There were, in total, 120 insurance companies not to be nationalized with a premium income of over £300m. per year."

He wondered whether the working-class policyholder would be any better off under the Labour Party proposals. The main administrative expense was the cost of premium collection and he doubted whether the plan would reduce that sum. The Industrial Assurance Act of 1948, with its National Insurance death grant, removed most of the future need for petty life-of-another policies for funeral expenses — such policies were limited to a maximum of £20 on the life of a parent or grandparent. According to a survey made by the Industrial Life Offices Association in 1947, of the 4s. 3d. spent weekly on industrial assurance by the average insured household, only 1s. 2d. was for funeral expenses, and the great bulk of all new industrial assurance business consisted essentially of endowment or whole life policies on the life of the policyholder or spouse.

A meeting was held on 27 July, 1949, at 11 Downing Street, between members of the Labour Party Committee and the Co-operative National Committee,[1] for the purpose of discussing points put forward by the Co-operative representatives at the previous meeting. A subsequent letter, however, from Michael Young indicated that the Co-operative delegates had been expected to bring forward further suggestions. Mr. Gill, the principal speaker for the Co-operative delegates, pointed out how difficult this was, as the memorandum which had been promised by James Griffiths on 7 April, amplifying the general proposals set out in *Labour Believes in Britain* had not been forthcoming, so that the Co-operative Movement was in no better position to discuss details of the Labour Party proposals than they had been at the meeting at Downing Street on 30 May. The Co-operative

[1] Present, representing Labour Party:

Herbert Morrison	Tom Driberg
Aneurin Bevan	Alice Bacon
James Griffiths	Morgan Phillips
Hugh Dalton	Michael Young
Sam Watson	

Representing the Co-operative Movement were:

T. H. Gill	C. C. Hilditch
R. Southern	A. Davies, CIS Chairman
Jack Bailey	L. Cooke, CIS Director
C. W. Fulker	R. Dinnage, CIS General Manager

253

representatives emphasized that if the Labour Party disregarded the alternative proposals submitted by the CIS, then the Co-operative Movement must insist on the CIS being excluded from any scheme of nationalization. Herbert Morrison, in reply, made it quite clear that the setting up of a separate industrial assurance board to compete with the CIS and other offices, was not a practical proposition. The General Manager of the CIS then outlined the details given in a memorandum. The CIS Committee had suggested that a form of negative control of investment would be sufficient to meet the objection put forward by James Griffiths that insurance funds had in the past been invested either to the disadvantage of certain sections of the community, or in what had been regarded as anti-social and undesirable securities. The CIS proposals were that there should be a minimum support for Government securities in investment portfolios, and that there should be greater publicity with regard to the types of security held and for there to be prohibition of investment in certain classes of security regarded as socially undesirable. Herbert Morrison accepted the view of the CIS representatives that their suggestions for the control of investment were merely precautionary and would not involve the Government in any responsibility for the security of the funds of insurance offices. Mr. Dinnage, the CIS General Manager, also dealt with the question of compensating the shareholders in proprietary companies in the event of nationalization, and pointed out that it would be manifestly unfair that in the event of nationalization CIS policyholders should have to bear any part of the cost of such compensation. Aneurin Bevan referred to what he termed " pressure groups " and insisted that insurance offices were one of the biggest anti-Labour pressure groups in the country. Until they had been disposed of, the Labour Government would not be strong enough to come out openly with a policy which would allow the Co-operative Movement to exist side by side with nationalized industries. The CIS representatives commented:

> " We pointed out the obvious weakness in such an argument since it meant that, first the CIS, and possible other Co-operative interests, would have to be sacrificed before the Labour Party felt that it had sufficient control of the pressure groups to be able to withstand any further pressure, with the result that if at some stage in the future they decided that the Co-operative Movement could co-exist with nationalized industries, it would be a very much truncated Co-operative Movement."

Herbert Morrison summed up the meeting by saying that he would convey to the Labour Party Executive that the Co-operative Movement did not approve of the present proposals of the Labour Party, and that the Co-operative representatives felt that the alternative suggestions put forward by the CIS would meet all the considerations which appeared to underlie the Labour Party proposals for nationalization, and that if despite the advice of the Co-operative Movement, the Labour Party was undeterred, then the Co-operative Movement would insist on the exclusion of the CIS from nationalization, and that finally if this were not granted, the Co-operative Movement would have to consider whether they should publicly oppose the Labour Party.

The CIS point of view was put simply but forcibly by the General Manager in a letter to Jack Bailey, the Secretary of the Co-operative Party, on 8 August, 1949:

> "You will appreciate that my position in regard to the question of nationalization of insurance is that of technical adviser and ever since the discussions commenced I have tried to give advice which is free from personal or political bias. My standard of judgment has been — would the proposals benefit CIS policyholders ...?" He added: "The bulk of the cost of industrial assurance arises from the payments to agents ... It should be clear, however, that employment of agents by the Board will not reduce those costs unless the agents collect more premiums per £1 of wages ..." (The Labour Party was letting it be assumed that they could at one and the same time reduce costs and leave agents' terms unaffected.)

In a further letter, the General Manager stated:

> "I fully realise the dilemma in which we as Co-operators are placed, but nothing will convince me that in the long run anything will be gained by endorsing plans which we feel are inherently unsound from the consumers' point of view. The Labour Party would like us to endorse their present plans — we can't agree. They started by wanting to nationalize industrial assurance by separating it from the other classes of business. We went to great pains to show that this would be practically impossible, and as this was later confirmed by their discussions with the agents they accepted our advice. My view is that as both proposals are almost certain to be to the disadvantage of the policyholder we cannot support either."

Life offices hold the position of trustees for policyholders and their funds belong by and large to the policyholders: hence insurance funds " are not the correct vehicle for social or economic experiments; still less are they a suitable instrument of political favour or prejudice. In taking over those funds the State would acquire substantial holdings in many companies quite unconnected with existing or proposed nationalization schemes."[1]

Michael Young wrote to the General Manager of the CIS on 23 September, 1949, asking for comments on " the enclosed note which I have drafted as a purely personal venture." The note was entitled " The Possible Mutualization of Industrial Assurance " and referred to the two kinds of industrial assurance offices — the proprietary offices and the mutual offices, including the collecting societies. The proposal was that all the proprietary companies should be " mutualized," that is, converted into mutual offices: " Industrial assurance would then be run on a co-operative basis with the consumers, i.e., policyholders, owning the assets and receiving all the profits." The directors of the mutual offices would act as trustees for the policyholders, as was the case with Co-operative societies, and their sole duty would be to promote the policyholders' interests: " The main object of making this proposal is to meet the objections of the Co-operative Movement to the scheme outlined in *Labour Believes in Britain*." (The suggestions from Michael Young for " mutualization " included giving increased powers to the Industrial Assurance Commissioner, such as the duty of preparing schemes for amalgamation of offices, and for buying out the shareholders of the proprietary companies.)

The General Manager of the CIS replied on 24 September, 1949:
" ... I feel that I can quite safely say that I do not think you would be wise to assume too readily that ' the Co-operative Movement could hardly object to a policy for converting the whole industry into one that was co-operatively run.' As I see it your plan would not mean that the CIS would be run by the Co-operative Movement, and as you should by now be aware, one of the strongest objections the Movement has to the Labour Party proposals is that it would take away from it the power to run its own Insurance Society for the benefit of Co-operators. Your revised suggestions would only temporarily delay this procedure and from that angle I cannot see that they are likely to any more acceptable . . . so far as I can see you appear to

[1] Sir James Grigg, " Nationalization of Insurance " *National Provincial Bank Review*, August, 1949.

have largely accepted our alternative proposals as a basis for meeting many of the criticisms levelled at Industrial Assurance to that point we are on common ground. Having done so, you then made additional proposals for the purchase of shares, appointment of Directors, and eventual compulsory amalgamation, with so far as I can see, 'mutualization' becoming another name for 'nationalization,' and with what we believe to be all its attendant disadvantages."

A meeting between representatives of the Co-operative Union and the Labour Party National Executive Committee took place on 24 October, 1949, at the House of Commons. Herbert Morrison was again in the chair, supported by James Griffiths, Aneurin Bevan and Hugh Dalton, and other members of the Labour Party Policy Committee. The Co-operative representatives included the Chairman, Directors and General Manager of the CIS. A question was put by the CIS representatives:

"The memorandum . . . appears to postulate certain conditions under which the CIS might retain its independence . . . Do you still refuse to exclude the CIS unconditionally and permanently? "

Answer: "Yes."

Question: "The heading of Section 6A refers to the inclusion of all industrial life offices. Is it now the intention to include the 131 small societies previously excluded? "

Answer: Mr. Griffiths stated that they proposed to include all societies — "including the 131 previously excluded."

Of the 12 trade unions included in the National Federation of Insurance Workers, nine unions declared themselves opposed to the nationalization of industrial assurance at a conference held on 27 October, 1949. The nine unions concerned represented about 25,000 of the 40,000 agents and other insurance workers in the Federation. The three remaining staff unions in the Federation neither supported nor opposed nationalization. There were two fears which seemed to have weighed heavily with the insurance workers generally — the refusal of the Government to consider pension schemes for the bulk of workers in industries already nationalized made insurance workers afraid that under nationalization they would lose such pension rights as they had, or might hope to obtain from private industry; moreover, the Government's hostility to profit-sharing schemes in the gas industry after nationalization could equally apply to insurance agents. In effect, by the autumn of 1949, the insurance agents were suddenly having second thoughts about nationalizing industrial assurance. Transport House was now suggesting that Lord Beveridge had underestimated the difficulty of separating industrial and general insurance business. The *Financial Times* commented on 24 November, 1949: " In face of persistent opposition by the Co-operative Movement, the socialists have now modified their proposals for the nationalization of industrial assurance." The decision had been made known in a statement issued by the National Executive Committee of the Labour Party on 23 November:

" The National Executive Committee of the Labour Party at its meeting today considered the subject of industrial assurance. After full discussion, it was decided that the proposal outlined in *Labour Believes in Britain* to convert industrial assurance into a public service should be implemented on the basis of mutual ownership. In applying this policy, the guiding principle will be that the interests of the policyholder should be paramount. Thus the proprietary companies in the field of industrial assurance will be owned by the policyholders themselves instead of by private shareholders. The interests of industrial assurance staffs will be safeguarded. These two recommendations will be included in the programme of the Labour Party for presentation to the people at the next General Election."

The *Financial Times* correspondent anticipated that a State Insurance Board would be part of the Labour Party's proposals, and that this body would so rigidly control investment that in the end, " it is doubtful whether there would be any noticeable difference — apart from preserving the identity of the Co-operative Insurance Society — between ' mutualization ' under such conditions and outright nationalization." *The Times,* of 25 November, also thought that the abandonment of the Labour Party's programme for a " super Pru " was in part the refusal " of the leaders of the Co-operative Movement to sacrifice their own insurance company . . ." *The Times* noted that the CIS was already owned by its policyholders, and that the Labour Party's plans for mutualizing the industrial assurance offices would not affect such mutual offices — the Co-operative Insurance Society was " a company which by a slight change could be wholly mutualized." The companies earmarked for mutualization could be converted into collecting societies, and so have their investments subject to all the restrictions of trustee securities; but the consequent loss of earnings from invested funds would probably more than offset the saving on

258

dividend and tax. It was hard to foresee any advantage could be gained that could not be achieved with far less trouble by a statutory limitation of industrial assurance dividends, with compulsion on the part of the companies to return the bulk of their surpluses to policyholders:

> "It must not be imagined that the conversion of the millions of customers of the industrial assurance companies into joint-owners and risk-bearers would give them any semblance of real control over the mutualized companies. Self-government would be as much of a fiction in a mutualized Prudential as it was in the Prudential Approved Society and as it has for long been in the large collecting societies."

The Central Executive Committee of the Co-operative Union met in Manchester on 1 December, 1949. Representatives of the National Executive Committee of the Labour Party were present including James Griffiths, J. Reeves, and Michael Young. Mr. A. Davies, the Chairman of the CIS, with other directors and the General Manager were also present. An official statement after the meeting announced:

> "In the course of a most friendly discussion the whole subject of industrial assurance was explored. It is understood that the Co-operative Movement will now consider the further observations of the Labour Party and that in the near future the Movement will decide whether or not the latest proposals of the Labour Party can be supported."

It was envisaged that a Board of Insurance Commissioners would be set up to take over the private companies and to arrange for control by policyholders. A period of grace of five years would be allowed to the CIS and other mutual companies to bring down their expense-ratios. If by that time they had not made themselves as efficient as companies controlled directly by the insurance commissioners, they would be subject to take over like the rest. The question was put by the CIS directors to James Griffiths:

> "If the plan is adopted and each company retains its own name, is it intended to continue after five years, or is this a step to nationalization?"
>
> *Answer:* "At the end of five years the Board will report that those which have proved they are efficient, can continue as they are. Some, especially the smaller offices, will not be able to attain sufficient efficiency."

The General Manager of the CIS wrote a memorandum at this stage in December, 1949:

> "However unsatisfactory the position may be in many

259

respects, it can scarcely be denied that our continual pressure for the maintenance of the independence of the CIS has achieved a good deal when it is remembered that the original intention was to take over and nationalize the CIS along with 13 other offices. Although the long-term position is still uncertain, nevertheless, it seems to me our efforts have been far from fruitless."

A joint meeting of the Boards of the CWS and the SCWS (meeting as shareholders of the CIS) was held in London on 7 December, 1949, on the subject of mutualization of insurance. A resolution was passed that:

"This joint meeting expresses its regret that the Central Executive of the Co-operative Union have accepted the principles contained in the statement of the Labour Party, as conveyed by the Labour Party delegation, before obtaining the views of the CIS ... that if the Labour Party decides to proceed with its proposals for the mutualization of industrial assurance, the Co-operative Movement should reserve its judgment until the details are known, the CIS (with the approval of the CWS and the SCWS Boards) at this stage reserving its rights in the matter ..."

The General Manager of the CIS commented that all the evidence seemed to indicate that mutualization was a settled policy of the Labour Party, and that nothing the CIS could say or do would now alter this proposal, particularly having regard to the decision of the Co-operative Union. It therefore seemed to him a mistake to refuse to have further discussions with the Labour Party after all the negotiations that had taken place. Having recognised that mutualization was an irrevocable decision of the Labour Party, it was now incumbent on the CIS to again consult with the Labour Party to secure the best interests of the Society.

Michael Young took up his pen once more in December, 1949, with a draft entitled "Industrial Assurance as a Public Service — a Proposal for Mutual Ownership by the Policyholders." The preamble explained that the draft was not for popular consumption:

"Note to Policy Committee: this draft pamphlet has been prepared under the guidance of the expert sub-committee under the chairmanship of Jim Griffiths, adapted in the light of the recent decision of the NEC in favour of mutual ownership. The draft is not intended as a popular presentation but as a solid document which would be read by insurance staff and serve as a basis for general propaganda in the coming months."

Michael Young went on: "The Labour Party is not wedded in any doctrinaire fashion to one particular type of common ownership; in this case ownership by the consumers — the policyholders — is the most suitable form of common ownership to adopt." Industrial assurance was again brought before the bar:

"Industrial assurance had been more strongly criticised over a longer period — if we perhaps except coal — than any other section of any British industry. Inquiry has followed inquiry. Private investigators have marched in to underline official commissions, and never once has it been given a clean bill of health. Again and again have the main defects been pilloried — profiteering, excessive competition, high cost and overselling."

Apparently, one of the reasons for seeking to establish mutual offices owned by the policyholders, instead of offices owned by the State, was to safeguard the overseas earnings of the insurance industry. Michael Young referred to the statement by Sir Stafford Cripps on 12 November, 1945, in which he had said that the Government had no intention of interfering with the transaction of insurance business by private enterprise, save to the limited extent to which insurance at home might be effected by proposals relating to personal social insurance and industrial injuries. Sir Stafford Cripps had added: "It is the desire of the Government that insurance should be, in the future, as in the past, dealt with on an international basis and as business of an international character."

Sir Arnold Wilson was also quoted:

"The salient characteristic of industrial assurance is the existence of vast aggregations of capital in a very few hands, with unlimited power, exercised in secrecy and uncontrolled by any external agents, to give or withhold financial assistance in any country, at home or abroad, to any industry or trade."

The Labour Party, said Michael Young, "wants only to protect the policyholders. Opponents of Labour declare that in future the funds of its industrial assurance offices will be controlled in such a way that profits will be reduced. This is not true." Michael Young then put this question-begging argument:

"Policyholders share in profits today, and will obtain all the profits when there is mutual ownership. It would therefore be wrong if profits were to be reduced as the result of State control: for it is the policyholders who would suffer. In the future, as partners in mutual offices, they will not be worse off;

they will be better off. For the duty of the directors of the offices will be to promote the interests of the policyholders."

The draft pamphlet, to re-quote Michael Young, "was not intended as a popular presentation, but as a solid document." Despite this assertion, the document included rather specious analogies comparing industrial assurance contracts with a free market for consumer goods:

"The consumer of potatoes would be similarly entitled if she had to go on buying potatoes from the same greengrocer for the rest of her life once she had bought the first pound. That is the way it is with insurance. Pay the first premium and you are committed to pay maybe another 2,000 premiums in the next 40 years."

The draft then outlined future proposals for control of the insurance industry. The existing mutual offices engaged in industrial assurance would be "expected to improve their service to their members." The deadline would be at the end of a five-year period:

"The success of these offices in securing an improved service will be reviewed five years after the Act comes into effect. During this period these independent offices will be put on their mettle to show what they can do to meet the criticisms levelled at industrial assurance in the past. It will be open to any of these offices, if their members wish, either to amalgamate with other independent offices or to be taken in with the new mutual offices which will be created out of the proprietary companies."

The Industrial Assurance Board to be set up would arrange to buy out the shareholders in the proprietary offices, to vest the property in the hands of policyholders, and to appoint new directors to the boards of the offices concerned — "The offices will not be converted into friendly societies, since that would involve a limitation upon their scope for investment." Industrial premiums would be collected from door to door, "but this is not to say that the same number of agents will be required. In fact it will be possible, as the result of the re-organisation to do the work with fewer agents." Compensation would be paid to agents for the full value of book-interest. The draft moved towards its conclusion with a reference to the Beveridge Report:

"The collectors now visiting at short intervals most of the houses in Britain have become in thousands of cases the friends and advisers of families with whom they deal. Many of them are in effect travelling citizen's advice bureaux. They regard themselves as servants of the public. They can find in a new

1940

relation a better opportunity and not a worse, of living up to that ideal."

Michael Young added:

"The defects of industrial assurance were not the faults of insurance staff. The defects are the faults of the system. The insurance staff can now help to settle this long-standing question of controversy and introduce a public service which will be fair to themselves and fair to the policyholders."

Michael Young's pamphlet, with the title *The Future of Industrial Assurance: Labour's Proposals for Mutual Ownership by the Policyholders*, was published in January, 1950. The *Manchester Guardian* commented favourably that the statement set out the case for tackling industrial assurance, but the remedies proposed were hardly comprehensive. In the words of the Beveridge Report: "It was inevitable that the democracy of the collecting societies should become a syndicalist organisation of agents, an association of the sellers of insurance rather than of the buyers." More details were required on how the "mutualized" companies were to be democratically governed. In effect, the proposal to set up a public board in order to regulate the business more closely than through the existing Industrial Assurance Commissioner would create a smaller number of larger units; the Cohen Report had recommended this course as more attractive and practicable than outright nationalization — "eight or ten privately-owned Pearls instead of a single State-owned Prudential." There was also an unequivocal pledge that no limitation would be imposed on the freedom of companies to invest their funds as they thought fit. In theory, there could be a possible cheapening of the cost of industrial assurance, but the saving could not be large, as the principal cause of high costs — the collection of small premiums on the doorstep — was left untouched, and any wasteful form of competition between agents of rival offices would probably be just as keen between a score of mutually-owned offices as it would be between the existing companies, mutual or proprietary. In fact, all the faults attributed to the existing system would be produced in the new system. The only exception would be in the reward received by shareholders of the proprietary companies, but the sums which went to these shareholders would represent only a minute gain to policyholders numbered in millions. Even Sir Arnold Wilson had written "the radical defects of industrial assurance could not be surmounted or palliated by any change in the relative positions of shareholders and policyholders."

All, it was claimed, would benefit under the new proposals: policy-holders and agents, insurance funds and their investment (which would remain emphatically in private hands); but the State would still "guarantee and accept complete responsibility for all existing policies." The circle would be squared. The General Manager of the CIS wrote to the Secretary of the Co-operative Union on 18 January, 1950, stating that the CIS could not agree to collaborate in the revising of the Michael Young pamphlet.

Nearly three years later, Ian Mikardo, then MP for Reading, spoke on the subject of the Co-operative Movement on 30 November, 1952. The *Insurance Mail* of 10 December, 1952, commented: "We believe that this is the first indication on which it has been publicly declared that it was the Co-operative Movement which was responsible for the revision of the Labour Party's policy for industrial assurance in 1949." In June, 1953, the Labour Party published a further statement, entitled *Challenge to Britain*. The section on industrial assurance noted the grave defects in the organisation of many private agencies and the serious social and economic objections to the control by giant companies of a large part of the nation's private savings, but it did not indicate these objections in detail. The Beveridge Report was again referred to, as was the 1949 policy statement *Labour Believes in Britain*:

> "Nothing has happened since to cause us to revise our opinion. On the contrary we are convinced that a publicly-organised industrial assurance service would give better value and security to policyholders, sharply reduce administrative costs and provide a channel for further savings."

No mention was made of nationalization or "mutualization." It was concluded: "Labour believes that these two problems affecting private insurance — the future of industrial assurance and the transfer of relative pensions should be the subject of a special examination." The General Secretary of the Co-operative Union wrote to Morgan Phillips, then Secretary of the Labour Party, on 26 August, 1953, on the statement *Challenge to Britain*. He commented on industrial assurance:

> "It is difficult to ascertain exactly what is intended under this head ... In the present statement reference is made to a publicly-organised industrial assurance service.
> *Question:* Is the Labour Party now in favour of nationalization or mutualization or some other form of social ownership?

Further question: What are the intentions of the Labour Party regarding the Co-operative Insurance Society? It is recalled that in a private and confidential statement made by Mr. Griffiths to the Co-operative Union Central Executive Committee on 1 December, 1949, recognition of the mutual character of the Co-operative Insurance Society was categorically expressed.

Question: Is it the intention of the Labour Party to stand by this statement? "

Michael Young contributed an article to the *Socialist Commentary* in October, 1953, entitled " the Unanswered Challenge." He wrote: " The case for public or mutual ownership of industrial assurance is . . . stronger than ever." Michael Young went on:

" How vastly irritating therefore (particularly to me since I spent nearly a year of my life at Transport House working out the plans for taking over insurance) to find this inaccurate statement — ' In our 1949 policy statement, *Labour Believes in Britain,* we advocated public control over all this industry. Nothing has happened since to cause us to revise our opinion.' "

He then remonstrated:

" Horrible! *Labour Believes in Britain* did *not* put forward public control. It put forward public ownership. If the Party had not revised its opinion on this why not propose it again, instead of some ridiculous examination? We are not all school-children. This industry has been investigated dozens and dozens of times, and the only reason for proposing another is to conceal the shaming fact that no action at all is going to be taken. Better to leave out all mention of the subject than to fill out the programme with such hypocrisy as this."

. . . From thenceforth proposals for the mutualization or national-ization of industrial assurance were omitted from official Labour Party policy statements.

It might well be that the retreat from the proposals for nationalization of industrial assurance, after thirty years of intermittent campaigning for its take-over, raised the first doubts over the ideology of national-ization. Certainly, from this period, " nationalization " became less of a rallying-cry and more a reproach, and with its more violent opponents, a smear word.

What few published references there are to the outcome of the campaign accredit the change of heart of the Labour Party largely to the hostility of the insurance agents.[1] Perhaps the task force of agents could see the innate contradictions of the nationalization proposals just as clearly as their employers. Whatever the balance of forces, the CIS played a critical role out of keeping with being merely one insurance office in many. In the last resort, the confusion over industrial assurance would have been cleared if the Labour Party had been able to distinguish more clearly between social insurance schemes and an insurance industry.[2]

(v) The New Building

Living in a society approaching urban saturation, we are confronted more and more with architecture. The CIS chief office building in Manchester is a great fact; it was the first important post-war building to be constructed in the centre of the City. The site chosen was in a bombed-out area not quite blighted, but seedy and certainly decayed, with the frontage of the new building to overlook a district once known waggishly as Angel Meadow.[3] The immediate vicinity remains

[1] For a highly critical account of nationalization see R. Kelf-Cohen *Nationalization in Britain* (2nd edit. 1961), p.319.
   " The reception by the public of the ' shopping lists ' [of industries earmarked for nationalization] was cool to the point of hostility and in some cases such as industrial assurance, the workers engaged in the industry were so antagonistic that nationalization was hurriedly changed to mutualization."
   H. Hopkins, *The New Look: A Social History of the Forties and Fifties* (1963), p.371.
   " [The Labour Party] cowered before the prospect of opposition from 60,000 agents organised in 400 anti-nationalization committees . . it vacillated, compromised and finally collapsed."
[2] W. A. Robson sees this distinction in another context in his authoritative *Nationalized Industry and Public Ownership* (2nd edit. 1962), p.19.
   " We are not concerned here with social insurance schemes since these are more a social service financed by taxation masquerading as insurance rather than a form of public enterprise of an industrial or commercial character."
[3] Angel Meadow was a square bounded by Rochdale Road, Cheetham Hill Road, Gould Street and Miller Street. It contained 33 acres and 70 years ago it accommodated 7,000 people at a density of 200 per acre, but the real density was even greater as much of the area was covered by works, warehouses and railways: " Angel Meadow, neglected, forgotten, as it now is [1897] has seen better days." The top storeys of many of the houses in the area had long, narrow windows — showing evidence of hand-loom weaving. In Angel Meadow at that time there were no houses with baths and there were no public baths near at hand. The only social centre in the area was Charter Street Ragged School. The general conditions of sanitation and housing in Manchester were bad " but to arrive at Angel Meadow conditions you have to compound with the peculiar ingredients of the atmosphere of our City, the persons and homes . . . the self-assertive and penetrating scents of the fried fish and chip shops and the nauseous exhalations . . . " The general death rate in Angel Meadow 1888–1890 was 50.9 per thousand. In 1894 the total number of paupers in Angel Meadow was 687, of whom only 83 had come from " own homes ": 2,500 were living in common lodging houses. " I conclude by urging the necessity for more systematic action on the part of the State as well as municipalities and of private philanthropic institutions, if slums like Angel Meadow are to be abolished."
   Extracts from J. E. Mercer, *Conditions of Life in Angel Meadow* (1897). Paper read to Manchester Statistical Society.
   The author of the 1897 pamphlet could hardly have foreseen that a small insurance office then in Long Millgate was to beautify Angel Meadow within a further lifetime.

a confusion of railway stations and buildings, bridges, gas holders, a river and culverts, with a rash of more recent bald patches used as car parks. The tall tower of Strangeways Prison overlooks this industrial detritus.

The CIS management, having decided on a tall building, demonstrated in its scheduling, planning and design all the qualities of sound insurance practice. Before quoting for a unique form of insurance cover, comparability studies should be undertaken; adequate precautions should be taken against forseeable hazards and allowances earmarked for contingencies; discretionary margins made for providing adequate room for expansion of such business — the planning for the CIS building took into account all these considerations. The true value of the new building to the CIS is not just its imposing structure, but rather the thought-transfer that an insurance office which puts its own house in such efficient order must also be capable of providing worthwhile service to its policyholders.

Visually, the CIS building does not act as a mere backcloth to an industrial landscape, but rises as a very three-dimensional impression. Unlike many of our curtain-walled office blocks, it could not be erased easily from the mind's eye, although its line-perspective and its texture change, as indeed they should, in varying conditions of light, and from different approach routes.

Preliminaries to New Building

With the continued growth of the CIS, it became necessary to consider new premises for chief office. Owing to war-time conditions and subsequent restrictions on building, it was impossible to make any progress, and by the 1950s, the CIS was operating from ten different offices in Manchester.

The natural location for the new building appeared to be a site close to the existing main premises in Corporation Street. It was, however, considered wise to explore the possibility of moving to the suburbs of Manchester, because the building was to be an administrative head office, not generally to be used by the public. It was believed too, that away from the centre of the City, both site and building would be cheaper. It was also expected that staff would be easier to recruit.

The surburban site which appeared to offer the greatest advantages in terms of pleasant location, good transport, reasonable costs and a large potential labour force, was at Wythenshawe. The staffing position was felt to be particularly attractive as the Society was mainly concerned with recruiting women, and it was known that large numbers of office workers commuted daily from Wythenshawe to central Manchester. In common with other employers, the CIS was suffering from a rather high rate of turnover of female staff, and expected that continuing losses in its chief office personnel could be replaced by local workers.

However, the result of a pilot survey of the availability of clerical workers, conducted by the CWS Market Research Unit, indicated that girls were not interested in working in Wythenshawe, and preferred to travel into Manchester for shopping, and other social amenities. The report was so positive that the proposal to move to a suburb was abandoned.

In January, 1953, the Board of Directors appointed two of their members to meet the Planning Officer of Manchester to discuss the question of a site. By that time, the CIS had dispensed with the Wythenshawe project and had turned to the possibility of building in Miller Street, Manchester, as part of the property was already owned by the CWS, and one side of Miller Street had been completely cleared through bombing; but before taking any decision, the Corporation of Manchester was consulted with regard to plans for future development of the City. The Corporation indicated two sites in which they would like the CIS to be interested, one of them being the Piccadilly site, but it was made a condition that development there would have to include shops and a hotel in the scheme. The CIS Board were interested in the Manchester Piccadilly proposals, but they had reservations whether a hotel as an integral part of that development would be a suitable investment for the Society's funds. By 1957, planning permission was secured to build a new office on the corner of Dantzic Street and Miller Street, Manchester.[1]

---

[1] *Miller Street*
Miller Street is one of the oldest thoroughfares in Manchester. It existed before the days of Elizabeth I — a case of land enclosure was dealt with in October, 1588 — " William Byrche not having taken down his encroachment in the Mylner's Lane hath forfeited 30 shillings to the lord." On a plan dated 1650, the thoroughfare was named Mill Lane and it included six almshouses of the Mayes Charity, founded in 1621. The almshouses were situated on part of the present site of the CIS Chief Office.

It was on land abutting Millers Lane that a steam engine was installed in a cotton mill about 1783 by Richard Arkwright. The actual site was in Simpson's Factory Yard on the west side of Miller Street, north of the present offices of Baxendale and Company.

By the end of the 18th century, Millers Lane had become known as Miller Street (Laurent's Map 1793).

Baxendale and Company began business in nearby Hanover Street in 1863 and removed to Miller Street in 1869.

[*Continued at foot of page 269*]

In the meantime, the CIS Board had appointed for the proposed development, G. S. Hay, the chief CWS architect in Manchester. Departmental managers of the CIS indicated the type of accommodation they would require, and it was concluded that the building ought to accommodate a staff of about 3,000 persons.

Work-study flows, probable rates of growth of various departments, the changes likely to come about by computerized systems, meant that the new chief office was to be regarded as a workshop which would become more and more mechanised.

The first plans involved a long, three-storey building, with a centre block rising to 17 storeys, but Manchester Corporation indicated that in amended plans it was proposed to widen Miller Street more than had been originally intended; moreover, a building of 17 storeys would not be approved.

At the time of consideration of the preliminary plans for the new chief office, there had been considerable criticism of the style of architecture of new office blocks being built in London. It was realised that the new building was likely to be one of the largest and tallest buildings in the country, if not in Europe, and it would be the subject of much interest and probable criticism. Given the circumstances, the CIS Board felt that it would be wise to secure alternative designs and they considered that some form of competition should be held, but that failing this, an associate architect should be appointed

[Continued from foot of page 268]

Dantzic Street
Dantzic Street was so named in the 18th century — there is reference to the street in deeds of 1790 and the name appears on maps of 1836 and 1848. There is some confusion over the history of Charter Street which was the name given to the continuation of Dantzic Street beyond the west side of Miller Street. The *Manchester Evening News* of 6 May, 1936, referred to the street name:

"Some time in the 1860s, a merchant named Lowther ordered goods from a spinner, asking that they be delivered to an address in Charter Street.

Mr. Spinner had either (1) an objection to anything that reminded him of Chartists or (2) no wish to deal with such an unsavoury neighbourhood as it was then, and he declined the order, saying he would take good care none of his yarn went to such a place as Charter Street!

After the property owners and residents petitioned the town authorities, and the result was that part of Charter Street became and remains to this day Dantzic Street."

The above account appears to be a legend based on a possible misconception — there does not seem to be any valid reason, either in the 1860s or the 1960s, for anyone to associate the word "Charter" with the Chartists of the 1840s — more probably the name was to commemorate the town Charter (Corporation Street is adjacent). Moreover, Charter Street Ragged School was founded during the 1860s and perpetuated the name, apparently without opposition from local residents. In fact, Charter Street was so named until 1907, when it was re-named Dantzic Street. There is another surviving Charter Street, situated in a nearby area which continues to cause some confusion as Charter Street Ragged School, now a Women's Hostel, still keeps its original title.

to work with the CWS architect in designing the elevation and interior of the building. The President of the Royal Institute of British Architects was approached for advice concerning the arrangements for a competition, but the CIS directors intimated that they did not wish to commit themselves to accept the design adjudged to be the best, and reserved the right to select another entry if they so preferred. The RIBA indicated that they could not sponsor a competition on such conditions, and so the CIS Board made independent approaches to a number of leading architects, enquiring whether they would collaborate with the CWS architect in the design and erection of the new building. It was finally decided to invite Gordon Tait of Sir John Burnet Tait and Partners to act as associate architect. The two architects produced the design of the building, and they suggested that a structural engineer should be engaged who would design the frame of the structure and associated foundation work.

The Corporation of Manchester, having previously objected to a proposal for a 17 storey building, was prepared to consider fresh plans limiting the height to 14 storeys. These revised plans were approved in principle. At that stage, it was felt that a deputation including the architects, engineers and one of the directors, should visit North America to investigate the problems which might arise from the construction of tall buildings[1] incorporating full air-conditioning — which the Board was anxious to install if at all possible provided that the cost was not prohibitive.

As a result of this study of American buildings, and careful costing, it was decided that a full air-conditioning system should be introduced, and so the architects were asked to review their design and to re-submit a scheme based on the use of a higher and more centralised building than they had originally proposed. They were recommended to give consideration to the development of a single large block of between 20–25 storeys. A further recommendation was that the Board should appoint a premises controller, who would take part in all discussions during the construction and equipping of the building, so that he would be fully conversant with its operation and maintenance. The Board took this advice and it proved to be a most far-sighted recommendation.

[1] The first skyscraper in the world is generally taken to be the ten-storey Home Insurance Building erected in Chicago in 1883. There is no precise definition of the minimum number of storeys to qualify as a skyscraper; the nature of the building site and building material (the skyscraper is constructed on a steel frame) are more important determinants.

The provisional plans for a much taller building were submitted to the City Surveyor, and despite his previous views, he approved them; the City Architect intimated that he would have preferred an even taller building. Eventually, in consultation with the City authorities, new plans were prepared by the architects and approved by the Corporation. The scheme included a smaller block for the CWS and a meeting hall sited between the two main blocks.

Apart from the urgent necessity of providing adequate centralised premises for a rapidly-growing insurance office, the CIS Board was anxious that the new building should add to the prestige of the Society, the Co-operative Movement generally, and improve the appearance of the City of Manchester. Further, it was expected that the first-class office accommodation would add to work-satisfaction, and would help to attract more high-quality staff.

The successful tender for the building contract was submitted by John Laing and Son.

A good deal of investigation took place before the selection of external materials was finally settled. Stonework in Manchester soon becomes polluted, despite the introduction of smokeless zones. Hence it was decided to use glass, aluminium and steel as external materials, and that strict attention should be paid to regular cleaning. The service tower, a reinforced concrete structure 400 feet high without windows, would require a special treatment. It was to be clad in mosaic which, to a large extent, is self-cleansing. Before reaching a decision on the facing material, a party visited Milan to inspect several tall buildings. As a further inducement, the cost of mosaic was found to be less than a quarter of the cost of more traditional materials such as marble, granite or slate facing. From the outset, the management had decided that office areas should be left as open as possible, and that services should be funnelled into a separate tower which would act as a spine to the main building.

Considerable research was undertaken to arrive at the best design and materials for internal finishing of ceilings and floors. Special light fittings were developed and erected so that air circulation could be examined and part of the circulation system was directed through the light fittings.

At that stage of development, it was decided to consult members of the Design Research Unit under the leadership of Professor Misha Black. A group of CIS officials visited the head offices of a number of Co-operative organisations in Europe to study their decor and furnishing. The CIS Organisation and Methods Section assisted with office layout and records control, and the Design Research Unit submitted designs for office furnishing, which included desks based on specific requirements. Building "mock-ups" and "prototypes" had been essential preliminaries in many respects before decisions were taken; for instance, a good deal of experimentation by means of mock-ups had to be undertaken before a satisfactory solution as regards light, sound and air-conditioning was achieved in areas where privacy was essential. The Post Office installed a system of telephones to meet the special requirements of communications in the tower block. It will be apparent to anyone who has visited the CIS chief office that non-acceptance of the obvious was an important aspect of the planning and design of this new building.

The Board felt that a certain proportion of the total cost should be set aside for artistic features. Professor Misha Black was authorised to approach certain artists to submit proposals for motifs in the entrance hall and forecourt. A mural by George Mitchell in the entrance hall is in the form of a bas-relief built up of sections in polyurethene moulds, faced with bronze flake and backed by fibreglass laminates. In the cafeteria, there is a frieze by Vincenzo Apicella extending over 200 feet, which depicts landscapes of cities in different parts of the world. Paintings and drawings by British artists were bought to enliven committee rooms, staff restaurants and certain offices.

The staff of 2,500 started to move into the new building on 1 August, 1962. All files and equipment were moved during the night and at weekends, and work went on as usual.

Since the completion of the CIS building in 1962, several other edifices have out-topped it,[1] but the CIS building remains important not merely for its altitude statistics; it has been a continuing source of interest to architects:

> " It would not be difficult to erect a building of moment in Manchester whose post-war effort has produced tragically few good buildings. What is so very heartening is, that before the English curtain wall follows its American counterpart into the history of the mid-century, the City has acquired an example of outstanding quality, and (much more important) a precedent has been set by big business to give our major northern City

[1] There are points of comparison between the new CIS Chief Office and the history of American skyscrapers. F. W. Woolworth built his 792 feet high gothic tower after the Metropolitan Insurance Company refused him a loan. At that time (1913), the Metropolitan building (700 feet) was the tallest in the world. Other skyscrapers have since surpassed the Woolworth altitude, but the Woolworth Building has retained its fame as it has been classified as an American national historic monument.

the best design and quality available. Much redevelopment is afoot in Manchester. The CIS has given us a first-class yardstick against which to measure it.[1]

The working situation within the building became the subject of an investigation carried out by two research workers from Liverpool University.[2] This environmental study included a caveat in its findings — " Considering that there was virtually no overall design responsibility other than that exercised by the building owners, it is rather remarkable that the result is so successful." It is difficult to agree with the authors that this problem of shared responsibility for design was so difficult to disentangle — there is nothing untoward in the owners of a building taking overall design responsibility. Large open office spaces have tended to be avoided by a number of other office managements: barely more than half of the total staff in the CIS building are housed on the five floors of the podium. " If office staff do have strong feelings about the size of their working area," commented the Pilkington Unit investigators, " then it might be expected that in the CIS building, where the staff have been divided between such very different conditions, these feelings would be apparent. In fact they have not been demonstrated . . ." The authors then speculated that given this evidence, the CIS could have designed a building of possibly ten floors instead of the present 25. In that case, the staff would be more compactly related and the proportion of office to circulation space increased. Such a building would have been less costly, " but the Society would have lost its soaring symbol and new-found trade-mark." Nevertheless, the investigators found the total environment to be quite impressive:

" The ultimate way of evaluating an environment can only be in comparison with other buildings. Without doubt this is the best building in which the Pilkington Research Unit has worked; it represents a significant advance on most other British office buildings, and in terms of building design and office environment, illustrates the office building of the enlightened present and the future . . . The CIS building is a

[1] " Manchester's Skyscraper," N. Keith Scott, *The Architect and Building News*, 16 January, 1963.
A number of other specialist articles appeared in professional journals, e.g., " Skyscraper for Co-operators " *Interior Design and Contract Furnishing*, January, 1963.
[2] Peter Manning and Brian Wells, members of the Pilkington Research Unit in the Department of Building Science of Liverpool University. See also " Psychology in the Office " — Brian Wells, *The Guardian*, 23 October, 1962, and " Subjective responses to the lighting installation in a modern office building and their design implication," *Building Science*, Volume 1, 1965.

major advance on the "routine" office block and, without doubt, among the two or three most beautiful office buildings in the country."

The impression was also felt that the building was a considerable social success. The authors concluded: " It is the most striking prestige symbol in the business centre of the North, and its permanent publicity value must be enormous."

A further investigation into the lighting of the building made some startling observations. Access to daylighting is generally considered an important condition for a good working environment. The investigation found that the strength of beliefs about daylighting and access to a view was independent of physical context, expressed in terms of the individual's working distance from the nearest window, and that people tended to overestimate the proportion of daylight that they thought necessary for efficient work at increasing distances from windows:

> " If the only valid argument appears to be that people demand daylighting as a necessary constituent of an acceptable environment, then it may well be the case that one can build very much more deeply than has been regarded as desirable and still produce satisfactory conditions."

During May, 1964, an investigation was made into the influence of offices size on the individual and on supervisory and managerial processes,[1] but the conclusions drawn were rather slender and self-evident:

> " The results showed that people working in large open areas are better disposed towards them than are people working in small semi-enclosed ones. This seems to suggest that some form of prejudice is operative such that people are either better disposed to what is familiar or less well-disposed to what is unfamiliar . . . Considerable social consequences have therefore been found to result from different types of space provision, and that these differences justify further investigation of the building as a management tool."

Some Specifications of the New Building

The significant dates in the construction of the building were: 4 August, 1959 — contract starting date; 1 January, 1960 — first

[1] *Office Design — A Study of Environment.*
Edited Peter Manning, Pilkington Research Unit, Department of Building Science, University of Liverpool (1965).

concrete placed in base slab; 28 June, 1960 — structural steel work commenced at ground level; 12 September, 1961 — structure completed; 1 August, 1962 — occupation of building commenced.

Superficial area of buildings	..	572,000 square feet
Cubic capacity of building	..	8,555,500 cubic feet
Tender cost per square foot	..	£6 19s. 2d.
Tender cost per cubic foot	..	9s. 3½d.

The buildings stand on a bed of solid sandstone estimated to be 100 feet thick.

The scheme comprises a 26-floor office block, a 14-floor office block and a 1,000 seat conference hall. The site area is approximately three acres.

The concrete spine behind the main tower is 400 feet high, and when completed was the highest occupied building in the United Kingdom. The tip of the tower is 530 feet above sea level, and on exceptionally fine days, it is possible to see the Jodrell Bank radio telescope in Cheshire, and the Welsh Mountains. The 25th floor, which is 330 feet above pavement level and 380 feet above the basement floor level, is mainly an observation area with special glass fitted so as not to interfere with the performance of binoculars or telescopes.

The service tower is clad in 14 million pieces of Italian mosaic. All other cladding is of glass and aluminium curtain walling.

The major problem in setting out the building was to meet the specified tolerance of one inch in verticality in the lift shafts. (This was achieved over a height of 365 feet by plumbing optically, using a theodolite, through two four-inch square holes left purposely in the service tower lift lobby floor slab.)

Engineering plant in the main building includes fully automatic lifts at speeds of 800 feet per minute. There is also an automatic vertical chain conveyor, the first of its kind in Britain, for the distribution of documents and mail.

The podium floors of the building have a total floor area at each level of about one acre. In all, the total floor area of podium and tower is nine acres.

The entire building is designed on a 5 ft. 2 in. module which determines the centres of the curtain walling mullions and of all internal division walls.

The weight of the building is estimated at 100,000 tons.

Contact with ground level during building operations was by radio telephone. On the other hand, the contractors observed, that " for handling small quantities of loose material, notably sand, it was not found possible to improve on the wheelbarrow."

There are 62 fireproof steel rolling shutters in the building fitted with a mechanism which incorporates a fusible link, which closes the shutters automatically in cases of fire.

The window-cleaning gear includes gondolas run on mullions which are electrically-controlled by the operator. Window cleaning is a full-time job.

The building is fully air-conditioned. There are no windows that open and the building is sealed against dust and draughts. Air is drawn in from the roof of the main building at the rate of 250,000 cubic feet per minute. This air is filtered, washed and then passed through an electric filter to remove microscopic dust. The humidity is then adjusted and the air is finally controlled for temperature depending on the season. There is a complete change of air in the building every half hour. (Air control has had beneficial effect on members of staff suffering from respiratory troubles.) The effect of clean air on staff absences, general fitness, and rate of labour turnover was soon apparent.[1]

The use of air-conditioning also made electronic equipment a much more practicable proposition. It is possible to inspect the filters in the air-cleaning system to show the smoke and other particles that are trapped in the Manchester atmosphere. The original plans for the installation of a roof weather station had to be postponed in March, 1963, because of the sulphurous fumes emitted by chimneys in close proximity to the building. These fumes would have a corrosive effect on the meteorological equipment.

To avoid dirt being taken inside during periods of snow, melting coils have been embedded in the forecourt. The precipitation of snow is detected by two separate methods — a photo-electric cell responds to reflected light from the snow surface and a proximity switch responds to a critical level of snow layer. There is an automatic scanning and data-logging system for premises control. This equipment is combined with remote control with indication facilities for all the principal items of mechanical plant in the building.

[1] Absentees in ten scattered buildings, between December, 1961 and February, 1962 — total staff, 2,100, 2,008 absences; average rate of absence 5.88 per cent. In the new building, December, 1962 to February, 1963 — 2,560 staff, 1,214 absences; rate of absence 3.31 per cent, showing an improvement of 43.7 per cent during the severe winter months. Labour turnover 1961 — 19 per cent in old building; 1962 — 14 per cent, including five months in new building 1963 — 12 per cent.

There is a radio telephone service installed at the top of the CIS building for contacting the members of the Manchester midwives' service.

The CIS sign at the top of the service tower has letters of 7 ft. 7 in., which are visible for ten miles.

Press Cuttings — New Building

September, 1960 — Steel spidermen fit the new Torsheer bolt which has superseded rivetting and which is machine-tightened by compressed air.

Digging of the site took six months. To date 200,000 tons of earth and rock have been excavated. A 180 ft. Bailey bridge was erected to enable lorries to get into the site.

November, 1960 — A concrete testing-laboratory was built on the spot. The spidermen get paid 1d. per hour extra for each 10 feet of altitude.

January, 1961 — The sway at the top of the building will be a maximum of 2 in. at 70 m.p.h. wind speed. The wind stresses were worked out at the Imperial College of Science, April, 1961. No navigation light is required at the top of the building.

September, 1961 — In all 200,000 sq. ft. of glass used. (Compare Great Exhibition of 1851, with over 1m. sq. ft.)

December, 1961 — A press photographer wins the Encyclopaedia Britannica Prize Award for his shot entitled " High Tea " taken at top of CIS steelwork.

January, 1962 — Conveyor system to any floor at 80 ft. per minute which routes documents by means of magnetically recorded memory tabs — as trays pass each floor the code recorded on the tab is read electronically.

March, 1962 — A floor completed every two weeks. Began 17 May, 1960, and completed structure 484 days later. Excavations began August, 1959. A huge glacial boulder was unearthed in excavations. It was too big and hard to blast and too heavy to move, so that the workmen buried it deeper below the 60 ft. level.

The CIS has its own climate with an interior temperature 75 degrees Fahrenheit and 50 per cent humidity.

Fourteen miles of mullion form the tracks for window-cleaning equipment.

Two thousand five hundred tons of steel structure was only five-eights of an inch out of plumb. The 50 ft. square service tower carries a greater part of wind stresses and acts as a torque box to the steel-framed office block. Structural steel of CIS building nearly all the new universal beams and columns — first rolled in Britain less than four years ago. A 1/60 scale model was erected to help estimate torsional properties of the tower.

April, 1962 — A full-time gardener was appointed.

May, 1962 — The first operative worker in the CIS building will be the computer.

Eight lightning conductors will act as a lightning umbrella to surrounding property. The cone of protection will have an angle of 45 degrees from its height so diameter of protection will be 800 ft.

August, 1962 — Continuous flow, washing-up kitchen equipment for the first time in Britain. The air in the kitchen is changed thirty times per hour, and in cafeteria area, six times per hour.

It took two years to design remote control system of temperature checking and data-logging equipment. Automatic logging by electric typewriter.

September, 1962 — Fire precautions — ceilings plastered with small grey boxes which automatically telephone the fire brigade, locate the fire, shut off air-conditioning and isolate area with steel shutters. They also start fire pumps and ring warning bells. There are 1,800 detectors in 40 fire sections.

Report on CIS in *Guardian* — 23 October, 1962

... A prestige building. High buildings abroad reassured the clients; also the reputation of Burnet, Tait and Partners reassured Manchester Corporation. "I would put the Board Room floor and the clerks' dining room amongst the most beautiful modern interiors in the world." The *Guardian* thought the scale and dignity of the building was affronted by its illuminated sign "pinned to its collar . . . A prestige building labels itself."

Co-operative News — 27 October, 1962 — The first time that Royalty has ever opened a Co-operative building.

Cabinet Maker — 1 November, 1962 — Nylon coating for furniture is a technique about ten years old. It costs about 25 per cent more than the best stove enamel and the thick coating reduces metal preparation costs. It reduces coldness of metal and avoids abrasion.

Punch — 26 December, 1962 — " Curious that employees of the CIS Manchester Branch, now moved into a new glass skyscraper,

WHAT GOES INTO A SKYSCRAPER

TOPPING OUT

OPENING CEREMONY

This Plaque was unveiled by
H.R.H. The Prince Philip, Duke of Edinburgh K.G.
on the occasion of the Official
Opening of these premises on
Monday, 22nd October, 1962

Top : Entrance Hall

Left : Section of the Cafeteria

Above : Recreation Room

Top left : Committee Room

Top right : Coffee Lounge

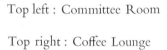

Above : Officials' Dining Room

Middle left : Recreation Area

Bottom left : Office Area

Above : Visitors' Dining Room   Top right : Observation Floor

Below : Boardroom   Bottom right : Control Room

A staff car park now occupies the bottom left foreground

should have been warned not to let the passing public see them — in their braces. Can any article be more symbolic of insurance?"

Electrical Times — 17 *January*, 1963 — Thermostats mounted on outside of the building to control the temperature by sensing solar radiation as well as atmospheric conditions and providing local adjustment to the overall temperature controlled at the plant source. Every four hours an electric typewriter prepares a log sheet. The scanning equipment is at 200 points for noting actual temperature. The neon signs consume 15 units of electricity per hour and are switched on by solar time-switches with an over-riding photo-electric cell catering for abnormal darkness during daytime hours.

January, 1963 — The building has a fall-out shelter with enough air for three days.

March, 1963 — The CIS pipes in Musak via GPO to the document store in the basement to compensate workers for loss of natural daylight

Electrical Review — 29 *March*, 1963 — A proportion of interior lighting is left on all floors after business hours so that it shall not have a patchy after-dark appearance that breaks the outline of a tenanted office block.

October, 1963 — A medal was awarded to CIS architects.

Punch — 25 *September*, 1963 — Misha Black on *Design 2,000 A.D.*

"Profits are secure enough so company self-esteem centres around its athletic, cultural and artistic prowess. The annual cricket match between the Prudential and the Co-operative Insurance Society is followed, by the Board, with the delectable anxiety which only the Ashes once provoked. No office building now lacks its swimming pool, theatre, gymnasium . . . In the end the office will become largely recreational and academic . . . one way of returning profits to the profit creators."

The Official Opening

The plaque to commemorate the official opening is inscribed:

"This Plaque was unveiled by H.R.H. the Prince Philip, Duke of Edinburgh K.G., on the occasion of the official Opening of these premises on Monday, the 22nd October, 1962."

The following list of people were presented to the Duke of Edinburgh:

Mrs. A. Wild
Mrs. R. Dinnage
Mr. S. L. Kassell
Mrs. S. L. Kassell
Mr. A. E. F. Lovick, J.P.
Mrs. A. E. F. Lovick
Mr. L. Cooke, O.B.E., J.P.
Mrs. L. Cooke
Mr. R. Taylor, J.P.
Mrs. R. Taylor
Mr. G. S. Hay
Mr. G. Tait
Mr. A. E. Beer (Consulting Engineer)
Mr. G. K. Medlock, J.P. (Engineer and CWS Director)
Mr. O. Castick (Engineer)
Professor M. Black, O.B.E. (Design Research Unit)
Mr. W. Kirby Laing (Contractors)
Mr. M. McKinnon (Contractors Agent)
Mr. W. Broderick
Mr. A. P. Pickwell (Workman employed by Contractors)
Mr. H. Seeley, D.S.C. (Investments Secretary)
Mr. R. J. Browness (Premises Controller)

Mr. Albert Wild, J.P., Chairman of the CIS, and Mr. Robert Dinnage, General Manager, received His Royal Highness. Representatives from overseas Co-operative and insurance organisations included visitors from Finland, Israel, Canada, Denmark, United States, Turkey, Pakistan, Sweden, West Germany, France, Switzerland and Holland.

(vi) *International Co-operative Alliance and Reinsurance Bureau*

The International Co-operative Alliance set up an Insurance Committee in 1921, formed at the instigation of Joseph Lemaire, who was at that time General Manager of the Belgian Co-operative, La Prevoyance Sociale. It was felt that every insurance society in the international Co-operative Movement, however small, should be in a position to reinsure some portion of its risks within the Movement. Before 1921, Co-operative societies had to have recourse to independent insurance offices for this type of cover. Joseph Lemaire invited representatives from Co-operative insurance societies to a meeting in Rome in April, 1922, to which the Belgian, Swedish, French and Dutch Co-operative insurance societies sent delegates. (Certain Italian representatives were also present but it was discovered that in fact they were not members of a *bona fide* Co-operative insurance society.) Co-operative movements of Germany, Denmark, Norway, Switzerland and Czechoslovakia all indicated their agreement with the idea of establishing closer relationships, but were unable to arrange to be represented at the meeting. The CIS could, at that time, see no purpose in such a forum and they consequently declined to send a delegate. The Rome conference weighed the possibility of forming an international Co-operative reinsurance society, or alternatively an international organnation for the study and furtherance of Co-operative reinsurance. It was felt that it would not be advisable to undertake immediately any direct reinsurance contracts with member-societies, but that societies should furnish data as to the business undertaken, the results achieved, the methods adopted of conducting business, and generally to exchange views, which it was hoped would lead ultimately to Co-operative reinsurance.

The CIS remained unconvinced over the merits of the new moves. A letter from the Secretary of the International Co-operative Alliance in January, 1923, inviting the CIS General Manager to a meeting at Ghent, was not entertained — " In our opinion the time is not opportune for studying the subject of international Co-operative insurance." Nor did the CIS agree to attend a committee for the study of Co-operative and workers' insurance at Brussels in 1927; but a change of attitude was shown when the CIS sent two representatives to a conference on international Co-operative insurance held in Stockholm during that summer. In October, 1927, La Prevoyance Sociale invited the CIS to enter into a reciprocal reinsurance treaty. The CIS General Manager was sympathetic, but on balance he thought it was not wise at that time to reinsure any portion of CIS risks with foreign Co-operative insurance societies, as there were " much better reinsurance facilities at home." La Prevoyance Sociale sent a deputation to Manchester in the summer of 1928, and again asked the CIS to underwrite some of the fire risks of the Belgian organisation. The Co-operative Union of Canada also requested the CIS to extend its operations to Canada, but the invitation was declined. Eventually, in September, 1928, the General Manager and Fire Manager of the CIS agreed to inspect the class of property insured by La Prevoyance. In November, a visit was made to Belgium; the risks covered by La Prevoyance were inspected and the buildings covered were found to be of excellent construction, with the result that a treaty was entered into with liability not to exceed £4,500 on any one risk. These initial developments prompted the Insurance Committee of the ICA to form an Executive Committee to discuss international Co-operative insurance.

A request was received from the Madras Provincial Co-operative Union in December, 1928, and the CIS agreed to provide facilities at chief office for a representative to study insurance, but the CIS would not entertain a suggestion to open a branch in Madras. In 1929, it was recommended that a treaty should be drawn up with Kansa, the Finnish CIS. Also in 1929, a treaty was entered into with L'Assurance Ouvriere of Paris, and the CIS General Manager attended a Leipzig meeting on international reinsurance. The Swedish CIS (Folksam) seconded one of their staff to be attached for a period at the CIS chief office in Manchester. Additional lines of reinsurance were entered into in 1931 with La Prevoyance Sociale, as the CIS General Manager felt that the Belgian Society was working on a sound basis, but the New Zealand and Australian Co-operative societies who invited the CIS to undertake direct insurance in their countries had to be advised that the CIS was not empowered to transact business abroad.

La Prevoyance Sociale intimated in 1933 that they intended to undertake accident and motor car insurance, and were anxious that one of their representatives should have the opportunity of visiting the CIS chief office to gain some insight into the methods of running such a department. Raymond Lemaire, the son of the then General Manager of La Prevoyance Sociale, subsequently spent several months with the CIS.

A fire reinsurance treaty had been entered into with Bulgarian co-operators in 1930, but in 1933, the Bulgarian Government placed an embargo on currency export, with the result that the CIS had a frozen credit of £860 in the Central and Co-operative Bank of Bulgaria. The General Manager tried to arrange with the CWS, who also traded with Bulgaria, for the deposit to be used for the purpose of discharging CWS accounts, but the National Bank of Bulgaria continued to block the accumulated reinsurance fund surpluses. By 1940, the amount involved was nearly £6,000. The CIS also suffered from foreign exchange controls imposed by other countries — the Reichsbank declared a six months' moratorium on German long and middle-term debts abroad in the summer of 1934, which had dire effects on CIS holdings of German securities.

The Hassneh[1] Insurance Company of Palestine extended its business to fire, accident and motor in 1935, and a reinsurance treaty was drawn up with the CIS from March, 1937, in respect of workmen's compensation, personal accident and third party insurances.

Since 1929, when the CIS was finally won over to the advantage of working with foreign Co-operative insurance societies, the General Manager of the CIS has continued to act as chairman of the ICA Insurance Committee and of its Executive Committee. Up to the outbreak of the second world war, although a number of the largest European Co-operatives, namely La Prevoyance Sociale, Folksam of Sweden, and the CIS, had established contact through the Insurance Committee, and were ceding amongst themselves shares of their surplus fire reinsurance business, these exchanges were only on a very limited scale, and there was no organised system of arranging reciprocal participation among members of the ICA generally. On the outbreak of war, the few exchanges which were in force were automatically cancelled, but on the conclusion of hostilities, the Co-operative insurance organisations of Britain, Sweden and Belgium, took the first opportunity of resuming their pre-war connections. As the success of these arrangements became apparent, the members of the Insurance Committee of the ICA felt that the exchange of reinsurance business could be considerably extended amongst their other Co-operative insurance members. Accordingly, at their annual meeting in 1949, the Executive Committee appointed a sub-committee to consider a proposal that an international Co-operative reinsurance company should be established to deal with the reinsurance programme of all Co-operative organisations throughout the world.

The sub-committee consisted of representatives from the CIS, La Prevoyance Sociale, and Folksam, and the committee members, after thoroughly investigating all aspects of the matter, concluded that in view of the insurmountable difficulties which existed at that time in obtaining adequate capital reserves for an international organisation, and bearing in mind the currency restrictions and the heavy expenses of management which would be involved, it would not be practicable to proceed with the establishment of a separate Co-operative reinsurance organisation. They recommended, as an alternative, that the best method of providing for Co-operative insurance organisations to share in each other's surplus business, was to encourage all such organisations to place at least part of their reinsurance treaties with other Co-operative organisations. It was felt that in the case of many of the

[1] *Hassneh* — Burning bush.

283

small insurance organisations, it should be possible for the whole of the treaties to be placed co-operatively, whilst other larger concerns would only be able to dispose of a proportion of their treaty through Co-operative reinsurance channels. A portfolio of Co-operative re-insurance business would thus be created which could form the nucleus of a separate international Co-operative reinsurance company, should the time ever arise when the formation of such an organisation became possible, and desirable. It was on the basis of these ideas that the International Co-operative Reinsurance Bureau was established with Mr. J. L. Nuttall, the Deputy General Manager of the CIS, acting as Chairman and Secretary of the Bureau.

The aim of the Bureau was to promote and develop exchanges of business between existing insurance Co-operatives, and to extend to the smaller organisations the benefit of practical underwriting know-ledge and skill which the older organisations had acquired. And with a ready awareness of the need for international economic and social development programmes, the Bureau was to render all possible assistance by way of technical advice, training facilities and reinsurance, in the establishment of insurance Co-operatives in the developing countries.

At the outset, although a small amount of accident and marine business was reinsured, the bulk of the business exchanged was fire, and this has continued to be the case. It must be emphasised how-ever, that the members of the Bureau are primarily direct writing offices, and consequently each restricts its acceptance in any reinsurance contract to such a proportion as will produce no greater net commit-ment on any one risk that it would be prepared to retain if it were writing a direct line on the risk. The Bureau aims to extend its activi-ties so that all members will eventually have the opportunity of sharing in the reinsurance business of each Co-operative organisation throughout the world.

The Bureau operates by means of correspondence, supplemented by occasional personal visits by members. The Secretary of the Bureau, through whom the offers of reinsurance are made, has no authority to bind any of the members to accept any offer. The general practice differs from that of independent brokers and profes-sional reinsurers, who, in placing their clients' treaty contracts, offer participation to any office they consider will be in a position to offer reciprocity. The Bureau procedure however is quite different, for it has acquired a knowledge of the resources and general underwriting policy of the various member-offices, and in view of the special relationship which exists between them, takes these factors into account when deciding whether or not to recommend participation in a treaty, and, if so, to what extent, to any particular member-office of the Bureau.

Membership of the Insurance Committee is open to Co-operative insurance societies, but other insurance organisations may be admitted, provided that their objects and methods are in conformity with the Co-operative Movement. Such societies can only become members of the Insurance Committee with the consent of the central Co-operative organisation in their respective countries.

From the early 1950s, the Reinsurance Bureau has been progressively involved in its other important task of advising and assisting in the establishment of insurance Co-operatives in developing countries.

The possibilities which might exist for the successful launching of an insurance Co-operative are largely determined by the strength of the indigenous Co-operative or trade union movement. Delegations from the Bureau have visited many countries, and have found on investigation, that before an insurance Co-operative could be established and be successful, changes would be required in the commercial and social regulations of the countries concerned. In the interim period, facilities for the training of selected officials have been made available at a suitable Bureau office.

It has been found, however, that in some of the developing countries there does not exist the necessary potential for a successful Co-operative insurance organisation. The only insurance business which has seemed likely to succeed, would be very large insurance cover in respect of highly vulnerable risks, widely out of proportion to anticipated premium income. No new insurance Co-operative could hope to operate successfully on such a restricted portfolio, nor could Bureau offices prudently grant reinsurance facilities in such cases. The view of the ICA Executive Committee is that Co-operative insurance facilities should not be forced upon developing communities as a matter of principle. In the case of many such countries, the standards of living are not yet sufficiently high for the individual members of the population to require insurance facilities at the level of sophistication in more mature economies. Although cover may be required for the products of farming Co-operatives, neither the volume nor the spread of these risks provide a suitable portfolio of business on which a successful insurance society could be established. The first consideration when advancing Co-operative activity in such a community is to evaluate and support general programmes aiming at improvements in the standard of living of the local population. When the community attains a sufficient measure of economic viability, and the Co-operative Movement and its individual members begin to acquire sufficient possessions and assets to demonstrate the need for insurance, Co-operative insurance facilities can then be reasonably considered. It is fallacious to set up an insurance society for the purpose of accumulating funds for the general development of a Co-operative Movement — the lesson of the history of the CIS is that a Co-operative Movement must come first before Co-operative insurance can grow. Obviously, there can be no worse publicity for Co-operation in any country, than for it to establish an insurance society which subsequently fails and thus undermines confidence in Co-operative principles. In many cases, the benevolent support of the government in the inititial stages of forming a Co-operative insurance organisation is most important, provided it does not interfere with the basic principles, and eventually is prepared to allow a society to stand on its own feet.

From time to time, a suggestion for the creation of a separate reinsurance company has been raised. Experience has shown, however, that it would be most unlikely that Bureau members as a whole would be prepared to cede all their reinsurance business to such a company, or could in fact handle all the reinsurance requirements of the largest societies. Any alternative to the present system of voluntary exchanges of reinsurance is gradually becoming impracticable, on account of the tendency in newly-developing countries of establishing government reinsurance pools, in which a quota of business has to be placed compulsorily by all insurers operating in the country concerned. Where such pools have been established, no concessions have been made to Co-operative insurance organisations, who are treated in the same fashion as non-Co-operative companies. Nevertheless, since 1949, there has been a record of continued progress in the amount of Co-operative reinsurance business undertaken. By early 1967 the total annual premiums relating to the insurance business exchanges between Bureau offices, was over £4m., the total number of reinsurance contracts then in force was over 500, and the total number of Bureau offices exchanging business with each other was 35, located in 22 different countries. In addition, the Bureau has been the means of disseminating much information among the older-established member companies.

What are the actual processes of sponsoring international Co-operative insurance organisation? Normally, technical assistance is required in under-developed countries for a limited period until such time as suitable local officials can be trained to take over responsibilities for their Co-operative insurance organisations. Over the years, the CIS, Folksam, La Prevoyance Sociale, and others, have assisted in this work, and the CIS has seconded officials to Australia, Ceylon, South Africa and Malaya. In 1947, the CIS was approached by the Co-operative Movement in New South Wales for assistance in the formation of an insurance Co-operative. A. Robinson, the CIS Accountant, went to Australia, and on his return, he recommended that the New South Wales Co-operative Society should establish its own insurance society. A member of the CIS London branch staff, L. G. Boyd, was invited to organise the company and become its first General Manager. More recently, arrangements were made by the ICA Reinsurance Bureau for a trainee from Malaya to receive instruction in fire business at the office of the Australian CIS. A successful Co-operative insurance organisation set up in Ceylon in 1951, under the guidance of Donald Bell, the present Manager of the CIS Fire and Accident Departments, was ultimately nationalized ten years later. During the period between 1948 and 1953, the CIS received many enquiries from Malayan Co-operative sources regarding the creation of an insurance Co-operative, which was formed with the advice of the CIS and commenced business with life assurance. Subsequently, at their request, the CIS seconded to Malaya one of its assistant district managers to help establish an agency organisation with a view to expanding the business. In the meantime, the CIS in Manchester accepted a trainee seconded by the Malayan CIS to gain experience in the transaction of fire and general business. The CIS Actuary has continued to act as adviser to the Malayan Society since its establishment. In many other cases, overseas officials have received intensive training with the CIS — for instance, towards the end of the second world war, the CIS accepted a trainee from the Co-operative Movement in Iceland. He subsequently became the first general manager of the Iceland Insurance Society called Samvinnutryggingar.

Shortly after the second world war, a CIS delegation was asked to visit the Farm Bureau Insurance Society, Columbus, Ohio.[1] The American company, which is based on producer Co-operation, made overtures to the CIS for reinsurance business, but there were immense technical difficulties to be overcome. In effect, the CIS would have been required to open an office in the United States, and become a licensed insurer. Not only was there a shortage of dollar funds at that time but also a further complication — the insurance authorities in

---

[1] The company now operates under the name " Nationwide."

the United States contended that the CIS was not a true Co-operative because it had share capital. This meant that the CIS could not establish a branch office in the United States; but on further legal advice it was decided that the CIS was entitled to establish a subsidiary licensed company in the United States. A Company on these lines was established and registered in New York State to transact reinsurance business — " We had to think of a name and decided that we could not do better than ' Rochdale.' . . . "

In 1947, the CIS received a request for reinsurance facilities from co-operators in Canada. A very small organisation had been established in Toronto to grant fidelity insurance cover in respect of Co-operative employees. Reinsurance facilities were granted, and led to a CIS deputation visiting Canada. This small group in Toronto grew into what became known as the Co-operators' Insurance Association, which does practically all its reinsurance business with the CIS and the International Co-operative Reinsurance Bureau. For many years, the policies of the Canadian company bore a note that they were guaranteed by the CIS of England. In Regina also there is a flourishing Co-operative Insurance Society, which covers Western Canada and maintains close relationships with CIS Manchester.

In many cases, appeals for assistance from the CIS have taken the form that the CIS should commence operations abroad, but it has always been held by the CIS that a more healthy and permanent development would result from the establishment of indigenous Co-operative insurance societies which would be more likely to receive support from their local members than a foreign-based Co-operative organisation. If CIS business in an overseas country became successful, it would almost inevitably lead to a request from the local Co-operative Movement to take over the venture, with all the difficulties and complications that would be involved; but in cases where the business did not develop, the CIS would be left in an invidious position.

(vii) *Changing Patterns of Investment of Insurance Offices*

Usually, investment of the life funds of insurance offices in British Government securities tends to be confined to periods when either the yield is relatively high, or the business outlook is uncertain, and caution is being exercised in regard to other types of investment. These two periods often coincide. The extent in any one year of investment in debenture and preference stock also tends to be influenced by the degree of activity in the new issues market, rather than by any deliberate policy on the part of investment managers to increase or restrict these types of holdings. During the late 1950s, the "swing into equity" intensified and culminated in a dramatic rise in ordinary share prices, but during the 1960s, greater caution generally has been observed by insurance companies investing in ordinary shares, although investment in real property has grown over the period — and this has included appreciable holdings of ordinary shares as well as debenture stocks of the property development companies.

The mortgage field also has been an area of growing importance in the investment of life funds. But there is considerable fluctuation, because building societies are the main source of house purchase mortgage funds, and the demand for these from insurance companies, at least as far as home mortgages are concerned, tends to be greatest at times when building societies are short of loanable funds.

Board of Trade quarterly figures show that total invested funds of the life assurance companies are the largest of all the institutional investors[1] (but the Jenkins Committee supported the life offices in their shyness about disclosing the market value of their investments.)[2]

---

[1] *The Radcliffe Committee on the Working of the Monetary System*, Cmd. 827 (1959) found that the insurance companies could finance one-fifth of all public and private investment.

[2] *The Company Law Committee*, Cmd. 1949 (1962).

Proportions of total assets of the CIS held in different types of investment and in cash

(Book Values)

	1950	1951	1952	1953	1954	1955	1956	1957	1958	1959	1960	1961	1962	1963	1964	1965
	%	%	%	%	%	%	%	%	%	%	%	%	%	%	%	%
Mortgages	17·75	22·17	21·61	20·35	18·83	19·71	20·82	21·34	21·78	21·63	21·96	20·87	20·62	19·62	18·90	19·35
Policy Loans	0·35	0·40	0·53	0·60	0·64	0·69	0·74	0·79	0·78	0·74	0·72	0·70	0·72	0·71	0·71	0·75
Other Loans	3·47	3·47	3·12	2·73	3·01	3·48	4·76	6·45	6·65	9·83	9·27	8·99	7·43	7·35	6·34	5·98
British Government Securities	52·86	47·64	45·54	42·99	38·78	34·10	29·81	25·62	24·05	21·53	19·90	17·97	19·18	18·64	20·46	20·67
Municipal County and Public Boards	2·61	2·44	2·36	2·11	1·77	1·43	1·45	1·11	1·08	0·97	0·95	1·07	1·24	1·53	2·37	2·47
Commonwealth Securities	0·82	0·75	0·57	0·34	0·51	0·53	0·69	0·68	0·65	0·68	0·59	0·56	0·41	0·39	0·39	0·33
Foreign Government	0·76	0·12	0·32	0·69	0·64	0·64	0·43	0·41	0·36	0·33	0·29	0·13	0·11	0·13	0·13	0·19
Debenture Stocks	3·07	3·06	3·06	4·07	3·49	5·40	5·56	5·77	5·65	6·74	6·10	6·20	5·74	5·04	4·92	5·66
Preference Stocks	4·09	3·71	3·69	5·06	7·21	7·96	7·55	6·55	6·05	4·57	5·49	5·22	5·21	5·39	5·81	6·24
Ordinary Stocks	4·78	4·95	5·67	7·70	12·03	12·10	13·05	13·86	14·66	16·52	17·93	21·73	22·71	22·75	22·72	22·82
Associated Companies	4·06	3·85	4·26	2·32	2·15	2·67	3·82	3·23	4·27	2·58	2·14	1·96	1·83	4·38	4·21	1·90
Properties Rent Charges	2·23	4·11	5·10	7·49	8·42	8·95	9·04	11·66	11·60	11·39	11·95	11·95	12·16	11·63	10·82	11·63
Cash and Deposits (including Debtor Account)	3·15	3·33	4·17	3·55	2·63	2·34	2·28	2·53	2·42	2·49	2·71	2·65	2·64	2·44	2·22	2·01

The table of invested funds and cash balances of the CIS over the period 1950–1965 shows important variations in the portfolio:

(1) Gilt-edged securities which took up 52 per cent of total funds in 1950, fell to 20 per cent in 1965. This move out of gilt-edged was a counterpart to the five-fold increase in holdings of ordinary stock, which illustrates the importance of equity shares as an inflation hedge. It should be noted that the increase in preference share holding was merely 50 per cent over the period — in 1950 the proportions of ordinary stock and preference shares in the portfolio were equal whereas in 1965, ordinary stock was almost four times as large as preference shares. (The trend and place of debentures is similar to preference stocks.)

(2) Since the late 1950s, there has been an increase in municipal stock and a fall in Commonwealth securities. Foreign Government securities are now negligible. Indeed the only items which have remained in fairly constant proportion between the years 1950 and 1965 are mortgages and municipal stock. Over the period there was a doubling of the proportion of policy loans but the total remains small. It should also be noted that "Other Loans" have doubled their proportion over the period. The cash ratio has been falling during the 1960s to a figure of 2 per cent.

(viii)   The CIS and Investment within Co-operative Movement

To what extent does the investment of CIS funds differ from that of other insurance offices? The branch managers of the CIS have the duty of acting as advisers on insurance to Co-operative organisations. They try to persuade societies to be fully insured, and they point out that the retail Co-operative societies are, for practical purposes, the sole beneficiaries of the surplus which arises from the non-life business of the CIS — which is the only insurance office in the country where profits in the fire and general departments are returned to the policy-holders. Co-operative societies therefore benefit in normal years from the fact that the CIS trades profitably with the public at large and returns some of the profits from non-life business to the retail societies as policyholders.

An investment policy for the CIS developed after the second world war.[1] During the war-period a dynamic investment policy was hardly applicable because the CIS felt impelled to support Government issues. In common with other insurance offices, the CIS issued savings bond policies which provided for the sum due on death or maturity to be paid in savings bonds, on the understanding that the premiums as received would be invested in one of the series of savings bond issues. Unfortunately for the CIS, in most cases when the claims fell due the bonds were standing at a discount, and eventually the CIS had to agree to redeem in cash the face value of the policies. After the second world war the time arrived when it was possible to con-template a wider investment field, and the CIS Board was asked to consider a new policy which included the revolutionary recommenda-tion (for the CIS) that there should be a substantial increase in holdings of ordinary shares. Approval was given for the purchase of sound industrial preference and ordinary shares to the extent of £700,000 during 1946. As a result of these purchases, the CIS held approximately 4.4 per cent of its funds in preference shares and 1.4 per cent in ordinary shares. Acquisition of real estate in urban centres was also considered. The administration of investment was re-organised from the beginning of 1947, and all investment matters thenceforth were dealt with in the General Manager's Department. Mortgage debenture stock of a cinema circuit was acquired in 1947, and the investment limit for industrial securities was extended to £2m. Further, the General Manager was authorised to initiate investment negotiations in respect

---

[1] B. Holgate, the first fully-qualified Actuary for the CIS, confirmed to the writer that during the 1920s there had been no co-ordination between the investment department and the Actuary, and no impression of a flexible investment policy.

of any suitable property: the type of real property considered most suitable was premises occupied in whole or part by Co-operative societies.

James Darroch referred at this time to the developing investment policy :

> " Hitherto we have been guided by the principle that no part of our funds should be invested in businesses which are directly or indirectly in competition with the Co-operative Movement, but the expansion of the Movement in recent years has been such that few, if any, trades or businesses remain outside its scope, and we have been compelled by circumstances to review our position and revise our opinions without, I think, violating our principles. And so we have made extensive purchases of ordinary shares in what may be termed the gilt-edged of the industrial market, which although subject to considerable price fluctuations, should maintain high interest rates."

The obvious arguments in favour of this course of action were that the CIS could not hope to compete as regards premiums and bonuses with other offices, and that inflation could have a disastrous effect on financial stability. Further, it was pointed out that there seemed no reason why CIS policyholders should not share in the profits of the companies in which many of them were employed.

Investment in ordinary shares inevitably led to a great deal of ill-informed criticism. Accusations were made that the CIS was indulging in anti-Co-operative and anti-social activities.

The policy of the CIS with regard to investment in the Co-operative Movement was clearly set out in the report of the Co-operative Union Financial Policy Committee in 1951. Therein it was stated that the CIS invested a proportion of its new money in first-class mortgages, and that preferential consideration was given to applications from Co-operative societies for mortgage advances:

> " It must be emphasized that the CIS has not unlimited funds available for this type of investment; therefore societies must not assume that their requirements for liquid capital will be met automatically from this source. Further, the CIS is not normally prepared to make loans for unspecified periods or for short terms."

When the steel industry was de-nationalized in 1953, the CIS decided that it should hold a stake in one of the nation's major industries — which it was felt would show a good return for policyholders.

The CIS therefore made application for United Steel shares, and was alloted a sum which made the CIS the largest shareholder. This investment was assumed to have certain political implications, and caused consternation in the Movement, and in many local branches of the Labour Party and other organisations.

From time to time, general enquiries for finance to improve say the working capital, or liquidity position of a Co-operative society, are received by the CIS. Normally, this type of finance is properly the province of the CWS Bank, but for some years, there has been an arrangement with the Co-operative Union that any societies which were known to be seeking capital for legitimate and sound expansion have been referred to the CIS. In 1956, the CIS submitted a memorandum to an independent commission investigating the nature and scope of finance provided by the CIS for retail and other Co-operative societies. By that date, the CIS was prepared either to purchase, or to lease back, or to grant loans, to enable societies to acquire property. Until the early 1950s, there had in fact been very little demand from retail Co-operative societies for financial assistance. The question of retail societies finding suitable points of sale for Co-operative dry goods trade had financial implications, and in October, 1956, a Co-operative Dry Goods Trade Association held conferences which were attended by CIS representatives. In a talk given by a CIS director in February, 1959, further reference was made to the complaint that the CIS was not lending or investing funds in the Co-operative Movement at a sufficiently preferential rate of interest. The CIS felt that far too much emphasis was being placed on the rate of interest to be paid on capital employed in connection with schemes of development. It had frequently been possible to show that if the success or failure of a proposed development depended on a slender margin of say one per cent in the rate of interest, then the proposition could not be justified on any grounds whatever.

The canons of investment policy followed by the present-day CIS are in no way unique — its policy is based on sound economic principles. The main concern of the CIS is the continuing investment of life funds which constitute 96 per cent of its total funds. (The contingency of having to realise investments to meet distant future claims under life policies means that the investment policy of a life office differs fundamentally from say that of a bank. Moreover, surplus cash for investment is likely to grow each year and therefore investment policy should as far as possible be a continuous one.) The first duty of the CIS is to invest funds to the best advantage of its policyholders. Any other considerations must remain secondary. This does not mean that the CIS does not seek opportunities for investment which are mutually beneficial to policyholders and to the Co-operative Movement. On the other hand, no investment would be made, however advantageous it might be to the CIS policyholders, if it could be shown conclusively that the investment would be detrimental to the Co-operative Movement as a whole.

Within these limits, the CIS has always been willing to provide the Retail Movement with a certain amount of capital. Normally, the only type of investment the CIS can make with the Movement is in respect of property. For a period, the CIS was prepared to grant mortgages, but in recent years it has preferred to purchase the freeholds and lease the properties back to the retail societies concerned. One lesson to be learned from the history of the CIS is that until the CIS adopted well-established investment principles and procedures, the CIS made little progress; in the words of the General Manager — " We must trade profitably, but having made these profits we divide them on Co-operative principles."

(ix) *Recent Trends*

The *CIS Review* ceased publication between the years 1939 and 1947. On its re-issue in 1947, it could comment that the CIS had grown to third in size of the industrial/ordinary life offices in terms of premium income. By 1953, the CIS had attained the lowest expense ratio of any of the insurance companies or larger societies, despite the fact that the CIS transacted the second largest volume of new industrial assurance business. A series of articles appeared in the new *CIS Review*, outlining the growth of the various branch offices.[1] Manchester Branch was opened in May, 1961, at 119 Portland Street, and was in effect the first branch to be opened since 1926 — for a period Manchester Branch had been absorbed into Chief Office, and was not reinstated until the 1950s.

The premium income of the CIS more than doubled from £32m. to £76m. between 1952 and 1962. In 1961, Portsmouth was the first district office to achieve new ordinary life sums assured of over £1m. in a year.

---

[1] Glasgow Branch was the first branch to be opened, followed by Newcastle 1902, London 1905, Cardiff 1906, Edinburgh 1908, Nottingham, Birmingham and Plymouth 1919, Bristol and Southampton 1922, Liverpool 1926. (The first CIS office in Yorkshire was opened at Bradford soon after 1900; Leeds became a fully-fledged Branch after the first world war.) See pp.182-4 for branches in Ireland.

Punched cards had been used since 1923, and from 1950, industrial life policies and subsequently ordinary life policies were mechanically printed. In 1962 began the changeover to printed motor policies. Lapsed industrial life proposals and punched cards, dating back to the inception of the Society, amounting to 19m. cards in all, were destroyed, after having been microfilmed for record purposes.

Investment in freehold and leasehold properties continued to grow from the early 1960s, and long-term agreements were entered into with property companies. In January, 1962, the CIS joined with other insurances offices in contributing towards a £100m. fund for export credit finance. The CIS also supported an international study of the relationship of the cholesterol level in blood to coronary heart disease. Sub-standard lives, previously unacceptable for ordinary life policies, were considered from the end of 1963, and the Society participated in a reinsurance pool for such cases.

In 1961, for the first time, sums of new ordinary life business (£54m.) exceeded those of industrial life (£53m.). A large volume of pension or group life business which has become a post-war feature of many offices has not been developed at the CIS, as the pension schemes of the Co-operative Movement are nearly all on a self-administered basis.

In the early days of industrial assurance, it was found advisable to charge higher premiums for various occupations such as miners and sailors, but for many years it has been the practice of large companies, including the CIS, to charge one general scale of premiums.

The CIS became the second largest British industrial/ordinary life office in 1963. The expense ratio increased slightly in 1962 from 24.86 per cent to 25.38 per cent — due to the full effect of salary revisions in 1961, and the extra cost of financing the building of the new chief office: profits were £9.9m. in 1962, compared with £18m. in 1961. There was a loss on the general accident and motor accounts in 1962, also on fire — for the first time for many years, as much storm damage had occurred. Ordinary life business, however, rose by 50 per cent in the first quarter of 1963, coinciding with the move into the new chief office. But there was no room for complacency — the CIS share of ordinary life business in Britain was 4 per cent, but the CIS was in touch with 20 per cent of the households.

The concluding remarks in business histories are never satisfactory. If they are pertinent, they are bound to involve present personalities by inference, if not by name. Almost without exception, the business-house histories that reach publication stage are concerned with firms that have survived and grown. They are therefore a biased sample, and hence, in many cases, the editorial problem of dealing with personal references does not arise, because too often the accounts are written as eulogies and end like travelogues: their saving grace is that they remain largely unread. Making personal remarks is presumptuous at the best of times, and to pontificate about a firm made up of thousands of working lives, after a brief look through its windows from the outside world, is rank conceit. Such remarks would be a reminder of the dangerous ease of theorizing without facts, or of interpreting facts with too limited theories. And yet business history can, and should wherever possible, raise and question generalizations thrown up by Economics and Economic History, Business Administration and other study-disciplines, if business history is to add a further dimension to business studies; for the moment, business history in Britain promises to fulfil a useful purpose as a much-needed link between Economics and Business Administration — the number of reputable business-house histories have increased appreciably since the second world war, but a general business history of Britain over say the past century has yet to be written.

The single incontrovertible fact about history is that it can be written only in the present. Writing about the contrived past and the imaginary future is romantic, but not history. Nor would there be any purpose in writing *now* from say the viewpoint of 1940; we should re-write history each generation, and we cannot dissolve the process of arriving at the historic present. History has lessons for the future, but in the future other things are never equal; shadow-boxing is energetic, but not very productive. None of these contentions should dissuade or debar the historian from making preliminary remarks about the recent past as roughage needed for the digestion of future historians — business or otherwise.

Given these reservations, what does this business history tell us about the CIS, and its social and economic environment? Perhaps it is safe to suggest in 1967, that the completion of a century of Co-operative Insurance coincides with a critical stage in the development of the CIS. Its relationships with the Co-operative Movement have always been fraternally sensitive — a Co-operative Movement at large which is in the throes of re-thinking its ideology. The CIS likewise should take stock of its own position within the insurance industry and with the general public.

Insurance is a "growth" industry with enviable increments of new business and rising productivity indices.[1] The general economic climate brought about by a full employment policy in Britain since the second world war has helped the insurance industry — rising prices; wider prosperity; larger inventories of savings, property and capital goods; extended human longevity.

The CIS begins its new century with distinct advantages: it has achieved a new image of professionalism and modernity; it has a highly efficient field staff; it has a sympathetic market within the Co-operative Movement; it is productivity-minded and activated.[2] But on further inspection, each of these efficiency quotients contains possible hazards. The CIS is now the second largest industrial/ordinary insurance office in Britain, with a life premium income in 1967 of £61m., a non-life account of £22m., making a total of £110m., including income from investments. Its assets at the end of 1967 amounted to £447m., hence size and growth, coupled with the question of administrative cost, are obvious preoccupations of the CIS management. It has been said that prestige of a large business corporation rests on its ability to explore, to experiment, and to innovate. The question arises — how far can the insurance industry and the CIS innovate in the future? It seems obvious that any marked innovation will be in the processing of data rather than in the covering

[1] Many of the techniques now being used in present-day control systems in business were derived from insurance underwriting. Insurance was the first industry to apply mathematics (used in annuity tables) to business. Actuarial science developed, particularly over the course of the 19th century, and was widely applied in life assurance at a time when other industries and technologies, such as civil and mechanical engineering, had to rely on rudimentary calculations, sometimes even on a rule-of-thumb basis. If the engineer was the prime mover in showing the need for cost accountancy from the end of the 19th century, insurance paved the way for present-day business numeracy with all the offshoots of systems analysis and data processing. Concepts of discounted flow techniques and probability computations, which are now widely applied in business, can be traced to the actuary matching future premium income to risk liabilities over the term of the insurance policy. (Similarly, investment analysis became a feature of insurance with the "move into equities" from the inter-war years.) Moreover, insurance was using what later became known as management ratios much earlier than industry generally — which had to await the development of cost accountancy as a basis for its financial control systems.

[2] The CIS reduced its chief office staff in a period of expanding business in 1966. Under a productivity agreement authorised from January, 1967, the savings are being shared between policyholders and staff.

of new forms of risk. Mechanisation must not, however, be at the cost of incentive. The CIS agents are human agents and not processing devices. So far, the CIS has adhered to a policy of developing the enlightened self-interest of its field staff as a sufficient incentive for growth, and the agents have responded as a volatile hard-selling force who are the foundation of the success of the CIS. The supervisory ratio for the CIS agency staff has always been low compared with other industrial/ordinary insurance offices — agents are eager to further their own business interests, and CIS chief office certainly supports their efforts by providing excellent publicity material. But the "knocker" remains golden. What seems to be lacking is any systematic market research backing for any specific target area. Each district explores its own territory, but there is little scientific investigation using sampling techniques of income and occupation distribution, age-structure of population, to evaluate the insurance potential of a new town or settlement area. With further mechanisation there is a suspicion that the computer has an inbuilt (although diminishing) resistance to "one-off" processing — the danger to be avoided is any undue influence by the computer on the type of business that is acceptable. The computer is, however, helping motor insurance administration, but motor premium rates are approximations because it is not possible to make any objective assessment of risk.

The CIS has increased its ordinary life business at a surprising rate during the post-war years; for instance, no other British office achieved 100,000 new ordinary life policies in 1964 except the monolithic Prudential, but six offices had a greater increase in ordinary life premium income than the CIS. One company with 11,500 new policies in 1964 derived £3.4m. increase in premium income compared with an increase for the CIS of £2.9m. on 103,000 policies. However, the average sum assured on CIS ordinary life policies is now showing appreciable increases compared with the more immediate post-war years.

The new CIS image also has constraints. Because the CIS is becoming more widely known, it has to adopt the role expected of a prosperous commercial institution — it has to assume certain public responsibilities beyond the confines of the Co-operative Movement (the CIS has, for instance, sponsored a number of research projects at universities). J. K. Galbraith, the Atlantic economist, has suggested that "countervailing external powers" are tending to replace market competition. He identifies them as the State, organised labour, and public opinion. If his analysis is valid, the CIS is in at least four worlds, as one must not forget the Co-operative Movement that gave paternity to the CIS.

Many of the qualities of the CIS growth are question-begging — as are many of the theories of economic growth. If you grow successfully, you have them — but an evaluation of these qualities shows that self-criticism and analysis can often clear the paths to expansion. Perniciously, the very fact of sustained progress may mask the limited potentialities of its well-marked paths. Growth, we are all told, signifies change. It is immaterial that patterns of development may be along well-established lines, rather than into new ventures. What *is* important, but tends to be overlooked, is that growth, irrespective of means or direction, should throw up questions relating to administrative re-organisation. Many once-large firms have suffered from administrative inertia, often resulting from the policy gap between the founder-entrepreneur and subsequent generations of managers. This is one problem that the CIS by its nature has avoided. Changes in policy were always imminent, just because questions were constantly being posed by members and institutions of the Co-operative Movement. The CIS, especially since 1945, has been well aware when administrative change is needed. In many instances, departmental re-organisation has been the answer to short-term operational needs; in other cases the administrative concomitants of long-term appraisal and planning have been recognised and implemented with more radical effects. Thus, in 1949, the CIS investigated the probable consequences of increased mechanisation on local office procedure; and in 1962, an administration department was formed, partly to incorporate the computerised data processing which had been growing during the intervening years. It was hardly significant that the 1949 investigation misconstrued future developments; what is indicative is that the CIS at that early date had the right attitude in accepting change (we should guard against any prescience over past generations of businessmen who were not so confronted as we are with the processes and problems of change).

Probably the most important growth factor for the CIS was the take-over of the agency organisation of the Planet Collecting Society — a decision which was made only after intense self-questioning of identity, purpose and direction. Taking into account the Planet infusion, the stage-development of the CIS over its first century can be thought of as fourfold. An initial, simple organisational structure survived without noticeable adjustment until well beyond the CWS

299

take-over in 1913. Functional departmentalization had to be delineated with more sophistication after the Planet merger in 1918. Diversification of insurance services and affiliation with the International Co-operative Movement grew during the inter-war years. The present stage is one of re-organising the organisation, which began after the second world war, when the CIS took its place as a leading insurance office and institutional investor. It is significant, bearing in mind the protracted discussion in the early years of the CIS with regard to entering the Industrial Assurance field and the reluctance to issue weekly premium policies, that in 1965 the CIS took a major decision to cease issuing any further weekly premium policies.

Corporate resources exert their own pressures for fuller utilization, materially, and in managerial terms. An office of the size of the CIS is constantly looking for growth opportunities, not only in its new business with policyholders, but also for the investment of its considerable funds. One might hazard that the complexion of resources of an organisation shapes a firm's history, just as much as conscious management decisions. The CIS cannot contract out of being an institutional investor; its decision-areas and policies are to a certain extent size-determined. The first question in business should always be " What are we producing and How? " The second question is " Why? " The last question is " Where are we going? " You must state your aims in every form of enterprise; only then can you measure attainment in achieving those ends. Good service is a worthy ideal which can breed efficiency; and the search for efficiency can also bring its own brand of idealism. One can be successful in business without necessarily creating " organisation men " or buying souls. On this score, the CIS has given itself a worthy aim — Complete Insurance Service.

In sum, what are the main factors in the successful growth of the CIS? They are obvious and simple — clear aims, limited objectives, and most critical of all, entrepreneurial skill in decision-making. Paradoxically, the avowed policy of " Complete Insurance Service " does not contradict any of the above factors, which still characterise the CIS.

Perhaps the most important service provided by the CIS when looked at from the hindsight of the next century will be its international affiliations. International Co-operative reinsurance is small as yet, but socially important in terms of the world community. Under-developed countries look for expertise, and it is necessary that these countries should receive disinterested advice. Already the imports of non-industrial countries are rising faster than world trade as a whole, despite the growing gaps between the richest and poorest nations. The CIS is not only the secretariat for international Co-operative re-insurance, it also gives ready assistance and advice to Co-operative Movements abroad, struggling to provide insurance cover. The CIS is welcomed because it does not seek empire, nor are there any strings, shareholders or politics. This is all to the good — there will be few Laodiceans in the years that are left to us of the 20th century.

APPENDICES

Appendix I

A Note on Insurance and Economic History

Insurance has received scant notice in recent works on British economic and social history, in contrast to say banking. Insurance and banking are however distinct industries. There is no home-service banking, and unlike banks, "the insurance offices cannot create credit" has commented the British Insurance Association.[1] Both industries are heavily involved in the provision of funds for industry, but the canons of investment policy adopted by banks and insurance offices differ. The banks reconcile liquidity with profitability and security; the insurance offices are in addition concerned with matching their investment portfolios to their long-term liabilities to life policyholders. The use of banking services increases the rapidity of circulation of monetary claims and balances. In theory, the introduction of banking into a static model of the economy would engender inflation; in practice, banking also affects the production side of the receipts-expenditure equation, and there is some level of banking which is the optimum for production and consumption quotients.[2]

Both banking and insurance contribute heavily to the invisible items in the external balance of payments of the U.K. economy, but there has been little distinction drawn between their respective roles in studies of recent economic history.

The amount of general insurance (apart from personal accident insurance) depends upon the volume of production and the amount of property owned in the economy. Broad correlations have been drawn between industrial production and fire insurance, based on the value of real property insured and calculated from official statistics published from the 1780s until 1869 during the period of a statutory fire insurance duty. Since 1869, however, there have been no statistics of the value

---

[1] British Insurance Association, Memoranda of Evidence Vol. 2, p.38, *Radcliffe Committee on Working of the Monetary System*, Cmd.827. (1959).
Although this assertion is substantially valid, the insurance offices, as institutional investors, can increase monetary demand through adding to net savings the proceeds from realisation of securities. But it would be difficult to determine whether these sales to the public are paid for out of current income or idle balances.

[2] Changes in the ratio of net bank deposits to gross domestic product are not an indication of the direct influence of banking on the economy. The ratio rose from 1920 to 1949, subsequently the trend has been downward.
Key Statistics of the British Economy 1900–1962, London and Cambridge Economic Service.

302

of property insured against fire (except in the metropolitan area of London). This dearth of statistical evidence of insurance is also noticeable in the authoritative works on British economic history. In W. Ashworth's *Economic History of England 1870 to 1939*, there are, for instance, 27 references to banking and only ten references to insurance — but the limited number of insurance references include some interesting comments on the period 1871–1875. The annual average of insurance earnings contributed to the external balance of payments during that period is given as almost one-third of the income from shipping and from foreign investment. The estimated income from foreign investment and business services, *including* insurance and shipping, was equal to 63 per cent of the value of home-produced exports. (The percentage rose to 87 per cent during the period 1891–1895, and was still as high as 75 per cent in 1911–1913.) Professor Ashworth adds that the chief source of this estimated income was interest and dividends on investment and earnings of shipping. He comments — " It is unlikely that earnings from insurance and from trading and banking services grew any faster than those from merchandised exports — more probably they grew less."[1] An inference which could have been drawn from the above figures is that, on *external account*, the contribution of service industry generally was not only approaching the total value of manufactured goods exported during the late 19th century, but that this heavy proportion of external service income was a harbinger for 20th century trends in the *internal* economy.

The insurance industry became an institutional investor from the inter-war years, and increased appreciably its holdings in equities from 1932 with the introduction of a cheap money policy. By 1936, over £1,500m. had been invested, of which one-quarter to one-third was in railways and industrial or commercial enterprise,[2] but with minute exceptions, this trend is ignored in economic histories of the period: there is little reference to the insurance industry in Professor Pollard's standard work on the British Economy from 1914.

In the remaining works of authority on the recent economic and social history of Britain, such chance remarks as there are, mainly relate to fire insurance and beginning of national insurance. Obviously these two subjects are mentioned because relevent statistics and other data are available. In the definitive work on British historical statistics — *Abstract of British Historical Statistics* by B. R. Mitchell and Phyllis

[1] Ashworth, op.cit., p.159.
[2] Ashworth, op.cit., p.369.

Deane — there is a chapter on banking and insurance which includes twelve tables, but ten of these refer to banking. Of the remaining two tables, one is concerned with fire insurance over the years 1789 to 1869, and the other table with new capital issues on the London money market, 1870 to 1939 — there is no other reference to insurance in the work. Nor is there any appreciable assessment of the social significance of insurance in other reputable works on social history and development. Where references occur, they are almost entirely restricted to the development of national insurance. Admittedly, there has been sound scholarship shown in a study of the growth of the friendly societies in the 19th century, but of the army of industrial and ordinary life agents which grew in the second half of the century, and the many millions of policyholders visited at their households, there has been little mention by economic and social historians. In the *Survey of Social Conditions in England and Wales* by A. M. Carr-Saunders, D. Caradog Jones and C. A. Moser, there is a single bald statement on insurance to the effect that industrial assurance premiums increased 250 per cent between 1938 and 1954, but no inferences are drawn. In the book *Changing Social Structure of England and Wales 1871 to 1951* by D. C. Marsh, there is no reference whatsoever to insurance. In *Condition of the British People 1911 to 1945*, a Fabian Society study by Mark Abrams, there is at least an awareness and appreciation of the link between income and insurance arrangements. The survey shows that as late as 1913–14, expenditure on items other than food, shelter and clothing in the average working-class family budget was negligible (2s. 3d.). By 1937–38, it had risen to almost 16s. per family and was absorbing 30 per cent of the whole increase in money income between 1913 and 1938. Within the figure of 16s., voluntary insurance took up 2s. 4½d. and State insurance 2s. 0¾d. (In the middle-class family budget of 1937–38 voluntary insurance took up over 10s. per household.) Mark Abrams concluded that the average working-class family in the mid-1930s generally had enough to meet its overheads including insurance, but unfortunately these averages often remained outside the grasp of many. As late as 1936, 19m. people in Britain remained practically propertyless, but almost all concerned had taken out industrial assurance policies.

As further evidence of the protracted lack of interest in the social and economic implications of life assurance, one has to go back to Seebohm Rowntree's study of poverty in York in 1899 as one of the few published sources making a specific reference to insurance as an expenditure item in working-class budgets.[1] In York at that time, there were ten part-time insurance agents and at least 75 full-time agents engaged in the collection of weekly life assurance premiums. (Forty of the agents were employed by one company, the others by nine smaller companies.) Seebohm Rowntree commented:

> "It has not been possible to ascertain exactly what total sum is collected weekly, but judging from information received regarding the weekly takings of about half the agents, it is clear that the total sum paid for life insurance by the wage-earning classes of York is *not less* that £400 per week or about 8¼d. per family.[2] (The average weekly premium paid to the leading company concerned was about 2d. and the average sum assured about £10.)

Appendix II

Insurance and Inflation

Probably the more important influence for the insurance industry (as for most other industry) is the *trend* rather than the existing general *level* of prices. The trend of prices during the 20th century has of course been upward. What is unique is not so much the direction of movement of prices — the tendency has been for prices to rise throughout history, with the possible exception of the 19th century; a fact which has tended to distort our general attitude towards price levels and movements — rather it is the extent of the rise in prices, especially since 1939. Price and cost-inflation over the past quarter of a century have had drastic effects on the insurance industry; in conjunction with increasing human longevity, inflation has made bonus distribution an institutional feature of life assurance practice. Inflation has also affected the scale of new insurance business, but it is difficult to state the extent categorically. It does, however, appear to be the case that in the converse of inflation, viz.; slump and unemployment conditions, the insurance industry does not suffer as much in terms of regression as many other industries, particularly primary industries. Indeed, first evidence shows that the insurance industry continues to expand throughout boom and slump conditions,

[1] There is however a short reference to the prevalence of industrial assurance during the 1930s in C. L. Mowat, *Britain Between the Wars* (1955), p.500, which quotes data on weekly expenditure on insurance premiums in four family budgets — the insurance premiums paid out varied from 8d. to 3s. 2d. in incomes from 39s. to 26s.
See also P. Massey, *Portrait of a Mining Town* (n.d.) pp.62–3.

[2] B. Seebohm Rowntree, *Poverty — A Study of Town Life* (2nd Edit., London (n.d.))

without any marked interruption.[1] From the early 1930s, the marked increase in unemployment caused life offices to experience heavy lapses and surrenders of policies, but during the years of recovery from 1936, new business grew for the CIS, as for the other offices, and lapses tended to fall. It may, however, be remarked that at no time during the period of depression did the CIS and the other industrial assurance offices cease to expand. In particular, it is interesting to relate the ratio of life assurance premiums to national income during periods of falling incomes and employment. The ratio rises during slump conditions because of the effect of the contractual nature of life assurance premiums. Moreover, there was sales pressure in some offices in the early 1930s which brought in a high level of new business during the slump years, even though agents knew that much of the business was not maintainable. *New Dawn,* the monthly journal of the USDAW, referred in 1935 to the fact that a quarter of a million colliers were idle, and that engineering and shipbuilding industries were in a state of paralysis — " But our fertile plot never fails to produce increased crops. Each year shows more policies, more premiums, more profit and investments growing by leaps and bounds."[2]

Another important factor relating inflation to insurance is the effect of inflation via the rate of interest earned on investment by insurance offices. In the equity share market the principal long-term price trend has been upwards (although the market faltered during the mid-1960s) and the most persistent feature in the UK economy since the end of the second world war, apart from inflation, has been the need for a high rate of capital investment to improve the productivity of industry and so raise the conversion factor of the economy. In general, the proportion of insurance office assets held in equity shares and freehold property, although of increasing relative importance, has not been large. In this sense, only a proportion of the assets has been used as a hedge against inflation. Nevertheless, the limited holdings of equities are necessary to set against " with profit " policies, which are demanded by policyholders as their private hedge against inflation.

Inflation followed the two world wars. Between 1919 and 1920, the rate of total money incomes rose over 25 per cent — far more

[1] See W. H. Chaloner, *National Boiler* 1864–1964 (1964)
   " Dividends were paid uninterruptedly on a rising scale through the Great Depression . . . "
   There was often a time lag in the effects of boom and depression on the National Boiler's affairs. In both of the years 1930 and 1931, it was stated that " The profit balance for the year was the largest in the history of the Company."
[2] *New Dawn,* 9 February, 1935.

than the rise in the cost-of-living index. On the other hand, after the second world war, total personal incomes increased by only 4 per cent between 1946 and 1947, but new ordinary life business rose by a much higher rate than in the corresponding period after the first world war. The continued increase in life assurance premiums after 1946 has been due, not so much to the rise in incomes, but to the increase in the proportion of personal incomes, and more particularly of the margin of income, going into life assurance. But the relationship between insurance premium income and total personal income shows a less well-marked increase over the past half-century than figures of the actual monetary increase in sums assured would tend one to suppose.

There is little reliable information as to the trend of the ratio of premiums to total personal saving. It used to be taken for granted that the percentage of income saved rose as real income increased, but this is no longer so widely held. What has been accepted is the part played by life assurance in restraining inflation. Saving through the medium of life assurance has increased steadily since before the first world war. Wage-earners and certain individual middle-class groups have now become the most important source of personal savings, but it cannot be taken for granted that this would have been so marked in the absence of the pressure exerted by life assurance. Saving by wage-earners and the lower-middle classes, unlike that done by the rich, say during the early 20th century, can hardly be described as automatic, and it is this contrast which gives point to the claim that institutional savings in general, and life assurance in particular, are indispensable to the economy in the provision of a high level of capital investment and in the struggle against inflation. This claim is the stronger the more the Government of the day seeks to prevent a redistribution of income during inflation in favour of receivers of profits. The more progressive the Government, in fact, the greater is its need of a thriving life assurance industry.

It may be noted that the disadvantage of life assurance which is deplored by the policyholder during inflation — its failure to provide a hedge against the rise in prices — is the vary factor which, together with the characteristic of an unvarying level of premium, make life assurance such an effective disinflationary force. If it were possible for sums assured to vary with the price level, a large part of life assurance's disinflationary effect would be destroyed, and it is conceivable that life assurance might even accentuate both boom and slump.

A falling expense-ratio usually occurs in a period of deflation, since it may be possible to reduce some items of expense while premium income continues to increase (because of the tendency for the insurance industry to be counter-cyclical). Nor have expense ratios risen during the two decades since the second world war — the insurance offices have made their policy-processing more efficient,[1] conjointly with selling more life business in real as well as nominal terms.

In 1954, total premium income from life and annuity business for offices in the United Kingdom was 2.9 per cent of the national income; by 1964, the proportion had risen to 3.8 per cent. In 1965, net life premiums (premium income after reinsurance arrangements) received by member companies of the British Insurance Association totalled just over £1,000m., compared with just under £500m. in 1955.

Appendix III
Some Recent Developments in Certain Branches of CIS Business
(1) *Fire Insurance*

Out of a total fire insurance premium income of £4m. in 1967, £107m. was in respect of Co-operative society business — approximately one-third the total account.

The CIS has no records to indicate the insurable value of premises or of stock figures for all the premises in the Co-operative Movement. (This could only be obtained by physically checking every Co-operative society policy, but this would not indicate the true insurable value.)

Neither is there information on the amount of self-insurance by Co-operative societies — all that can be said in general terms is that the CIS insures practically the whole of the Co-operative Movement in respect of fire insurance, but some retail societies carry their own risks in respect of some of their smaller shop properties.

(2) *Life Assurance*

Is there any evidence available which would give a broad indication of the percentage of say CIS life policyholders who are members of local retail Co-operative societies? The query was put to a member of CIS management, who explained:

" We have no information on this at all — many local retail

---

[1] "Another problem brought about by inflation is that, as the life assurance industry is relatively ' labour-intensive,' it is difficult for it to avoid the effect on costs of rising wage-rates." H. B. Rose " Life Assurance within the field of Savings since the War," *Journal of Insurance Institute of London* Vol. 51, 1963 p.52.

(Professor Rose has some doubts whether life assurance will expand any more rapidly than total personal income unless the proportion of income saved continues to increase. Even so, he believes that the task of life assurance may be to compete more strongly with other forms of saving.)

societies supply our district managers with lists of new members which our agents canvass, and because of this (and also because other Co-operative members may be more sympathetic to us than non-members if approached on a "cold canvass" or through another connection) we have probably a higher proportion of Co-operators amongst our policyholders than in the general population in the relevant age groups (a very high proportion of new policies is on lives aged 25–35, where the membership of retail Co-operative societies is perhaps not as high as in older age groups). Canvassing of retail society new members is, however, nowadays a comparatively minor way of getting new business — far more comes from existing policy-holders and connections of existing policyholders."

(3) *Fidelity*

The premium income in respect of Fidelity insurance forms part of the Accident account and in 1967 totalled £305,000. Of this total, nearly £53,000 was in respect of premiums paid by Co-operative organisations covering Fidelity risks of their employees

The recent tendency has been for Fidelity insurance to be issued to employers on a "blanket" basis, and the CIS issues such policies to Co-operative organisations covering all their employees with a maximum sum insured for any one period of insurance.

(4) *The Motor Account*

Motor insurance comes under heavy fire from a critical public — it is significant that when the British Insurance Association wished to improve the public image of insurance, it commissioned McKinsey to investigate motor insurance; the CIS was one of six offices offering themselves as guinea pigs in this operation.

The McKinsey investigation forecast that the value of claims for 1970 will be double the 1963 figure. If pushed to extreme, increases in "no claims discount" vitiate the whole principle of insurance. The nearer the lucky are to come to being excused contributions, the more the principle of insurance is flouted, and the situation arises where it becomes cheaper for an individual to bear his own risk. In motor insurance this is illegal, but the good driver who foots his own bill rather than sacrifice a high "no claims discount" is in a sense reverting to self-insurance. The remedy proposed by the American consultants of relating the premium more to the driver has now been adopted by the tariff offices. Factors such as occupation, district of use, type of car, are being considered alongside mileage — which is re-emerging in importance. (It should be remembered that the Vulcan Boiler Insurance Company adopted mileage as a criterion 60 or more years ago in motor insurance.) There is bound to be an approach towards a closer linking of premiums with individual risks and separate premiums for special risks. Motor insurance is being brought more into line with other branches of insurance. This can never of course be done in full with motor policies that are numbered in millions, but the aim must surely be to get as near the ideal as possible, by taking into account the maximum number of factors influencing the risk, and demanding that the computer shall give each the appropriate weighting.

It is believed that the CIS was the first major British insurance office to apply computer techniques to motor insurance; by the end of 1967, the entire business had been so converted. Electronic computers have been applied to the preparation of policy and endorsement documents including the calculation of premiums, renewal papers and the appropriate accounting documents. Since 1963, six local offices have been opened to handle motor claims business in order to relieve the Birmingham and London branches. The premium income of the Motor Department had quadrupled within the decade 1954 to 1963. Although the trend in the Motor Department is for an increased use of mechanisation in the handling of day-to-day routine procedures and in the producing of statistical data, the CIS readily admits that it does not know nearly enough about the constitution of motor insurance business and the influences which are exerted upon it. When the CIS decided to install a computer, an opportunity was created for making a statistical analysis of the motor business, but it was not until 1966 that a statistician was appointed who would confine himself to non-life work — for some years at least on motor statistics. At the time of writing it is doubtful whether this statistical work would enable any violent departure from prevailing market rates. There is however some hope arising from the fact that following a recommendation of the McKinsey Steering Committee, a Statistical Bureau has been set up covering the whole of the Company motor insurance market and this should lead to a more sensible rating policy.

(5) Marine Business

In January, 1964, a separate Marine and Reinsurance Department was founded on the basis of business which had been introduced in 1953.

(6) Premises Department

The new Premises Department was formed in 1962. The first CIS premises controller was appointed in March, 1959, to act as the client's representative during the construction of the new chief office and subsequently to manage it.

The unit expenditure on the complete operation and maintenance of CIS chief office building compares very favourably with other offices in Britain and in America. Unfortunately, with the exception of the Americans, building owners and managers tend to keep their operating costs a close secret.

It is not usual for a building manager to be responsible for such a wide variety of skills as that of the CIS premises controller, whose duties include engineering, catering, branch and estate management, security, etc.

It has become increasingly the policy of the CIS to pay more attention to the investment aspect of branch and district office properties. Previously, suitability as a branch or district office had been the main criterion.

(7) Agency Department

In 1963, a field staff sales training officer was appointed and canvassing officials have since attended intensive sales training courses at chief office. CIS district offices are larger than those of most other insurance companies in the sense that they each service more agents. In addition, CIS district managers generally have more authority than their counterparts in assessing and arranging payment of claims.

(8) Administration Department

The Administration Department was set up in 1962, for the purpose of co-ordinating work at the district offices with the appropriate departments at chief office. The Department was also concerned with the introduction of mechanised motor accounting system at district offices.

In the Industrial Life Department, microfilm was used in lieu of the retention of lapsed proposal forms, and a manual check on the financial details or some 16,000–18,000 weekly proposals for industrial life was transferred to magnetic tape computer. Mechanised systems similar to those for motor and ordinary life branch business are being extended to fire and accident business. Eventually, the intention will be to introduce random access devices to permit immediate access to all master record cards including industrial life cards. Document reading to permit accounting data to be fed into the computers at high speed is also a possible future development.

The Organisation and Methods Section was set up in the first instance to assist in planning and organising the move into the new building. The O. and M. Section was responsible for the installation of audio typing and other clerical and administrative systems. O. and M. staff have also worked in liaison with outside consultants on the subject of clerical work measurement and re-organisation.

Board of Directors on 29 August, 1967

Chairman	Albert E. F. Lovick
Directors	Harry Afford
	Ronald Byrom
	Frank Cooke
	Kenneth Albert Noble
	Sydney James Phillips
	Herbert Arthur Toogood
	William Tom Welch
	R. Stewart Thomson

List of Chairmen from 1867 to 1967

1873 – 1874	J. R. Shepherd
1875 – 1880	William Foster
1881 – 1908	William Barnett
1909 – 1912	Thomas Wood
1913 – 1914	John Shillito
1915	Thomas E. Shotton
1916	George Woodhouse
1917 – 1918	T. B. Stirling
1919	Washington Hemingway
1920	George Woodhouse
1921	George Hayhurst
1922 – 1932	Sir Thomas Allen
1933	Sir. George Riddle
1934 – 1943	Arthur Judd
1944	John W. Sutton
1945 – 1952	Aneurin Davies
1953 – 1961	S. Leonard Kassell
1962 – 1963	Albert Wild
1964 –	Albert E. F. Lovick

Prior to 1873 there does not appear to have been an appointed Chairman of the Board.

Full-time Principal Officials

1873 – 1919	James Odgers
1919 – 1943	Joseph P. Jones
1943 – 1947	James Darroch
1947 – 1967	Robert Dinnage F.I.A.

In December, 1967, Harry Seeley F.C.I.S. A.C.I.I. became General Manager and Secretary on the retirement of Robert Dinnage.

INDEX

Accident Insurance, 42, 101, 127, 189
— Collective Scheme, 119
Accident Offices Association, 130-1, 132, 220
Acts of Parliament—
— Poor Law Amendment Act (1834) 70
— Friendly Societies Act (1834), 70
— Industrial and Provident Societies Act (1852), 16, 71
— Joint Stock Companies Act (1862), 26
— Manchester Police Regulations Act (1866), 20n
— Metropolitan Fire Brigade Act (1866), 20n
— Stamp Act (1870), 232
— Life Assurance Act (1870), 44, 74, 77, 85, 87
— Friendly Societies Act (1875), 76
— Industrial and Provident Societies Act (1893), 104
— Friendly Societies Act (1895), 152
— Highways Act (1896), 189
— Assurance Companies Act (1909), 133, 177, 178, 234
— National Health Insurance Act (1911), 98n
— Courts (Emergency Powers) Act (1914), 149
— Industrial Assurance Act (1923), 176-7, 178, 202, 234
— Industrial Assurance Act (1929), 203
— Road Traffic Act (1930), 191, 220
— Road Traffic Act (1934), 191
— Prevention of Frauds (Investments) Act (1939), 222
— Industrial Assurance and Friendly Societies (Forfeiture) Act (1940), 223
— Assurance Companies Act (1946), 229
— Industrial Assurance and Friendly Societies Act (1948), 235-6, 250, 253
Actuaries, Institute of, 228

Actuary, CIC, Appointment of, 77
— CIC, 84, 85, 92, 96, 102, 129, 159, 165, 181, 195, 200
Administration Dept., CIS, 311-12
Advertisements, CIS, 30, 40, 43, 54, 67, 101, 165, 179, 192
Agency Manager, CIS, 166, 222
Agricultural and Horticultural Society, Co-operative, 49
Albert Life Insurance Co., 53, 74-5
Albert Mill Co., 45
Alexander, A. V. (Lord), 177, 178, 202, 223
Allen, Sir Thomas, 211
Alliance Life and Fire Insurance Co., 45, 48, 80
Amalgamated Society of Carpenters and Joiners, 44
Ancient Order of Foresters, 39
Angel Meadow, Manchester, 266
Apicella, Vincenzo, 272.
Arkwright, Richard, 268n
Armagh, railway accident, 84
Articles of Association, CIC, 26, 31, 57, 60, 77, 81
Arrears, premiums, life assurance, 176, 181, 182, 195
Associated Electrical Industries, 194
Association of All Classes of All Nations, 14, 70
Association of British Fire Offices, 59n
Assurance Ouvrière, Paris, 282
Australia, Co-operative insurance, 287
Aviation insurance, 196n

Babbage, Charles, 232
Bacon, Alice, 251
Baernreither, J. M., 68n
Bailey, Jack, 255
Bain, Sir Edward, 194
Balloon Street, Manchester, 125n
Banbury Co-operative Society, 34
Barnett, William, 43, 82, 89, 93, 94, 117, 118, 120-3, 135, 138
Barou, P., 235n
Bathgate Co-operative Society, 29

INDEX

Baxendale and Co., 224, 268n
Baxter, R. Dudley, 7–8
Beard, John, 204n
Bedlington Co-operative Society, 48
Belfast, 163
— Fire office, 55
— Working Men's Co-operative Society, 29
Beswick Co-operative Society, 126
Bevan, Aneurin, 254, 257
Beveridge Report, 235, 236, 240, 243, 244, 247–8, 262–3
Beveridge, Sir William, 226, 235, 245, 251
Bevin, Ernest, 197
Black, Professor Misha, 271–2
Blackley, Canon, W. L., 68n
Block system, premium collection, 154
Blyth, 164
Bolton Co-operative Society, 69n
Booth, Charles, 8, 9n
Borrowman, James, 20, 21, 22, 24, 36, 40, 47
Braddock, John, 164n
— Mrs. Bessie, 164n
Bradford, 112, 114
Bradford Provident Co-operative Society, 107
Bradford and Gass, builders, 125
Bradford-on-Avon Co-operative Society, 23
Bristol Co-operative Society, 69n
Bristol, CIS district manager, Lord Mayor of, 220
Brisbane Co-operative Society, 84
British Co-operator, 9, 10
British Engine Boiler Insurance Co., 229
British and Foreign Life Assurance Co., 45
British Industry Life Assurance Co., 74n
British Insurance Association, 223
British Metal Trades and General Assurance Collecting Society, 129
Brokenshir, J. 73n

Builders Guilds, 171–3
Bulgaria, 282
Burial Societies, 10, 71n, 73, 75, 76
Burnley Weavers Society, 98

Cambridge, stamp scheme, 184–185
Campbell, Alexander, 22
Canada, 288
Car and General Insurance Co., 189
Carlisle Co-operative Society, 141
Carlisle life table, 71n, 96
Carlyle, Robert (builders), 126
Carr-Saunders, A. M. 148n
Cassell Committee on Motor Insurance (1936), 220
Central London Fire Office, 65
Ceylon, 287
Chadwick, Edwin, 70–71, 73n, 74n
Challenge to Britain, 264
Channel Islands, 220, 228
Chartered Insurance Institute, 36n, 166, 228
Cheap money policy (1930s), 210, 217
Child life assurance, 87
Churchill, Winston, 151n
Citrine, Sir Walter, 204, 206
Clare Co-operative Society, 183
Clarion, The, 152
Clegg, C., 70n
Clynes, J. R., 151n, 202
Cohen Committee on Industrial Assurance (1932), 211–216, 232n, 243
Cohen, Sir Benjamin, 213–214
Colchester, CIS agent, Mayor of, 220
Collecting Societies, 6, 72
Collective fire insurance scheme, 102
Collective life assurance, 102–103, 119, 120–124, 167–168, 169–170, 195, 210, 224, 227
Community Friendly Society, 14, 15, 16n, 53, 59–60, 77–78
Conciliation, National Co-operative Board, 205
Consolidated Fire Office, 55, 56
Cooper, William, 23, 24, 27, 28, 31, 32

Co-operative Conference, Manchester (1867), 25
Co-operative Equitable Permanent Benefit Building Society, 45, 48, 66–67, 115, 129, 130, 186, 187
Co-operative Friendly Society, 49, 50, 57, 58, 59, 68
Co-operative House Building Scheme, 38
Co-operative insurance, abroad, 84, 85, 101
Co-operative Movement, early, 13ff
Co-operative Newspaper Society and Co-operative Printing Society, 22n, 56, 67, 91, 113, 114, 125, 126, 128
Co-operative Sickness Insurance Friendly Society, 145
Co-operative Societies, early, 10, 11
Co-operative Union, 113, 142, 162n, 251, 252, 257, 259, 292
Co-operator, The (Manchester), 22n
Co-operative Insurance Company (CIC), later Co-operative Insurance Society (CIS)—
— Agents, 35, 50, 54, 56, 64, 79, 80, 82, 86, 95, 101, 105, 107–108, 109–110, 115, 128, 135, 150, 164, 166, 180, 195, 197–198, 216–217, 229.
— Balance Sheet, 116, 230
— Branch Offices, 36, 127–128, 162n, 180, 183, 198, 294
— Chief Office, new, 266ff
— Chief Office, specifications, 274–277
— Chief Office, Press cuttings, 277–279
— CIC converted into CIS (1899), 103–105
— Co-operative Credit Guarantee Insurance, 40
— Fire Tariff, 32
— Interest and Profits, 33, 40, 47, 58, 78, 95, 100
— Life Assurance, 32, 33, 44, 77–96
— Premises, 36, 52, 56, 125–7

— Registration, 26–27, 28
— Relations with CWS, 117ff, 136–148
— CIS Review, 182, 211, 294
— Share Capital, 30, 31, 33
— Shareholders, 33, 47, 63, 81, 86, 87, 95, 109, 132, 148
— Staffing and Salaries, 32, 38, 41, 48, 50, 56, 63–64, 79, 84, 101, 112, 114, 115, 127, 165, 167
— Terms of Settlement with CWS (1913), 147
Co-operative Retail Societies—
— Banbury, 34
— Bathgate, 29
— Bedlington, 48
— Belfast, 29
— Beswick, 126
— Blaydon, 55
— Bolton, 69n
— Bradford, 107
— Bradford-on-Avon, 23
— Brisbane, 84
— Bristol, 69n
— Carlisle, 141
— Carnforth, 47
— Chester-le-Street, 35
— Clare, 183
— Coatbridge, 39
— Crosshouse, 20
— Derby, 99, 130
— Dewsbury, 48
— Dukinfield, 23
— Eastleigh, 122
— Enfield Highway, 187
— Exeter, 87
— Failsworth, 44
— Glasgow, 9
— Halifax, 11, 45, 122
— Hartlepools, 118, 181
— Hebden Bridge, 35, 40
— Hull, 23
— Kendal, 29
— Lewes, 48
— Lincoln, 50
— Liverpool, 164
— London, 168, 193
— Londonderry, 116

Co-operative Retail Societies—*cont.*
— Long Eaton, 116
— Manchester and Salford, 44, 49
— Middleton and Tonge, 28n
— Nottingham, 18
— Oldham, 18, 29, 39, 164
— Over Darwen, 29
— Plymouth, 11, 18, 162n
— Prestwich, 29
— Ramsbottom, 50
— Ripponden, 9, 18
— Rochdale (see Rochdale Pioneers' Society)
— Royal Arsenal, 180
— Scunthorpe, 187
— Sheerness, 130
— Sheffield, 87
— Shepshed, 29
— Shepton Mallet, 23
— South Suburban, 187, 201
— Sunderland, 118, 130, 141, 142
— Tralee, 163–164
— Winnington, 130
Co-operative Wholesale Society, 28, 29, 30n, 36, 38
— Banking Dept., 63, 171, 218, 293
— CIC Agencies, 39
— CIC, membership of, 38
— Development Bonds, 171
— Motor Dept., 179
— Motor Vehicle Manufacturing, 189
— Nationalization Industrial Assurance, 260
— Premises, 50, 55, 113, 115, 116, 126
— Shareholder in CIC, 60
— Shoe Works, Leicester, 47
— Soap Works, Durham, 50
— Trade Insurance Fund, 17, 38, 80, 106, 115, 139, 140, 141, 143, 164, 201
Corporation Street, Manchester, 125n
Cotton Spinners Mutual Fire Insurance Association, 59n
Coupon Insurance, 131–132, 197
Cripps, Sir Stafford, 261

Daily Herald, 196–7
Daily Mail, 192
Dalton, Hugh, 251, 257
Dantzic Street, Manchester, 125n, 219, 269n
Darroch, James, 114, 128, 135, 165, 180, 200, 208, 226, 230, 292
Defoe, Daniel, 75n, 98n
Depression, inter-war, 206, 216
Derby Co-operative Society, 99, 130
Design Research Unit, 271–2
Dewsbury Co-operative Society, 48
Dinnage, Robert (General Manager), 200, 208, 211, 226, 248, 251, 254, 255, 256, 259, 264
Directors, CIC, inaugural, 28
Dobson and Barlow Ltd., 65
Donations, CIS, 116
Douthwaite, John, 16
Dukinfield Co-operative Society, 23
Dyson, James, 28

Eagle Star Insurance Co., 191
Ealing Tenants Association, 113
Eastleigh Co-operative Society, 122
Economist (1821–2), 13, 21
Economist, The, 230
Eden, F. M., 73n
Edinburgh, Philip, Duke of, 279
Enfield Highway Co-operative Society, 187
Equitable Fire Insurance Co., 45, 48, 54
European Insurance Co., 53, 74n, 75
Exeter Co-operative Society, 87
Export Credits Guarantee Dept., Board of Trade, 235n

Fabian Society, 234n, 241, 247–8
Failsworth Co-operative Society, 44
Fay, C. R., 26n, 194
Female staff, CIS, 112, 114, 167, 212
Fidelity Insurance, 8ff, 33, 66, 86, 87, 98, 115, 130, 309
Financial Times, 258
Finland, 282
Fire Insurance, 93, 101, 168

Fire Insurance, Claims, 55
— Collective Scheme, 102n
— Companies, 55, 56, 63
— and Co-operative Movement, 17ff
— Department, CIS, 308
— Limits, 65, 91, 106, 130
— Losses, 57, 65–66, 80, 86, 94–95, 106
— Precautions, 65
— Rates, 58
— Reinsurance Treaties, 178
— Salvage, 201, 217
— Surveyors, 57, 61, 64, 112, 150
— Tariff, 54, 58, 106
Fire Offices Committee, 59, 60–61, 65, 66, 93–94, 101, 106, 108–109, 131, 132
Fire, Tenby, 20
Folksam, 282, 283
Ford Motor Co., Ireland, 183
Ford Motor, Model T, 190
Foresters, Ancient Order of, 71, 77
Friendly Societies, 6, 70–74
Friendly Societies, Report of Royal Commission (1874), 46, 71, 73, 75, 76, 97
Furnivall, F. J., 16
Future of Industrial Assurance, 246, 263

Galbraith, J. K., 298–9
Garnett, R. G., 13n
General Accident Insurance Co., 191
General Electric Co., 193
Gerrard of Swinton (builders), 126
Glasgow, City of, Assurance Co., 202
Glasgow Conference on Co-operative Insurance (1866), 24
Glasgow Co-operative Society, 9
Glass, S. T., 172n
Goderich, Lord, 16
Gosden, P. H. J. H., 70
Gostrakh, 196
Greening, E. O., 38, 49, 62, 79
Greenwood, Abraham, 22, 25, 28, 29, 32n, 51, 52, 53
Greenwood, Arthur, 244–6

Griffiths, James, 237, 238, 243, 244, 248, 249, 250, 251, 254, 257, 259
Groom, Tom, 152
Guarantee Society of London, 11

Halifax Building Society, 187
Halifax Co-operative Society, 11, 45, 60, 122
Halifax Flour Mill, 54
Hallam, H. D., 152
Hanover Street, Manchester, 125n
Hartlepool Co-operative Society, 118, 181
Hassneh Insurance Co., Palestine, 283
Hearts of Oak Benefit Society, 187
Hebden Bridge Co-operative Society, 35, 40
Heckmondwike Manufacturing Co., 45
Hecla Insurance Co., 51
Heysham, Dr., of Carlisle, 71n
Hilton, John, 28, 34
Hire Purchase Insurance, 193
Hobson, S. G., 172
Hollin Bank Mill, Blackburn, 55
Holyoake, G. J., 33, 45, 54, 90
House Property, CIC, 67, 83, 99, 129
House Purchase, 115, 119, 185–188
Howard, Abraham, 32, 35, 51, 53, 60
Howarth, Charles, 28
Hughes, Thomas, 16, 44, 70, 80
Hull Co-operative Provident Society, 23
Hulme, Manchester, fire (1878), 56, 58
Hunt, A., 152
Iceland, 287
Income Tax and CIC, 48, 113
Independent Labour Party, 152
Industrial Assurance, 88, 103, 109, 117, 120, 232
— and CIC, 46, 108, 133, 198
— Commissioner, 178, 182, 202, 206, 225
— Companies, 6
— Criticism of, 233–234
— Derivation of Term, 74

Industrial and General Assurance Co., 74

Industrial Life Offices Association, 253

Influenza, 166, 169, 170

Insurance Companies in Manchester, 36n

Insurance Institutes, Federation, 109

Insurance Record, 45

Interest-in-book, Agents, 82, 127, 156, 157, 159, 174, 175

Ireland, 163, 182–184, 208–209, 220

Ireland and CIS, 135

Ireland, Northern, 114, 182, 209

Irish Agricultural Organisation Society, 182

Irish Ford Motor Co., 183n

Isle of Man, 184

International Co-operative Alliance, Insurance Committee, 280, 283

International Co-operative Reinsurance, 280ff

International Co-operative Reinsurance Bureau, 284–286

Investment of Funds (CIC and CIS), 43, 66–67, 83–84, 91–92, 99–100, 107, 123, 129, 166, 170–171, 193–194, 209–211, 217–218, 227–228, 229, 291ff.

Japan, industrial assurance, 216

Jenkins Committee on Company Law, 289

Jews, 91

Jones, Joseph P., 114, 127, 134, 163, 212, 214–5

Jones, Lloyd, 16, 34, 62

Kendal Co-operative Society, 29

Kennet Committee on Manpower, 225

Kingsway, London, 193

Kirkwood, Andrew, 41n, 71n

Knight, James, 12n

Labour Believes in Britain, 239, 240, 241, 253, 256, 264, 265

Labour Party, 172, 196, 234, 237, 239, 246, 248–250, 253, 255, 293

Laing, John, and Son (building contractors), 271

Lapsing, of insurance policies, 76

Laski, Harold, 251

Laundries, Association of United Co-operative, 217

Leeds Co-operative Society, 136n

Leeman, F. W., 25n

Leicester, Industrial Web Manufacturing Society, 47

Lemaire, Joseph, 280

Lemaire, Raymond, 282

Levy, Hermann, 216, 230, 234n, 235, 237

Lewes Co-operative Society, 48

Lewis's Store, Manchester, 65

Life Assurance (CIC and CIS), 69, 74–77, 113, 114, 131, 178, 308–309

Life Assurance, Group, 170n, 192

Life Offices Association, 210

Life tables, Actuaries, 71n, 77, 85, 95–96, 178, 200

Lincoln Co-operative Society, 50

Lincoln Land and Building Society, 48, 84

Liverpool Co-operative Society, 164

Liverpool Victoria Friendly Society, 72, 239

Lloyd's, reinsurance treaties, 132, 164, 178, 189, 196n, 223

London, CIC, fire business, 83

London, CIS branch office, 127–8, 193, 222

London Co-operative Society, 168, 193, 220

London and Counties Friendly Society, 154

London and Lancashire Fire Office, 50

Londonderry Co-operative Society, 116

Long Eaton Co-operative Society, 116

Long Millgate (Manchester), 125, 126, 127
Loss-of-Profits insurance, 196
Ludlow, J. M., 16
Luytens, Sir Edwin, 193

Macdonald, Sir Arthur, 148n
Malaya, Co-operative Insurance, 287
Management ratios and expenses, 76, 105, 108, 174
Manchester College of Commerce, 27n
Manchester District Unitarian Sunday School Union, 59
Manchester Fire Brigade, 65
Manchester Grammar School, 91, 125n
Manchester Guardian, 22n, 241, 252, 263
Manchester, and insurance, 36n
Manchester and Liverpool District Bank, 28
Manchester Police Regulation Act (1866), 20n
Manchester and Salford Co-operative Society, 44, 49
Manchester and Salford Savings Bank, 8n
Marine insurance, 44, 55, 58n, 196, 217, 311
Marr, T. R., 96n
Mather and Platt Ltd., 59
McKinsey Corporation, consultants, 309–310
Means Test, 206
Mechanics' Institutes, Manchester, 16, 27n
Medical Officer and CIC, 78, 87, 106, 174, 179
Meison, F. G. P., 96n
Memorandum of Association, 26
Metropolitan Board of Works, 20n
Metropolitan Insurance Co. of America, 272n
Mikardo, Ian, 236–237, 264
Middleton and Tonge Co-operative Society, 28
Miller Street, Manchester, 125n, 268n

Milne, Joseph, 71n
Mitchell, George, 272
Morrah, Dermot, 74n
Morrison, Herbert, 238, 239, 248, 249, 251, 254, 255, 257
Morgan, Augustus De, 6
Mortgage advances, 113
Motor insurance, 188–191, 219–220, 309
Motor Insurance Bureau, 230
Motor Vehicles, 179
Municipal Mutual Insurance Co., 229
Mutual Insurance Office, 63
Mutuality Clubs, Co-operative, 201
Mutualization of Industrial Assurance, 246, 256–257, 260, 265

National Arbitration Tribunal, 226
National Boiler Insurance Co., 229
National Employers Mutual Assurance Co., 208–209
National Health Insurance, 98n, 145, 219
National Industrial Life Assurance and General Deposit and Advance Co., 52
National Insurance, Ministry of, 237
National War Bonds, 171
Nationalization of Industrial Assurance, 216, 232ff
— and Investment of Funds, 250, 254
Neale, E. Vansittart, 16, 24, 29, 40, 44, 49, 55, 61, 62, 63, 70, 78, 81, 82, 83, 87, 88–89
— and Co-operative Friendly Society, 53
Neill, Sir Thomas, 202
Newcastle-on-Tyne, 114
New Moral World, (1834–1845), 14
News Chronicle, 240–241
Newton, William, 16
Norman, Montagu, 220
Northampton life table, 71n
North British and Mercantile Insurance Co., 48, 64n
Northern Counties Fire Office, 55, 58
Norwich Union Fire Office, 48

Nottingham Co-operative Society,
18, 25n
Nuttall, J. L., 166

Odgers, James, 47, 53, 84, 87, 89, 90,
95, 107, 109, 114, 135, 138, 146
— Appointment of, 36, 37
— Fire Precautions, Paper on, 41–42
— Life Assurance, Paper on, 80
— Instructions to Agents, 48
— made Manager, 51
— Salary, 50, 112, 127
— Retirement, 162–163
— Tariff Negotiations, 61–63
Oddfellows, Manchester Unity of,
71, 72, 96n
Oddfellows, National Unity of, 77
Office Accommodation, 90, 113–114
Office Methods and Equipment, 85,
107, 112, 199, 200, 219, 230–231,
295
Oldham Co-operative Society, 18,
39, 164
Orbiston Community, 22n
Ordinary life assurance, 129, 77–96
passim, 179–180, 199
Organisation and Methods, 231,
271–272, 312
Over Darwen Co-operative Society,
29
Owen, Robert, 14, 15
Owenites, 14, 15

Paraffin oil and fire insurance, 32, 35
Pare, William, 33, 34, 35
Parliament, Co-operative Party,
Members of, 216
Parmoor Committee on Industrial
Assurance, 176, 232n, 246
Parmoor, Lord, 176n, 177
Pearl Assurance Co., 153n
Peddie, Lord, 252–253
Pension schemes, 192
People's Provident Office, 74n
Percival, James, 28
Phillips, Morgan, 248, 264
Pilkington Research Unit, Univer-
sity of Liverpool, 273–274

Pioneer Insurance Co., 153
Pitman, Henry, 22, 35
Planet Friendly Assurance Collecting
Society, 152–160, 299–300
— Take-over, 156–158, 159
— Agents, 158, 159
— Valuation, 160
— Ex-business, 174–175
Plate glass insurance, 133
Plunkett, Sir Horace, 183
Plymouth Co-operative Society,
11, 18, 162n
Police strike (1919), 164
Poor Law, 97
Poor Law, Royal Commission on
(1905–9), 97n, 136n
Post Office, 74, 172, 272
— Annuity Scheme, 66n, 76, 81,
185
Potter, Beatrice, 89
Potts, John, 28
Pratt, Hodgson, 81
Premises Dept., CIS, 311
Premium income, CIS, 294
Prestwich Co-operative Society, 29
Prevoyance Sociale (Belgium), 280,
281–282, 283
Pribicevic, B., 172n
Price, Dr., of Northampton, 71n
Priestley, J. H., 18n
Prince of Wales (later Edward VIII),
79
Profit-sharing, 67
Property deeds, CIS premises, 125n
Provident Clerks and General
Guarantee Assurance, 66
Provident Fire Office, 48
Prudential Assurance Co., 74n, 76,
88, 105, 126, 166, 298

Radcliffe Committee on Monetary
System, 289n, 302n
Ramsbottom Co-operative Society,
50
Rational Sick and Burial Society, 15,
16
Rational Society, 15
Raynes, H. E., 59n

Red Cross Insurance Co., 189
Redfern, P., 38n
Refuge Assurance Co., 112
Reinsurance, 45, 57, 224, 228
Reynolds News, 220
Ridley, P. E., 20n
Ripponden Co-operative Society, 9, 18
Robens, Lord, 226n
Rochdale, 89
Rochdale Co-operative Land and Building Co., 30
Rochdale Cornmill, 32, 47, 51, 54
Rochdale Equitable Sick and Burial Society, 14n
Rochdale Manufacturing Society, 32
Rochdale Pioneers' Society, 21, 24, 25, 28, 30, 35, 45, 60, 67, 168n, 218
— and Claims, 32, 83
— Surety, 11
Rowntree, B. Seebohm, 14, 304–305
Royal Arsenal Co-operative Society, 180
Royal Co-operative Friendly Society, 133
Royal Institution of British Architects, 270
Royal Insurance Co., 44, 133, 159
Royal Liver Friendly Society, 50, 72, 154, 239
Rusholme Board of Health, 67
Russia, All-Russian Co-operative Organisation Society, 196

Sadler, James (balloonist), 125n
Salvation Army Assurance Society, 212
Sampson, Anthony, *Anatomy of Britain*, 1n
Savings, personal, 8n
Scotland (and CIC, CIS), 34, 36, 86, 92–93, 100, 105, 108, 109, 115, 128, 134, 135, 165, 218
Scottish CWS, 36, 57, 80, 92, 100–1, 106, 129, 141
Scunthorpe Co-operative Society, 187

Sheerness Co-operative Society, 130
Sheffield Co-operative Society, 87
Shepherd, J. R., 32
Shepton Mallet Co-operative Society, 23
Shillito, John, 132, 142, 148
Simpson, J., 152, 154, 158, 222
Skyscrapers, 270n, 272n
Smethwick, CIS agent, Mayor of, 220
Smith, R., of Hartlepool, 118, 138, 139, 141, 143, 144–145
Smithies, James, 28
Snowden, Philip, 152
Social Conditions in North West, 96–98
Society for Promoting Working Men's Associations, 16
South Suburban Co-operative Society, 187, 201
Southern Co-operative Provident Benefit Building Society, 92
Spencer, Herbert, 6
Springhead Spinning Co., 50
Sprinklers, fire, automatic, 59n
Steel, denationalisation of, and CIS, 292–293
Stott, Samuel, 32
Strike, CIS District Office staff (1921), 179
Strike, General (1926), 170, 190, 194–196
Strikes, CIS (1928–1931), 203–206
Suffragettes, 193n
Sun Life Office, 87
Sunderland Co-operative Society, 118, 130, 141, 142

Tait, Burnet, and Partners (Architects), 270
Teetotalism, 81, 90
Tenby Co-operative Society, 20, 23
Thompson, W. T., 75n
Thorpe, W. (builder), 126
Times, The, 240, 241–2, 244, 258–9
Titt, George, 152
Tooley Street, London, fire, 20n

Trade Unions and CIS, 166, 197
— Amalgamated Society of Railway Servants, 131
— Amalgamated Union of Co-operative Employees, 127, 167
— Guild of Insurance Officials, 167, 206, 226, 251
— National Amalgamation of Life Assurance Workers, 180–1, 197, 235
— National Federation of Insurance Workers, 235, 257
— National Union of Co-operative Insurance Society Employees (NUCISE), 197, 205–6, 227, 238, 240, 251
— National Union of Co-operative Officials, 167n
— National Union of Allied and Distributive Workers (NUDAW/USDAW), 167, 181, 195, 197, 203, 204, 205, 224, 226, 239, 251
— National Union of General and Municipal Workers (NUGMW) 206
— Transport and General Workers Union (T & GWU), 206
— Workers Union, 159
Trade Union Congress, 206, 235, 239, 242
Tralee Co-operative Store, 20, 23
Tweddell, T., 136, 138, 143

Unemployment, 182
Ulster Agricultural Organisation Society, 182
Union Land and Building Society, 51, 58–9, 67
United States, Co-operative Insurance in, 287–8
Universal Insurance Co., 220, 230

Vaccination and Insurance, 35
Victoria Fire Office, 67
Valuations, CIC, quinquennial, 85, 86, 95
Vulcan Boiler Insurance Co., 114, 163, 229, 310

Wage cuts, 167
Wales, CIS and, 198–9
Walford, C., 30n
Watson, Sir Alfred, 213
War, Bonuses, 151
— Contingencies, 114, 149–151
— Damage, 224–5
— Evacuation, 225
— Life Claims, 223–4, 227, 228–9
— Outbreak of, 1939, 222
— Pay claims, 226
— Premium Income during, 228
— Risks, 223
Webb, Beatrice, 37, 176n
— Sidney, 223n
Weir, Lord, 223
Whitehead, James, 96n
Whitt, Rev. D. T., 67–8
Wilkinson, T. R., 97n
Williams, F. Austen, 180
Wilson, Sir Arnold, 216, 230, 234n, 235, 237, 243, 261, 263
Winnington Co-operative Society, 130
Workmen's Compensation insurance, 108, 133–4
Wood, T., 35, 36n
Woolworth Building, New York, 272n

Young, Michael, 248–9, 253, 256, 259, 260–3 passim, 265

Zurich Insurance Co., 191